VLADIMIR SOLOV'EV AND THE KNIGHTHOOD OF THE DIVINE SOPHIA

VLADIMIR SOLOV'EV AND THE KNIGHTHOOD OF THE DIVINE SOPHIA

SAMUEL D. CIORAN

Wilfrid Laurier University Press acknowledges the support of the Canada Council for the Arts for our publishing program. We acknowledge the financial support of the Government of Canada through the Canada Book Fund for our publishing activities.

Library and Archives Canada Cataloguing in Publication

Cioran, Samuel D., 1941-
    Vladimir Solov'ev and the Knighthood of the Divine Sophia

Includes bibliographical references and index.

ISBN 978-0-88920-042-5 (paper)
ISBN 978-0-88920-859-9 (PDF)

    1. Solov'ev, Vladimir Sergeevich, 1853–1900 – Criticism and interpretation. I. Title.

PG3470.S7Z56   891.7'3   C77-001365-1

Cover design by Leslie Macredie

© 1977 Wilfrid Laurier University Press

Every reasonable effort has been made to acquire permission for copyright material used in this text, and to acknowledge all such indebtedness accurately. Any errors and omissions called to the publisher's attention will be corrected in future printings.

No part of this publication may be reproduced, stored in a retrieval system or transmitted, in any form or by any means, without the prior consent of the publisher or a licence from The Canadian Copyright Licensing Agency (Access Copyright). For an Access Copyright licence, visit www.accesscopyright.ca or call toll free to 1-800-893-5777.

ACKNOWLEDGEMENTS

This book has been published with the help of a grant from the Humanities Research Council of Canada, using funds provided by the Canada Council. Further, I would like to thank the Canada Council for the research grant which enabled me to carry out the original research. My thanks also go to Miss Pat Goodall for her patient typing and retyping of the manuscript at various stages in its development.

CONTENTS

Preface 1

Introduction 5

PART I. SOPHIA'S PROPHET

1. The Public Solov'ev 11
2. The Private Solov'ev 39
3. The Affair of Anna Schmidt and Vladimir Solov'ev 71

PART II. EARLY DISCIPLES

1. The Symbolist Assessment of Vladimir Solov'ev 89
2. The Solov'evian Circle 105
3. A Dialogue on the Divine Sophia 121
4. The Beautiful Lady 139
5. The Woman Clothed in the Sun 163

PART III. THE APOSTASY

1. The Demonized Ideal 175
2. Farces and Fools 199
3. The Triumph of the Demonic Feminine 233

PART IV. THE FAITHFUL

1. The Church Controversy 247

Conclusion 273

Bibliography 275

Index 277

PREFACE

A philosophical and religious tradition in modern Russian thought bearing the designation of *Sophiology* has long been apparent. A number of contemporary writers[1] have alluded to its omnipresence in the metaphysical schemes of such prominent thinkers as Vladimir Solov'ev, Pavel Florenskij, Sergej Bulgakov and even Nikolaj Berdjaev. While there is some disagreement as to the precise origins and exact formulation of *Sophiology*, the general outlines seem fairly clear. As the word implies, wisdom lies at the root of the scheme. This wisdom is in the possession of God who in creating the universe did so with a clear purpose in mind. The universe, the world, history and mankind are not random creations but all possess meaning and are progressing towards specific ends. This purposeful journey appears to be directed towards an achievement of, or restoration of, oneness between heaven and earth, God and man. Mankind is capable of gaining this end if it can discern the purpose or wisdom of God's creation. Indeed, God Himself has sought to inspire man with the wisdom of His divine plan by providing him with archetypes or prototypes representative of the union of heaven and earth, such as the perfect Godman, Christ, and the perfect Church in which mankind as a whole is united with God.

God's purposeful scheme for the universe, the wisdom He displays in its formulation, was associated by a number of the abovementioned thinkers with Sophia, or the Divine Wisdom of God. The name of Sophia will be familiar from various gnostic sources, the Cabbala, as well as *Proverbs*. In a number of these sources Sophia is clearly assigned a feminine nature. However, for a portion of the so-called sophiologists, in particular Vladimir Solov'ev, the more abstract concepts of *Sophiology* surrounding God's Divine Wisdom, or Sophia, appeared to assume the unmistakable contours of a sacred feminine divinity. For many critics this archetype of a Divine Feminine, in the guise of Sophia, and displaying attendant motifs of a mystical eroticism, completely dominated and even distorted the more abstract and incorporeal scheme of *Sophiology*. Sophia, divine and indescribable, distant and alluring, fleshless yet fleshly, became

---

[1] See V. V. Zenkovsky, *A History of Russian Philosophy* (2 vols.; London, 1953); and N. O. Lossky, *History of Russian Philosophy* (London, 1952).

the practically tangible goddess of a religious and philosophical system.

The study that fills the succeeding pages concerns itself most particularly with the rise and fall of this specific feminine archetype within certain elements of Russian philosophy, belles-lettres and theology during the latter part of the nineteenth and the beginning of the twentieth centuries. Beginning with Vladimir Solov'ev, the idea and presence of Sophia, in her resultant manifestations as both the Divine and Demonic Feminines, is examined through the prism of the Russian symbolist poets and novelists such as Aleksandr Blok, Andrej Belyj and Valerij Brjusov. The study then concludes with a survey of Sophia's inspirational force in the theology of Sergej Bulgakov and the resultant controversy in the Orthodox Church. The atmosphere of knight-errantry which typified the devotional attitudes of Solov'ev, and the symbolists in particular, before the image of the Divine Sophia seemed particularly remarkable. Consequently, an attempt has been made to emphasize the specific motifs and vocabulary of chivalry attendant upon this feminine ideal.

While the idea of Sophia, or the Divine Wisdom of God, seems more aptly the object of philosophical or theological examination, the reader should note that the following study focuses primarily on the reflections of this feminine archetype among the representatives of literary symbolism in Russia at the turn of the century. To be precise, it was my intention to isolate the idea of Sophia within Vladimir Solov'ev's philosophy and poetry in terms which would facilitate an examination of the idea as borrowed by the Russian symbolists. In so doing, I wished primarily to display the responses elicited by the reactions and counter-reactions to Solov'ev's Divine Sophia. There seems little doubt that a discussion of Solov'ev's Sophia was instrumental in animating the literary ideas and literary relationships of prominent symbolists like Andrej Belyj and Aleksandr Blok in particular. Consequently, I make no claim to dealing with the entire body of Solov'ev's metaphysics or all of the ramifications of his *Sophiology*. The inclusion of Sergej Bulgakov, a theologian, in the final chapter, seemed natural, or, at least, irresistible, from the point-of-view of both an intellectual and literary curiosity. His early devotion to and defence of Vladimir Solov'ev's philosophy and poetry, as well as his intimate knowledge of the writings of the Russian symbolists, begged his inclusion in this predominately literary study. The same charges of heresy, deviation, gnosticism and even mystical eroticism which had been levelled at Solov'ev and the symbolists' because of their devotions before the Divine Feminine, were used later to attack Father Bulgakov by the more conservative elements in the modern Orthodox Church.

I have made a very conscious attempt to provide fairly detailed outlines of the major works under discussion. This I did in deference to an English-speaking audience who is not apt to be familiar with the more arcane realm of Russian symbolism in particular. I trust students of Russian literature, philosophy and theology will bear with me in this.

Finally, if this is the place to warn readers of what to expect in the text, then it seems only fitting to issue a counter-warning of what they will not find. Hopefully, I have made it clear that my primary interest is the literary fate of a religious idea despite the necessary inclusion of both philosophical and theological material. In addition, I do not pretend to, or attempt to, discuss the entire tradition of *Sophiology* and its numerous representatives in modern Russian thought. This is a task more demanding of time and paper and one which this literary historian gladly surrenders to the philosophers and theologians who do not fear pricking their fingers in counting the number of angels to be accommodated on the heads of pins.

INTRODUCTION

The Russian symbolists found this world of time and space a pale reflection and imperfect echo of eternal, infinite reality. In sunset and whisper they sought the hint of revelation that could lay bare the golden chains strung tenuously between heaven and earth. Their search, they hoped, would provide them the means for earth's spiritual transformation. Andrej Belyj's early poetry is particularly expressive in its call to discovery: "Let us fly to the horizon: there the crimson curtain/ gleams in the unending dawn of eternal day./ Quickly to the horizon! there the crimson curtain/ is all spun of phantasy and fire." ("Za solntsem", 1903). Perhaps even more illustrative of this quest-motif are his verses inspired by the Argonauts' search for the golden fleece contained in that "manifesto-poem" of Russian Symbolism, "Zolotoe runo" (1903):

> Suffused with fire is the heavenly vault...
> And, lo, Argonauts trumpet to us
> on horns of flight...
> Take heed, take heed...
> Enough of sufferings!
>
> Don your armour
> Of fabric fraught with sun!
>
> The ancient Argonaut
> summons to follow,
> he calls
> on a horn
> of gold:
>
> "To the sun, to the sun, whoever loves freedom,
> "let us fly into the ether
> "of azure blue!..."
>
> And enveloped in radiance
> our winged Argo,
> in full flight,
> overtakes
> the luminary body of day,
> torchlike set alight anew.
>
> Once again it overtakes
> its golden
> fleece...

Unlike their decadent colleagues, the Russian Symbolists had no desire to create independent worlds of artificial experience in order to insulate themselves from the coarseness of existence. They were irrevocably commited not only to the creation of a new spiritual culture, but ultimately to the restoration of union between heaven and earth, to the creation of the Heavenly Jerusalem. Unwilling to abandon the conditional in favour of the unconditional world, they felt earth must be penetrated with heaven and not simply rejected.

Inasmuch as the symbolist world-view was generated from an awareness of the disparity between two antipodal realms, everything was viewed as a series of antinomies to be resolved and therefore restored to oneness in the great symbolist synthesis. The Russian symbolist poet, however, was not only the triumphant herald of this design, but also the victim of its inherent laws of unresolved duality. Every positive archetype spontaneously generated its negative counterpart. Thus Christ begat Antichrist, the Woman Clothed in the Sun demanded her opposite in the Harlot, Jerusalem spawned Babylon, the Godman created his own foil in the Mangod. Behind this multivalency, the major categories of Good versus Evil, Cosmos versus Chaos, etc., become apparent as the basic antipodes animating the struggle between opposites. If the Platonic mirror catches the divine reflections of perfect ideals, it must also be allowed, in the symbolist scheme of things, that a mirror is a double reflector, trapping also the demonic images of the imperfect anti-ideals below. As Belyj, for one, was only too aware, the symbolist poet is this very double-mirror in his intermediary position between cosmos and chaos: "In the wretched heart much evil/ is consumed and dissolved./ Our souls are mirrors,/ reflecting gold." ("Solntse", 1903). Thus, it is his fate to determine the resolution of the "ideal" and the "anti-ideal", the thesis and antithesis. The irony of his role can thus be explained: he is the ambiguous priest *cum* sacrificial victim of his own symbolist religion. In this light one can begin to comprehend the frequent allusions to being "on the divide," "at the cross-roads", the offspring of a fateful generation or, in the words of Dmitrij Merezhkovskij, the "children of night" existing between the dusk of the old culture and the dawn of the new: "We are the steps over the abyss,/ Children of gloom, we await the sun./ We see the light, and like shadows/ We perish in its rays." ("Deti nochi", 1896).

Within their essentially Platonic scheme of things, the symbolists needed an intermediary at the intersection of the two worlds who would guide them to the perfect harmony they longed for. The prime candidate for this role would seem to be Christ, the traditional link between heaven and earth in his dual aspect as human and divine harmoniously united in a single individual, who in the Second Coming would announce the Millenium. However, it was not the Christological archetype which inspired many of the symbolists in their initial search. Christ's role was usurped by the Divine Feminine who assimilated all the traditional functions of Christ to herself in what was essentially an atmosphere of apocalypse at the turn of the century. For Andrej Belyj she was the Woman Clothed in the Sun or Eternity, for Aleksandr Blok the Beautiful Lady, for L. L. Ellis-Kobylinskij the Holy Virgin, for the theologians Pavel Florenskij and Sergej Bulgakov the Divine Sophia, but all of these epithets were merely aliases for a single feminine archetype. Rather than Christ, it was the more vividly emotional anima-projection who shaped the religio-poetic aspirations of the Russian symbolists.

The Russian philosopher-poet, Vladimir Solov'ev, provided Russian Symbolism with many of its major philosophical concerns. In fact, it is my contention that he is responsible for its seminal pattern: the conception of the Divine Feminine within a symbolist scheme of transfigurative synthesis which informs the work of many of the major symbolist writers. The Beautiful Lady of Aleksandr Blok's poetry cannot be fully comprehended without prior knowledge of Solov'ev's conceptions of Sophia, the Divine Wisdom of God, nor do all the ramifications of Belyj's concern with The Woman Clothed in the Sun emerge clearly without reference to Solov'ev's Divine Feminine. Once having examined Solov'ev's theories on Sophiology in the latter part of the nineteenth century, one is struck by the analogous theories of many later writers and intellectuals like Dmitrij Merezhkovskij, Pavel Florenskij, Sergej Bulgakov and even the strange Anna Nikolaevna Schmidt who have either been influenced by the thought of Solov'ev or have arrived at the same conclusions by independent means. Certainly, the fact that all of these writers and thinkers chose the Divine Feminine as the symbol and content of their systems is worthwhile examining in itself as evidence of what must be considered one of the most remarkable, if not unique, traditions in modern Russian culture.

PART I

Sophia's Prophet

Vladimir Solov'ev (1853-1900)

Chapter 1

THE PUBLIC SOLOV'EV

In 1873, at the age of nineteen, Vladimir Sergeevich Solov'ev announced a platform of philosophical research and action to his fifteen-year-old cousin, E. K. Romanova, whereby all of Christendom would be transformed. While the goal which this manifesto of faith and action proposes may seem naive and idealistic, Solov'ev's unmistakably serious attitude and his rational proposals reveal a manifest conviction of the possibility of its realization.

The letter is divided into three significant moments which Solov'ev dissects in a clearly analytic fashion. These three distinct points are significant not only because the number "three" proved the magical cipher for all of Solov'ev's work, but also because, from the very beginning, it is possible to discern in the youthful philosopher a consciously rational attempt to deal with what had been regarded as a completely unrational subject, namely religion. Thus, Solov'ev proceeds in this letter from the awareness of an imperfect situation to an analysis of the reasons underlying it in order to arrive at a programme of action. In later years this same programmatic approach typified the symbolists' attempts to discover and formulate a theory of symbolism which would provide for the transformation of the world and the salvation of mankind.

A realization of the imperfect nature of all things was Solov'ev's earliest observance:

> From that time when I first began to have conceptions of anything, I was aware that the existing order of things (but above all the social and political order, the relations of people among themselves, which define all of human life), that this existing order was far from being what it should have been, that it was based not on reason and justice, but, on the contrary, moreso on meaningless chance, blind force, egoism and constrained submission.[1]

Faced with this, Solov'ev believes that two reactions are usual: either one is "practical" and adapts oneself to the system, or one becomes essentially a Byronic type who expresses contempt and seeks with-

---

[1] See Solov'ev's letter to Selevina (nee Romanova) on 2 August, 1873, in Pis'ma Vladimira Sergeevicha Solov'eva, ed. E. L. Radlova (Moscow, 1908-1923), III, 87.

drawal. However, Solov'ev immediately pronounces a third unequivocal position which he maintained throughout his life:

> A conscious conviction in the fact that the present condition of humanity *is not such as it should be*, means for me that *it must be changed, transformed*. I do not recognize the existing evil as eternal, I do not believe in the devil. Recognizing the necessity for transformation, I consequently feel myself bound to devote my entire life and all my powers to the end that this transformation might be in fact carried out.[2]

The unselfish and boundless devotion to a seemingly unattainable ideal should be remarked upon immediately in this passage. The youthful romantic is clearly prepared to dedicate his entire life, to swear an oath of eternal allegiance to a glorious task. It was this very willingness for self-sacrifice, for total and uncompromising obeisance before seemingly impossible ideals which subsequently exerted such a fascination on the young, impressionable symbolists and earned Solov'ev the designation of the "poor knight". Moreover, when ultimately Sophia, or the Divine Feminine, became representative of this ideal of transformation, the same symbolists could not help but see in Solov'ev's actions and pronouncements the rebirth of a chivalrous knighthood of old which was once again engaged in a "holy war", in a contemporary "crusade" to liberate the world. The symbol adorning this modern-day knight's shield would be none other than that of Sophia, the Divine Wisdom of God. Indeed, as will be shown in the following chapter, Solov'ev himself was responsible for introducing this very concept of knightly devotion and sacrifice in his poetry and causing it to reverberate throughout the later writings of the symbolists.

The question is, of course, *by what means* this transformation might be carried out. Solov'ev believes that the means are to be found in Christianity and its truths. But this only poses a further question. People must act according to the Christian truth, but although they know what the convictions of Christianity are, they do not have any clear awareness of what the Christian truth is. Alluding obviously to the prevalent positivist and anti-religious spirit characterizing much of the Russian intellectual scene in the 1860's and 1870's, Solov'ev points out that contemporary attitudes oppose Christian truth. The reason for this state of affairs is quite apparent to him as well:

> The problem is that Christianity, although unconditionally true in itself, has possessed up until the present time... only an entirely one-sided and insufficient expression. With the exception of a few select minds, for the majority Christianity was merely a matter of simple, semi-conscious belief and undefined feeling, and had nothing to offer to the *mind*, did not penetrate reason. Consequently it was

[2] Ibid., 88.

enveloped in an irrational form that did not conform to it and was burdened down with all manner of senseless rubbish.³

This one-sidedness, this mystical or irrational exclusiveness, must be ended and the means of doing so will be akin to putting old wine into new skins by seeking out a new form for the inherent truth of Christianity: "The task which stands before us is: to introduce the ancient content of Christianity into a new form that corresponds to it, i.e., one that is rational and unconditional."⁴

The new form which Solov'ev envisages for his revitalized Christianity is to be composed of a grand synthesis of all of man's rational thought, a stupendous assimilation of knowledge in support of the Christian truth in order to resolve all rational and philosophical objections against what up until now has been only irrational superstition. Why should Western philosophy and science not be in support of, rather than in opposition to, Christianity?:

> Now it is as clear to me as 2 x 2 equals 4 that the great development of Western philosophy and science, apparently indifferent and often hostile towards Christianity, in actuality has only formulated for Christianity a new and worthy form for it. And when Christianity actually is expressed in this new form, appears in its true mode, then that which until now has been obstructing its penetration into the general consciousness, namely its fleeting contradiction with rationality, will disappear of its own accord.⁵

When Christianity becomes, therefore, the actual conviction of people, a way of life, then obviously all will be changed, transformed. However, Solov'ev confesses his awareness that this goal is still a long way off, the object of a protracted and gradual process. For the time being he must occupy himself with the theoretical side of the problem, produce a philosophical or rational basis for his view of a transfiguring Christianity. The final lines of the letter have an ironic ring, for Solov'ev admits that many will no doubt consider him mad or unbalanced to harbour such convictions, but claims: "... the madness of God is wiser than human wisdom."⁶ The accounts of Solov'ev's religious "madness" were to become legion not only during his lifetime, but even long after.

The manifesto which Solov'ev so simply and forthrightly expounded in this early letter did not change during the entire course of

---

³ Ibid., 88-89
⁴ Ibid., 89.
⁵ Ibid., 89.
⁶ Ibid., 90. As has been pointed out to me, Solov'ev was no doubt referring to the passage in 1 Corinthians, 1:25 (which in English reads "... the foolishness of God is wiser than men ..."). However, he has actually paraphrased the passage as it appears in the Russian version to read "madness" [bezumnoe] rather than "foolishness" [nemudroe].

his life. Its points of reference formed the basis upon which he was to construct his broad philosophy of Christianity with its doctrines of "Godmanhood", the "Universal Church", "Theocracy" and so on. However, perhaps one of the most important aspects of this first statement of faith and action is the positive attitude which Solov'ev assumes in his basic assessment of the world situation and the possibility of achieving a transformed Christian society. It should be recalled that he states quite clearly: "I do not recognize the existing evil as eternal, I do not believe in the devil."[7] Here he implies a non-dualistic system in which evil is transitory in comparison to the eternal nature of good. Furthermore, he goes on to protest against those who would attempt to destroy force by force or would use force to transform the world. The Christian truth is "passive" in that it must attract, it must be an inner action: "I know that all transformation must take place *from* within—from the human heart and mind."[8] In other words, facing the fact that bringing the Christian truth to open consciousness in people will demand a lengthy process, Solov'ev, nonetheless, implies a belief in the attainment of his grand vision of "Godmanhood" by peaceful, evolutionary means, by a positive revelation or apocalypse in which force alone will not be exerted over evil. However, as his hopes in the achievement of a peaceful revelation diminish and his fears of the violent and catastrophic apocalypse increase towards the end of his life, when the cosmos can no longer *absorb* chaos in a peaceful process of universal history—as implied in his Sophiology—he comes to feel that man will have to witness the violent confrontation of cosmos and chaos, for the latter can be subdued and absorbed only through force. What is remarkable in this later phase is that Sophia and Sophiology, as such, seem to fade in both the poetry and theosophy of Solov'ev, even as they subsequently do with Aleksandr Blok and Andrej Belyj.

The grand goal which Solov'ev set himself was to be achieved principally through rational thought, as the philosopher explained in his letter. He viewed as prejudice, and an innate enemy of Christian truth, the exclusive right of mysticism and irrational logic to define the nature and function of Christianity. This intense awareness no doubt accounts for the extremism in Solov'ev's apologetic works, namely, their ultra-rational, ultra-theoretical approach to proving the existence of God and defining the progressive nature of true Christianity. The attempt to seek out and express the rationally attractive basis of Christianity necessarily results in the discovery and revelation of Sophia, the Divine Wisdom of God. However, at the same time as her function is invariably accepted by Solov'ev as a rational neces-

[7] *Ibid.*, 88.
[8] *Ibid.*, 88.

sity in the operation of his scheme, she invariably masks a mysterious transformation, a mysterious relationship, a mysterious union whether divine or terrestrial. Thus, she may be considered the mysterious symbol of a rational process.

The feminine archetype of Sophia, or Divine Wisdom, more than any other single concept, occupies the centre of Vladimir Solov'ev's theosophy and poetry. A great deal of confusion surrounds Solov'ev's many definitions of this figure because she apparently represents so many categories in his thought and his poetry. In the principal theoretical works dealing with the nature of Sophia[9] a shallow reading finds Sophia an independent spirit at one moment, and at the next inextricably part of the nature of the Godhead, of Jesus Christ, the Holy Virgin, the World-Soul and even of the Universal Church and Humanity. The wealth of aliases that accompany her, of course, often add to the same confusion. In her theosophical hypostases she appears under the appellations of "Divine Wisdom of God" or "essential Wisdom of God"; her concrete celestial designation is often "Aphrodite Urania" or the "Eternal Feminine", while as "Sophia" she combines both these concrete and abstract modes into a single manifestation. Her earthly reflections are correspondingly multiple: abstractly she is known as the "World Soul", while in her concrete manifestations she assumes the titles of both "Aphrodite Anadyomene/Pandemos" and "Mother Nature."

Much of the confusion arises from the fact that the celestial and earthly designations of Sophia are erroneously considered coequivalent, coeval. To consider the World Soul the same as the "Divine Wisdom of God" or Aphrodite Anadyomene essentially of the same nature as Aphrodite Urania is an idolatry which worships the graven image, or manifested likeness of God, rather than the spirit behind the manifestation.

Solov'ev's "visions" of Sophia were both rational and irrational as may be judged by comparing his theosophy and poetry. Practically from the very beginning of his investigations she appears as the central issue of the question, the riddle to be solved, the key to the mystery of God and the purpose of Christianity as revealed by God. His studies in the nature of the Divine Wisdom of God were both rational and intuitive. He set himself to examining not only the major philosophical systems of Western culture, but the esoteric writings of the mystics and Gnostics as well. At the same time, Solov'ev's rational search was supported by his own mystical or intuitive visions. His

---

[9] The three principal works which underlie Solov'ev's conception of Sophia, the Divine Wisdom of God, and of primary concern here are: *Chtenija o Bogochelovechestve*, which was serialized in the journal *Pravoslavnoe obozrenie* from 1877-1881; *La Russie et l'Eglise Universelle* (Paris, 1889); "Smysl ljubvi," first serialized in *Voprosy filosofii i psikhologii*, 1892-94.

most famous poem "Three Meetings" ("Tri svidanija", 1898) records three supposedly actual meetings with or visions of Sophia. The first took place in a church during a religious service; the second appeared to him while he was reading gnostic-cabbalistic literature in the British Museum in London where in 1875 he had made a special journey specifically to study sophiological literature. This second vision directed him to the Egyptian Desert where he subsequently witnessed Sophia's third appearance. While the mystical and prophetic were obviously of great personal importance to him as inspiration for carrying on his theoretical work, his specific task called for a "rationalization" of the Christian truth and not merely the recording of religious experiences. The importance of a rational or theoretical basis for expounding Sophiology is quite apparent in the following excerpt from a letter written to S. A. Tolstaja on 27 April, 1877. While displaying Solov'ev's all-out theoretic effort in the study of Sophia, it also discloses his deep conviction that mere mystical experience is insufficient without a coherent and well-developed system to place it in:

> I did not find anything special in the library [i.e., the British Museum]. In the mystics there were many affirmations of my own ideas but no new light and, what is more, they almost all possess an extremely subjective character and, so to speak, rather drivelling at that. I found three specialists in Sophia: Georg Gichtel, Gottfried Arnold and John Pordage. All three had personal experiences almost the same as my own, and this was the most interesting fact, but especially in theosophy all three are rather weak; they follow Boehme, but are inferior to him. I think Sophia had to do with them more for their innocence than for anything else. Consequently, only Paracelsus, Boehme and Swedenborg still prove to be the real people, so that I am left with a large field.[10]

Solov'ev appears to believe that there must have existed or still does exist some divine condition or a divine model of truth from which man has strayed. In order to rediscover this archetypal condition one must return to the very beginning, to the origin of the cosmogonic process. Solov'ev wastes no time in doing so, for in his very first article, "The Mythological Process in Ancient Paganism" (1873), he deals specifically with the questions of monotheism and polytheism as they relate to the development of both the mythological process, and the origin of "religion" as such.

Ostensibly setting out to discount the "nature-theory" of the origins of mythology, which generally states that the appearances or manifestations of nature were responsible for the formation of myths and worship in a polytheistic shape, Solov'ev, in fact, outlines the working area for an eventual formulation of Sophiology. On the basis

[10] Pis'ma V. S. Solov'eva, II, 200.

of his study of ancient religion, in particular the Vedic tradition, Solov'ev argues that the original or primeval religion must have been monotheistic, believing in an "unconditionally single, purely spiritual divinity."[11] But if the original divinity or Godhead was unconditionally one and purely spiritual, a freely creative spirit, subsequently man's perception of the single, unique Godhead fragmented His oneness, provoking not only a plurality of gods for aspects of the original Godhead, but falsely hypostatizing the plural aspects in place of the original and single god in an attempt to satisfy his desire for knowledge of God in his entirety through taking the material appearances of divinity for divinity itself. This basic view of the course of religion underlies all of Solov'ev's subsequent positions on Godmanhood and the Universal Church contained in his philosophy of Sophia.

Although in this first article Solov'ev does not proceed beyond this analysis of the history of religion and mythology, it becomes apparent in retrospect what precisely he had in mind. Obviously, Judaeo-Christian tradition represented the first two phases in the history of modern religion as opposed to that of ancient mythology. The Hebrew tradition provided the first monotheistic phase and Christianity, as the second phase, complemented it with a human Christ in order that the third and future phase, the marriage of God and man, spiritual heaven and material earth, might be consummated, thereby returning to that primeval oneness or total-unity.

Consequently, the Christian truth which Solov'ev seeks to theorize and expound, is the truth of oneness, the all-oneness of total-unity between God and man, heaven and earth. However, the loss of this vision has to be rectified; man must be presented with the development from exclusive and original divine oneness through false material multiplicity to a marriage of the two in a new and single union of heaven and earth.

Now, many critics have blithely stated that Solov'ev's original vision of Sophia and the return to oneness owe a great deal to the Gnostics without in fact stating precisely why or providing any details. Arcane and complex as it might seem, nonetheless it may be worthwhile to examine in some detail the Gnostic scheme. This is well worth the pains involved inasmuch as it will not only fill the lacunae in Solov'ev's own Sophiology, but show rather convincingly that the "Sophia-Mythus" of the Gnostics provided the archetype for Solov'ev's own vision of a unity lost and restored, of paradise lost and regained. Doubtless there are other "sources" equal in importance to gnosticism when dealing with Solov'ev's Sophia. He himself specifically made mention in his correspondence of others such as Boehme,

[11] "Mifologicheskij protsess v drevnem jazychestve," in *Sobranie sochinenij V. S. Solov'eva*, ed. S. M. Solov'eva and E. L. Radlova (2nd ed.; Petersburg, [1911]), I, 11.

Paracelsus and Swedenborg. However, I have isolated specifically the Gnostics with reason. Solov'ev's "Gnostic poems" (discussed in the following chapter) are not only obviously important in themselves, but made an impact on young symbolists like Aleksandr Blok and Andrej Belyj. Belyj, in particular, made much of what he personally believed to be Solov'ev's indebtedness for Sophia to the Gnostics.[12] Finally, one of the most vehement reasons for attacking the "heresy" of Sergej Bulgakov's theology in later years was the supposedly pernicious influence of Gnosticism.

The end of all Gnosis was the acquisition of Wisdom and consequently the pivotal point in the Gnostic scheme was the role played by personified Wisdom or Sophia. The dwelling place of Sophia was in the Middle Kingdom (the Ogdoad), between the superior and entirely spiritual kingdom (the Pleroma) and the inferior material kingdom (the Hebdomad or Seven Spheres of psychic substance).[13] In the Ogdoad Sophia was not only the Mediatrix between the spiritual and material kingdoms, but projected the Types or Ideas of the Pleroma into the Hebdomad. The mystery that confronted the Gnostics was to explain why Wisdom, originally of a "pneumatic and spiritual essence", originally dwelling in the Pleroma, should be banished to the Middle Kingdom and be plunged into sorrow and longing. The solution of the mystery was traced to Ignorance and indicated the "Path of Self-Knowledge" or "self-analysing reflection" as the remedial process. In order to become one with the spiritual mind, the physical mind had to be purified. For this purpose, the soteriological drama of Christ's deliverance of Sophia from her ignorance and suffering was formulated.

While there are many variations on the cosmology surrounding the Sophia-Mythus, Hippolytus' outline should provide the basic model. The originating cause of the universe is a Monad, unbegotten and imperishable, incomprehensible, the source of the generation of all existing things and usually designated as the Father. (There was dissent among the Valentinian Gnostics as to whether the Father could beget alone or whether there was a spouse, Sige, for this purpose). The Father is not subject to time or space; he is solitary and self-existing, reposing within himself. In his solitariness he projects and conceives the dyad Nous and Aletheia (Mind and Truth). In their turn they project or conceive the syzygy of Zoe and Logos (Life

[12] See Andrej Belyj, "Vospominanija o A. A. Bloke," in *Epopeja*, No. 3, 1922, 228ff. Belyj even makes a detailed comparison between Blok and the Gnostics. *Ibid.*, 232ff.

[13] This conception was presumably drawn from the text in *Proverbs*, viii and ix: "Wisdom built for herself a House and rested it on Seven Pillars," and "She is in the lofty Heights; she stands in the Midst of the Paths, for she taketh her seats by the Gates of the Powerful Ones, she tarrieth at the Entrances." This reading doubtless provided the source of her appellation for Solov'ev and the other symbolists as the *Deva raduzhnykh vorot* ("Maiden of the Resplendent Gates").

and Word) who produce Anthropos and Ecclesia (Man and Church). This creation of pairs or Aeons continues until there are some 28 or 30 Aeons in the Pleroma (depending whether the Father, or Bythe, and Sige are included). The youngest of these Aeons is called Sophia. Noting that all the Aeons produced their offspring by syzygy or conjugal intercourse, she determines, in imitation of the Father, to produce an offspring without a partner or intercourse and yet create a work in no way inferior to the Father's. But while all things exist simultaneously in the Unbegotten One, in the begotten Aeons the female is projective of substance and the male is formative of this substance. Consequently Sophia can only produce a formless substance, a shapeless, imperfect mass. The rest of the Aeons are thrown into dismay at this abortion of Sophia's presumptuous work and fear that it might destroy the harmony of the Pleroma. The Father allays their fears and consoles the sorrowing Sophia. He orders a further projection through the syzygy of Nous and Aletheia whereby Christ and the Holy Spirit are projected who are to restore Form, remove Sophia's abortion and console the distraught youngest of the Aeons. With the birth of Christ and the Holy Spirit, Sophia's shapeless abortion separates from the entirety of the Aeons; in order to maintain the harmony of the Pleroma the Father creates a separate realm outside it called the Ogdoad, but in no way inferior to it. When Christ and the Holy Spirit have given form to what was formless and consoled Sophia in the Ogdoad, they return to the Pleroma. Now, in honour of the Father, the Aeons jointly project a single Aeon, "The Joint Fruit of the Pleroma" who is also to be called Jesus. Meanwhile Sophia, who is outside the Pleroma, is in search of the Christ who had brought her comfort and given form to the formless and she is terrified that she will perish if she remains separated from him. She sends her supplications to the Pleroma where the Christ and the Aeons have pity on her and send the "Joint Fruit" to her in order to rectify her four passions of fear, sorrow, perplexity and entreaty. But the Joint Fruit, or Jesus, perceives these passions to be eternal and therefore unsuitable for destruction, and consequently rectifies her passions by converting them into substantially extant essences: fear becomes animal desire; grief is made material; the passion of perplexity becomes the passions of the daemons; but conversion, entreaty and supplication are made into the path to repentance and power over the animal essence. Generally speaking these converted "passions" combined to form a realm inferior to the Ogdoad called the Hebdomad. Sophia is able to exert her energy and influence from the intermediate realm of the Ogdoad on the inferior realm of the Hebdomad.

The Demiurge, who is senseless vigour and action, believes itself to be the Creator of this inferior physical world, whereas in fact

Sophia is its cause and inspiration. Thus Sophia is the power from which the animal and material creation originally derived its present condition. Sophia is called spirit, whereas the Demiurge is named the "Soul". However, the Demiurge does have control over material manifestations and physical forms in the Hebdomad.

Sophia's realm, the Ogdoad, is divided up into Aeons in imitation of the Pleroma and she becomes the mother of all living things, while the Joint Fruit of the Pleroma is the Logos. The Ogdoad is now known as the Heavenly Jerusalem and this Jerusalem is Sophia whose spouse is the Joint Fruit, while the Demiurge is charged with projecting souls in the lower kingdom. Bodies for these souls are fashioned by the Demiurge from the "devilish essence" (i.e. clay) and this becomes material man. However material man's soul can be inhabited by the Logos from above, that is, from the Joint Fruit and from Sophia together. If man's soul is fashioned by the Demiurge in the likeness of the Ogdoad, and inhabited by the Logos, man will become immortal and rise to the Heavenly Jerusalem, which is the realm of Sophia, and which of course was created in the likeness of the original Pleroma.

From this brief outline of the Valentinian system of Gnosis, the major motifs informing Solov'ev's Sophiology may be extracted without undue difficulty. The conception of Bythe or the Father as the all-in-one, self-existing and incomprehensible monad parallels the similar concept of Solov'ev's Godhead. The creative mode of syzygyies, or unions of pairs from which the Aeons emerge, underlies the creative development of the philosopher's own cosmology. In particular the Sophia-Mythus serves as the model of perfect totalunity, of harmony once extant, lost and finally restored. The restoration of total-unity and harmony is reflected in the divine image of Sophia who, in union with the Joint Fruit or Jesus is reinstated to her perfect divine nature. This is the divine example of perfect union which is to inspire material man. The Demiurge is clearly the archetype for Solov'ev's "World Soul" which functions precisely in the same manner, namely as creatrix of physical forms, of earthly souls which may then be inspired with and inhabited with the descending logos to become likewise divine and immortal. This latter marriage of the divine and the earthly is the formula, of course, for Solov'ev's Godmanhood in which Sophia herself serves as the eternal image of a syzygy that has been effected between herself and Jesus. The reader will also recognize the "feminine" and "male" roles which are to be interpreted in a similar fashion by Solov'ev, namely, that the feminine role (as in Mother-Nature, or the great Earth-Mother) is to produce the physical matter, while the male role is to fertilize or give form to this matter. These functions will be described metaphysically as the "passive and active principles" in the Solov'evian schema. But above all, without this primeval structure of syzygy, of the union of polar natures, upon which the Gnostic view is based, nothing positive can be created.

In both his *Lectures on Godmanhood* and *La Russie et l'Eglise Universelle* Solov'ev defines Divinity or Godhead as an unconditional, spiritual, single being who possesses completeness, explains all things and is explained by himself. He is the unique universal organism that contains all things within himself in harmony. God is one in all and possesses all in his unity. This unity or totality presupposes a plurality, but one that is reduced to oneness in God. However, in order to explain God better, in order to understand his nature better, Solov'ev also seeks recourse to the concept of the Holy Trinity. The three major aspects of God are: 1) the pure or primordial act; 2) the secondary act or manifested action; 3) the state of perfect enjoyment of itself. These three aspects, which in Christianity assume the names of Father, Son and Holy Spirit, possess no separate or independent being outside of the single principle of the Godhead. As hypostases they are consubstantial and indivisible.

In the beginning the Godhead perceived the idea or thought of creation. The action or act of creation is represented by the Father who, in fact, creates. The Son signifies the result of the creative act, the passive principle of that which has received form. Finally, the Holy Spirit designates the third aspect which is essentially the enjoyment of creation and the return of creation to the creator, thus crowning the concept of the three-in-one. These three aspects of hypostasis are pure possibility within the Godhead; they do not exist separately, but only as the three inherent aspects of a single God. While Solov'ev attempts to explain the roles of the three aspects in the more or less theologically traditional fashion, he produces a new theological concept in order to define the unique substance of this divine Trinity, the absolute objectivity of this Three-In-One.

> It is one; but not being capable of being one thing among many, a particular object, it is the universal substance or *all-in-oneness*. In possessing it, God possesses all in it, it is the plenitude or the absolute totality of being preceding and superior to all partial existence. This universal substance, this absolute unity of all is the essential wisdom of God (Khocmah, Sophia). Possessing in her the hidden power of all things, she herself is possessed by God and is so under a triple mode.[14]

Solov'ev then offers support for this view of Sophia as the divine principle of *all-in-oneness*, which is the Wisdom of God, the unique thought or idea which he possesses, by quoting from *Proverbs* 8:22ff. which further illustrates his meaning, namely that God possessed Wisdom or Sophia in the beginning of his way, before his work of

[14] V. Solov'ev, *La Russie et l'Eglise Universelle* (2nd ed.; Paris, 1906), 233.

creation, and that he possesses her eternally. Apparently, then, in the concept of Sophia, Solov'ev discerns not a fourth hypostasis of God, but rather a completely independent idea of the special relationship of the Holy Trinity, and God's "plan" of total-unity, the Wisdom he displays in his purpose.

If God's operative or active principle is the divine principle of all-in-oneness, of total-unity, then Sophia's function is to represent in a passive fashion the divine manifestation of this total-unity. To better understand this passive and reflective nature of Sophia (and subsequently the feminine principle embodied in the Holy Virgin Mary, the Universal Church and the World Soul) Solov'ev introduces the concept of two unities in every organism, the first active and producing, the second passive and being produced:

> In every organism we have of necessity two unities: on the one hand the unity of the active principle which reduces a multiplicity of elements to itself as to one; on the other hand we have that multiplicity which has been reduced to a unity as a definite image of this principle. We have a unity which produces and a unity which is produced, or a unity as a principle (in itself) and a unity which is manifested.[15]

The first principle of active union, the producing principle of oneness is the Word or Logos and is possessed by God and subsequently by Christ. They are the agents who possess oneness unconditionally. The second principle of produced oneness finds, however, its embodiment in Sophia. She is the produced, the manifested idea of total-unity: "Sophia is the body of God, the substance of Divinity permeated by the principle of divine oneness."[16] The fact that Sophia is the *passive* and *manifested* symbol of the total-unity of the divine principle is extremely important in understanding not only Solov'ev's philosophy and poetry, but also that of the succeeding symbolists as well.

When God conceived the creation of the world, the idea he possessed in his wisdom was the idea of Sophia, namely that of all-in-oneness. Solov'ev points out this conception, as has been mentioned, on the basis of the passage from *Proverbs* which he also reinforces by reference to the uncanonical text of *The Wisdom of Solomon*. If the world is to be created in the divine principle of the likeness of Sophia, it is necessary to understand why God creates the world, and thus, Solov'ev again seeks recourse to an ever-expanding conception of Sophia.

Chaos is willed to exist by God outside of himself: "But God loves chaos in its nothingness and he desires that it exist, for he will be able

---

[15] Solov'ev, "Chtenija o Bogochelovechestve," *Sobranie sochinenij V. S. Solov'eva*, III, 114.

[16] *Ibid.*, III, 114.

to return this rebellious existence to unity. He will be able to fill the infinite void with his abundant life. Therefore God grants liberty to chaos."[17] Sophia or the Divine Wisdom of God is explained, in this relationship between the divine oneness or cosmos of God and the extra-divine plurality or chaos, as the "play" of his Divine Wisdom. Obviously, God could by the mere force of his omnipotence return the chaos of the extra-divine to total-unity in the divine realm. Sophia's "play", in regard to the extra-divine world, is explained as the means for God to display the truth of his absoluteness:

> She "plays" by evoking before God the innumerable possibilities of all the extra-divine existences and by absorbing them anew into this omnipotence, his absolute truth and his infinite grace. In this play of his essential Wisdom the one and threefold God, by suppressing the power of potential chaos, by illuminating its shadows and by penetrating its abyss, is aware of himself from within and proves to himself for all eternity that he is more powerful and more true and better than all possible beings outside of himself. It is manifested unto him by this play of his Wisdom that all that is positive belongs to him by fact and by right, that he possesses eternally in himself an infinite treasure of all the real forces, of all the true ideas, of all the benefits and of all the graces.[18]

But if this particular "play" of his divine Wisdom is only a *potential* vanquishing of the chaos of the extra-divine world, then God seeks an *actual* realization of absorbing this chaos and its plurality into his oneness. God is not content to preside over all while remaining within himself and merely asserting his potential power, truth and grace. By his love he desires yet another nature that can become as absolute and unconditional as he is: "If in his power and his truth *God is all*, he wants in his love that *all should be God*. He wants that there should be outside of himself another nature which might become progressively that which he is for all eternity—the absolute all."[19] Consequently, Sophia's divine and potential play described above will be initiated in fact in the extra-divine world. This is God's Divine Wisdom: "In order to arrive by itself at the divine totality, in order to enter into a free and reciprocal association with God, this nature must be separated from God and at the same time united to him. Separated by its real basis which is the Earth, and united by its ideal summit which is Man, it is especially in the vision of earth and man that eternal Wisdom has laid out before God its play for the future."[20] Just as Sophia represents the produced oneness in the divine sphere and the potential unifying of the extra-divine or

---

[17] Solov'ev, *La Russie* . . ., 231.
[18] Ibid., 229.
[19] Ibid., 230.
[20] Ibid., 230.

chaos with the divine, so also will she symbolize the possibility of an actual produced oneness taking place between the creaturely and divine worlds.

The nature of the material world which God creates in his Divine Wisdom is explained by Solov'ev as simply the *reversal* or *transposition* of the divine and is separated from the divine by the laws of time, space and mechanistic causality. However, since outside of God it is impossible to conceive of the real existence of any being other than God, these three conditions must be considered conditional: "... these three conditions are nothing real and positive, they are only a negation and a transposition of the divine existence in its principal categories."[21]

If the world created out of chaos or the extra-divine is the reversal of the divine, then the three conditions of time, space, and mechanistic causality tend to fracture and dissolve the exemplary total-unity and oneness of the divine realm. This force supposes the existence of a *will* which in turn supposes the presence of a *soul*. Consequently, this soul of the natural world, this "World Soul", provides the basis of extra-divine nature or chaos.

Confusion has arisen over the identity of this World Soul. She is often confused with Sophia or the Divine Wisdom of God, but in fact she represents the opposite of Sophia. Just as Sophia is divine, immovable, fixed and eternal, the World Soul is extra-divine, and subject to the conditions of time and space: "... as this world is the opposite or the reverse of the divine totality, the World-Soul itself is the opposite or antitype of the essential Wisdom of God."[22] Just as Sophia represents the unconditional all-in-oneness, the absolute and spiritual body of God, the "Queen of Heaven", so the World Soul represents the conditional and material body of the natural world: "This World Soul is the single created being and the first of all the created beings, the *materia prima* and the true substratum of our created world."[23]

However, in the same way that in his Divine Wisdom God created the world out of the extra-divine in order to return it to his oneness, so also the World Soul is created in the image of Sophia, as the prototypic Wisdom of God. It is absolutely necessary that the World Soul be conceived of as a freely operating spirit in the extra-divine world, just as God is in the divine. Consequently, the World Soul is essentially a dualistic spirit, one that can exist outside of God's oneness, or within it:

> In her quality of pure and indeterminate power the World Soul possesses a double and variable nature (*i aoristos dyas*): she is capable of

[21] *Ibid.*, 234-235.
[22] *Ibid.*, 235.
[23] *Ibid.*, 235.

desiring to exist for herself, outside of God, she is capable of putting herself at the false point of view of chaotic and anarchical existence, but she is also capable of submitting before God, of attaching herself freely to the divine Word, of returning all creation to perfect oneness and of identifying herself with Eternal Wisdom.[24]

As Solov'ev expresses her free and dualistic nature in Lecture X of *Lectures on Godmanhood*, she is "participating in God's oneness and at the same time embracing the entire multiplicity of living souls."[25] She includes in herself both the divine principle of oneness (because God, in his Wisdom, allowed her to exist independently and be capable of returning the natural world to oneness) and the principle of created being which she controls exclusively and can desire to control outside of God. The first instance gives her freedom from the time, space and casuality of the creaturely world, whereas the second allows her independence from God. But the obvious role for the World Soul to assume, of course, is that of a potential source of Sophia, of the Divine Wisdom of God: "As an act of creation she does not exist eternally in herself, but she exists for all eternity in God in the state of pure power, as a hidden basis of Eternal Wisdom."[26]

Indeed, in her positive assumption of the earthly role of Sophia, or the divine principle of total-unity, the World Soul can actually become the active, producing principle, or Logos, which creates oneness. In this role she complements the first hypostasis of the Godhead, namely the Father, who is the principle of creative all-in-oneness: "This potential and future Mother of the extra-divine world corresponds as an ideal complement to the eternally actual Father of the Godhead."[27]

In her earthly condition of chaos and plurality the World Soul experiences the desire for oneness. As a result the Word (the divine and active principle) reveals himself to her at creation in the vague idea of the one and indivisible world. Thus, her relationship with God is defined by three states of time:

> The state of her primitive absorption into the oneness of the eternal Father—her eternal subsistence in him as pure power or simple possibility, is henceforth defined as the *past* of the soul; the state of her separation from being with God by the blind force of chaotic desire constitutes her present; and the return to God, the new reunion with him, becomes the object of her aspirations and her efforts—her ideal future.[28]

This temporal progress of the World Soul represents no less than the content of world history or the world process: "The gradual realiza-

---

[24] Ibid., 235-236.
[25] V. Solov'ev, "Chtenija o Bogochelovechestve," III, 140.
[26] V. Solov'ev, *La Russie...*, 235.
[27] Ibid., 235.
[28] Ibid., 238.

tion of this striving, the gradual realization of the ideal total-unity composes the sense and purpose of the world process."[29]

This "play" of God's Divine Wisdom, or Sophia, has created an illusory and transposed world as an antitype to the divine realm. However, Solov'ev can also reverse the point-of-view and claim that Sophia's "play" in creating an inferior or chaotic world of possibilities, has in its turn evoked a superior and cosmic world which operates as a divine model of truth for its inferior version:

> We have seen, in effect, how Eternal Wisdom evoked the possibilities of irrational and anarchical existence in order to oppose to them the corresponding manifestations of absolute power, truth and goodness. These divine reactions which are only a play in the immanent life of God, are fixed and become real existences when the anti-divine possibilities which provoke them cease to be pure possibilities. Thus, to the creation of the inferior or chaotic world necessarily corresponds the creation of a superior or celestial world.[30]

Thus, the World Soul appears, not as Sophia herself on earth, but rather as her potential spirit, her potential agent. By uniting with the Word or *Logos*, the World Soul will be submitting to God's Divine Wisdom and the principle of total-unity. Sophia is the initiation of this world process because she is the manifested symbol of divine oneness. At the same time, she is also the completion of the process in which the potential oneness of the extra-divine world has already been realized archetypally:

> If She [i.e. Divine Wisdom] exists in God substantially and for all eternity, she effectively realizes herself in the world and is incarnated there successively in returning it to an increasingly perfect unity. She is "reshith" in the beginning—the fruitful idea of absolute unity, the unique power which must unify all; she is "Malkhouth" ($Βασιλεία$ Regnum) in the end—the Kingdom of God, and the completely realized unity of the Creator and of creaturely being. She is not the World Soul,—the World Soul is only the vehicle, the means and the substratum of her realization.[31]

The closest Sophia comes to the World Soul is when the World Soul unites with the *Logos*, for it is in the action of the *Logos*, the active principle of oneness, that Sophia makes herself known to the World Soul. United with the *Logos*, the World Soul can progressively raise herself to an identification with Sophia, but that, of course, can only be consummated at the end of cosmic history, namely in the union of Heaven and Earth. However, in spite of the fact that Sophia is not the World Soul, she still stands in a special relationship to the world: "Khocmah, $χοκμα$, and Divine Wisdom are not the World

---

[29] V. Solov'ev, "Chtenija o Bogochelovechestve," III, 144.
[30] V. Solov'ev, *La Russie* ..., 239.
[31] *Ibid.*, 241-242.

Soul, but rather the guardian angel of the world covering with her wings all the creatures in order to elevate them gradually to true being just as a bird covers its young. She is the substance of the Holy Spirit who is borne over the shadowy deeps of the nascent world."[32]

The consummation of the work of the World Soul is in the creation of man. This creation crowns the world process and initiates the historical process. However, it should be borne in mind that directly or indirectly the World Soul is responsible for the creation, not only of man (in both his masculine and feminine counterparts), but also for mankind—society as well. Man can be conceived by the World Soul only when she is in a completely receptive condition, a state of humility wherein she recognizes the Word and seeks to found the Kingdom of God within herself.

Man possesses the total-unity of God within himself and is created in the likeness of God. Nevertheless, as a rational and conscious being he must resolve to possess this divine principle outwardly as well, that is, consciously. Born of the will of the World Soul and bearing the concealed divine principle, man is the perfect dual son of two natures, the one material, the other divine:

> Accepting and bearing in his consciousness the eternal divine idea and at the same time by his factual origin and existence inextricably connected with the nature of the external world, man appears as the natural intermediary between God and material existence, the bearer of the all-uniting divine principle to the elemental plurality—the builder and organizer of the universe.[33]

In fact, man alone can become the effective agent of Sophia on earth, for only through him by virtue of his dual nature can be initiated a series of deliberate and rational actions whereby he transforms the earth and returns it to the World Soul penetrated by light and life-giving spirit. In the same way he can, by his rational acts, make the heavens descend to earth: "If by him—by his reason—the earth has been elevated to the Heavens—by him also—by his action, the heavens must descend and fill the earth; through him all the extra-divine world must become a single living body—the total incarnation of Divine Wisdom."[34]

The progress of man towards total-unity, or the universal process as Solov'ev designates it, is outlined in "Triple Incarnation de la Sagesse Divine" (Part III, Chapter VII of *La Russie et l'Eglise Universelle*). This "triple incarnation of Divine Wisdom" or Sophia is schematized in a series of ascending triadic configurations of the Three-In-One principle. These triads essentially operate in imitation

---

[32] Ibid., 242.
[33] V. Solov'ev, "Chtenija o Bogochelovechestve," III, 150.
[34] V. Solov'ev, *La Russie . . .*, 257.

of the divine model offered by the Holy Trinity whose special nature finds expression in the manifested idea of Sophia.

The first three-in-one is proposed at the lowest level of universal history, or the history of mankind in the triad of man + woman = society. This is "natural humanity" as it has resulted from the offices of the World Soul and will form the basis for a more idealized and elevated "divine humanity": "The reason and conscience of man, the heart and instinct of woman, finally the law of solidarity or altruism which forms the basis of all society—are only a prefiguration of the true, divine-human oneness, a germ which must yet grow, flourish and bear its fruit."[35] Immediately discernible in this lowly, but germinating configuration is the same three-in-one principle which Solov'ev used in defining the Godhead. The terms "man", "woman" and "society" only represent a triple hypostasis of a single, potentially united mankind. For, it is not individual man who in isolation from his fellow-man will strive to unite Heaven and Earth, but mankind as a single, homogeneous and united principle. To this end Solov'ev does not hesitate to emphasize the importance of collective oneness: "It is only through society that man can attain his definitive goal—the universal integration of all extra-divine existence."[36] Thus, natural man represents the germ of the Father's hypostasis, namely, the primordial act, the active and producing principle; woman is the Son's hypostasis, namely the passive and receptive principle; whereas society is the enjoyment of this relationship between producing and produced, the spirit of free relativity.

Stated otherwise, man can receive the *Logos* or principle of total-unity and actively attempt to objectify it in his complementary half, woman, and therefore create society which is the extension of the total manifestation of man. In spite of these three moments, however, the man-woman-society triad represents only a single human being, total-unity in oneness. The concept of Sophia once again enters the discussion in order to symbolize the specific nature of this three-in-oneness which is the blue-print for the next stage in universal history: "The successive development of this germ is accomplished by the process of universal history; and the triple fruit which it bears is: the perfect woman or nature made divine, the perfect man or the Godman, and the perfect society of God with men—the definitive incarnation of Eternal Wisdom."[37]

However, just as God created a divine or celestial realm displaying his essential Wisdom in order to disclose the false point-of-view of the World Soul and the illusory nature of the material world, he

---

[35] Ibid., 259.
[36] Ibid., 258.
[37] Ibid., 259.

must also provide a divine archetype for the perfect man, the perfect woman and the perfect society for mankind. This exemplary three-in-one is Christ, the Holy Virgin and the Church. Just as mankind is born of both a divine and earthly principle (in the image of God and as son of the World Soul), both Christ and the Holy Virgin possess a dual nature. This divine principle is suggested by the names "Christ" and "Holy Virgin", whereas their earthly nature is implied in their names as "Jesus" and "Mary". Furthermore, the Logos, the active or producing principle of oneness, is imparted to Christ (as the perfect Godman) and the passive and produced principle of oneness is imparted to the Holy Virgin (as the perfect woman or nature made divine). In other words, Christ, the Holy Virgin and the Church are the divine-creaturely hypostasis of the three-in-one, the manifested Logos which serves as a model for mankind. Through them, humanity is reunited with God. Once again this is the triple manifestation of Divine Wisdom operating through Christ, the Holy Virgin and the Church:

> Humanity reunited with God in the Holy Virgin, in Christ, in the Church, is the realization of the essential Wisdom or of the absolute substance of God, his created form, his incarnation. In truth, it is one and the same substantial form (designated by the Bible as *semen mulieris, scilicet Sophiae*) which is produced in three successive and permanent manifestations, in actuality distinct, but essentially indivisible, by being called Mary in its feminine personality, Jesus in its masculine personality—and preserving its proper name for its total and universal appearance in the perfect Church of the future, the Betrothed Bride of the divine Word.[38]

Ultimately, therefore, Solov'ev seeks a collective oneness of all mankind, a humanity penetrated by conscious and rational knowledge of what God's Wisdom consists of, namely, the plan for uniting all of mankind through Christ, the Holy Virgin and the Church to God which will produce a synthesis of Heaven and Earth in Godmanhood. The consummation of this Godmanhood through a Universal Church would signify no less than the perfect incarnation of Sophia: "And his reunion with God, however necessarily triple, nonetheless constitutes only a single divine-human being—the incarnate Σοφία of whom the central and most perfectly personal manifestation is Jesus Christ; the feminine complement—the Holy Virgin, and the universal extension—the Church."[39] Sophia presides over every single stage in this cosmic process which has as its object the unification of God and mankind. Just as she represented the divinely manifested principle of three hypostases, indivisible and consubstantial in a single God, she also represents the culmination of universal history which is the extra-divinely manifested principle of three hypostases indivisible

[38] Ibid., 261.
[39] Ibid., 260.

and consubstantial in perfect humanity or the Universal Church. Thus, in her role of the divine Wisdom of God, she stands as the fixed and eternal meeting point of Heaven and Earth, as the ultimate incarnation of total-unity in which the union of the divine and the extra-divine is viewed in the following manner: "... by producing an existence which is semi-terrestrial and semi-celestial, capable of embracing in its unity the totality of created being and by rejoining it to God through a free and living tie, by incarnating in a created form the eternal divine Wisdom."[40]

The concept of love also poses an important problem in understanding the nature of Sophia, especially in her role as mediator between Heaven and Earth in the process culminating in the marriage of the divine and extra-divine, in the formulation of the heavenly and earthly syzygy. Being herself the product of a divine syzygy, of the three-in-one union of Father, Son and Holy Spirit in the indivisible and absolute oneness of God, it follows naturally that as the symbol of all-in-oneness she should be present in the concept of earthly love.

In his article "Smysl ljubvi" ("The Meaning of Love")[41] Solov'ev outlines the nature and role of love. His analysis is both metaphysical and ethical, for it deals not only with the meaning of love in the relations of individuals, but also in the larger context of his theories on Godmanhood and the Universal Church.

The first of five articles on the subject briefly treats the various existing theories of the meaning of love, all of which Solov'ev refutes by more or less logical and rational argument. Consequently, on the lowest level, he refuses to view "sexual love" as merely a biological function whereby the species is maintained. At the highest level he also attempts to prove by reference to various biblical theories that in both sacred and secular history sexual love is not an instrument of historical purposes intended to advance the human species.

In the second article Solov'ev focuses attention on the human individual and his relations with other individuals. The positive aspect of sexual love must be sought out in the individual life and man as the highest form of intelligent life must be the source of truth in this regard. This truth that each individual possesses inwardly is the "positive oneness of all things." Once man discovers his justification and affirmation of the truth of all-in-oneness, he cannot affirm himself separately, egoistically, outside of it. This truth of all-in-oneness is the same truth which God expresses in his divine Wisdom, in Sophia. Solov'ev now calls it "love": "Truth, like a living force possessing the inner being of man and in actual fact leading him out of a false self-affirmation, is called love."[42] Love provides the means

[40] Ibid., 248-249.
[41] "Smysl ljubvi" was serialized in *Voprosy filosofii i psikhologii*, 1892-1894.
[42] V. Solov'ev, "Smysl ljubvi," in *Sobranie sochinenij V. S. Solov'eva*, VII, 15.

for defeating man's false egoism, for overcoming the attraction to a false and chaotic Mangodhood in which man affirms his sovereignty and independence outside of God. Sexual love, therefore, offers man a chance of defeating the temptation of egoism by recognizing the unconditional worth of another being outside of himself. Solov'ev describes this union, this microcosmic syzygy, in the following terms:

> Only in this, so to speak, chemical union of two beings which are of the same species, of equal worth and yet completely dissimilar in form, is the creation of a new person possible (both in the natural order as well as in the spiritual order), the actual realization of a true, human individuality. Such a union, or at least the closest possibility of one, we find in sexual love, and therefore we grant it an exclusive significance as the requisite and irreplaceable basis of all future perfection, as the unavoidable and constant condition whereby only man can genuinely abide in truth.[43]

Already it is possible to see that Solov'ev's theory of love is yet another formulation of the major concepts in his Sophiology. Only "sexual love" can meet all the requirements of his larger plan. For in "sexual love" there is a meeting of two equally significant individuals, of the same nature or species, but at the same time differing in form—in other words a man and a woman. This is of course a reflection of the various triads already discussed, the syzygy of Christ and the Holy Virgin in their divine aspect, of Jesus and Mary in their human aspect, and, of course, of man and woman in their natural aspect. Following the same triadic contours whereby out of the syzygy of Christ and the Holy Virgin arose the Church and out of the syzygy of man and woman arose society or the prototypic perfect humanity, Solov'ev also praises the "offspring" of two equal and yet qualitatively different subjects which is the result of love or the perfect union to produce the perfect oneness. Obviously, homosexuality and lesbianism are denied any valid status in Solov'ev's theory, not on purely moral grounds, but because they do not represent a union of opposite qualities, of two principles of male (active and producing) and female (passive and produced) conforming to his metaphysical scheme. In this article Solov'ev significantly denies a purely "mystical love". The reasons again are dictated by his final purpose. A mystical love is not a true love because each of the celebrants completely loses his or her identity by submitting themselves to a nirvanic state of non-differentiation. This would, of course, deny Solov'ev's attempts at a triple manifestation of divine Wisdom wherein the indivisible aspects of total-unity can be distinguished and comprehended. Obviously, it would also detract from the *free*

[43] *Ibid.*, VII, 19.

and *rational* meeting of God and perfect humanity to create a *conscious* Godmanhood.

In the third article he returns to a closer analysis of his term "sexual love" to clear away any possible misunderstanding. In fact, as the reader may already have surmised, Solov'ev's conception of "sexual love" is hardly orthodox: "I call sexual love (for want of a better term) the exclusive devotion (reciprocal as well as unilateral) between people of differing sex who are capable of being in the relationship of man and wife between themselves, in no way prejudging hereby the question or meaning of the physiological aspect of the affair."[44] Apparently, then, Solov'ev's major concern is for the meeting of two equal but differing principles. The "sexuality" of love is not the physiological union (which Solov'ev wishes to deny as the exclusive meaning of love), but rather the generic aspect, the man/woman aspect which naturally accords with the syzygal aspect of his entire philosophy. Consequently, love has the following task:

> The task of love consists of *justifying in fact* that meaning of love which at first is given only through emotion; a combination of two given, conditional beings is required, who would create of themselves a single absolute ideal individual. ... A realization of this oneness, or the creation of the true man as a free union of the male and female principles, preserving their formal particularization yet overcoming their essential separation and disintegration, this is the genuine and imminent *task* of love.[45]

Thus, while Solov'ev does not wish to affirm sexual love merely as a physical act, he also wishes to avoid any mystical or "platonic" love as an exclusive alternative. However, he does not deny sex altogether; rather he sees it as a logical consequence of his own conception and not as the prime mover. At the same time he does not completely disavow the significance of mystical love, for it can offer that ideal inspiration and noble thought which is partner to any genuine syzygy. Obviously, he wishes to steer the middle course between the two extremes, seeking the hermetic synthesis of the earthly and divine.

The fourth article is no doubt the most significant and far-reaching of all five. Here Solov'ev presents love as the universal vehicle which enables mankind to overcome all. Death signifies disintegration, separation and loss; it is preeminently the spirit of chaos, the content of "negative infinity." Love, however, can deliver man from death, can obviate death's presence. If a condition of separateness and division exists, then death and disintegration ensue, but the condition of oneness and total-unity implied in the androgynous union of the sexes through true love can bring about eternal life. True

---

[44] *Ibid.*, VII, 22.
[45] *Ibid.*, VII, 24.

love makes eternal life possible, but exclusively physical love can mean death, because it is only passing and incomplete. The problem is how to effect the genuine union that is required by true sexual love. Characteristically, Solov'ev presents the solution in terms of a synthesizing triad—three principles which will enable man to realize his essentially androgynous nature. The first principle, or category, of love is the biological one suggested by lower forms of nature, namely, the furtherance of the species in the physical act. The second is the socio-moral principle which places the relationship in a societal structure. However, it is the third principle alone which offers the genuine means for man to achieve wholeness. This is the divine principle of man's union in God. This final union with God is no less than the ultimate goal for which all the triads discussed earlier present a blueprint.

Recognizing that true love has not yet been attained, let alone the ultimate Godmanhood, Solov'ev realizes the necessity for basing true love on faith or belief. This faith will be confirmed once man can see himself as an individual, a unity, and deny any egoism by completely affirming the worth of another individual outside of himself, uniting with the other individual in the love of God and thereby entering into ideal union with God. Ultimately, God is the object of any genuine love or union, but Solov'ev realizes that at the present time, this ultimate syzygy cannot be consummated. The object of our love (in the ideal sense) is still differentiated from the empirical fact of our instinctive love, although the two are connected or, in fact, one:

> This is one and the same person in two differing modes or in two different spheres of being—the ideal and the real. The first is for the time being only an idea. However, in genuine, faithful and perceiving love we know that this idea is not our wilful fabrication, but that it expresses the truth of that object, only not yet realized in the sphere of external real appearances.[46]

What is this "idea", this "ideal object", of both our earthly and God's divine love? It is, of course, no less than that very ideal oneness towards which the world is striving. God's love is oneness or the desire for oneness. This is why he created the world out of chaos—so that in his boundless love another being, another nature might become as absolute as he is, so that the creaturely world, or chaos, might be returned or reunited with the divine world and the cosmos. Thus, Divine Wisdom or Sophia once again appears at the intersection of God's love and God's thought in the idea of total-unity. Man finds the expression of the heavenly object of his love in the feminine spirit of Sophia: "The heavenly object of our love is only one, forever and for everyone one and the same: the eternal Divine Feminine."[47] The fact

[46] Ibid., VII, 44.
[47] Ibid., VII, 47.

that Sophia seeks and finds her delight in the sons of Man, that in man she finds the worthy agent for producing that unique all-in-oneness of which she is the eternal expression, suggests that the "othersidedness", or all that is outside of God but is becoming, is being elevated to God, as the spirit of perfect femininity. However, it is not enough that the archetype of the Divine Feminine or Sophia exists eternally only so that God can love her. She must inspire and return man's love as well; she must be an active force in his life:

> For God his othersidedness (i.e., the universe) possesses from the beginning of time the image of the perfect feminine, but he desires that this image should not be for Him alone, but that it should be realized and incarnated for every single being capable of uniting himself with it. Towards such a realization and incarnation strives the Eternal Feminine herself who is not merely an inactive image in the mind of God, but a living spiritual being possessing all the fullness of powers and actions. The entire world and its historical process is the process of her realization and incarnation in a great multiplicity of forms and stages.[48]

If earlier, Sophia appeared to be an entirely passive symbol, a theological principle designed to express the nature of God's Three-In-Oneness, the indivisible nature of the celestial and earthly triads, the concept of a perfect humanity and finally the spirit attendant upon the consummation of Godmanhood, Solov'ev now provides her with the active role of the spirit of Love. Love is the reason underlying God's Wisdom; it is the mysterious force whereby the free and conscious union of God and Man can take place. The Divine Feminine is not merely the recipient of man's love, but she in turn must inspire us to concrete works and we must be inspired by her love for us to those actions leading to the realization of total-unity.

But since the world is still in a state of imperfection, still in a condition of becoming, we must discern two loves, or a two-fold love. We love that ideal being which we seek to invest in our ideal world (the world of perfect humanity and, consequently, Godmanhood) and we love that human creature of nature (the feminine object of this material world) which offers the personal material for this realization. Solov'ev defines this as an ascending and a descending love: the former envisages the divine nature of Sophia, namely Aphrodite Urania, whereas the latter turns to the earthly nature of Sophia in the World Soul or Aphrodite Pandemos. As a result, earthly woman offers the opportunity for a manifestation of potentially divine love, a true love that is in the process of becoming divine oneness:

> The complete realization, the transformation of the individual female being into a ray of the Divine Feminine that is indivisible from her

[48] Ibid., VII, 46.

radiant source, will be an actual fact and not merely subjective, but an objective union in it of the living and immortal image of God."⁴⁹

Love provides the emotional, the inner force for the realization of the universal syzygy envisaged by Solov'ev.

This is the main content of the fifth and final article on the meaning of love. Since all histories and all processes, whether universal, world, or historical contain a potential or actual movement towards oneness, then this ultimate fact of God's Divine Wisdom, or Sophia, may be expressed in the single word "syzygy". The desire to be reunited, the desire to be all-one, describes the true nature and direction of the world. Consequently, the "meaning of love" is only a question of understanding the larger plan of God's Wisdom. Thus, it is not the strictly ethical or social relationship of man and woman (or only peripherally so), which informs Solov'ev's obsession with syzygy, with ultimate union between the divine and extra-divine. Syzygies, or unions and syntheses, are the basic content of Solov'ev's entire Sophiology, the operative force behind the movement from the lowest forms of life to the highest expression of Godmanhood; "sexual love" is yet another manifestation of this Solov'evian *Idea*.

Just as Sophia was the theological formulation construed by Solov'ev at all the other key points of syzygal union throughout the the system, she now absorbs the function of love through the Divine or Eternal Feminine which may be considered, in fact, no more than another hypostasis or aspect of Sophia's nature and function as God's Divine Wisdom.

Solov'ev feels that the uniqueness of his Sophiology is also the uniqueness expressed by the Russian spirit in its intuitive perception of the nature of Sophia:

> In dedicating its most ancient temples to Saint Sophia, the substantial Wisdom of God, [the Russian people] have given to this idea a new expression which is unknown to the Greeks (who identified Σοφία with the λόγος). By intimately linking Saint Sophia to the Mother of God and to Jesus Christ, the religious art of our ancestors distinguished her manifestly from one and the other, by representing her in the features of a particular divine being. It was for them the heavenly substance overlaid by the appearances of the inferior world, the luminous spirit of regenerated humanity, the guardian Angel of Earth, the future and definitive appearance of the Godhead.⁵⁰

According to Solov'ev, then, Sophia is not to be identified solely with Christ or even with the Holy Virgin. The Russian people, so he believed, have intuitively known Sophia represents neither of these individual divine figures, but rather perfect humanity or the Universal Church:

---

⁴⁹ Ibid., VII, 45-46.
⁵⁰ V. Solov'ev, *La Russie...*, 263-264.

> Thus, beside the *individual* human form of the divine,—beside the Virgin-Mother and the Son of God,—the Russian people have known and loved, under the name of Holy Sophia, the *social* incarnation of the Godhead in the Universal Church. It is to this idea, revealed to the religious sensibility of our ancestors, to this truly national and absolutely universal idea that we must now give a rational expression. It is a question of formulating the living Word that ancient Russia has conceived and that the new Russia must pronounce to the world.[51]

The uniqueness of the Russian and Solov'evian Sophiology is therefore to be found in the "social incarnation of the Godhead in the Universal Church,"; humanity reunited with God in the Holy Virgin, in Christ, and in the Church, represents the realization and incarnation of God's Divine Wisdom. This is precisely the interpretation which Solov'ev draws from *Proverbs* (8:22ff.): "Then I was by him, as a master workman/: And I was daily his delight, Rejoicing always before him;/ And my delight was with the sons of men." Sophia or Eternal Wisdom finds her delight (or "play") in the sons of men, for in the perfect humanity to come she can be fully realized:

> "Eternal Wisdom which is in principle the unity of all, and entirely the unity of opposites,—a free and reciprocal unity—finally finds a subject in which and by which she can realize herself completely. She finds it and rejoices. *My delight*, she says, *my delight par excellence, is in the sons of Man.*"[52]

In tallying up the aspects of Sophia's hypostases it is impossible, therefore, not to include practically every stage in Solov'ev's rational scheme for transforming all of Christendom. She expresses the unique relationship of the indivisible Three-In-One nature of the Godhead; God has Sophia before him in creating the extra-divine world; the World Soul is the potential material or corporeal expression of Sophia's own manifested oneness which can become purified and elevated to an identity with her; she is implicit in the three successive manifestations of God's incarnation through Christ, the Holy Virgin and consequently the Church which natural man, natural woman and society, or collective humanity, have as a divine archetype before them; her mode of operation is "true love" which is attached to the Divine Feminine and which operates potentially in every single feminine individual on earth; finally the ultimate and perfect incarnation of Divine Wisdom receives its complete expression in the reunion of perfect humanity with God in Godmanhood.

It is quite apparent that Solov'ev was intent upon creating two differing and opposing realms, the divine and the extra-divine. But he also sought to provide a constant bridge between them, to allow for a free and conscious, yet inspired, meeting of the two. The creaturely

[51] *Ibid.*, 264.
[52] *Ibid.*, 255.

world is a mirror of the divine, but as a reflection, of course, reversed or transposed. The divine world has to attract the extra-divine to a union through the truth, idea and goodness of its example. All the forces and spirits of the divine find their false opposites or antitypes in the extra-divine. But the meeting of the two is prepared for by Sophia. She is the bridge, the manifested perfection that operates between the two realms. The Gnostic formulation is no doubt the most expressive account of this possibility of union, presenting as it does the potential or possible account of the entire cosmogonic process which Solov'ev treats in his discourses. In the meeting and subsequent marriage of each pair of divine and extra-divine types and antitypes, she acts as the marriage-broker who prepares, conducts and concludes the androgynous syzygy. That this consummation should be expressed as "androgynous" follows quite logically when it is borne in mind that Solov'ev's first and positive apocalyptic vision was one in which he envisaged, not the destruction of chaos or the extra-divine natural world by the divine, but rather a *free, conscious* and *reciprocal* union of the two in which the entities of perfect Mankind and perfect God would join indivisibly, but distinctively. This can be the only purpose of the entire universal process, for as Solov'ev argues, if it were merely a matter of suppressing chaos and restoring it to oneness, God could not perform this act with a single display of his omnipotence. Consequently, God's love in his Divine Wisdom is for another nature to exist outside of him and to know him, his truth, idea and love and become as He himself.

Thus, Sophia is God's expression of his celestial plan of unity. At the same time, she signifies man's desire to know God's Divine Wisdom, to become conscious of what that Wisdom is. If ultimately Sophia is God's attempt to know man, then Sophia is also man's attempt to know God. As Solov'ev astutely points out in "The Meaning of Love", the Bible expresses "sexual love" (in both its physical and philosophical sense) as "knowing", to have "knowledge" of another person, thereby implying the necessity of union or syzygy in order to attain perfect knowledge.

Chapter 2

THE PRIVATE SOLOV'EV

By the time the first major critical appraisal of Vladimir Solov'ev, *Sbornik Pervyj. O Vladimire Solov'eve* (Moscow, 1911), appeared eleven years after his death, the concept of his dual character as philosopher and poet had been firmly established. In "The Problem of East and West in the Religious Consciousness of V. S. Solov'ev", Nikolaj Berdjaev laid out the opposing sides of Solov'ev in terms of the *daytime* or rational and the *nighttime* or mystical Solov'ev.

As the daytime philosopher Solov'ev had attempted to outline in rational and theoretical terms his revelation of the Divine Wisdom of God, his own teaching on total-unity based on a sophiological interpretation of cosmic and world history. Devoid of all rhetoric and spontaneity, this daytime philosophy was designed to woo the mind rather than the heart which was what Solov'ev originally stated as his purpose in his manifesto-letter to E. K. Romanova. This theoretical revelation was to be understood as a *public* statement, the rational basis for some positive action in the area of ecumenism and ethics. However, in a plan as vast and religious in nature as Solov'ev's, one suspects some original source of pure inspiration, some personal conviction constructed on inner revelation or personal and immediate experience. The source of this mysterious flame which was supposed to ignite the lamps of man's rational knowledge was to be found in the nighttime Solov'ev, the mystic and poet who had been the recipient of a personal vision of the divine Sophia herself. The interplay of the philosophical search of the daytime and the mystical quest of the nighttime is clearly stated by Solov'ev himself in the following poem:

> In morning mist with steps uncertain
> To mysterious and wondrous shores I journeyed.
> The dawn contended with the final stars
> And dreams still hovered—and seized with dreams
> My soul beseeched the unknown gods.
>
> In the cold white day along a lonely path,
> As before, I proceed to an unknown land.

> The mist disperses and the eye clearly sees
> How difficult the mountain path and yet how far,
> How far is all of which I have dreamed.
>
> Until midnight with unfailing steps
> I shall ever proceed to desired shores,
> There on the mountain where beneath new stars
> All aflame with triumphant fires
> Awaits me my sacred temple.
> ("V tumane utrennem nevernymi shagami...", 1885)

From the poem it is clear that the first and irrational impulse is a child of night's dreams and reveries. The consummation of the dreams' promises falls not in the daytime, but, once again in the night, at midnight when the journey comes to an end as the poet reaches his promised temple. In between lies the difficult and steep path of rational revelation which is to be traversed in daytime—certainly the atmosphere of Solov'ev's theoretic writings. Ironically enough, this single poem sums up better than any other the poet's premonition of his spiritual *curriculum vitae*. On the basis of a personal and intuitive revelation, which is outlined in his poem "Three Meetings", Solov'ev embarked upon a life-long campaign to prepare and preach a rational and philosophical conception of the Christian truth, an attempt to facilitate the foundation of the Heavenly Jerusalem within the framework of a serene and rational apocalypse without the horrifying spectres of destruction usually associated with the end of world history and the fusion of heaven and earth. However, increasingly disillusioned and resigned towards the end of his life, Solov'ev turned more and more to the irrational and mystical impulses of this nocturnal aspect of revelation in his visions of Pan-Mongolism and the threat of the Antichrist. The measured and confident tact of the daytime philosopher submitted increasingly to the visions of the poet of night. Thus, the poet-philosopher was brought full circle from the revelatory state of nocturnal dreams through the long and arduous philosophical apology for Christian truth back to the final mysterious consummation of his vision at midnight.

While the rational thinker made himself known in his theoretical writings, public and university lectures, as well as his personal efforts to bring about an ecumenical union of the Eastern and Western branches of Christianity, the mystic Solov'ev was revealed to many not only in his poetry, but also in his eccentric life-style and private views. Many are the personal accounts and reminiscences of Solov'ev's occult interests. As a young man, he apparently took a very active interest in spiritism and frequently participated in seances. His letters give ample evidence of this preoccupation with mediumistic practices. It gave rise to earnest arguments with N. Strakhov,[1] the

---

[1] In Vladimir Solov'ev's correspondence can be found numerous references to his

positivist; it attracted him to the circle initiated by A. K. Tolstoj (and carried on by A. K. Tolstoj's widow after his death in 1875) who himself had been very deeply immersed in occult studies; it provided part of the basis of his friendship with the Slavophile Aksakovs who were like-minded. While in London in 1875, he made a special visit to the then famous English medium, Charles Williams, although in his correspondence he voiced some doubts about the character and success of both the medium and the seance. In fact, Solov'ev appeared to be rather disappointed on the whole with most of the professed mediums he encountered in both London and Paris, judging from his letters.[2]

Among others, Prince Evgenij Trubetskoj tells of the extremely delicate and nervous constitution of Solov'ev.[3] Apparently, he was often sick and feverish and it was especially during these bouts of illness that he was particularly susceptible to visions and hallucinations. In fact, Solov'ev considered himself to be a very sensitive medium and often confided to friends the nature of his contact with the spirits. In his reminiscences one Russian intellectual, who was also doing research in the British Museum at the same time as Solov'ev was there, gives a rather startling description of the young philosopher's activities both in and out of the library in London. This chance acquaintance often observed Solov'ev at work in the reading room and his curiosity was aroused by the abnormal manner of the philosopher. Solov'ev would sit for hours over a single text on the Cabbala that contained mysterious and fantastic drawings and symbols. To Janzhul's question of why he was so absorbed in this single book, Solov'ev's reply was apparently that "... in a single line of this book there is more intelligence than in all of European science..."[4] Especially arresting, however, is the account of the following episode that relates most directly to Solov'ev's mediumistic abilities and eccentric behaviour:

> Incidentally, I would add to this [i.e., Solov'ev's visit to Williams] that to the latter individuals, that is, to the young girl, Schtudnitz and to my wife, by way of a special sign of trust, Vladimir Sergeevich frequently and in a most serious manner announced that in all the decisive and important instances of his life he acted according to the

own interest in the occult and mystic. His letters to N. N. Strakhov are of special interest in this regard. Strakhov appears to have taken a negative view of such delvings into the supernatural and Solov'ev feels compelled to defend this realm of knowledge. See in particular the two letters to Strakhov of 2 March, 1884, and 12 April, 1887, which are contained in Pis'ma V. S. Solov'eva, pod. red. E. L. Radlova (Petersburg, 1908-1923), I, 17-18 and 32-34, respectively.

[2] See his letter to Dmitrij Nikolaevich Tsertelev, on 22 August (o. s. 3 September), 1875, in Pis'ma V. S. Solov'eva, II, 228.

[3] See Pr. Evgenij Trubetskoj, "Lichnost' V. S. Solov'eva," in Sbornik Pervyj. O Vladimire Solov'eve (Moscow, 1911), 45-74.

[4] "Vospominanija L. I. Janzhul", Russkaja starina, No. 3, 1910, 482.

directions and advice of the spirit of a certain Norman woman of the XVIth or XVIIth century, who appeared to him when he wished and gave the appropriate directions on how to act or what to expect. I repeat again that he announced this several times—avoiding us, the men, who would have held him up to ridicule for such announcements.[5]

Quite obviously there was a hidden side to Solov'ev's life of which few people knew a great deal. The person who did have knowledge of the most intimate and uncirculated details of his strange habits and occult visions was his brother, Mikhail Sergeevich Solov'ev. Apparently in the private papers and correspondence of the deceased philosopher, M. S. Solov'ev uncovered such incredible and compromising material that he felt forced to destroy most of it in order to preserve the intellectual and moral reputation of his brother. One of the scandalous facts that leaked out was recently presented by Nikolaj Valentinov in his posthumously published memoirs, *Two Years with the Symbolists*.[6] Valentinov intended to destroy the myth of Solov'ev's "saintliness" by exposing him as a mentally unbalanced pervert. According to Valentinov, M. S. Solov'ev found a series of intimate letters addressed to Vladimir Solov'ev and signed merely with the letter "S". However, it was quite apparent that the letters were in Solov'ev's own easily recognizable handwriting. Apparently he had written these erotic letters to himself and signed them "S" which was construed as "Sophia". However, Valentinov's "exposé" was by no means new, for this rather amazing set of circumstances had been documented by two other sources. It was known that Solov'ev did indulge in "automatic writing" much as Yeats did, and claimed to be sensitive to emanations and telepathic messages from other realms. Of particular interest is the fact that a later symbolist writer, Georgij Chulkov, claimed that he had seen some specimens of Solov'ev's "automatic writing" in the 1920's. Apparently, then, not all of Solov'ev's compromising private papers were in fact destroyed.[7] They may exist to this day in some appropriately hidden and mysterious Soviet archive. Andrej Belyj also testified to the existence of such curious letters throughout his own memoirs.[8] Perhaps M. S. Solov'ev only wanted to give the impression that the papers had been destroyed in order to put a stop to the vicious rumours concerning Solov'ev's strange and erotic loves. These sinister rumours increased during the final year of his life because of his so-called "mysterious affair" with a certain Anna Nikolaevna Schmidt, who also had mysti-

[5] Ibid., 481.
[6] Stanford, California, 1969.
[7] See fn. 16 of Chapter III.
[8] See Andrej Belyj, "Vospominanija o A. A. Bloke," in *Epopeja*, No. 1, 1922, 140, 142.

cal visions and saw herself as the incarnated Sophia, descended to earth for union with Vladimir Solov'ev. This particular relationship and Anna Schmidt's teachings will be dealt with in detail in the following chapter.

Although an opposition can be developed between the author of the poetry and the philosophy, the two were never essentially divorced. The rational and irrational revelations inspired and nurtured each other throughout his lifetime. Born of a single and united conception of God's Divine Wisdom, the poetry and philosophy travelled distinct but parallel paths throughout his life until they finally merged in the poetic sermon, "A Short Tale of Antichrist". If the irrational inspiration was usually submerged in his theoretical statements, the same was generally true of the theorized content of his poetry. However, Solov'ev no doubt viewed ethics and aesthetics as the legitimate offspring of metaphysics, in his rational mode, at least, and accordingly midwifed the theoretical birth of poetry in the following terms:

> The task of poetry, and of art in general, does not consist of "decorating reality with pleasant contrivances of the living imagination", as it was stated in classical aesthetics, but of incarnating in *sensible* images that very higher meaning of life to which the philosopher gives definition in rational concepts, which is preached by the moralist and realized by the historical agent as the idea of good. To the artistic sensibility is immediately revealed in the form of sensible beauty that same perfect content of being which is gained through philosophy as a truth of contemplation.[9]

At least Solov'ev does not seem to claim any special rights for poetry and its intuitive perception of truth. It appears to be only another mode, another agency for revealing and describing the ultimate. Significant, however, is the connection between philosophy and poetry that is struck in this definition, for, in fact, the goals and functions of the two are identical. If Solov'ev's rational philosophy of Christianity was intended to move the world closer to the divine principle of total-unity, then poetry was also the handmaiden of the same master, the external and fixed vision of God's Wisdom, another means of revealing the otherworldly and the divine:

> While history is still continuing, we can have only individual and fragmentary *premonitions* (anticipations) of perfect beauty; the arts existing today, in the greatest of their works catching glimmers of eternal beauty in the flux of our reality and continuing them further, anticipate, allow us to have premonitions of a reality that is for us otherworldly and drawing nigh, they serve in this fashion as a transition and connecting link between the beauty of nature and the beauty

[9] V. Solov'ev, "Poezija F. I. Tjutcheva," in *Sobranie sochinenij V. S. Solov'eva*. VII, 124.

of the future life. Art comprehended in this manner ceases to be empty amusement and becomes an important and edifying work, but not at all in the sense of didactic sermonizing, but only in the sense of inspired prophecy.[10]

The poet is at the intersection of two worlds, the perfect and the imperfect, the heavenly and the earthly. As a child of both divine and material principles, as the agency whereby material nature has to be transformed and united with divine being, the poet-man "... must without fail penetrate *into the homeland of fire and word* in order to bring forth from there the proto-images of his creations and at the same time that inner enlightenment which is called inspiration and by means of which we in our material reality can discover the sounds and colours for the incarnation of ideal types."[11] Amplifying this idea even further, Solov'ev views poetry as the offspring of rational contemplation in which he enters into *direct communication* with the images of the divine world:

> And man, as one who belongs to both worlds, can and must by an act of rational contemplation concern himself with the divine world, and finding himself yet in a world of contention and vague apprehension he must enter into communication with vivid images from the kingdom of glory and eternal beauty. But in particular, this positive although incomplete knowledge or penetration into the reality of the divine world is characteristic of poetic creativity.[12]

It would hardly seem presumptuous, in retrospect at least, to read into this "communication with vivid images from the kingdom of glory and eternal beauty" Solov'ev's own personal encounters with Sophia recorded in his poetry. Quite obviously, he did not view this supernatural communication as anything other than totally legitimate insofar as it served the ultimate purpose of transforming the world. Divine revelation, intercourse between the divine and extra-divine realms, religion, the inspired and immediate expression of rational contemplation—these are no less than the essential ingredients of any alchemical art that will be compounded eventually into a symbolist aesthetic for the succeeding generation of poets. Moreover, there can be little doubt that Solov'ev's choices of expounding specifically a Christian truth and employing Christian archetypes greatly influenced the later symbolist poets into electing an essentially Christian symbolism as the basis of their art.

Solov'ev even went so far as to state the actual themes of poetry, the internal and external aspects of lyrical poetry:

---

[10] V. Solov'ev, "Obshchij smysl iskusstva," in *Sobr. soch. V. S. Solov'eva*, VI, 84.

[11] V. Solov'ev, "Chtenija o Bogochelovechestve," in *Sobr. soch. V. S. Solov'eva*, III, 118.

[12] *Ibid.*, III, 118.

> The general meaning of the universe is revealed in the soul of the poet in a two-fold fashion: from its external side as the beauty of nature, and from the internal side as love, and namely in its most intensive and concentrated expression—as sexual love. These two themes: the eternal beauty of nature and the infinite power of love together make up the essential content of pure lyricism.[13]

Isolated from any over-all conception of Solov'ev's theoretical work these two themes appear as rather vague and generalized categories of the poetic corpus. The "beauty of nature" and "love" seem to be indiscriminate commonplaces for the definition of poetic content, at least until they are viewed in connection with Solov'ev's theoretical Sophiology, whereupon they immediately assume very distinct and specific contours. Solov'ev's own peculiar interpretation of "love" or more specifically "sexual love", presents the entire spectrum of Sophiology as the process of divine and earthly syzygy which he outlined in his article "The Meaning of Love" discussed in Chapter I. Similarly, the "beauty of nature" is not merely the inspiration of an artist infatuated with the sensible forms of beauty, but introduces once more his theoretical Sophiology in which the World Soul, or nature, becomes the earthly matter of the divine Sophia or Wisdom of God, inspired with the divine principles, striving for union with the divine world and potentially the purified and resplendent body of Sophia. Consequently, philosophy and poetry are one in their rational and irrational content. The same feminine archetype that Solov'ev filled with such a rational and detailed theological content in his theoretical writings—whose theosophical features, contours and epithets are so fully developed in rational theory—in his poetry is only mystically and vaguely shaded. However, in spite of her vague contours she still bears the unmistakeable mark of the philosophical Sophia.

The knightly devotion and zeal of Solov'ev's desire to embark on a life-long quest for the transformation of mankind has already been alluded to in discussing his early correspondence in the previous chapter. The same missionary-like fervour is easily discernible in the very earliest verses where he views himself, in a Christlike fashion, as the receptacle in which all of mankind's sufferings are contained:

> I imagine, as though a heavenly emissary,
> That all passions, all human afflictions,
> All grief and sufferings, all the spite of the ages
> Have I encompassed within my own breast.
> ("Nochnoe plavanie", 1874)

Echoing the "daytime" pursuit of the Universal Church and Godmanhood, were the philosopher's verses of "holy crusade" in which he

---

[13] V. Solov'ev, "O liricheskoj poezii," in *Sobr. Soch. V. S. Solov'eva*, VI, 247.

announced his readiness to sally forth and do battle with the spectres of evil. These verses of chivalrous militancy were, to be sure, more typical of the end of his life when disillusionment no doubt reinforced his visions of apocalyptic struggle:

> Heir to the sword-bearing host!
> You are faithful to the banner of the Cross.
> The flame of Christ is in your steel,
> And sacred is your menacing speech.
>
> The Lord's bosom is replete with love,
> And it summons us all alike...
> Yet before the dragon's fiery maw
> You perceived: the cross and sword are one.
> ("Drakon", 1900)

Many of Solov'ev's verses were similarly explicit as to his metamorphical role of knight to the Divine Sophia or her earthly representative, the World Soul: "Earth-mistress! Your beauty is incorruptible,/ And your radiant knight is immortal and mighty." ("Na tom zhe meste", 1898). But more typical perhaps of this aspect of Solov'ev's verses was the mood of doubt, despair and impotence. Lines such as the following contributed more effectively to his designation as the "poor knight": "Impotent mind, chained to earth's dust,/ Has summoned in vain the incorruptible dream." ("Vostorg dushi raschetlivym obmanom...", 1884). During his lifetime, Solov'ev's idealistic quest was crowned not with glorious success, but with humiliating defeat: "I proceed like a timid lamb,/ Delivered up for sacrifice." ("Tam, pod lipoj u reshetki...", 189?). Yet Solov'ev was unwilling to admit defeat even at the end of his life when all seemed hopeless. Surveying the ruins of his philosophical edifice he nonetheless preserved unsullied and unmarred the emblem of the Divine Sophia emblazoned on his knightly shield:

> Forever it remains unique! Though in the slumbering temple
> The infernal gleam shines in darkness and thunder resounds in silence—
> Though all has fallen round,—still the banner will tremble not,
> And the shield will not be moved from the crumbled wall.
> ....
> Only the emblem alone of an incorruptible testament
> Between heaven and earth stood as once before,
> And from heaven the same light illuminated as of old
> The Maiden of Nazareth and the serpent's vain poison before Her.
> ("Znamenie", 1898)

This fervour of his devotion to the Divine Sophia was Solov'ev's abiding legacy to the younger Russian symbolists.

The major categories of Sophia's hypostases in Solov'ev's poetry are three in number, as suggested by his theoretical articles: 1) Sophia the perfect eternal, and divine archetype who although fixed and immovable in her divine perfection, can move freely between the heavenly and earthly worlds; 2) the World Soul, or nature, the feminine principle of matter which can receive the *logos* and become divine—the earthly mirror of Sophia; 3) earthly woman, the feminine complement to the masculine principle, out of whose union arises society, the first syzygy leading to the ultimate union of heaven and earth. In keeping with the philosophical views of the poet, the only constant and fixed star is Sophia, whereas the extra-divine feminine principle in nature or womanhood is "free" to accept God's Wisdom and strive for union with Him, or to assert itself contrary to the divine principle of total-unity.

The best known and most remarkable verses inspired by Solov'ev's irrational visions of, and visitations from, Sophia are contained in "Three Meetings". The poem was composed in late September of 1898 under the impetus of some particularly profound mystical experience Solov'ev underwent over a period of three days, but nevertheless contained, according to Solov'ev's own eccentric comment "... in humorous verses the most significant of all that up until the present time has happened to me in life". The peculiar and perhaps misleading inappropriateness of couching "the most significant" events of Solov'ev's life in "humourous verses" is further deepened by his description of the longish poem as "... a little autobiography that a few poets and a few ladies found pleasing". The poem is suspended between shallow farce and profound revelation, swinging from the ridiculous to the sublime, like Solov'ev's hideous laughter that both repelled and attracted with its curious mixture of monstrous absurdity and prophetic naiveté. The prologue is serious enough:

> Prematurely triumphing over death
> And having overcome time's chain with love,
> Eternal friend, I do not summon you,
> But you, however, sense my trembling song ...
>
> Believing not in the deceptive world,
> Beneath the coarse covering of matter
> I perceived the incorruptible porphyry
> And came to know the brilliance of divinity.
>
> Was it not thrice you showed yourself to human eyes—
> Not in a movement of the mind—Oh no!
> Whether a presage, help, or a reward,
> Your image came in answer to the summons of the soul.

The dichotomy of divine and extra-divine, heavenly and earthly, is clearly established and the poet's attraction to another, more real, more ideal, world underscores his Platonic posture in these first three verses. However, this serious atmosphere is disturbed, not by the first revelation, but rather by a humorous account of the poet's first "love affair" when he was nine years old, the appearance of a "rival" and suggestions of a duel to decide things.

The first real vision of Sophia occurs in 1862 when the poet is still nine and replaces his "earthly love". This is the least remarkable of the three visions insofar as it takes place within predictable circumstances, namely the interior of a church, possibly during evening service amid the intoxicating incense, icons and music. Perhaps a passing hallucination in a feverish and sickly child with an overactive imagination:

> The altar is open... But where the priest, the deacon?
> And where the crowd of praying people?
> The flood of passions—it has suddenly dried without a trace.
> Azure is all about, azure is in my soul.
>
> Penetrated with a golden azure,
> Holding in your hand a flower from unearthly lands,
> You stood with a smile of rays of light,
> Nodded to me and disappeared into the mist.

The second visitation from Sophia occurs thirteen years later when, as a young university lecturer, Solov'ev has gone to study in the British Museum in London. The reader will recall Janzhul's testimony regarding his bizarre reading habits and his concentration on Gnostic literature, as well as his own confession that he was reading all he could about Sophia:

> More and more often I am alone in the reading room;
> And believe it or not as you will—God sees
> That mysterious powers have selected for me
> All that I could but read of her.
> . . . .
> And, lo, once—it was towards autumn—
> I said to her: oh, flowering of divinity!
> You are here, I sense it—why have you not revealed
> Yourself to my eyes since childhood years?
>
> And no sooner had I conceived this word—
> When suddenly all was filled with a golden azure,
> And once again she stood radiant before me—
> But only her face—it alone.

Another hallucination caused by overwrought nerves and tendentious reading? At any rate, this time Sophia speaks to him when he beseeches her to reveal herself totally. She directs him into the Egyptian Desert where presumably he will once again receive a visitation. Solov'ev immediately brings his affairs to a halt in London and leaves for Cairo via Paris without stopping en route. A satirical description of his Cairo hotel and the Russian and foreign clientele ensues which spills over into a grotesque caricature of himself wandering about in the desert wearing a top-hat and overcoat. He is attacked and tied up by some Bedouins, who probably take him for the devil, but then subsequently released. By now night has fallen and he finds himself alone in the desert, the eerie silence broken only by the mournful call of a jackal. At this moment of deepest despair and trepidation Solov'ev finally receives his third vision:

> And a long while I lay in cruel slumber,
> When lo there sounded: "Awake, my poor friend!"—
> And I awoke; but when I had fully awoken—
> The earth and heavens all around breathed of roses.
>
> And in the purple of the heavenly brilliance
> With eyes filled with azure fire
> You gazed like the first gleaming
> Of the universal and creative day.
>
> What is, what was, what is to come in all eternity—
> All this was here embraced by a single motionless gaze...
> Below me the seas and rivers grew blue,
> And the distant forest, and the heights of snowy mountains.
>
> I saw all, and all was but one—
> But one image of feminine beauty...
> The boundless entered into its measure—
> Before me, within me—are you alone.
>
> Oh, radiant one! I am not deceived by you:
> I saw all of you in the desert...
> In my soul those roses will not fade,
> Wherever the world surge may rush!

This third vision is the complete and undying revelation of Sophia that Solov'ev is to bear with himself for the rest of his life. The first two were preparations for this third and ultimate manifestation which is to serve as his constant inspiration in creating his philosophical and poetical Sophiology. As Solov'ev makes clear in the prologue and epilogue to the poem, this vision of Sophia has revealed an essentially Platonic situation wherein this world is but an imperfect reflection of the divine, a deceptive covering thrown over true reality. The poet, a captive of this sham, has received a direct and indisputable revelation of reality. The fore-knowledge of the poet's inconstancy and the Divine Feminine's immovable and constant nature should be remarked upon here as Solov'ev does himself in the lines, "Eternal friend, I shall not name you,/ And you forgive my inconstant song." This explains a great deal in the relationships of both Solov'ev and

Blok with their divine, feminine symbols. It is not Sophia or the Beautiful Lady that degenerates into the demonic archetype of Hecate, the moon goddess of an erotic and destructive sub-lunary flux, but rather the poet himself who in describing his own fall causes the divine vision of light to become sullied and imperfect. The special importance of this in the case of Blok will be seen in a subsequent chapter. However, Solov'ev himself defines the essential relationship between Sophia and her poet as that of the slave of inconstant earth in revolution about the exemplary sun, but in danger of enchantment by the sun-goddess's reflected but deceptive beauty in the baleful moon-goddess.

The feminine inspiration of Solov'ev's poetry, while unmistakably the Sophia of his theosophy, never appears under that name. Her titles are numerous, but invariably as vague and indefinite as her actual presence. Among the poetic designations which directly refer to her are: "eternal friend", "queen", "goddess". Most often she is simply addressed as "thou" (uncapitalized) which in itself does not always distinguish her from her earthly incarnations in the World Soul or Woman. She is, of course, the divine spirit invested in both the "Eternal Feminine" of Solov'ev's poem "Das Ewig-Weibliche" as well as the "Eye of Eternity" in the poem so titled.

However, as befits the mysterious and elusive nature of her poetic incarnations, more often than not we have only intimations of her presence, echoes and reflections and fleeting encounters with what is little more than an incorporeal and ethereal being. Even though in his third encounter with Sophia Solov'ev says that she finally revealed herself to him in all her radiance and perfection, the poet takes great pains to keep the mysterious revelation private and personal, as though its complete divulgence would destroy the vision itself.

The atmosphere of divine visitation and revelation is usually unmistakable in these poems. The immanent appearance of Sophia is invariably presaged by the colour symbolic of revelation—azure. The range of blue from pale through purple attends any sudden manifestation of Sophia. In "Three Meetings" blue or azure suffuses each encounter. Of the first, Solov'ev writes, "Azure is all about, azure is in my soul". Sophia herself is filled with azure: "Penetrated with a golden azure...". Finally the third emerges "in the purple of the heavenly brilliance/With eyes filled with azure fire...". Elsewhere we find "All in azure there appeared today/Before me my queen", and "An azure eye/Through the gloomily suspended clouds...". While azure is the most ecstatic colour of revelation in Solov'ev's vocabulary, it is not the only one. Sophia, as the spirit of light and brilliance in contrast to gloom and darkness, is often described simply in terms of brilliant light or the colour gold. This last is present in several of

Solov'ev's most significant poems, including "Three Meetings", together with azure and suggests the mystery revealed of that alchemical compounding of heaven and earth that not only penetrates Solov'ev's poetry, but proved the direct inspiration of Andrej Belyj's first book of poetry *Gold in Azure* (1904).

Unable or unwilling to produce Sophia's name, Solov'ev at one time presents a completely Gnostic and metaphoric portrait of this divine principle. In the poem, "My queen possesses a lofty palace", we find a paraphrase of Sophia directly based on Chapter 8 of *Proverbs*:

> My queen possesses a lofty palace,
> It stands on seven golden pillars,
> My queen has a seven-pointed crown,
> In it are precious stones without number.
>
> And in my queen's green garden
> There bloomed the beauty of roses and lilies,
> And in the transparent wave the silver stream
> Catches the reflection of curls and brow.
> ("U tsaritsy moej est' vysokij dvorets...", 1885)

However, the most Gnostic of Solov'ev's poems are the posthumously published verses of "The pure lily among our thorns" which disclose in indirect metaphors her syzygal function in the union of heaven and earth:

> The pure lily among our thorns,
> In the gloomy abyss the bright pearl,
> In the evil flame the unburning bush,
> In the general flood the ship secure,
> The bright cloud in the evening gloom
> Gleaming brilliant as God's elect,
> The rainbow reconciling heaven with earth,
> The faithful ark of divine promises,
> The precious phial of heavenly manna,
> The unassailable height, the one who bears God!
> Protect our world with your resplendent veil,
>   Blessed one from on high,
>   All illuminated
>   With light and the word!
> ("Lilija chistaja sredi nashikh ternij...", 1883)

This Gnostic obsession with syzygy may be considered the direct inspiration of other of Solov'ev's "occult" poems, such as "The Song of the Ophites" and the ecstatic prose poem or invocation to the Gnostic Sophia that was found in his album after his death. In his article on Vladimir Solov'ev and Anna Schmidt,[14] Bulgakov reproduces this

---

[14] See S. N. Bulgakov, "Vl. Solov'ev i Anna Schmidt," in *Tikhie dumy* (Moscow, 1918), 71-114.

prayer and expresses an appropriate doubt as to whether it is of Solov'ev's own making or a translation of some obscure Gnostic original:

> In the name of the Father, Son and Holy Spirit.
> An-Soph, Jah, Soph-Jah.
> With an unutterable, terrible and almighty name I adjure the gods, demons, peoples and all living beings. Gather into one the rays of your power, enclose the source of your desire and be the participants of my prayer: let us exert ourselves to catch the pure azure of Zion, let us discover the priceless pearl of Ophira, and may the roses and lilies be united in the vale of Sharon. The most holy Divine Sophia, the essential image of beauty and the joy of the all-high God, the radiant body of eternity, the soul of the world and the unique queen of all souls, with the boundlessness of thy unspeakable and gracious first and beloved son I beg of thee: descend into the prison of the soul, fill our gloom with thy brilliance, with the fire of thy love having melted the shackles of our spirit, present unto us light and freedom, in a visible and substantial way manifest thyself unto us, incarnate thyself in us and in the world, resurrecting the fulness of the ages, that the deeps may be encompassed and that god may be all in all.[15]

This is the only instance, in published form at least, where Solov'ev addresses Sophia outside of his rational treatises with her Gnostic and theosophical designation. Significantly enough, however, Solov'ev probably never intended to publish this prayer-poem and although he may have transcribed it from some obscure Gnostic hymn, it actually appears to be a synthetic creation incorporating several Gnostic systems in its Sophiological theosophy. The symbolism, as Bulgakov points out, is much the same as that of "The Song of the Ophites" which was written at approximately the same time.

Aside from the ecstatic outpourings of these few hymns, Solov'ev's descriptions remain generally vague concerning Sophia's actual appearance. As though revelation had smote him dumb and left him filled with an inner ecstasy that could only be expressed in imperfect speech, the details of her description are mysteriously lacking. In fact, a close examination of all his poems will reveal only three physical features of her appearance recurring over and over as leit-motifs. Most often he dwells on her eyes or hypnotic gaze. In "The Eye of Eternity" Sophia appears in one of her divine hypostases as the perfect symbol of all-in-oneness, as the magnetically attractive eye or gaze of eternity that draws man to Godmanhood:

> Alone, alone above the white earth
> Gleams a star,

---

[15] First published in the sixth edition of Vladimir Solov'ev's *Stikhotvorenija*, pod. red. S. M. Solov'eva (Moscow, 1915), and later reproduced in Bulgakov's article on Solov'ev and Schmidt in *Tikhie dumy*, 74.

> And across the distance, along an aetheric path
> > It draws all to itself.
>
> Oh, no, why? In a single motionless gaze
> > Are all wonders
> And the mysterious sea of all life,
> > And the heavens.
>
> And this gaze is so close and so clear—
> > Peer into it,
> You will become yourself—boundless and beautiful—
> > The King of all.
> ("Oko vechnosti", 1897)

This radiant eternal gaze is found throughout his poems, as in "The Azure Eye" or in "I see your emerald eyes...". Its suggestions of eternity and infinity are the essence of the third revelation in "Three Meetings": "You gazed like the first gleaming of the universal and creative day... / What is, what was, and what is to come for all eternity—/ All this was embraced here in a single motionless gaze...".

The second "concrete" feature is simply the image of Sophia's radiant and smiling face: "Holding in your hand a flower from unearthly lands,/ You stood with a smile of rays of light...". In the second vision in "Three Meetings" Solov'ev specifically remarks that he sees only her face: "And once again she stood radiant before me—/ But only her face—it alone". This combination of hypnotic eyes and radiant visage has suggested to a number of critics like Sergej Bulgakov and K. Mochulsky an unconscious association with the general appearance of the Holy Virgin icons in Russian Orthodox churches in Kiev and Novgorod especially.[16]

The only other specific feature comes in two or three references to Sophia's golden curls, for instance in the posthumous poem "Near, far, neither here, nor there":

> The voice of the fatherland in magical speech,
> In the light of azure eyes,
> The reflection of the fatherland in ethereal rays,
> In the gold of wondrous curls.
> ("Blizko, daleko, ne zdes' i ne tam...", 1898)

---

[16] Special attention should be drawn to Pavel Florenskij's mystical text Stolp i utverzhdenie istiny (Moscow, 1915). Chapter XXIV, entitled "Birjuzovoe Okruzhenie Sofii i Simvolika Golubogo i Sinjago Tsveta," (pp. 552-576) is quite astonishing insofar as Florenskij provides an almost identical religious symbolism of colours and iconography in the spiritual realm as the symbolists arrived at in the aesthetic depiction of the Divine Feminine. This particular chapter would seem to substantiate all the religious and spiritual claims for the poetic archetype of Sophia.

It seems strange to speak of "golden" curls. None of the best known Russian icons depict a "blonde" Holy Virgin, although of course the epithet could have another source, or could refer to a golden tiara or even the golden plate covering the Madonna as decoration. The only reason I mention this is that Blok's Beautiful Lady possesses, among her other rare features, golden curls. Blok may well have transferred this image from his wife, Ljubov' Dmitrievna Mendeleeva who was blonde. Perhaps it is merely a coincidence, but one that is nonetheless curious.

Complementing the rather obscure and vague features of azure or emerald eyes and radiant, smiling visage are other equally obscure and mysterious epithets. The poet hears from time to time indistinct echoes, rustlings and summonings from another world which he takes to be Sophia's voice:

> Somewhere far away flowers are blooming,
> A magic voice rings and summons
> ....
>
> The voice of the fatherland in magical speech
> ....
>
> Once again I caught the fading summons
> Of my mysterious friend.

But Sophia is also felt in silence, the silence which is the music of the spheres: "And in the transparent silence of immovable harmonies/ You are reflected". Just as Solov'ev perceives Sophia's hidden presence in otherworldly echoes, so also does he receive knowledge of her in images of transparency and reflection:

> The indistinct ray of a familiar gleaming
> ....
>
> Once more the reflection of an unearthly vision
> ....
>
> Again I sense above me the wing of an unseen shadow
> ....
>
> And in the transparent wave the silver stream
> Catches the reflection of curls and brow
> ....
>
> The reflection of the fatherland in ethereal rays,
> In the gold of wondrous curls.

In the interim between the end of Solov'ev's first series of recorded revelations that terminated in the late 1870's and their continuation towards the end of his life, the reader encounters mainly the echoes and reflections of Sophia rather than her full manifestation. The poems of the 1880's and early 1890's offer a record of the poet's striving to reestablish their communication. All that he can discern, however, is the spectral shadow that one finds for instance in "Wingless spirit, filled with the earth":

> The indistinct ray of a familiar gleaming
> The barely audible echo of an unearthly song—
> And the former world in an unfading radiance
> Arises anew before a sensitive soul.
>
> Only the dream remains—in a heavy wakefulness
> You will await with langorous longing
> Once more the reflection of an unearthly vision,
> Once more the echo of a sacred harmony.
> ("Beskrylyj dukh, zemleju polonennyj...", 1883)

Attention has already been drawn to the atmosphere surrounding Sophia's appearances as reflected in the colours of azure and gold. In "Three Meetings" the actual physical surroundings were rather bizarre, moving from the interior of a church, to the British Museum, to the Egyptian desert, but at least they were defined. In the shifting landscapes of Solov'ev's later poems, she loses this localized habitation altogether. The mystery surrounding her is dwelt on in the poem "Near, far, neither here, nor there":

> Near, far, neither here nor there,
> In the kingdom of mystical reverie,
> In a world invisible to mortal eyes,
> In a world without tears and laughter,
> There, goddess, for the first time
> I came to know you in the misty night.

Sophia, thus, becomes connected with the revelation of nighttime, in an ambiguous world of reverie, "neither here nor there". She is not at all a rational and concrete being here, but part of that inscrutable realm where dream and revelation merge:

> One has but to slumber in daytime or waken at midnight—
>   Someone is here ... We are together—
> Directly into my soul peer the radiant eyes
>   In sombre nighttime or day.
> ("Lish' zabudesh'sja dnem...", 1898)

Curiously enough, day and night become one as Solov'ev here indicates—the rationality of day is obscured by the poet's slumber whereas the awakening at midnight suggests the enlightening of the irrational. What emerges is a murky and indistinct condition of waking dream or dreaming wakefulness. This is no less than Sophia's world suspended between the divine and extra-divine, where the two principles of light and darkness meet and create a new condition of being. This perceptual syzygy wherein the poet merges heaven and earth in his dreamlike state is borne out in the final stanza of the same poem, where he gives intuitive expression to divine oneness:

> Only light and water. And in the transparent mist
>   Your eyes alone are gleaming,
> And long since united, like the dew in the ocean
>   Are all the days of life.

This murky, dreamlike landscape is found in many of Solov'ev's poems. In "Waking Dream" (1895) the azure eye gleams "through the gloomily suspended clouds" and eventually becomes lost in them. Elsewhere the poet received his premonition of Sophia in the same fashion: "Through the gloom from afar a mysterious power/ Is sent to me by your silent light".

However, this world of dreams and reveries, of gloom and darkness, can also be maleficent. In one of his earliest articles Solov'ev was struck by the fact that "In the vital and primeval language possibility or pure matter is called *night*."[17] But of course this possibility is two-fold. While night can be seen in its positive aspect as the potential of Sophia's divinity, it can also generate the gloom and pessimism of despair as the realm of the moon-goddess or spirit of Hecate, something Solov'ev himself points out in the following poem:

> What an oppressive dream! In a mass of mute visions,
>   Crowding and hovering about,
> In vain I seek that blessed shadow,
>   That has touched me with its wing.
>
> Yet I have but to submit to the press of evil doubts,
>   Be seized with numbing grief and terror,
> When again I sense above me the wing of an unseen shadow,
>   Her words ring forth as before.
>
> What an oppressive dream! A mass of mute visions
>   Grows, grows and blocks the road,
> And barely audible is the distant voice of the shadow:
>   Believe not what is passing, love and forget not.
> ("Kakoj tjazhelyj son! V tolpe nemykh videnij..." 1886)

The ultimate stage in this dreamlike vagueness, this compounding of echo, reflection and premonition in which all is reduced to the absolute zero-level of preception is to be found in what is possibly Solov'ev's most elusive poem, written shortly before his death in 1900:

> By a secret path, woeful and dear,
> You have made your way to the soul, and—thank you!

---

[17] See V. Solov'ev, "Mifologicheskij protsess v drevnem jazychestve," in *Sobr. soch. V. S. Solov'eva*, I, 13.

> Sweet it is for me to draw near in my desolate memory
> To the silent shores veiled with death.
>
> With an incomprehensible thread the heart is still tied
> To insignificant images, to weeping shadows.
> Something begs to be said, something left unsaid,
> Something is coming to pass, but not here, not there.
>
> Former instants with a soundless step
> Have drawn nigh and suddenly taken the veils from the eyes.
> Something eternal is seen, something indivisible
> And by-gone years are like a single hour.
> ("Les Revenants", 1900)

It is well worth emphasizing the fact that Solov'ev's poetic landscape is often forbidding, fraught with mists and vague apprehensions. The premonitions of an unearthly realm appear in the midst of shadows and gloom, as a constant reminder of an imperfect world penetrated by rays from another, higher and more perfect. The poet discovers himself "In a land of frosty blizzards, amid grey-headed mists..." and "Under the alien power of the oppressive blizzard". His quest for perfection begins "In the morning mist with failing steps..." and he perceives Sophia "in the corrupting conflagration of the earthly murk..." as "... dark clouds in a threatening mass/ Envelop the azure...".

This Solov'evian vision becomes essentially the world of Blok and his Beautiful Lady. While the theosophical aspirations which underlie Solov'ev's vision of Sophia may not be identical in Blok, or even present for that matter, there can be little doubt that they share the same landscape of inspiration and despair.

It is possible now to draw up a summary of both the epithets and functions of Sophia in her divine hypostasis in Solov'ev's poetry. Her actual designations vary from the indefinite "thou" on the one hand to the title of "Eternal Feminine" at the other extreme. In between is a variety of somewhat vague titles ranging from "eternal friend" to "queen" and "goddess". Her physical aspect too is vague and indefinite, except for her eyes and smile, veiled in the revelatory azure. Usually the poet receives only hints of her existence, her summoning call, her fascinating reflection or shadow. Associated with her is a mysterious, but often forbidding landscape of night and gloom. The state of communication is one of waking dream and ecstatic revelation. Generally, her poetic contours reveal the same concerns as her theosophical definitions. As the eternal symbol of achieved oneness, she stands immaculate and perfect before the poet. She is the key to the union of heaven and earth, the archetype of divine syzygy that inspires the poet, that reveals to him the divine truth of oneness. Fixed and immovable in her perfection and constancy, she does not waiver in her relationship with the poet, but the imperfections both within and surrounding him distort his perceptions of her, just as the steady light of a distant star appears broken and refracted by its passage to earth.

Like Sophia, the World Soul maintains her theosophical function in her poetic formulation. As the feminine principle of nature she receives the designations of Earth-Mistress, or Fairy-Mistress, and is even specifically called the World Soul. Like Sophia, quite often she is simply addressed as "thou". In general she represents earthly nature in its entirety and is present in all of Solov'ev's poems addressed to the natural world. Although theoretically she is potentially divine or demonic, she invariably appears as the former. The spirit of material manifestation, the creatrix of the extra-divine world, nonetheless she is divinely inspired: "And beneath the passionless mask of matter/Burns the divine fire everywhere". However, she is still a dualistic principle, chained to the material principle of earthly nature and darkness, yet attracted to the divine principle of God's Wisdom and light:

> Oh, how much of the pure azure in you
> And how many the black, black clouds!
> How brightly above you shines God's reflection,
> How wearisome and scorching the evil flame in you.
>
> And how in your soul with unseen enmity
> Two eternal forces have mysteriously united,
> And the shades of two worlds like a distraught crowd
> Pressing to you have wondrously become entwined.
>
> But one believes: flickering in thunder there will pass
> Amid this gloom the divine word
> And a black cloud in mighty torrents
> Will burst into the desolate vale.
>
> And with radiant dew it will wash it,
> Will soothe the fire of hostile elements,
> And the heavenly vault will disclose all its radiance
> And illumine in stillness all the beauty of the earth.
> ("O, kak v tebe lazuri chistoj mnogo...", 1881)

Solov'ev invests his poetic vision of Mother Nature or the Earth-Mistress with the same prototypic and potential likeness to Sophia as he does in his theoretical articles. The future of the World Soul lies in her total union with the divine world:

> Earth-Mistress! To you I have bowed my head,
> And through your fragrant veil
> I sensed the fire of a kindred heart,
> I heard the trembling of the life of the world.
> In the mid-day rays with such a burning delight

> Descended the blessing of the radiant heavens,
> And freely flowing river and rustling forest
> Bore a melodious greeting to the silent gleam,
> In the manifest sacrament again I see the union
> Of the world soul with an otherworldly light,
> And from the fire of love life's suffering
> Is borne away like fleeting haze.
> ("Zemlja-vladychitsa! K tebe chelo sklonil ja...", 1886)

The poet's reverential pose before her comes close to the attitude of lover to beloved, a reflection, of course, of his relationship with Sophia which becomes more familiar and sympathetic with his Earth-Mistress, who is, after all, only semi-divine like himself and therefore more approachable.

This special relationship between the poet and the World Soul reaches its most passionate expression in a series of poems addressed to Lake Saimo in Finland where Solov'ev often retired for work and contemplation. In these poems, which include "Saimo" (1894) and "On Saimo in Winter" (1894), the lake becomes synonymous with the World Soul striving between her two fates:

> The lake splashes with impatient waves.
> Like the swelling tide in the sea,
> The disharmonious element surges towards something,
> Contends something with a hostile fate.
> ("Sajmo", 1894)

The "something" towards which the lake is striving is, of course, oneness with the divine realm and identification with Sophia, the Divine Wisdom of God. The prevalent water imagery in Solov'ev's poetry offers the best means of elucidating the uncontained, disunited nature of the World Soul, which in its ceaseless motion reveals unrest and the striving towards unity. Its reflective qualities carry the potential mirroring of the heavenly realm. This striving for syzygy in nature is affirmed in most of Solov'ev's poems, but pre-eminently in his "water poems":

> The wave disunited with the sea
> Knows no peace,
> Whether it beats in the frothing spring,
> Or flows along in the river—
> Ever complaining and sighing,
> In chains or unrestrained,
> Longing for the boundless
> Bottomless blue sea.
> ("L'Onda dal Mar' Divisa", 1884)

The most expressive of the World Soul's titles is given in "On Saimo in Winter", where she receives her most perfect poetic and theosophical appellation, the "radiant daughter of sombre chaos".

The "daughter of sombre chaos" because God brought her forth out of chaos to rule over its earthly embodiment and "radiant" because she is the potential, earthly counterpart of God's Wisdom, Sophia:

> You are all enveloped in luxuriant fur,
> Becalmed you lie in unresisting sleep.
> The radiant air does not waft of death here,
> This transparent, white silence.
>
> In serene and profound repose,
> No, I did not seek you out in vain.
> Your image is the same before the inner eye,
> Fairy-Mistress of the pines and rocks.
>
> You are unsullied like snow beyond the mountains,
> You are full of thoughts like the winter night.
> You are all in rays, like polar flame,
> Radiant daughter of sombre chaos!

This is perhaps Solov'ev's most complimentary poem to his Earth-Mistress. For its brief instant, nature has become so pure as to be practically the perfect earthly counterpart of Sophia—which is, after all, the ideal role of the World Soul which Solov'ev envisaged in his theoretical writings and expresses here in poetic terms. The transcendental vision of Sophia has been reflected in the lake and then for a fleeting moment caught in the frozen ice, ideally embodied or incarnated in the "radiant daughter of sombre chaos".

However, it was not always that the World Soul could offer such a perfect image of Sophia. She could be seduced by the false powers of time and space:

> Death and Time rule on earth—
> Do not call them masters;
> All, swirling about, disappears in the gloom,
> Immovable alone is the sun of love.
> ("Bednyj drug! istomil tebja put'...", 1887)

In 1898 returning to Pustynka where some twelve years before he wrote "The Earth-Mistress", Solov'ev was prompted to write another poem commemorating that occasion once again addressed to her. This poem recalls his troubled and inconstant vision of the divine Sophia over the years, while at the same time trying to resurrect and reaffirm his faith, not only in the potential immortality of the World Soul, but in himself as well:

> Earth-Mistress! with former emotion
> And with tenderness of love I bow over you.
> The ancient forest and river ring for me with youthful song...
> All that is eternal in them has remained with me.
>
> There was, true, a former day, cloudless and bright,
> From the heavens poured a torrent of rejoicing rays,

And everywhere among the trees of the ice-covered park
Glittered the spectres of mysterious eyes.

And the spectres have departed, but the faith unchanged...
And lo the sun has just peeked out from the clouds.
Earth-Mistress! Your beauty is incorruptible,
And the radiant knight immortal and mighty.
("Na tom zhe meste", 1898)

Thus the faith in nature's potential divinity, which he glimpsed in the frozen surface of Lake Saimo, remains. Sophia's presence in the World Soul is hinted at in the "spectres of mysterious eyes", but apparently the complete and perfect vision of her has been lost. Nonetheless, the World Soul is to be her natural and earthly agent, filled with her inspiration.

The question of the relation between the World Soul and Sophia is just as important in Solov'ev's poetry as it is in his theoretical writings and causes some confusion of the two images. In the third edition of his poetry (Moscow, 1900), Solov'ev added a preface intended to clarify this problem and at the same time refute—with typically Solov'evian irony—certain criticisms of his poetry. It seems that particularly the poems he addressed to a "lake" (obviously Lake Saimo) had been interpreted as possessing erotic overtones. Of course, these poems, which in fact represented his personal relationship with the feminine spirit of the World Soul incarnate in the lake and consequently with her divine archetype Sophia, could indeed lead to such a confusion. In a humorous mood, Solov'ev readily agrees with the criticism and says he should be more exact about such things, but puts a barb to his humour by reference to the even more romantic and erotic Lamartinian verses: "If one is inspired by a *lake*, then one should speak thus: 'Oh, lac! l'année à peine a fini sa carrière...'".

Then, however, Solov'ev attends to the more serious aspect of the question which is connected with two poems in particular, "Das Ewig-Weibliche" and "Three Meetings". He expresses certain misgivings to the effect that they could lend themselves to a charge of "subversive or pernicious sacrilege". The substance of such a charge would be that the feminine principle in both is being elevated to Divinity, to the level of God Himself. Without entering into a theosophical discussion, he seeks to define his position and "not lead the reader into any seduction". To clarify his stance he produces the three principles which guide his poetry:

> 1) the transference of carnal animal-human relationships into the superhuman realm is the greatest abomination and the cause of final destruction (the flood, Sodom and Gomorrha, the "satanic depths" of recent times); 2) the worship of feminine nature in itself, that is, the

> principle of ambiguity and lack of differentiation is susceptible to falsehood and evil no less than to truth and goodness, and represents the greatest madness and major cause of the degeneration and collapse which reigns at present; 3) there is nothing in common with the former stupidity and the latter abomination in the true worship of the eternal feminine which has genuinely received the power of God for all eternity and which has genuinely imbibed the plenitude of goodness and truth, and through them the incorruptible radiance of beauty.[18]

In her apocalyptic manifestation as the Woman Clothed in the Sun, the Eternal Feminine will do battle with the dragon or serpent who must be defeated. However, Solov'ev foresees the ultimate victory of this "Eternal Beauty":

> ... in the end Eternal Beauty will be fruitful and the salvation of the earth shall issue forth out of her when her deceptive likenesses shall disappear like the sea-foam that gave birth to the simple-natured Aphrodite. My verses do not serve the latter even with a single word, and this is the sole and inalterable worth which I can and should claim on their behalf.[19]

It is interesting that Solov'ev is telling us at this point not to beware the Antichrist, the false and deceptive likeness of Christ, but rather the "Anti-Sophia", the deceptive likeness of Sophia. However, the message is fairly clear. What Solov'ev celebrates in any feminine principle other than Sophia, what he celebrates in the World Soul or nature or earthly beauty, is not that earthly material nature itself, but rather the reflections, echoes and premonitions of the divine Sophia, who is invested there in potential form. As stated earlier, to worship the Earth-Mistress purely for herself is tantamount to idolatry, but discerning in her the potential for divinity, seeing in her the divine principle at work is to worship God alone. The distinction between the two Aphrodites is clearly drawn in Solov'ev's poem "Das Ewig-Weibliche" (1898). Here he addresses the sea-devils who were at first subdued by the birth of Aphrodite Anadyomene. The atmosphere surrounding her birth is remarkably similar to the atmosphere usually accompanying Sophia's manifestations:

> Do you not recall the roses over the white foam,
> The purple reflection in the azure waves,
> Do you not recall the image of a beautiful body,
> Your confusion and anxiety and fear?

Because the sea-devils were able to corrupt the image of this earthly Aphrodite with death and sow the seeds of hell in her, divine Aphrodite, or Sophia, must now descend upon earth to preside over its apocalyptic union with heaven:

---

[18] "Iz predislovija k tret'emu izdaniju," in *Stikhotvorenija Vladimira Solov'eva*, pod. red. S. M. Solov'eva (5-oe izd., Moscow, n.d.) XIV-XV.

[19] Ibid., XV-XVI.

> Let it be Known: today the Eternal Feminine
> In an incorruptible body is descending to earth.
> In the unfading light of the new goddess
> Heaven has become one with the deeps.

The distinction between this celestial image and its earthly counterpart is clearly stated:

> All wherewith the earthly Aphrodite is beautiful,
> The joy of homes, and forests and seas—
> All this will be replaced by an unearthly beauty
> More pure, powerful, real and perfect.

This poem expresses Solov'ev's growing conviction that the World Soul has been seduced by the evil forces of chaos, that it is no longer possible to achieve his theosophical conception of a radiant and positive apocalypse. In order to do this the World Soul would have had to be transformed—elevated to divinity. The descent of Sophia to announce the union of heaven and earth only partially masks the final conclusion Solov'ev reached in "A Short Tale of the Antichrist". He became convinced that the final revelation could not come without the preceding reign of Antichrist, the seduction of the earth by chaos. Redemption, therefore, is no longer an historical process, but the abrupt end to that process.

These views on the confrontation of cosmos and chaos were summarized by Vladimir Solov'ev during the final two years of his life and gathered together in his last major work, *Tri razgovora* (*Three Conversations*)[20] which also had "Kratkaja povest' ob Antikhriste" (A Short Tale of the Antichrist") appended to it in 1900. The principal question which the philosopher wished to probe was the nature of evil:

> Is *evil* merely a natural insufficiency, an incompleteness which will disappear by itself with the growth of good, or is it a genuine *force* which *rules our* world through deception so that in order to wage a successful struggle against it one must have a rallying point within a different order of being? .... My task here is ... apologetic and polemical: I wished as far as possible to present those living aspects of the Christian truth which are connected with the question of evil and upon which a mist is descending from various quarters, particularly in recent times.[21]

The discussion of the nature of evil is incorporated into a series of polite conversations in which a Politician, Prince, Lady, General and a certain Mr. Z participate. Obviously, Mr. Z represents Solov'ev's

---

[20] First serialized in *Knizhki nedeli*, 1899-1900, and then issued separately at Petersburg, 1900. The text quoted here is contained in *Sobr. soch. V. S. Solov'eva*, X, 81-221.

[21] V. Solov'ev, "Predislovie," *Tri razgovora*, X, 83.

position while the others provide the ideological stimulus for a confrontation of views.

In the first discourse, the topics are the concepts of resistance or non-resistance to evil, just wars and unjust wars. Whereas the Prince, an idealist and pacifist, abhors war under any circumstances, Mr. Z supports the morality of war for a just cause, as in the defence of the weak, abused or betrayed, or for self-defence.

In the second discourse the Politician makes a long and passionate plea in support of the concept that peaceful politics represent progress, a view questioned once again by Mr. Z who, in the third conversation presents his rebuttal.

Interpreting progress in an antithetical fashion, he claims that "a noticeable and accelerated progress is invariably a *symptom of the end*".[22] When queried on this point he responds that he has in mind the end of the historical process which has been increasing its pace. When one of the company protests that no doubt Mr. Z will now speak about the Antichrist, he replies that indeed the Antichrist is the most important aspect of this concept. Elaborating this point, he claims that according to all the biblical texts Antichrist will not be an obvious denial of Christianity, but rather a false version of it, claiming that *it is the genuine, the most beneficial Christianity*. This question of the Antichrist seems very much to concern the differentiation between a "good peace" and a "peace at all costs" which the Politician in particular has been supporting. Mr. Z singles out the most illuminating words of the scriptures to support his own case: "Thinkest thou that I come to bring peace on Earth? I come not to bring peace but a sword". Commenting on these words of Christ he proposes that Christ came to bring truth to the earth—and truth, like good, divides rather than unites.

Continuing his argument Mr. Z uses the evidence of death to prove to the Politician that the latter's concept of progress as the achievement of international peace does not represent progress at all, because at present all life ceases with death. Consequently, what meaning can progress have faced with the spectre of death. Affirming the existence of evil as genuine, Mr. Z wishes to propose actual resurrection, or conquering the Kingdom of Death, as the remedy. At this point, he recounts a story by the aged monk Father Pansophius which is entitled "A Short Tale of the Antichrist".

This Tale was obviously constructed in order not only to present Father Pansophius' (i.e. Solov'ev's) prophecy of final things, but in particular to reveal the true nature of evil and the falsity of Tolstojan "passive resistance" to it. The story begins with a description of how Pan-Mongolism conquers most of the Western world, not only by

[22] *Ibid.*, X, 159.

virtue of its superior numbers, but because of the disunity among Western European nations. Once subjugated, however, these nations work together secretly and finally overthrow the Asiatics. Among themselves they form a European United States and rule themselves as a single nation.

At this time there appears a brilliant young man who, because of his vanity, secretly conceives of himself as the supreme Mangod, the "real" Messiah greater than Christ. The devil naturally plays an important role in inculcating both these ideas and the powers necessary to support them. So brilliant are his socio-political writings, *The Revealed Path to Universal Peace and Prosperity*, that most of his former opponents acclaim him the greatest among them. The voices of the faithful few who suspect something evil in him are lost amid the general acclaim. He is soon elevated to one of the highest political offices, where he continues to distinguish himself by subduing dissident factions throughout Europe and Asia with a minimum of fuss and bloodshed and introducing peaceful, beneficial social policies for all. Finally, he is elected the supreme Emperor and succeeds in removing all political and social dissension, bringing apparent peace and prosperity.

Having gained dominion over the political and social sectors, he now desires to do likewise with religion, particularly with the Christians. Noting the long dissensions among their estranged factions, he calls together the leaders of the three major creeds, Catholic, Protestant and Orthodox. He offers to reconcile their differences and unite them all under his leadership. Using material and spiritual bribes, he gains much support at a great ecumenical congress, but the leaders of the three branches, together with a few followers, refuse to join him unless he professes his true Christian faith and expresses his belief in the Second Coming of Christ. Since, however, he has come to despise Christ and considers Him merely his own precursor, the Emperor refuses. The Elder Ioann, leader of the Orthodox, is the first to denounce him as the Antichrist, whereupon Pope Peter II follows suit. Both are immediately struck dead by the Emperor's magician, Apollyon.

Ernst Pauli, leader of the Protestants, takes their bodies, together with the few remaining faithful Christians, and hides in the mountains around Jerusalem, where the Emperor has built his palace. Finally, the Emperor is overthrown in rather bizarre circumstances. The Jews had supported him originally because they were led to believe he was Jewish. When they discover by chance that he is not even circumcized, they rebel. With the aid of his magician the Emperor manages to escape, but he and his entire army are engulfed in a mighty earthquake and lake of fire while fighting the Jews. The Jews flee towards Jerusalem filled with terror and seeking salvation from the God of Israel. Here is the apocalyptic conclusion to the Tale:

> When the holy city was in their sight, heaven was split asunder by mighty lightning from east to west and they saw Christ descending unto them in kingly robes and with wounds from nails on his outstretched hands. At the same time from Sinai to Sion a mass of Christians made its way, led by Peter, Ioann and Paul, and from various directions came running yet other rejoicing crowds: these were all the Jews and Christians who had been condemned to death by the Antichrist. They had come back to life and would reign with Christ for a thousand years.
>
> With this Father Pansophius wished to bring to an end his tale, which had as its subject not the universal catastrophe of the universe, but merely the resolution of our historical process which consists of the manifestation, apotheosis and destruction of the Antichrist.[23]

In *Three Conversations* and "A Short Tale of the Antichrist" Solov'ev apparently comes to the realization of the genuine power of evil. At least, in order to rouse people as his less impassioned writings seemed unable to do, to make evil seem real and threatening and to remove passive resistance to it, he utilized the apocalyptic imagery of *Revelation* and the threat of Pan-Mongolism. His Antichrist displays all the arguments and attitudes of the Politician and the Prince from *Three Conversations* who were in favour of peace as a sign of progress and passive resistance to evil. For Solov'ev, these represent the progress of Antichrist and not of Christ. He had striven all his life for an ecumenical union of the disparate branches of Christianity, for the creation of a genuine Theocracy which would be the preparation for Godmanhood. In this tale he shows that it takes a threat from without, the presence of manifest and not merely potential evil, to cause nations, peoples and faiths to put aside their differences and unite. Thus, it seems that in "A Short Tale of the Antichrist" Solov'ev embodied a final vision of the confrontation of good and evil, a catastrophic holy war to be waged against the Antichrist in the name of Christ. Only through this destructive apocalypse could his Sophiological plan for Godmanhood be effected.

It is worthwhile noting that Sophia has disappeared almost completely. Solov'ev's warning no longer concerns her deceptive likenesses, but the Antichrist. It is the Second Coming of Christ that is proclaimed here and not the descent of Sophia. This does not indicate that his hope for the union of heaven and earth was dead, but rather that his original vision of a *radiant* and *serene* apocalypse—with Sophia at its head—was to be replaced with a darker vision of impending cataclysm before the final proclamation of God's kingdom on earth could be uttered. Here Christ reassumes his traditional role in

[23] Ibid., X, 220.

the forefront of the cathartic upheaval preceding the Heavenly Jerusalem. The Christ at the head of the Red Guardsmen in Aleksandr Blok's "The Twelve" (1918) has doubtless much in common with Solov'ev's vision here. In both poets' work, so manifestly dominated by the Divine Feminine, this Christological archetype is absent until they reach a climactic vision of Christ at the end of their lives.

The third love which Solov'ev treats in his verses is earthly woman. Here I have in mind those poems which are inspired by his own love affairs. The two most notable were Sophia Petrovna Khitrovo in the early 1880's and Sophia Mikhajlovna Martynova in the early 1890's. The details of these two melancholy encounters are not particularly important to any understanding of their relationship to either the divine love of Sophia or the love of the Earth-Mistress. As in these two other types of love, the relationship between the poet and his human mistress could be predicated on his theoretical writings.

As Solov'ev stated in "The Meaning of Love", woman is the natural complement to man, the feminine nature necessary to achieve the first human stage of syzygy which will lead ultimately to society, the Universal Church and Divine Humanity. Like the World Soul, woman can also become divine, become the incarnation of Sophia, or her symbol of manifest oneness. This is, in fact, the role which Solov'ev seeks for his earthly loves in his poetry. He calls on this human love, this woman, to perceive the true nature of the world, the division between the divine and the extra-divine:

> Dearest friend, do you not see
> All that we perceive—
> Only reflects and shadows forth
> What our eyes cannot see?
>
> Dearest friend, do you not hear
> In the clamour of everyday life—
> Only the unstrung echoing fall of
> Jubilant harmonies?
>
> Dearest friend, do you not sense
> That the essence of the world lies hidden
> Only in that which heart to heart
> Carries its silent greeting?
> ("Milyj drug, il' ty ne vidish'...", 1892)

This first human unit of syzygy, this first step towards union, is potentially divine or demonic depending upon its direction, just as the World Soul can unite with the *Logos* or with matter.

In what is apparently the first poem addressed to Sophia Petrovna Khitrovo, Solov'ev is over-enthusiastic about the possibility of human-divine love. She is addressed in the superlatives usually reserved for Sophia herself:

> More beautiful and graceful than the desert gazelle,
> And thy words are infinitely profound—
> Touranian Eve, Madonna of the Steppes,
> Be thou our intercessor before Allah.
> ("Gazeli pustyn' ty strojnee i krashe", 188?)

This is a rather weak and overwrought poem, not at all typical of those which, rather than elevating, usually deplore the waywardness of his earthly love. His relationships with Khitrovo and Martynova were especially debasing and, although we have no other witness to the fact, the poems addressed to Martynova in the early 1890's provide rather eloquent testimony of his estimation of her. From an ecstatic and divine beginning, she rapidly assumes the proportions of the archetypal "living deception", a betrayal of her divine counterpart:

> Oh, what meaning have all the words and speeches,
> The ebb and surge of these feelings
> Before the mystery of our otherworldly meeting,
> Before eternal, immovable fate?
>
> In this world of Falsehood— oh how false thou art!
> Among deceptions you are the living deception,
> But then it is with me, it is mine, that joyous moment,
> That disperses all the earthly mist.
>
> Even should you not believe in this meeting,
> It is all the same—I shall not argue with you.
> Oh, what meaning have all the words and speeches
> Before eternal, immovable fate?
> ("O, chto znachat vse slova i rechi...", c1892)

The same theme of the imperfection of earthly love runs through a number of poems from the same period:

> Dear friend, not in the least do I believe
> Either your words, your emotions, your eyes,
> And I do not believe myself, I believe only
> The shining stars in the height.
> ("Milyj drug, ne verju ja niskol'ko...", c1892)

In short, his affair has proved but a deception of the feelings, a poor imitation of that divine syzygy he seeks.

Although it may be overstating the case to say that Solov'ev's earthly love proved demonic rather than divine, nonetheless the oppressive power of "erotic" love, that is, a love of passion between two people not leading to divine syzygy, could prove fatal. In the poem "New Year's Greetings" (1894) Solov'ev, having finally disentangled himself, looks back:

> Whether it was a fateful power or our impotence
> That clothed a radiant love in evil passion—
> Let us be thankful that the cup has passed.

> Passion has burnt itself out, we are free once again.
> ("S Novym Godom", 1894)

A single verse sums up without any further need for comment Solov'ev's attempt to transform his earthly passion into a divine love, to penetrate time and space with the divine passion of eternity and infinity:

> Impotent mind, chained to the earthly dust,
> In vain has summoned the incorruptible dream.
> ("Vostorg dushi raschetlivymi obmanom...", 1884)

The bitterness of disillusionment, the torment of impotence, and the threatening spectre of earthly passion enveloping the heavenly vision, so eloquent in these lines, also form an integral part of the Solov'evian legacy of Sophiology left to the naive romanticism of symbolism's first flourishing. The Knights of the "Beautiful Lady" and the "Woman Clothed in the Sun", Aleksandr Blok and Andrej Belyj, in their turn found the bitter in the sweet.

Chapter 3

THE AFFAIR OF ANNA SCHMIDT AND VLADIMIR SOLOV'EV

One of those bizarre mysteries in Vladimir Solov'ev's personal life that profoundly influenced the lives of symbolists like Andrej Belyj and Aleksandr Blok was the curious relationship between that philosopher-poet and Anna Nikolaevna Schmidt. It is unlikely that the details of their fascinating encounter will ever be fully elucidated, so obscured are they by lack of information and distorted by rumour. Solov'ev's "mystical romance" with Anna Schmidt occupies a completely unique position with respect to his "earthly loves", for Anna Schmidt considered herself something in the nature of the earthly incarnation of his divine Sophia. Their relationship is not only interesting in the light of Solov'ev's poetry and philosophy, but well worth examining insofar as it seems to provide a seminal pattern to be repeated and mimicked elsewhere during the symbolist period in Russian literature. While none were apt to impugn Solov'ev's morals because of his rationale for Sophiology outlined in *Lectures on Godmanhood, La Russie et l'Eglise Universelle* and "The Meaning of Love", the personalized invocation of his lyrics addressed to Sophia was given an erotic interpretation by critics unable to distinguish between verses addressed to Sophia, the World Soul and his "earthly loves". In any event, the interpenetration of eroticism and religion in the philosophical and poetic work of Solov'ev provides a basis for understanding what happened in his "affair" with Anna Nikolaevna Schmidt, an "affair" which confounded his disciples with a bewildering actualization of theory and armed his opponents with a religious scandal.[1]

Anna Nikolaevna Schmidt (1851-1905) lived in Nizhnij Novgorod where she held various positions including that of domestic tutor as well as correspondent for several newspapers.[2] She was

---

[1] See in particular N. Valentinov, *Two Years with the Symbolists* (Stanford, California, 1969). Valentinov's book is aimed at showing the aberrations and excesses of a number of the symbolists. Particularly Belyj, Blok and Solov'ev come under heavy fire for their mystical eroticism. (Despite the English title, the book is in Russian).

[2] Anna Schmidt's collected works are assembled in A. N. Schmidt, *Iz rukopisej*

unmarried and lived a solitary life with a mother whose illnesses demanded constant attention. Her financial resources being extremely limited, she found life difficult and rather burdensome. Among her acquaintances and colleagues she enjoyed the reputation of being extremely hardworking and kind-hearted, if somewhat eccentric. She came to know Solov'ev and his work only during the final months of his life. Attracted to his philosophical-poetic ideas and believing that his visions and revelations were essentially identical with her own, she became convinced that there was some preordained and divine covenant to be fulfilled between them.

Before examining their personal relationship, perhaps it is best to outline and analyse Schmidt's own curious if somewhat obscure Sophiology in which she herself, apparently, plays the major role. This strange material is to be found in the chapter entitled "On the Present-Day Life of Margarita" in the single volume of her posthumously published manuscripts.[3] "Margarita" is the spiritual appellation adopted by Anna Schmidt.[4] God sent her twice to be reborn on earth, but her first incarnation is corporeal, whereas her second is spiritual. During the first, she was to have no conscious knowledge of her origins or purpose; only during the second would she be omniscient and aware of her spiritual nature. Her role in the first life is defined thus: "In her first life she knew herself only through the personal teaching of Jesus and lived on earth mainly in order that the human race might be born anew through her...".[5] If this parallels

Anny Nikolaevny Schmidt (Moscow, 1916). The only other significant publication which can be attributed to her appeared under a pseudonym: A. Timshevskij, "O budushchnosti," Novyj put', 1904, No. 6. Of special importance is the study of Anna Schmidt and Vladimir Solov'ev compiled by Sergej Bulgakov which takes account of the writings of both Schmidt and Solov'ev, although he tends to romanticize and over-dramatize their "misticheskij roman". See S. N. Bulgakov, Tikhie dumy (Moscow, 1918), 71-114.

[3] Iz rukopisej Anny Nikolaevny Schmidt. In view of the fact that this book is extremely difficult to obtain, I have chosen to quote liberally from it in order to give some idea of its contents which, if not exactly enlightening to the general reader, should offer at least some idea of the bewildering blend of religion, mysticism and personal revelation that typifies Anna Schmidt's Final Testament.

[4] Anna Schmidt's choice of "Margarita" as her spiritual name is of some interest. It signifies the "pearl" (see Matthew, 13:46; Revelations, 21:21) associated with the value of heaven, the twelve gates leading into Heaven and with Christ's Second Coming. In the Greek church it also denotes the vessel wherein the host is kept. Perhaps more significant is the fact that "Margarit" represents a collection of Byzantine sermons (slova) by Ioann Zlatoust and their translation into Old Russian. These homilies no doubt represent the "pearls of wisdom" inherent in Margarita's spiritual revelation.

[5] Iz rukopisej..., 163. The similarity between this description and Solov'ev's own theoretical outline of the unconscious feminine and passive principle of the world soul is quite remarkable. See the chapter "L'Ame du monde" (Chapter IV) in La Russie et l'Eglise Universelle.

Solov'ev's concept of the uncomprehending physical nature of the World Soul, then the spiritual nature of Margarita in her second life also appears to echo the spiritualization of the world-soul who has consciously received the Logos or divine principle: "... in her second life she was now beholden, by means of invisible inspirations, to recognize her spirit and all the as yet undisclosed secrets of the heavens in order to reveal them to herself and to her children, but to remain personally unknown to them".[6]

Apparently the preparations for her second and spiritual life on earth begin in 1848, the year of the "climax" of lawlessness and degradation" or, in other words, the manifestation and appearance of the Antichrist. In her second birth she receives her corporeality from her parents, but her spirit and soul arise directly "from whence she abided in Jesus Christ as in her first life."[7] The peculiar nature of this second birth is described by Schmidt in the following manner:

> ... only then as a babe was she differentiated from Him who as an infant was born outside of a mother, but now as a babe she was differentiated out of Him who was an infant also, but who is abiding together with her within His Mother, His eternal baptism was in Her, and she was differentiated from Him at the birth of what was only His human but not yet His eternal spirit .... According to this origin, she, as in the first life, was born without any conception of sin within herself.[8]

Although this passage is certainly confusing, its main idea is reminiscent of Solov'ev's Sophiology. In qualifying her second and spiritual life, she visualizes an original oneness of herself with or within Christ. Her differentiation, her heterogeneous nature is expressed not in their spiritual oneness, but only at *physical* birth, in a material context.[9] Already one can foresee a possible movement towards syzygy, towards androgynous union, in the offing. She appears to be the feminine counterpart, purified and spiritual, to the masculine Christ, while both in their oneness are the offspring of some celestial Mother, the birth-giving principle of Divinity.

In regard to Jesus Christ, Margarita appears to occupy simultaneously all the possible feminine roles—mother, daughter, sister, bride and wife. Nevertheless, her foremost and undeniably explicit role is that of wife or bride:

> She felt with all her heart that she occupied alongside Him the same exclusive place as His Mother, and that even in a different manner she loved Him more than His Own Mother, although in other things His

---

[6] *Iz rukopisej...*, 163.
[7] *Iz rukopisej...*, 163.
[8] *Iz rukopisej...*, 163-164.
[9] Compare with both Solov'ev and the Gnostic system. One will also recall the theory of androgyny expounded by Aristophanes in Plato's *Symposium*.

> Mother loved Him more, but that all the same it was only with her and with no one else that she was able to stand as an equal in closeness and devotion to Her Son. This was the beginning of the awareness that she was taken directly from Him, out of the soul of His Spirit.
>
> This alone was expected of her by the Father and no sooner had she come to this very feeling and, like Mary, who had come to love Christ with the love of a Mother without having seen Him, she loved Him with the love of a wife without having seen Him, and herself not comprehending her own love, He sent her eternal spirit to be incarnated in her.[10]

Although Schmidt was not supposed to have had any knowledge of cabbalistic or gnostic literature, according to Sergej Bulgakov,[11] the relationship of Christ and Margarita bears an astonishing similarity to Valentinian gnosticism and, of course, to Solov'ev's own concept of divine syzygy. Whether or not this notion of Christ and Margarita as bridegroom and bride, and of Christ's restoration to harmony of the fallen and despairing Sophia-Margarita was genuine revelation or gleaned at first- or second-hand from either gnostic sources or Solov'ev is, of course, a matter of pure speculation. However, most people acquainted with Schmidt were quite convinced that it was pure—or rather, pre-ordained—coincidence.

After undergoing a voluntary six-day trial and recording her testament, Margarita gained full knowledge of her heavenly family and now she waited for God to recognize that she had fulfilled the tasks for which she had been sent on earth and take her up to heaven. Once again the longing for union is expressed in the anthropomorphic terms of syzygy characteristic of Solov'ev and the Gnostics:

> All that a mother, wife and daughter experiences in unending separation from her children, husband, father and mother, she felt on earth and did not know how to bide her time until it was granted to her to press to her heart her children, the eternal, angelic babes, and her Beloved, and fall at the feet of her heavenly Father and her true Mother-Sister.... Her longing for Him [i.e. Christ] and her longing to be with Him was immeasurably greater than all that could retain her on earth.[12]

The revelation and profession of the testament of which she is the earthly agent is no less than the spirit of her son by Jesus Christ whom she calls the Neo-Israelite Church. She is to provide both the spiritual and material substance of her son by Christ and the process of this syzygy is quite overt:

> The acceptance and profession by her of the testament which today is delivered through her must give rise within her to the life of her future

---

[10] Iz rukopisej..., 166.
[11] Bulgakov makes this claim in Tikhie dumy, 74-114.
[12] Iz rukopisej..., 168.

> son and grant within her the fruition of his spirit, for all that is recorded by her today, is his spirit, and all this must be affirmed by the profession of faith and acts of the Neo-Israelite Church in order that her son might come to fruition within her. At the same time with this preparation of his spirit for his birth, she has conceived his body as well; she has conceived it in the heavens in her incorruptible body as soon as on earth her eternal spirit became settled in her; for from this time began her physical union with Christ under one form, with their blood flowing simultaneously from one to the other of their hearts which had become one.[13]

This "son" which is born of Margarita and Christ is, in its physical aspect on earth, the Church, or more specifically the "Neo-Israelite Church" as Schmidt calls it. This, of course, parallels Solov'ev's doctrine of the "Universal Church" or "Godmanhood" produced in its divinely symbolic form by the exemplary union of Christ and the Holy Virgin. The distinction between the physical aspect (i.e. Jesus and Mary) and the spiritual (i.e. Christ and Holy Virgin) is reached independently by both Solov'ev and Schmidt, so we are led to believe.

This physico-spiritual conception of the "Son-Church" underlies the two "mighty purposes" of Schmidt's Final Testament, concerned as it is with Armageddon:

> The foundation of the Neo-Israelite Church on earth outside of Margarita and the conception of the body of her son in heaven within her, these are the two mighty purposes of the Final Testament. They both lead to one and the same end desired of God; to the destruction of the tainted world.
>
> For the time has come to reveal why the son of Jesus Christ and Margarita has been born, about whom the Apocalypse prophesies, and who he shall be: he shall be the destroyer of the world, he has been born for the purpose of destroying all the works of the enemy of his Father.[14]

The time is near for the birth of this Son-Church, for the world is shaken at its foundations.

Just as the Gnostics and Solov'ev intentionally blur the distinctions between the various hypostases in order to reflect more nearly the oneness of the divine spirit and the manysidedness of Sophia, so in Schmidt's account we find a similar multiplicity of roles for the holy figures and, in particular, for Margarita. Clearly her progress from physical to spiritual incarnation, culminating in a divine syzygy with Christ and the birth of the Son-Christ which prepares the way for the final confrontation of good and evil, the destruction of the latter and the triumphant union of heaven and earth, offers an uncanny parallel to the course of universal history which Solov'ev outlined in *Three Conversations* (1900) and "A Short Tale of the Antichrist".

[13] *Iz rukopisej...*, 169-170.
[14] *Iz rukopisej...*, 170.

Moreover, Anna Schmidt's theme of destructive apocalypse, allied with a Sophiological view of world history, must have struck a particularly responsive note in Solov'ev, since during the final months of his life his own vision was becoming increasingly apocalyptic. Whereas Solov'ev's final conclusions on eschatology may have been fostered by the growth of pessimism about the positive course of universal history and a sense of impotence in the face of the divisions between the Eastern and Western branches of Christianity, Anna Schmidt's own vision was permeated with apocalypse from the very beginning. Furthermore, the bride-mother role of Margarita as the necessary vehicle for the culmination of history is much more overt. Although the successive stages of theosophical "marriage" and the resultant offspring of these syzygies are femininely inspired in both Schmidt and Solov'ev, Schmidt's projection of herself as the earthly incarnation of Christ's Bride and the Mother of their Son—the Neo-Israelite Church—obviously goes far beyond any claims that Solov'ev ever made for himself whether in his philosophy or his poetry.

The manner in which Schmidt visualized the culmination of her role on earth as Margarita is quite arresting especially when viewed in connection with certain requests made to Sergej Bulgakov concerning her correspondence with Solov'ev. The final summation of the life of Margarita is described by Schmidt thus:

> Just as the world was not created by itself, but by God, so also will it be destroyed not by itself but by the Son of God, Raphael. (And the first time the mother-Church lived on earth in order to give birth anew to all her children, but the second time,—in order to bear the destroyer of the world that her children might taste of the fruits of redemption.)
>
> Whether Margarita, incarnated for the second time, has died or not—is unknown, just as she herself is unknown.[15]

From all accounts, Schmidt discovered Raphael, or the earthly incarnation of Christ, in Solov'ev and made her views known to him by letter, asking to meet him personally. One can well imagine the speculation set off by Schmidt's overture once her views became known. It may be that no one other than Solov'ev himself knew precisely what Anna Schmidt first wrote to him concerning her visions and revelations. However, it is possible to speculate that his brother, Mikhail Sergeevich, who took possession of his papers, diaries and correspondence after his death in 1900, had direct access to these "secrets". It is also quite possible that Mikhail Sergeevich's son, Sergej Mikhailovich Solov'ev, as well as Aleksandr Blok and Andrej Belyj, who were close to the Solov'evs, were made privy to the intimate details of this affair. Apparently, any "compromising" evi-

---

[15] Iz rukopisej..., 171.

dence was destroyed by Mikhail Sergeevich in order to protect his brother's reputation, although several sources exist which claim to have seen examples of strange papers, letters and even specimens of automatic or mediumistic writing well after the death of the philosopher.[16]

A few years after Solov'ev's death, when Sergej Bulgakov wrote to Anna Schmidt asking whether she had any valuable correspondence from Solov'ev that might be published in the journal *Novyj put'*, she sent him copies of several letters but specifically requested that they were not to be published until some "mighty event" occurred or until after her death. One can only speculate as to her meaning—was she expecting the culmination of her relationship with Solov'ev, the birth of her metaphorical Son-Church and the end of history or perhaps some concrete manifestation of the fact that she was indeed the second incarnation of Margarita on earth? Of course, this is as much pure speculation as the intimations that, during their one brief meeting in the city of Vladimir, their "mystical romance" was physically consummated. Such was the nature of the succeeding years that this type of mystical, apocalyptic eroticism was to serve as inspiration for an entire series of works, the two best examples being Andrej Belyj's *Silver Dove* (1910) and Valerij Brjusov's *Fiery Angel* (1907).

The extant correspondence between Anna Schmidt and Vladimir Solov'ev is quite limited and entirely one-sided. It consists only of the letters from Solov'ev to Schmidt. Their correspondence took place during the last months of Solov'ev's life, from March until June of 1900. Before March of 1900 Anna Schmidt apparently had no knowledge of Solov'ev, his works or ideas, but upon becoming acquainted with them she immediately entered into an exchange of letters with him that seems much more energetic and forceful on her part than on his.

As far as can be estimated, she sent him, at the very least, some thirty letters and telegrams during the three or four months before his death. On the other hand, only some seven of Solov'ev's letters remain

[16] "I recently had the opportunity — in 1922 — to examine several mysterious specimens of handwriting by Solov'ev which have remained unpublished even until now. These specimens are a special type of writing by the poet-philosopher which he made automatically while in a state of trance. This state (medium-like) was characteristic of Solov'ev at times. The theme of Solov'ev's recordings invariably appears as a she, "Sophia," whether genuine or imagined, is another question. In any case the nature of the recordings is such that one need not doubt the 'demonism' of the experiences accompanying the spiritual experiment of this worshipper of the 'Maiden of the Radiant Gates.' See Georgij Chulkov, *Gody stranstvij. Iz vospominanij* (Moscow, 1930), 123. Chulkov's account is also substantiated by Andrej Belyj throughout his memoir literature, but particularly in "Vospominanija o A. A. Bloke," *Epopeja*, 1922, No. 1, 140.

(plus four empty envelopes and a single telegram, to be exact).¹⁷ All of his correspondence was despatched from his room at the "Hotel Angleterre" and addressed to her at the "Nizhegorodskij Listok" in Nizhnij Novgorod. Anyone reading his letters will be quite disappointed to find nothing particularly "mystical" or "erotic", despite curious hints at sealed papers, bizarre revelations and the like.

In the first letter, dated the 8th of March 1900, Solov'ev expresses his pleasure at hearing Schmidt's views on Christianity:

> Having read your letter with the greatest attention, I was happy to see how close you had drawn to the truth on a question of the greatest significance, incorporated into the very nature of Christianity but not yet formulated clearly either in the consciousness of the church or general philosophy, although individual theosophists do speak about this aspect of Christianity (particualrly Jakob Boehme and his followers: Gichtel, Pordage, Saint-Martin, Baader). Since 1877 I have found myself forced to deal with this question in public lectures, articles and books, maintaining a necessary caution. I think, on the basis of many facts, that the broad disclosure of this truth in the consciousness and life of Christianity and of all humanity is imminent in the near future, and your appearance seems to me to be very important and meaningful.¹⁸

Solov'ev goes on to say that he would like to become acquainted with the article she is presently preparing, with her autobiographical work, but mainly with Anna Schmidt herself. Since he is about to take a trip abroad, however, the meeting will have to wait until he returns. Further on, he discusses the problem of ecumenism:

> But even at this point I can dispell one misunderstanding in your letter, namely, concerning the Ecumenical Council. At the present time the question of its convocation can have no practical meaning whatsoever for the reason that there is no one who can convoke it: papal authority is acknowledged only by catholics, whereas imperial authority is divided among independent governments: Russia, Germany, Austria and Britain. And besides this, the task of ecumenical councils consists merely of conclusively formulating and professing those religious truths which have already been pronounced, whereas that truth which concerns you and me, still demands greater clarification.¹⁹

The letter ends with an expression of his desire to remain in contact with her. Obviously the letter is formal and polite, reflecting above all the rational thinker in Solov'ev, the rational proponent of Godmanhood and the Universal Church. Judging from his comments, it is

---

[17] The two principal sources for the correspondence between Vladimir Solov'ev and Anna Schmidt are: *Pis'ma Vladimira Solov'eva*, ed. E. L. Radlov (Petersburg, 1923), IV, 8-13; "Prilozhenie. Pis'ma V.S. Solov'eva k A. N. Schmidt," Iz rukopisej..., 281-288.

[18] *Pis'ma V. S. Solov'eva*, IV, 8.

[19] *Pis'ma V. S. Solov'eva*, IV, 9.

unlikely that Anna Schmidt had disclosed any of her "revelations" concerning her connection with him, but perhaps only those regarding the destiny of her own personal life and the course of the Neo-Israelite Church. It should be borne in mind that irrational or mystical revelation is the common denominator between Solov'ev and Anna Schmidt and, obviously, Solov'ev is interested in the appearance of another, independent individual who apparently experienced similar Sophiological revelations. Nevertheless, he avoids giving his complete and enthusiastic support to Schmidt's visions, seeking refuge instead from this strange woman in rational discussion.

In his next letter to her, at the end of March or the beginning of April 1900, he thanks her for her previous letter and also says that the papers which she has sent him he will keep sealed until she requests him to do otherwise. Apparently, she has told him of something that happened to her on the 4th of January, 1885. As far as may be gleaned from Solov'ev's comments, she had a vision or saw a strange being in a hotel where she was staying at that time. What exactly happened is not clear, but apparently the initials connected with this vision were I. R. and Solov'ev hazards the guess that they might stand for "Iuda Raskajavshijsja" (Judas the Repentent). However, he adds that the person probably had a different surname and it would doubtless be of little use to attempt to discover his identity from the hotel register. In conclusion, Solov'ev reiterates his desire to meet her when time allows.

The third letter is not of any great importance, but the fourth is rather tantalizing. On the 22nd of April, 1900, Solov'ev gently chides Anna Schmidt for confusing him at times with his older brother, Vsevelod Sergeevich Solov'ev, who ostensibly had some obscure dealings with Mme. Blavatsky and wrote something on this account. Solov'ev himself denied emphatically any interest in, connection with, or support for Mme. Blavatsky, her "miracles" and "tricks".[20] Then he makes a very interesting remark about the fact that Anna Schmidt has sent him a copy of a poem that he wrote sometime before and which, because it appears to be a "better version" than the one presently in his possession, he will use for the new edition of his poetry. He makes a rather vague, but curious, criticism of some remark that she has made concerning it: ". . . out of this most simple fact you are drawing some complicated conclusions."[21] Perhaps she drew

---

[20] In fact, Solov'ev had written an article on Mme. Blavatsky some eight years previously, in 1892, entitled "Zametka o E. P. Blavatskoj" in which it is apparent that he has read all of Mme Blavatsky's major works. His major criticism in the article is not of Mme Blavatsky or her popularization of Buddhism so much as it is his anxiety lest people turn entirely to Buddhism which he considers an incomplete and false teaching. The article is contained in Solov'ev, Sobranie sochinenij, VI, 394-400.

[21] Pis'ma V. Solov'eva, IV, 11.

some symbolic meaning from the poem (one of his mystical and Sophiological works?), or felt that she had intuitively selected a version that enlightened their relationship, according to her own mystical revelations concerning Margarita and Raphael. However, in this letter Solov'ev is not very well disposed towards her and rebukes her rather severely for something she has written him in the form of a "confession":

> Your confession arouses the greatest pity and speaks dolefully on your behalf before the Almighty. It is fine that you have written this now, but I beg you not to return to this subject again. When I depart for Moscow today, I shall burn the factual confession in both versions, not only for the sake of precaution, but also as a sign of the fact that all this is only ashes.[22]

What was Anna Schmidt's confession? Did it concern her self-avowed incarnation as Margarita and indicate Solov'ev as Raphael? Was it a recital of her revelations and tribulations? The fact that Solov'ev says that he will burn the confession because "all this is only ashes" offers food for thought. Does this mean that his own visions of Sophia have ceased and that, as he suggested in an earlier letter to Anna Schmidt, there is no longer any hope for the positive and non-destructive apocalypse leading to the Universal Church and Godmanhood? Does it mean that the only solution he sees is the catastrophic apocalypse which he outlines in "A Short Tale of the Antichrist" in which Sophia together with all of her attendant hypostases has completely disappeared? No doubt Anna Schmidt's personal conception of the divine syzygy of Margarita and Raphael and perhaps even of their terrestrial embodiment in herself and Solov'ev may have fallen on despairing ears. The mystery of it all is deepened by what follows.

Solov'ev relates a dream that an old woman once had concerning him in order to teach Anna Schmidt some inscrutably symbolic lesson:

> And concerning what is behind all those ashes I shall relate to you the dream of a certain old woman who died a long time ago. She dreamt that she was given a letter from me, written in my usual script which she called *pattes d'arraignée*. Reading it with interest she remarked that inside there was folded up yet another letter on magnificent paper. Unsealing it, she saw words written in a beautiful script and in gold ink, and at this moment she heard my voice: "here is my real letter, but wait before you read it". Then she saw that I was entering, bending beneath the weight of an enormous sack filled with copper coins. I fetched out of it and threw upon the floor several coins one after the other, saying: "when all the copper is finished, then you shall be ready for the golden words". I advise you, Anna Nikolaevna, to take this dream unto yourself as well.[23]

[22] *Ibid.*, IV, 12
[23] *Ibid.*, IV, 12.

Is Solov'ev referring to the premature nature of Schmidt's prophesies, her revelations concerning Margarita and the Church? Or to their own relationship, not yet consummated? At any rate, he does not appear very anxious to meet her immediately; although he offers to arrange a brief meeting with her in Vladimir on his way to Moscow, he clearly prefers to postpone their meeting until the end of the year. He adjures her not to discuss him with other people, but instead to pray as much as possible.

The meeting in Vladimir took place in late April, but no one knows what transpired during its brief hours. From Solov'ev's point of view, at least, it was probably not the portentous meeting of Margarita and Raphael, of the earthly incarnation of Sophia and the poet-Godman. In his first letter afterwards he is as formal as before. He feels, however, that she is disturbed about her behaviour at the meeting: "Here are a few words of reassurance. I am well, and as before I preserve towards you the same unchanged feelings, interests and sympathies; no unpleasant impression of the meeting with you has remained; in a word, all is as it was before".[24] He ends this short letter by promising to write more often.

In the final letter, dated the 22nd of June, 1900, Solov'ev seems to share Schmidt's premonitions of apocalypse: "I also think that the former historical thread has come to an end. But what lies ahead: it is not granted to us to have knowledge of the times and dates".[25] Then, he tells her that he is going to the south of Russia in a few days and that he cannot possibly meet her in St. Petersburg as she had apparently requested. Concerning her doubts in regard to supernatural phenomena, Solov'ev replies: "I am very happy that you yourself have some doubt of the objective significance of certain visions and inspirations or communications which you do not comprehend. To insist further on their doubtfulness would be, for my part, ungracious."[26] He then promises to write to her when he returns to St. Petersburg, probably in August.

This fragmentary correspondence gives some indication of the real nature of this much-vaunted "mystical romance". Clearly, Solov'ev was an unwilling "lover"; he sought to avoid direct contact with Anna Schmidt and apparently did not quite know what to make of her appearance and "confession". No doubt he was startled by the similarity between their sophiological revelations and premonitions of apocalypse, but at the same time he evinced no interest in playing Raphael to Margarita-Schmidt, despite the fact that she was to bear the Son-Church, the logical offspirng, after all, of Solov'ev's own views on syzygal union and the Universal Church.

[24] Ibid., IV, 13.
[25] Ibid., IV, 13.
[26] Ibid., IV, 13.

Obviously, Solov'ev himself must have been aware of his own paradoxical situation, caught as he was between rational and irrational expressions of God's Divine Wisdom and the eternal striving for oneness. His encounters with the Divine Feminine, whether in the form of the divine love of Sophia, the natural love of the World Soul, or the earthly love of woman, were all premonitions of a future that had yet to arrive, that would lead to the union of the spiritual and the physical, to the union of Heaven and Hell. How natural and yet ironic it was, then, within such a context that there should suddenly appear, in answer to Solov'ev's ardent entreaties for syzygal union with this feminine spirit, the earthly incarnation of that divine bride in the person of Anna Schmidt.

Anna Schmidt had the final word in their relationship. In an undated letter to a friend,[27] she gives a summation of her sentiments in regard to Solov'ev, the influence he exerted upon her life and the providential similarity of their revelations:

> ... above all else I understood that the root of my family misfortunes and those of every person (i.e. it is better to say the despair and disillusionment caused by insignificant worldly misfortunes) was the *division of the church*. And I began to pray in secret not for my family, not for myself as an individual, but for humanity that it might be the one Church. And in answer to my prayer there came that revelation which God gave me miraculously through the *invisible* agency of Vlad. Serg. and which in 1900 was miraculously confirmed by the oneness of his belief with mine (after 14 years). This signified that in a new revelation God granted as well the means of that union of the Church that I had prayed for.[28]

The "means of that union of the Church" that Schmidt had prayed for was, of course, Vladimir Solov'ev himself. While the metaphor may have been only illustratively sexual (in Solov'evian terms, the exemplary union of two people according to the divine principle of all-in-oneness), it had of course its erotic overtones which were seized upon at the time.

Among the articles of Anna Schmidt's faith, listed in her Final Testament, the seventh is of particular interest, for it appears to hypostatize Solov'ev himself:

> And he who has ascended to the heavens, and sits on the right hand of the Father; remaining in his incorruptible body in heaven, having been *twice incarnated on earth in the year 1853 in a human being*, but who twice received in 1876 a Divine Being in the vision of the Church in Egypt and soon shall descend to judge the quick and the dead, there will be no end to His kingdom.[29]

---

[27] Iz rukopisej..., 272.
[28] Ibid., 272.
[29] Ibid., 273.

Of course, it is Solov'ev who was born in 1853 (in his human form or first incarnation) and was transformed or reborn in his spiritual nature in 1876 when he had the vision of Sophia in the Egyptian Desert which he recorded in his poem "Three Meetings". Nor is Schmidt at all circumspect in stating that she is the daughter of God and, simultaneously mother and bride to Solov'ev, who has become Christ. Her designation of the divine natures in both herself and Solov'ev is no more or less than the perfect expression of Solov'ev's own principles of Godmanhood as outlined in Lectures on Godmanhood and La Russie et l'Eglise Universelle, and the function and end of love as presented in "The Meaning of Love". In this same letter, we find that Schmidt offers the "sources" which in fact have affirmed these beliefs of hers:

> Read in the light of this profession of faith the poems of Vladimir Sergeevich: only then will they become completely comprehensible to you. Note that all his life he had a premonition of and waited for an unknown person, his feminine *alter ego* who was living somewhere, with a dual nature, with a dual spirit, earthly and heavenly. This is especially clear in the poems: "Not by the will of fate . . ." ["Ne po vole sud'by, ne po mysli ljudej . . ."], "I see your emerald eyes . . ." ["Vizhu ochi tvoi izumrudnye . . ."], "Wherefore words . . .?" ["Zachem slova? V bezbrezhnosti lazurnoj . . ."]. That this person did not appear for so long was "amid deceptions the living deception"[30]; that she impeded the work of Vlad[imir] S[ergeevich] and that he died only with a faint hope; that he was tormented by the unearthly suffering of a fruitless expectation throughout all his lonely life—in all of this is my cardinal sin before him, before God, before humanity! But all the same I fear neither death nor the end of the world. I sense His blessed compassion, His inexpressible sympathy towards me when I say: "May no one love You as I do, for You have not forgiven anyone as much as You have me!".[31]

Here, in the final apotheosis, it is evident that Vladimir Solov'ev and Christ have become one for Anna Schmidt.

However, Anna Schmidt's mystical search for her masculine counterpart did not cease with the death of Solov'ev in 1900. Until her own death in 1905, she continued to seek what she assumed to be the further earthly incarnations of Solov'ev among the Russian symbolist poets. Georgij Chulkov, Aleksandr Blok and Andrej Belyj were confronted in succession by this earthly incarnation of Sophia. The Sophiological themes which had obsessed her in the works of Solov'ev led her to those early "disciples" of the poet-philosopher who took up the theme of the Divine Feminine with its attendant motifs of longing, syzygy and apocalypse. Having read Chulkov's first book of poems, *Kremnistyj put'* (1903), she paid him an unannounced

---

[30] This reference is from Solov'ev's poem "O, chto znachat vse slova i rechi..."
[31] Iz rukopisej..., 274.

midnight visit in Nizhnij Novgorod in 1903 and proceeded to read to him out of her manuscript, "The Third Testament":

> Anna Nikolaevna opened my book [of poems] and directed my attention to three poems—"O, the strange gaze of the medium" [O, Mediuma strannyj vzor] ... "I pray to you as to the sun, as to the day's radiance" [Ja moljus' tebe, kak solntsu, kak sijan'ju dnja".] ... and finally, my poetic rendition of "The Song of Songs" ["Pesn' Pesnej"]. This gives me the right to demand of you your consideration for my "Third Testament"—she said quietly and solemnly.[32]

The appearance of Blok's first poems in *Severnye tsvety* and *Novvj put'* in 1903 and the subsequent publication of his *Stikhi o Prekrasnoj Dame* the following year, drew Anna Schmidt's attention to him. According to the editors of the collected correspondence of Aleksandr Blok and Andrej Belyj,[33] a letter from Anna Schmidt to Blok, written on the 12th of March, 1903, is preserved in Blok's archives; "... she quite openly refers to the fact that she is the manifestation of none other than the earthly incarnation of the 'world soul', Solov'ev's 'Sophia-Divine Wisdom'".[34] In one of Blok's letters that was published in an earlier collection, but for some reason omitted from the later *Sobranie sochinenij* (in 8 vols., M.-L., 1960-63), he writes to his mother:

> Anna Nik. Schmidt, in spite of the fact that I have never answered her, has once again written "for God's sake, arrange our meeting" and so on. She has calculated out her days and it transpires that she will arrive here [Shakhmatovo] on the 11th or 12th [of May, 1904] for a day or two for a weighty conversation .... Anna Nikol. considers herself the incarnation of the World Soul, longing for God. Fortunately, she already knows from Serezha [Sergej Mikhajlovich Solov'ev] that my verses are not addressed to her. In any case, the situation is difficult ....[35]

She did in fact turn up at Shakhmatovo on the 12th of May, 1904, and departed the following day, having had her "weighty conversation" with Blok. In his letters and diary Blok describes the occasion: "A. N. Schmidt paid us a visit. She left a confusing but, in any case, a good impression of her extreme sincerity and *clarity of mind*, devoid of all *fiendishness* [*infernalnost'*], whether good or bad. She spoke of many subtle things which are *comprehensible only to me*."[36] Apparently, her meeting with Blok (and the prior intercession of his friend Sergej Solov-ev, nephew of Vladimir) convinced Anna Schmidt that he was

---

[32] Georgij Chulkov, *Gody stranstvij. Iz vospominanij*, 122-123.
[33] *Aleksandr Blok i Andrej Belyj. Perepiska*, ed. V. N. Orlov (Moscow, 1940), 33-34.
[34] *Ibid.*, 33, n. 2.
[35] Blok, "Pis'mo k materi," 4 May, 1904, in *Pis'ma k rodnym* (Leningrad, 1927), II, 120.
[36] Aleksandr Blok, *Sobranie sochinenij*, VIII, 102.

not to be her Raphael. At any rate, she received even less attention from Blok than she had earlier from the philosopher.

Andrej Belyj, the third member of the "Solov'evian Circle", together with Blok and Sergej Solov'ev, also came face to face with Anna Schmidt, but apparently did not excite her Sophiological mysticism as much as the others. After Solov'ev's death, Anna Schmidt began to hound the philosopher's gentle and hospitable brother, Mikhail Sergeevich, with her incomprehensible revelations and visions. He had taken the responsibility upon himself of publishing any of his brother's unfinished articles, papers, etc., and was greatly disturbed at the possible consequences of Anna Schmidt's former connection with his brother and her continuing activities. Belyj, who first met her through Mikhail Sergeevich and Olga Mikhailovna Solov'ev recalls the situation thus:

> M[ikhail] S[ergeevich] hesitated to publish those excerpts of his philosopher-brother's unfinished articles which were connected with the theme of the deceased's poem "Three Meetings", because some insane Schmidt in Nizhnij Novgorod conceived of herself as the "world soul" who had inspired the deceased Solov'ev; this maniac badly upset M. S.; he constantly feared the birth of some mystical sect out of the depths of his brother's philosophy under the influence of Schmidt's ravings.[37]

Belyj refers to Anna Schmidt as representing the "type of Solov'evian fanatic"[38] he was interested in as material for his satirical Symphonies; ostensibly with this purpose in mind he became acquainted with her and even exchanged letters with her as early as 1901.[39]

With her death in 1905, Anna Schmidt's name temporarily disappeared from the literary-philosophical scene in Russia.[40] However, the religio-mystical pattern of divine syzygy initiated in her "affair" with Solov'ev was firmly established. One has but to recall the farcical worship of Ljubov'Dmitrievna Mendeleeva (the wife of Blok) as an earthly incarnation of Sophia or the Divine Feminine by the Solov'evian triad of Belyj, Blok and Sergej Solov'ev,[41] or the demonic reversal of the theme in the love-triangle of V. Brjusov, Belyj and Nina Petrovskaja which was supposedly portrayed in Brjusov's novel *The Fiery Angel* (1907). The theme is manipulated over and over again by

[37] Andrej Belyj, *Nachalo veka* (Moscow-Leningrad, 1933), 119.
[38] *Ibid.*, 138.
[39] Belyj, "Vospominanij o A. A. Bloke," in *Epopeja*, 1922, No. 1, 141.
[40] To be revived later principally by Sergej Bulgakov who was behind the publication of her manuscripts. Bulgakov, more than anyone else, appeared to be fascinated by the spiritual possibilities of the "affair."
[41] The "Holy Trinity" of Sergej Solov'ev, Belyj and Blok, the role of Mendeleeva as Sophia and the enactments of this pseudo-serious farce are recorded particularly in Belyj, "Vospominanija o A. A. Bloke," in *Epopeja*, 1922, No. 1 Chapters I and II.

Belyj throughout many of his works. It is to be found in multiple variation in three of his four *Symphonies* (the first, second and fourth) as well as the novels *The Silver Dove* and *Petersburg*.

During his lifetime Anna Schmidt was one of the few who seemed to grasp the essence of Solov'evian Sophiology, the role of the feminine principle which, in fact, the Nizhnij Novgorod mystic attempted to assume. She also realized, of course, that this was the unique feature of Solov'ev's thought and immediately seized upon it in his poetry and philosophy, intuiting an indivisible link between the two that seemed to frighten even Solov'ev himself when she confronted the philosopher with the mystic, when she brought face to face the inherent eroticism of the poetic longing for union between Solov'ev and Sophia and the rational exegesis of the syzygy between heaven and earth.

PART II
Early Disciples

Chapter 1

THE SYMBOLIST ASSESSMENT OF VLADIMIR SOLOV'EV

For knights of the Divine Sophia Vladimir Solov'ev appeared as an enigmatic yet inspirational silhouette outlined against the sunset of the nineteenth century awaiting the sunrise of the twentieth. For most of the young symbolists this diurnal cycle represented their own predicament as well. Arrested in an ambivalent nocturnal atmosphere, trapped between the ecstatic premonitions engendered by sunsets and striving for the revelatory annunciation of the new day in the sunrise, the drama of Solov'ev's poetic-philosophical work became theirs as well.

Precisely what Vladimir Solov'ev meant to poets like Aleksandr Blok, Andrej Belyj, Sergej Solov'ev and Georgij Chulkov, as well as to philosopher-theologians like Sergej Bulgakov and Pavel Florenskij, is by no means beyond assessment. Most have made it abundantly clear exactly what it was that attracted them to Solov'ev. As in Solov'ev's own life-drama, however, there was both a public and a private aspect to the adulation paid to the philosopher-poet, a discussion of Solov'ev that was open to the public in the pages of the leading journals, and an understanding of him that cast the die for the personal lives and interrelationships of those who seemed to be most closely connected to the man's memory and work. While the public discussion was usually, if not always, rational, the private understanding bore those characteristic Solov'evian features of the bizarre and the irrational.

In the "memoir-literature"[1] of Andrej Belyj, which easily exceeds some two thousand printed pages ebbing and flowing at varying levels of veracity, Vladimir Solov'ev is perhaps one of the most constant figures to which Belyj pays homage. While Blok, Brjusov, the Merezhkovskijs and other leading figures of the time suffer at the hands of a brilliant but paranoid and megalomaniac memoirist who is constantly seeking to justify his own eccentric and somewhat mercur-

[1] *Nachalo veka* (Moscow-Leningrad, 1933), *Mezhdu dvukh revoljutsij* (Leningrad, 1934), *Na rubezhe dvukh stoletij* (Moscow-Leningrad, 1930). Of particular importance is Belyj's "Vospominanija o A. A. Bloke," *Epopeja*, No. 1, 1922, 123-273; No. 2, 1922, 105-299; No. 3, 1922, 125-310; No. 4, 1923, 61-305.

ial behaviour and views, Vladimir Solov'ev remains the "untouchable", the fixed emblem of his own symbolist values. The major portion of Belyj's assessment of Solov'ev can be traced back, however, to two of his more lucid and theoretically untrammelled articles, "Vladimir Solov'ev. Iz vospominanij" ("Vladimir Solov'ev. Reminiscences", 1911)[2] and "Apokalipsis v russkoj poezii" ("The Apocalypse in Russian Poetry," 1903).[3]

In the first of these Belyj goes back to his original meeting with this mysterious figure early in 1900 at the home of the philosopher's brother and sister-in-law, Mikhail Sergeevich and Olga Mikhajlovna Solov'ev, in Moscow. At that time Belyj was very close friends with the philosopher's nephew, Sergej Mikhajlovich Solov'ev, the son of Mikhail Sergeevich. This meeting was fraught with all the requisite mystery and significance for Belyj that one might expect under the extraordinary circumstances. Belyj had been invited to a private reading of Solov'ev's apocalyptically inspired "Tale of the Antichrist". He recalls:

> Then he read his "Tale of the Antichrist". At the words "John arose like a white candle", he also sat up as though stretching forth out of his chair. It seemed that lightning was flashing in the window. Solov'ev's face trembled in the lightning flashes of inspiration.[4]

Upon the conclusion of the tale, Belyj is so beside himself that he blurts out his own interpretation of the apocalyptic ties between Solov'ev's philosophical novel *Tri razgovora* (*Three Conversations*) and the "Tale of the Antichrist". Solov'ev looks upon Belyj's exegesis with special favour and interest and, when Belyj goes on to tell him that he has just written a work that resembles Solov'ev's in many ways,[5] the philosopher wants to send him home for it. However, since they have been reading all night, Olga Mikhajlovna intervenes and Solov'ev agrees to meet with his young "disciple" at the end of the summer. This meeting never took place because of Solov'ev's death. However, this inspiring meeting and the fateful likeness between the premonitions of the older man and the youth put a seal on Belyj's ecstatic regard for Solov'ev: "Subsequently Vladimir Solov'ev was for me the precursor of the fervour of religious searchings."[6]

Like all others who knew or had seen Solov'ev, Belyj too found it difficult to forget or ignore his eccentric "hoffmanesque" air. Forever

---

[2] In Andrej Belyj, *Arabeski* (Moscow, 1911), 387-394.

[3] First appeared in Vesy, No. 4, 1905, 11-28. Reprinted in Andrej Belyj, *Lug zelenyj* (Moscow, 1910), 222-247. The latter source is quoted in this text.

[4] Belyj, *Arabeski*, 394.

[5] This is probably a reference to one of Belyj's first works, a drama-mysterium entitled "The Antichrist" which was never published.

[6] Belyj, "V. Solov'ev...", *Arabeski*, 387.

embedded in his memory of the philosopher is the eerie ring of his childish laughter as well as an association with sunsets. In Belyj's *Kotik Letaev* (first published in 1922), written some sixteen years after Solov'ev's death, this association of the man with sunsets remains as fresh as it did at the time of his meeting and during the writing of these reminiscences: "Solov'ev was always beneath the sign of sunsets gleaming before him. Out of the sunset issued the sacred muse of his mystical philosophy (she, as he called her)".[7]

Solov'ev's physical appearance, in the devoted memory of Belyj, inspired the following romantic portrait:

> I remember him with fathomless penetrating eyes, with hair billowing about his shoulders, ironically calm to look at, thoughtful, enveloped with clouds of fire. Sharply, distinctly, his words were expressed like bursts of lightning and the lightning penetrated the future; and the heart was captivated with a mysterious sweetness when he bent comfortably over a manuscript, his visage like that of a biblical prophet.[8]

Belyj, himself committed to the spiritual transformation of the world and the active implementation of his own symbolist theories, saw in Solov'ev the same rationally theorized striving for transformation behind the mystical aura. Consequently, the metaphysical works which others, like Blok, found so boring, disclosed to Belyj the inescapably mystical roots of the rational philosopher:

> His muse became the norm of his life. One could say that Solov'ev transformed the striving towards the sunset into a duty, and to the disclosure of this duty are dedicated the eight volumes of his works where a sophisticated critical analysis is aligned with a diffuse, unfinished metaphysic and with an uncanny depth of mystical experience.[9]

One cannot help thinking how apt an assessment this is of Belyj's own theoretical writings!

The theoretically as well as mystically inclined Belyj obviously saw the connection between the rational theory and the irrational experience. This becomes quite apparent in his assessment of Solov'ev in the article "The Apocalypse in Russian Poetry". Here Belyj grasps the essential role of Sophia in the Solov'evian system. This article (which will be dealt with at length in another chapter) intends to outline the apocalyptic progress of Russian poetry leading either to worship of the Woman Clothed in the Sun (and, consequently, transformation and salvation) or to the deceitful adulation of the Harlot (leading to death and destruction). In it Belyj becomes obsessed with the idea of "tearing the mask" from illusory harmony

---

[7] *Ibid.*, 389.
[8] Belyj, "Apokalipsis...", *Lug zelenyj*, 223.
[9] Belyj, "V. Solov'ev...", *Arabeski*, 389.

and beauty or from the truth obscured by the "enemy". If this, then, is the duty of symbolism and himself, then it was Solov'ev who first descended into the pit to do battle with the beast and told not only of the lurking dangers but of the ecstasies waiting there:

> But from the immortal heights of Platonism and Schellingism Solov'ev glimpsed the rosy smile of the World Soul. He understood as well the ecstasy of the "Song of Songs" and the banner of the "Woman Clothed in the Sun". And lo, from the philosophical heights he descended into this world in order to warn people of the dangers threatening them, to show them those ecstasies which were unknown to them.... Powerful and majestic, he wrestled with the terror, it seemed as though he were turning not pages, but tearing the mask from the truth which was obscured by the enemy.[10]

Thus, not only did Belyj associate Solov'ev with the revelation of truth in a divine feminine incarnation, but he also perceived the dualistic nature of the World Soul, who was potentially divine or demonic. Furthermore, he openly recognized the function of union which Solov'ev had invested in his concept of Sophia as the Divine Wisdom of God: "Solov'ev attempted to indicate to us the attractive mask of falsehood tossed by the enemy over the Visage of She Who will unite the disunited heaven and earth of our souls into an indescribable oneness."[11]

For Belyj, then, Solov'ev appears not only as the watchful sentry who warns of the approach of Antichrist or "Anti-Sophia", but also as the formulator of the Russian poet's duty to reveal the genuine visage or nature of the Divine Feminine or Woman Clothed in the Sun who is to preside over the union of heaven and earth:

> Solov'ev indicated the mask of madness drawing nigh upon the world and summoned all those shaken by this spectre to become absorbed [in the eternal feminine] so as not to go mad. But to become absorbed in the eternal-feminine sources of the Soul means to manifest Her visage before everyone. Here begins the theurgic power of his poetry in which Fet's pantheism and Lermontov's individualism intersect with the radiant insights of the Christian gnostics.[12]

This concern for the exemplary, for the symbolic nature of Solov'ev as a person and a thinker, is precisely what seemed to obsess Blok in his public statements. However, it was the "living image"[13] of the man, the atmosphere of the mood of the man in his poetry, rather than the dialectics of his thought which appeared to inspire reverence in this reluctant symbolist. Although Blok never said as much in

[10] Belyj, "Apokalipsis...", Lug zelenyj, 224.
[11] Ibid., 228.
[12] Ibid., 229.
[13] See Blok's letter to Georgij Chulkov on 23 June (o.s.), 1905, in A. Blok, *Sobranie sochinenij* (Moscow-Leningrad, 1960-1965), VIII, 128.

public or in print, he did confide in a letter to one of his closest friends something that apparently he never disclosed in such blunt terms to his symbolist colleagues. There were "two Solov'evs" for him as well—the rational and the mystical. However, the rational Solov'ev had absolutely nothing to say to him. He recognized and esteemed the mystical Solov'ev alone, the Solov'ev of the nocturnal poetry:

> It is painful to speak to "Petersburgers", but not so to you (because you will understand *exactly* without any exaggerations), that this month I made an effort to get through Solov'ev's "The Justification of the Good" and there I found *nothing* other than several clever formulations of medium depth and inconceivable *boredom*. It makes me feel like doing everything *to the contrary*, for spite. There is Vl. Solov'ev and his poetry—a revelation unique in its kind, but there is also the "Collected Works of V. S. Solov'ev"—boring and prosaic.[14]

Blok wrote two articles on Solov'ev, the first entitled "Rytsar'-monakh" ("The Knight-Monk", 1910) on the tenth anniversary of Solov'ev's death; the second, "Vladimir Solov'ev i nashi dni" ("Vladimir Solov'ev and Our Times", 1920), on the twentieth anniversary. Both articles are extremely revealing, not only for their assessment of Solov'ev, but also for the light they shed on Blok who, as a poet, had been considered by most the direct heir, the most fervent disciple, of Vladimir Solov'ev.

In "The Knight-Monk", Blok, himself the target for so many ugly rumours during his life, begins by attacking all those scandalmongers and gossips who for various trivial reasons sought to discredit Solov'ev during and after his lifetime. He outlines those two aspects in Solov'ev which have most struck him. There is the Solov'ev of this world: "[he] routed the enemy with his own weapons: he learned to *forget* time; he simply pacified it by casting over the shaggy fur of the monster a light silver *fatus* of laughter; this is why that laughter was often so strange and terrifying..."[15] But the maximalist Solov'ev has also impressed Blok: "The other one—the otherworldly one—did not scorn and did not pacify. This was the 'honorable warrior of Christ'. He raised a golden sword over the head of the enemy. We all saw the radiance but either forgot it or mistook it for something else."[16]

Blok only saw Solov'ev once, in a funeral procession in 1900 for one of Blok's distant relatives. The inspired image he retains is not unlike Belyj's:

> In Solov'ev's gaze, which he by chance allowed to rest on me on that day, was a fathomless deep blue: an absolute renouncement and

[14] See Blok's letter to E. P. Ivanov on 15 June (o.s.), 1904, in Blok, *Sobranie sochinenij*, VIII, 105-106.
[15] "Rytsar'-monakh" in Blok, *Sobranie sochinenij*, V, 450.
[16] Ibid., V, 450.

readiness to execute the final step; this was no less than a pure spirit: surely no living person, but a representation; a silhouette, a symbol, an emblem... He walked slowly after an unknown coffin, into the unknown distance, knowing neither of the conditons of time and space.[17]

This is the image of the "otherworldly Solov'ev" that Blok prefers, the one that he is most willing to expand upon in the article as an emblem or silhouette for his own vague aspirations.

The exemplary nature of Solov'ev is recorded in the epithets which the younger poet affixes to him, namely that of "knight" and "monk". For he sees Solov'ev's prodigious effort in metaphysics and ethics as the "sword and shield" of the knight and the "good works" of the monk, they are "... only a *means*: for the knight—to wrestle with the dragon, for the monk—with chaos, for the philosopher —with madness and the mutability of life."[18] The nature of the work to be accomplished is significant, for Blok also understands where the efforts of Solov'ev's Sophiology are directed: "This is a unique earthly work: the work of liberating the captive Queen, the World Soul who is passionately languishing in the embrace of chaos and abiding in a mysterious union with the 'cosmic mind'."[19] In the light of the work which Solov'ev is trying to consummate, the eccentric nature of his behaviour must be understood in its proper context: "All the earthly romanticism, the strange eccentricity are only a fragrant flower on this picture. The 'poor knight', from an abundance of earthly enamourment, will lay it at the feet of the captive Queen."[20] In other words, Solov'ev may present an absurdly romantic or eccentric image of himself as a Quixotic "knight-monk", yet in spite of this, the authenticity of his visions and his romantic maximalism are indisputable in his works.

Like Belyj, who was also willing to accept the truth of Solov'ev's visions in "Three Meetings", Blok feels that the meetings with and premonitions of Sophia were quite genuine. The poem "Three Meetings" is not to be taken as an allegory, but as an image given by life itself, according to Blok. In typical fashion, he does not attempt to establish the validity of the visions themselves other than by saying that they must be genuine since they are all fixed on the axes of time and space. Instead, he goes on to describe the genuineness of the "image" afforded us by "Three Meetings" in a completely lyrical fashion: "...let it be the object of scientific scrutiny, its very essence

[17] Ibid., V, 446-447.
[18] Ibid., V, 451.
[19] Ibid., V, 451.
[20] Ibid., V, 450.

is not given to analysis; it pours forth an insubstantial golden light.In gold and cinnabar were written the words issuing forth out of Gabriel's lips: 'Ave, gratia plena.'"[21]

To preserve the honour and memory of Solov'ev, Blok exhorts his listeners and readers "... to joyfully remember that the essence of the world is from the very beginning beyond time and beyond space; that it is possible to be born a second time and cast off from oneself the chains and the dust...we must all, insofar as our strength allows, take part in the liberation of the Queen who is a captive of Chaos—the World Soul and our souls. Our souls are part of the World Soul."[22] Not only is Solov'ev an emblem of the essentially otherwordly nature of this world, but Blok also seems to be insinuating, in true Solov'evian fashion, that man's task is to liberate nature and the material world (i.e., the World Soul) from enslavement to mechanistic materialism.This exemplary image or portrait of Solov'ev is unmistakably suffused with a sense of apocalypse, a sense of being on the divide between two eras over which his enigmatic spirit presides: "... the new world is already at the threshold; tomorrow we shall recall the golden light sparkling on the border of two centuries that are so different. The Nineteenth Century has forced us to forget the very names of the saints; the Twentieth, perhaps, will see them face-to-face. This banner has been manifested to us Russians by Vladimir Solov'ev who stands before us still undeciphered and ambivalent."[23]

Ten years later in 1920, Blok delivered a rather ambiguous speech on the significance of Solov'ev entitled "Vladimir Solov'ev and Our Times". Here once again he apparently attempts to recapture and define the elusive nature of Solov'ev's significance as a silhouette on the border of two ages, moving from reaction and positivism to idealism and spirituality. Although very little is said in this speech, which reflects Blok's increasing fatigue and withdrawal after the Revolution, he makes some very interesting additions to his previous treatment. He compares Solov'ev's time to the first few centuries A.D. which witnessed the decay of Rome and the emergence of the new spiritual force of Christianity. In fact, this particular historical period does correspond better to the end of the Nineteenth and the beginning of the Twentieth Centuries in Russia, than to the period immediately preceding the French Revolution with which it is usually compared, according to Blok. Above all, there is a pervading notion of Solov'ev as a lonely, misunderstood figure caught between two warring forces

---

[21] Ibid., V, 453.
[22] Ibid., V, 453-454.
[23] Ibid., V, 454.

while bearing some enigmatic and all-reconciling power: "Vl. Solov'ev, for whom in life 'there was no shelter between two hostile camps', has not found this shelter even now, for he was the bearer of some part of this third power, of this new world, which, despite all, is approaching us."[24]

Some twenty years after Solov'ev's death Blok here looks back and considers that the best article ever written on Vladimir Solov'ev was Andrej Belyj's "Vladimir Solov'ev. Reminiscences." At first glance this may seem somewhat superficial, especially when one realizes the vast number of detailed articles and lengthy monographs that dealt with Solov'ev's life, thought and poetry. But comparing the content of Belyj's article and that of Blok, one realizes that it is above all the shadow cast by Solov'ev over their generation and the atmosphere he generated about him that proved of lasting memory for both of them.

One of the most interesting public discussions of Solov'ev was provoked by an article, "Poezija Vladimira Solov'eva" ("The Poetry of Vladimir Solov'ev", 1905) written by the young symbolist poet, Georgij Chulkov, one of the co-founders of "Mystical Anarchism". By no means a poet of talent or a thinker of genius, Chulkov nonetheless managed to inspire, in spite of himself, a revealing debate that centred on the meaning of Solov'ev's poetry and philosophy and their relatedness.

His article begins with a statement that the two aspects of Solov'ev, the philosophical and the poetical, represent a tragic split or dichotomy in the man. If Solov'ev's philosophy presents a single, homogeneous monolith, then in his poetry "the oneness and wholeness of the philosophical world-view is destroyed. The psychological diversity and complexity fragment that which logic has hammered out and in horror one sees the triumph of chaos over an organic order that mind and belief have sought to create."[25] In other words, Chulkov feels that it is impossible to conceive of Solov'ev's poetry merely as an expression of the philosophical system in its harmonious entirety. Although Solov'ev's rational expression of the divine idea is that of oneness, the irrational expression reveals a dark and somber duality that the poet is unable to overcome.

Chulkov goes into a brief analysis of the World Soul, for he believes Solov'ev's poetry to be inextricably connected with this teaching. The World Soul could exist in oneness with God but makes herself into an independent centre which then longs for union with God and desires to receive the Divine Logos. Chulkov singles out her

[24] "Vladimir Solov'ev i nashi dni," in Blok, *Sobranie sochinenij*, VI, 159.
[25] Georgij Chulkov, "Poezija Vladimira Solov'eva," in *Voprosy zhizni*, 1905, Nos 4-5, 102.

inability to consummate this union and sees her caught between the divine and the material. Consequently this dilemma provides, for him at least, the proof of a metaphysical contradiction and the affirmation of two absolute principles in Solov'ev's works. He is not convinced by Solov'ev's attempts to explain this apparent contradiction and believes that this "tragic split" reveals itself in his poetry in the confrontation of the first absolute—the oneness of God—and the second absolute—the duality of the World Soul.

Both the introduction to the third edition of Solov'ev's poetry (where he makes the important distinction between the heavenly and earthly Aphrodites) and "The Meaning of Love" Chulkov interprets to mean that Solov'ev denies all earthly love: "With gloomy insistence Solov'ev denies earthly love, opposing to it a cold love which has 'nothing in common with this folly' [i.e., earthly love]."[26] Furthermore, on the basis of his own interpretation of Solov'ev's poem "Tri podviga" ("Three Feats") he believes that "... only death solemnly promises a meeting with the Sacred Friend..."[27] and that "... the poetry of death celebrates its somber triumph in the verses of Solov'ev."[28]

In short, Chulkov's purpose was to show that in his poetry Solov'ev dared to make the confession which he was unable to in his philosophy, the confession that this world of nature and earthly love must be renounced since it is impossible to bridge the abyss between earth and heaven:

> We only wished to show that the spiritual mood that reigned in Solov'ev is unreconcilable with *love and creation here on earth*. Between the gleaming icy peaks and the flowering valleys yawns an abyss. Solov'ev did not know how to cast a bridge over this abyss just as all of *historical* Christianity did not know how.[29]

Chulkov views Solov'ev's life work as an unsuccessful attempt to reconcile the "religion of Christ with the religion of the Earth."[30]

Chulkov's crude generalizations on one of the most sensitive aspects of Sophiology provoked a great deal of controversy. His quotes from Solov'ev's poetry invariably were taken out of context and the confusion in his comments on "Three Meetings" show his failure to grasp the real dynamics of Sophiology in the relationship between Sophia and the World Soul. Sensitive as he was to the criticism of the leading symbolists of his day, Chulkov, curiously enough, in a later printing of the same article removed many of his questionable comments from the text as well as a series of references

[26] Ibid., 113.
[27] Ibid., 113.
[28] Ibid., 113.
[29] Ibid., 113.
[30] Ibid., 113-114.

to Belyj in particular.³¹ At the same time, however, there is little doubt that Solov'ev left himself vulnerable to this type of "Anti-Christ" criticism which his disciples subsequently admitted. One important aspect of the article, however, that appeared to be beyond attack concerned a comment made by Belyj in his article "O teurgii" ("On Theurgy", 1903) in which Belyj carelessly identifies the Sophia of "Three Meetings" with the Virgin Mary. Chulkov points out that Solov'ev himself specifically separated the two, although the Virgin Mary could be considered a sub-hypostasis of Sophia, or a principle of oneness in God's Divine Wisdom.

Chulkov's article appeared in the joint April-May number of *Voprosy zhizni* (*Questions of Life*) in 1905, and in the August number a rebuttal appeared in the form of an open letter entitled "A Reply to G. Chulkov on the Occasion of His Article 'The Poetry of Vladimir Solov'ev'", written by Sergej Solov'ev, the philosopher's nephew and the *de facto* leader of the "Solov'evian Circle". In general, he complains that Chulkov's analysis is onesided and often contradictory. However, he specifically attacks the statements "... only death solemnly promises a meeting with the Sacred Friend" and "... the poetry of death celebrates its sombre triumph in the verses of Solov'ev". He also takes exception to Chulkov's statement that Solov'ev opposed a "cold love" to an "earthly love". Since Chulkov made frequent reference to Solov'ev's poem "Three Feats", Sergej Solov'ev attempts to use the same poem as a basis of denial. He proceeds to show that, in fact, Solov'ev was not antipathetic to nature, but loved it dearly and viewed it as the first stage towards the ultimate feat of resurrection and immortality. It was potentially a divine and incorruptible beauty. In contrast to Chulkov, he believes that a single idea unites all of Solov'ev's poetic and philosophical works:

> A single idea indissolubly binds all the writings of Solov'ev, from the somber philosophical dissertations to the frivolous love verses. The union of marriage between the beautiful feminine and the blessed masculine, the flesh of Jesus's person and the Divine Word, the heaven and the earth...³²

There are three stages or three "feats of love" in the consummation of this union. While clearly expounding the philosophical ideas of his uncle, Sergej Solov'ev puts a much more antique or pagan stamp on them, in accordance with his interests at the time of writing the article. The first of these appears in the following manner: "From a love for nature begins a religion of life, its first stage is a creation in

---

³¹ See G. Chulkov, "O Sofianstve," *O misticheskom anarkhisme* (Petersburg, 1906), 45-68.

³² S. Solov'ev, "Otvet G. Chulkovu po povodu ego stat'i 'Poezija Vladimira Solov'eva'". *Voprosy zhizni*, 1905, No. 8, 235.

beauty, the first feat of love."³³ Sergej Solov'ev realizes that a religion of nature in itself leads to death just as sexual love alone is given to death and corruption. But once a religion of nature is infused with the Christian's hopes for a new heaven and earth, the first step has been accomplished.

The second feat of love begins with the realization that the serpent has seduced Eve (i.e. Nature) and sown the seeds of death in the earthly image of beauty. The material form of beauty must be purified by crucifixion to prepare the way for the ultimate feat: "If the first feat is the Transfiguration of the divine body on Mount Tabor, then the second feat is its crucifixion on Golgotha.".³⁴

The third and final feat is accomplished in the Christian fact of resurrection:

> "Defenseless, unarmed" before the 'dark genius of fate' the poor knight, the warrior of Christ, dares to sally forth for the third feat, whereby the holy deed of love will be consummated. The pagan world was not destined to free nature from hell's chains. Orpheus was supposed to lead Eurydice out of Erebus: but the new Orpheus, Christ, passing through the crucible of Golgotha, manifests the bright morning of the Resurrection, forming his flesh in beauty and immortality. Through the Transfiguration, through the crucifixion, to the Resurrection. This is the path of Christian Theurgy.³⁵

Sergej Solov'ev not only attempts to refute all of Chulkov's major points, but he also wishes to indicate, once again in a lyrical and exemplary vision, the role to be played by the true disciple of Solov'ev. The landscape and the motifs appear to be directly inspired by Belyj's "Severnaja simfonija" ("Northern Symphony", 1903):

> Nature is the captive princess jealously guarded by the dragon of sin. In the depths of the 'enchanted forest' filled with terrifying monsters stands her glass tomb. In it she lies, awaiting the bold act which will arouse her from her deep, age-old sleep. But few venture forth to wrestle with the monsters of the enchanted forest.... "The radiant daughter of somber chaos" slumbers in her native land of water and forest divinities. She is Undina, untrue, unfaithful, wanton, guarded by uncle Struj. But the knight presses on towards her liberation through a slumbering forest filled with demonic temptations and terrors.³⁶

This fairy-tale world that Sergej Solov'ev visualizes is certainly not without foundation. It is the *skazka*, no doubt that Vladimir Solov'ev alludes to in the somnabulent wakefulness or "waking dream" of a number of his verses.³⁷ But above all it does reflect faithfully the poet's

---

³³ *Ibid.*, 232.
³⁴ *Ibid.*, 233.
³⁵ *Ibid.*, 233.
³⁶ *Ibid.*, 236.
³⁷ See in particular "Sny najavu" (1895), "Kakoj tjazhelyj son! V tolpe nemykh

duty to free captive nature and elevate it to a divine condition wherein it resembles Sophia or perfect oneness. This is the inspiration for Sergej Solov'ev's allegorizations of Vladimir Solov'ev's poetical and philosophical Sophiology.

However, one important point should be raised. Although Sergej Solov'ev no doubt better understood and more vividly portrayed his uncle's desires and intentions, there seems to be an unwillingness on his part to recognize the grain of truth, albeit poorly argued, in Chulkov's statement concerning the undeniably paradoxical duality in Solov'ev's philosophy and the pessimism or rejection of this world which might well be implied in his ultimate vision of a destructive apocalypse engulfing the world in the reign of the Anti-Christ. Sergej Solov'ev was certainly the last of the Solov'evian triangle willing to give in to any doubts about realizing in concrete terms the positive Sophiology of his uncle. And as we shall see in the following chapter, he was the most adamant and dogmatic of the three. This would certainly go a long way to explain his "blindness" to conclusions which not only Chulkov, but Belyj and Blok appeared to have arrived at by 1905.

Chulkov's article provoked a response not only from Sergej Solov'ev, but from Aleksandr Blok as well. In a letter which he wrote to Chulkov on June 23, 1905,[38] Blok gives an outline of a counter-argument which he hoped to compose as a reply. The article, as such, did not materialize, although some of the main ideas do appear in the two articles which Blok wrote later and which have already been discussed. Like Sergej Solov'ev, Blok also disagreed adamantly with Chulkov's depiction of Solov'ev and his work as displaying a tragic split, an "ascetic world-view" and the "sombre triumph of death." In his letter Blok writes Chulkov that he intends to counter these points with: "1) the complete isolation and mystery with which the final years of Solov'ev's life were enveloped; 2) the face of the living Solov'ev, and 3) the knowledge of a certain silence terrifying to all, the knowledge in a form that more resembles intuition, instinct or smell (all these points are, of course, indivisible)."[39] As in his later articles, Blok has nothing to say on the theories of Solov'ev, on the metaphysics of Sophiology and apocalypse. He is more concerned with the atmosphere generated by the man. Searching for the sign of Solov'ev's investiture into another unearthly realm, Blok turns to the most idiosyncratic and disturbing feature of the philosopher's habits, his bizarre laughter:

videnij..." (1886), "Lish' zabudesh'sja dnem, il' prosnesh'sja v polnochi,—" (1898), "Les Revenants" (1900).

[38] See Blok, *Sobranie sochinenij*, VIII, 126-129.
[39] *Ibid.*, VIII, 127.

> Solov'ev's greatest poetic intensity is connected with the final three years [of his life], as well as the apotheosis of that laughter (benevolent rather than harmful) which he assimilated particularly from all the Solov'evs, made incarnate, "apotheosized,"—he rendered legitimate this choking laughter of his that bordered on stuttering; this laughter is one of the most essential elements of Solov'evianism in the personality of Solov'ev...[40]

Blok disagrees with Chulkov's pessimistic assessment of a "tragic split" and the "triumph of death" towards the end of Solov'ev's life. He believes that these signs of duality and ambivalence were a positive indication of the spirit of freedom which Solov'ev was gaining, of the "secret of *play* with mortal melancholy..."[41] In other words, it is as though Blok is saying that Solov'ev had gained the full knowledge of life and death, of good and evil at the end of his life, and the manifestations of these dualities, these ambivalent values overflowed in abundance through his work:

> *Knowledge* filled Solov'ev with an inexplicable ecstasy and rapture (after all, his verses possessed a *fateful significance*, you say, and this Fate filled him completely with the Inutterable, and not from abatement, but rather from overabundance did his most rich cup overflow when he died (and a tiny drop of which fell on me).[42]

As in his later articles, Blok also recalls the singular influence of the "living image" of Solov'ev on him in terms which are less restrained in this private correspondence than in his public articles. It is not only the deep impression of Solov'ev's appearance on him that he wishes to stress, but also the fact that in some inscrutable fashion a bond was sealed between the two of them, even though they did not know each other personally, that there took place a mysterious recognition between the two:

> I remember that face which I saw once in life at the funeral service of a relative. The tall figure in the doorway so that I spent a long moment in raising my eyes until I confronted him eye to eye. Probably some spirituality was expressed in my face because Solov'ev also gazed upon me with a prolonged bluish-grey stare. I shall never forget it—such was the atmosphere at that time.[43]

When Blok overhears in the procession a vulgar comment on the eccentric appearance of the hatless Solov'ev in a tattered old coat, his steel-grey hair exposed to the brisk February cold of a gathering snowstorm, he is almost overwhelmed with sudden anger. But just as mysteriously as he appeared before Blok in the snowflurries, just as enigmatically does he disappear from sight during the procession.

[40] Ibid., VIII, 127.
[41] Ibid., VIII, 127.
[42] Ibid., VIII, 128.
[43] Ibid., VIII, 128.

This sacred image Blok has obviously kept in secret for himself and he begs Chulkov not to show the letter to anyone for it contains, not theories, but the *"visage that lives within me..."*[44]

However, in an interesting "semi-confession", Blok reveals that he does know the power of death in Solov'ev's verses only too well, but at the same time this pall of mortality is penetrated and transformed by an even greater force—that of life. The symbol or principle of this death-conquering force is embodied in Sophia and the philosopher-poet can overcome all through Her: "This strength was given to Solov'ev by that Principle whereof I have dared to become enraptured, the Eternal Feminine, but to speak of It, means to lose It: Sophia, Mary, enamourment—they are nothing but dogmas, invisible cassocks, the filthy and bespattered boots of priests and vodka."[45] In other words, to call the "Beautiful Lady" by her theoretical names, to subject her to vulgar verbalization, to attempt to legalize and dogmatize Her manifestations, is tantamount to profanity for Blok who desires to possess her, as he does the "living image" of Solov'ev, within himself.

This letter to Chulkov, coming almost immediately after the breakup of the Solov'evian triad, offers a clue to the inherent disparity of character and belief among the three Solov'evian disciples.[46] It reveals Blok's mounting disinclination to verbalize the precise meaning of Sophia or the Beautiful Lady which brought him into direct conflict with Sergej Solov'ev's desire to dogmatize her manifestation and Belyj's own effulgent and exaggerated utterances on the question.

The final voice in this assessment of Vladimir Solov'ev was that of Sergej Bulgakov, one of the young idealists who made the philosophical journey from Marxism to Idealism at the turn of the century together with other intellectuals like S. L. Frank and N. Berdjaev. Writing in *Questions of Life* in 1905 on the occasion of the sixth volume of Solov'ev's *Collected Works*, Bulgakov attempts to establish the philosopher's significance.[47] Echoing the exaggersted rhetoric of the symbolist poets, he states his agreement with Professor Lopatin who compared Solov'ev's importance for Russian philosophy with that of Pushkin's for Russian poetry: "Solov'ev's philosophy, like the poetry of Pushkin, is profoundly national and at the same time, like everything profoundly national (and consequently not nationalistic) it is profoundly universal, it is the living

---

[44] *Ibid.*, VIII, 128.

[45] *Ibid.*, VIII, 128.

[46] The "Solov'evian Circle" will be discussed in detail in Chapter V.

[47] See Sergej Bulgakov, "Po povodu vykhoda v svet 6-ogo toma sobranija sochinenij Vladimira Solov'eva," in *Voprosy zhizni*, 1905, No. 2, 361 ff.

light of a living universal spectre; of the divine pleroma."[48] In particular Bulgakov praises Solov'ev's metaphysic because it is free from the systematic and academic rigidity of German philosophy, but above all, because, for the first time, the truths of religion are joined to those of philosophy in a system that contains practical considerations for life.

Bulgakov is especially impressed by the depth and breadth of Solov'ev's thought and feels that it was this very expansiveness, rather than the detail, which was fruitful in Russian thought in his time. Thus, Solov'ev represents a rallying point, a point of departure for the future. He is the "philosophical banner" under which all should come together. The rhetoric becomes eulogy in a final passage:

> Let us repeat, to comprehend, master and assimilate Solov'ev is the primary and requisite task for contemporary Russian thought. During his life few knew how to appreciate him. The millet seed must die in order to bring forth fruit. It was necessary to bear the heavy cross of denial and isolation and die beneath its weight in order that new shoots of life could break forth on the grave. Could it possibly happen that the Russia of the future, free and young Russia, will remain deaf to the summoning voice of Solov'ev![49]

In a later issue of *Questions of Life* that same year, Bulgakov joined the debate taking place between Chulkov, Belyj, Blok and Sergej Solov'ev.[50] Noting the rarity of a philosopher-poet, Bulgakov feels, nonetheless, that "... the content of poetic inspiration and philosophical insight are essentially one and the same."[51] Bulgakov, himself sensitive to Solov'ev's mysticism, praises Chulkov for appreciating not only the artistic qualities of Solov'ev's verses, but sensing their mystical mood as well. In what appears to be a somewhat *pro forma* approbation of Chulkov's efforts, Bulgakov also singles out the young symbolist's worthy attempts to deal with the Divine Feminine and World Soul. However, he expresses his distress at the fact that ultimately Chulkov seems to be ill-disposed towards Solov'ev—that he is playing the role of *advocatus diaboli* by showing everything in a distorted mirror. According to Bulgakov, Chulkov has no sense of the "whole" in Solov'ev, but has concentrated on the "parts" by examining separate motifs out of context without any attempt at general synthesis. Bulgakov takes issue particularly with Chulkov's conclusion that, while Solov'ev the philosopher does not deny all of the world, Solov'ev the poet does. Like Sergej Solov'ev and Blok, Bulgakov insists that the poet "teaches a love for life in his

---

[48] Ibid., 363-364.
[49] Ibid., 367-368.
[50] See Sergej Bulgakov, "Neskol'ko zamechanij po povodu stat'i G. I. Chulkova o poezii Vl. Solov'eva," in *Voprosy zhizni*, 1905, No. 6, 293 ff.
[51] Ibid., 293.

poetry."[52] Admitting that "grief" and "disillusionment" can be found in Solov'ev's verses, as indeed they can be in any great poet's, nonetheless he quotes from many other verses containing an affirmation of life. As a final rebuff, Bulgakov then presents a general outline of Solov'ev's philosophy and poetry in generally accurate terms. Just how well Bulgakov understood Solov'evian Sophiology and to what degree he himself fell beneath its sway, will become apparent in the final chapter of this book.

[52] Ibid., 295.

Chapter 2

THE SOLOV'EVIAN CIRCLE

A loosely organized circle or "salon" began to meet irregularly at the home of Mikhail Sergeevich and Olga Sergeevna Solov'ev, the brother and sister-in-law of Vladimir Solov'ev, in the closing years of the 1890's in Moscow. These people were not all avid disciples of Vladimir Solov'ev (who was in St. Petersburg most of the time anyway) but, in obedience to the fashion for organizing literary and cultural salons where the intelligentsia met to exchange ideas or simply gossip and find entertainment, Mikhail Sergeevich and his wife were the unobtrusive and kindly hosts of gatherings which saw many of the leading literary and philosophical minds under one roof. Within this group, however, there emerged a much more intimate and closely allied circle of friends and relatives who became increasingly devoted to the ideas and writings of Vladimir Solov'ev. The absolute hard-core of this inner "Solov'evian Circle" was made up of Mikhail Sergeevich and his wife, their son Sergej Mikhajlovich, Andrej Belyj (Boris Bugaev) and later, Aleksandr Blok. After the deaths of Mikhail Sergeevich and his wife in January of 1903, the circle was reduced to Sergej Solov'ev, Belyj and Blok.

Most of the information we have concerning the affairs of these arch-Solov'evians is found in the memoirs of Andrej Belyj.[1] Although these memoirs are by no means the most unbiased and trustworthy account of the inner workings of the Solov'evian Circle, they represent the only extensive first-hand one that we have. Fortunately, some of Blok's letters and notes contain a compensatory if fragmented perspective on some events, but there is essentially no material extant to provide with any consistency the view-point of the third member, Sergej Solov'ev.

Belyj was acquainted with Sergej Solov'ev and his parents before the death of Vladimir Solov'ev. It will be recalled that he gave an enraptured account of his meeting with the philosopher in the spring

[1] Of primary interest are Andrej Belyj's memoirs contained in "Vospominanija o A. A. Bloke,": *Epopeja*, 1922, No. 1 (123-273); 1922, No. 2 (105-299); 1922, No. 3 (125-310); 1923, No. 4 (61-305).

of 1900, several months before his death in July of the same year.[2] Thus, even before Solov'ev's death a kinship of apocalyptic premonition existed between the elder man and the young would-be symbolist. After Solov'ev's death, the twenty-year-old Belyj and Sergej Solov'ev, only fifteen, spent most of their time together reading his poetry and philosophy and discussing it between themselves and with Mikhail Sergeevich who was editing his brother's notes and works for a multi-volume edition. At this time they had no knowledge of Aleksandr Blok who, in fact, was distantly related to Solov'ev. In the summer of 1901, Sergej Solov'ev met him for the first time and discovered a kindred spirit, a fellow Solov'evian. Although Belyj and Blok did not meet for several years to come, they carried on an impassioned correspondence and read each other's works with consuming interest.

The youthful Sergej Solov'ev and Belyj were intoxicated with the philosophical and poetical Sophiology of Vladimir Solov'ev, but in their naive romanticism they were especially attracted to the Solov'evian arch-symbol, the Divine Feminine, with her mysterious sunsets and apocalyptic sunrises: "The symbol of the 'Woman' became the dawn for us (the union of the heaven with the earth) intertwining with the gnostics' teachings on concrete wisdom, with the name of the new muse that joined mysticism with life".[3] Solov'ev became for them the precursor, the "Bogoslov", and as the slogan for the new age dawning in the twentieth century, they chose his annunciation of Her appearance on earth: ". . . but we, the youth, we attempted to connect the sound of the sunset with the breaking of dawn in the poetry of Vladimir Solov'ev; his four-line verse was the slogan for us: 'Let it be known that today the Eternal Feminine/Is descending on earth in an incorruptible body./In the unfailing light of the New Goddess/The Heavens have become united with the deeps.'"[4]

The year after Solov'ev's death was spent in close discussion of his works and romantic and vague attempts at preparing the way for the union of heaven and earth or the "Future Theocracy". The nature of the Solov'evian mystique was such that the two made frequent "pilgrimages" to the philosopher's tomb in Novodevichij Monastery in Moscow, sat the nights through making apocalyptic prognoses in order to witness the symbolic dawning of the New Jerusalem in the effulgent sunrise and wandered through the snow-swept streets at night to savour the mysterious and purifying catharsis of the nocturnal blizzard which was to prepare for the new day.

Frequent visits were paid to the Solov'ev family estate at Dedovo where those white cow-bells had been transplanted which had so

[2] See Part II, Chapter I, p. 90.
[3] Belyj, "Vospominanija o A. A. Bloke," 1922, No. 1, 139.
[4] Ibid., 1922, No. 1, 139.

inspired Vladimir Solov'ev on the former estate of A. K. Tolstoj at Pustyn'ka (subsequently the estate of Sophia Khitrovo). Certain lines in these verses, compounded of spiritual resignation and physical weariness, which obscure Solov'ev's abiding faith in the future, became sacred for the young Solov'evian disciples:

> On menacing, sultry
> Summer days
> They yet remain
> Slender and white.
>
> Spectres of spring
> Although consumed
> Here you are faithful
> Otherwordly dreams.
>
> Malice forgotten
> Sinks in the blood.
> The new-washed sun
> Of love arises.
>
> Brave designs
> In a sick heart,
> White angels
> Have risen all around.
>
> Slender and ethereal
> They still remain
> On sultry and oppressive
> Burdensome days.
> ("Vnov' belye kolokol' chiki", 1900)

The memory of Vladimir Solov'ev was so overwhelming for the impressionable Belyj and Sergej Solov'ev that it led to such bizarre rituals and excesses as Belyj describes in his memoirs:

> I recall Dedovo: four of the most unforgettable days spent here between examinations flew past; the mysteries of eternity, the graves, so it seemed, rose up in those days. I recall the night that S. [ergej] M. [ikhajlovich] Solov'ev and I spent on a boat in the middle of the utterly still pond—reading the Apocalypse in the light of a candle flickering in the wind; from the east arose the first streaks of light; with this first light Mikhail Sergeevich Solov'ev, who had not slept all night, joined us: together with him we slowly made the rounds of the estate; we stopped before the cottage, remarking with love on that spot where there were planted, or rather transplanted, the white bells of Pustyn'ka..⁵

These white *kolokol'chiki* defined for the young symbolists their own special mission, their own unique nature: "These white cow-bells—I saw them later in bloom—appeared to us as the symbol of the *white*,

⁵ *Ibid.*, 1922, No. 1, 144.

mystical strivings towards the future".⁶ The "whiteness" of Andrej Belyj's pseudonym is no doubt connected to this same apocalyptic symbolism and was supposedly formulated for him by Mikhail Sergeevich Solov'ev, doubtless in accord with the mystic associations of the white lilies, white bells, snow blizzards and so on that recurred in their poetry and thought.

This period, from March to July of 1901, Belyj considered the climax of their romantic symbolism. However, in July of 1901, Belyj received a letter from Sergej Solov'ev in which the latter described his first meeting with his distant relative, Aleksandr Blok, a young student, the same age as Belyj, but living in St. Petersburg. Both Belyj and the youthful Solov'ev made the most of this totally unexpected encounter with a "soul-brother" who was destined to become the symbolic fulfilment of their Solov'evian triad:

> ...with amazement S. M. informed me that A[leksandr] A[leksandrovich Blok], like us, refers quite concretely to the theme of Sophia, Divine Wisdom; he draws a connection between the teaching on Sophia and the revelation of her visage: in the lyrics of Solov'ev; and from the letter it emerged: A. A. independently of all of us had arrived at the same conclusions as we had on the crisis of contemporary culture and the rising dawn; those conclusions he arrived at abruptly, falling into that "maximalism" that was characteristic of him; it emerged, according to Blok, that the new era is revealed; and the old world is collapsing; the revolution of the spirit proclaimed by Solov'ev is beginning....⁷

From this first meeting between Sergej Solov'ev and Aleksandr Blok in the summer of 1901 grows the tangle of events that eventually brought Blok and Belyj together in the Solov'evian triad, only to separate and then suffer many years of ambivalent contact.

A regular correspondance ensued principally between Blok and the Solov'ev family, though Belyj, accepted as a member of that family, had the opportunity to read Blok's letters and the poems he frequently enclosed in them. In fact, it was Mikhail Sergeevich and his wife who were responsible for making Blok's early poetry known among the literary elite of Moscow at that time.

The mystery of Blok's sudden appearance as an unknown "disciple" of Solov'ev was deepened by further coincidences. In the early part of January, 1903, Belyj and Blok were inexplicably taken by a simultaneous impulse to write to each another. Although they had known each other for the past year and a half and obviously were interested in each other, they had never met or even written. Then, suddenly, their first letters crossed in the mail, both expressing the same desire to become acquainted. This event had an enormous effect

⁶ Ibid., 1922, No. 1, 145.
⁷ Ibid., 1922, No. 1, 149.

on Belyj, though less on Blok. Belyj always made much of this symbolic coincidence in his memoirs, taking it as a sign of their common mission to transform the world:

> The letters, in all probability, met in Bologoj, crossed each other; the cross sign of the letters became a symbol of the crossing of our paths —from which subsequently I both suffered and took joy: yes, Blok's and my paths were thereafter to cross in various ways; the cross lying between us was at times the cross of brotherhood, at others the swords with which we struck each other: we quarreled more than once and embraced more than once.[8]

Almost immediately after this first exchange of letters, an event took place to shatter the first Solov'evian Circle. In January, 1903, Mikhail Sergeevich Solov'ev died and his wife committed suicide within hours of her husband's death. This was, of course, an enormous shock to the three youths who had been so close to them, not only as relatives and friends, but also in the common bond of Vladimir Solov'ev who united all their interests. However, even without the benevolent leadership of Mikhail Sergeevich and his wife, the Solov'evian "troika" of Sergej Solov'ev, Belyj and Blok continued to nourish itself on Solov'evian Sophiology. The frequent pilgrimages to his grave and verse-readings at his tomb were now expanded to include those of Sergej Solov'ev's parents.

Meanwhile, however, Blok was still in St. Petersburg and had not yet made the personal acquaintance of Andrej Belyj. With the death of Sergej's parents to whom many of Blok's poems and letters were addressed, his correspondance with Belyj increased. The closeness of this youthful triad, despite the obvious disadvantages of separation may be judged by the events surrounding Blok's projected marriage to the beautiful Ljubov' Dmitrievna Mendeleeva whom many, and in particular Belyj and Sergej Solov'ev, considered to be at least the earthly incarnation of Blok's mysterious verses to his "Beautiful Lady", if not indeed, Sophia herself.

When after a prolonged and not unstormy courtship Blok finally persuaded Ljubov' Dmitrievna to marry him in August of 1903, he asked Belyj (whom of course he had never met) and Sergej Solov'ev to be the two ushers at his wedding. How natural it must have seemed to all three poets that they be attendant on this "mysterious marriage", or prototypic divine syzygy, between one of their number and this earthly incarnation of divine beauty. Once again the nature of the time or "the atmosphere" was such that in their Solov'ev-inspired romantic mysticism they should interpret this "marriage" as the natural and long-awaited consummation of Sophiology. In his memoirs Belyj recalls the significance they attached to marriage, especially after

[8] *Ibid.*, 1922, No. 1, 158-159.

reading Solov'ev's "The Meaning of Love", and it is entirely in the spirit of the philosopher himself. Sophia descended was symbolized for them in the image of that woman who loved them. Her "partner" was the Christ-figure: "Manifesting more and more her visage to the world, she is active in the gaze of the woman who loves us; the relations of man and woman are the symbol of other relations: Christ and Sophia".[9]

Under the influence of such ideas these young symbolists were prepared to carry them to their natural conclusion at the first opportunity. However, this is not to say that they were totally unaware of the possibility of the deceptive mask of Antichrist or "anti-Sophia" which could be lurking behind this vision of heavenly beauty. Belyj, at least, claims that Solov'ev's equivocal relationship with Anna Nikolaevna Schmidt and especially the mysterious signature "S" which Solov'ev apparently recorded in his transcriptions of automatic writing could well have masked Sophia's fallen counterpart, the demonic aspect of Akhmaoth:

> I indicated earlier the confusion produced in us by the addresses of "S" to Vladimir Solov'ev, by the flamboyant rough drafts of his philosophical treatises where there were outlined the strange, amorous lines in a mediumistic handwriting and where stood the signature of either "S" or "Sophie"; the nature of this "S" we have tried to puzzle out. Who is she? A woman? Sophia Petrovna [Khitrovo] with whom Solov'ev was acquainted? A being of the spirit world who whispered the mysteries of a new testament? What did the name mean to him? "Sophia—Divine Wisdom?" Her reflection in passion or Akhmaoth sacrificially falling into chaos in order to arise in the radiance of God's word?[10]

In their enthusiasm, however, Belyj and Sergej Solov'ev in particular desired to, and therefore did, see the divine aspect of Sophia in Ljubov' Dmitrievna. Nonetheless, in the estimation of the paranoid Belyj, this courtship of the earthly Sophia did not last very long, for she soon removed her mask to reveal the "anti-Sophia" beneath.

Nevertheless the charade continued on and off for almost a year and a half, especially after the mysterious atmosphere generated by the wedding. Belyj was prevented from attending by his father's death, but its bizarre details were conveyed to him by Sergej Solov'ev who was present as an usher.

According to Belyj, the overly sensitive Solov'ev wrote of the atmosphere surrounding the wedding as being fraught with an inexplicable mystery, like the consummation of some divine behest or the sacred ritualizing of his uncle's projected syzygy. The mystery was deepened by the presence of a Count Razvadovskij, a Pole who took

[9] Ibid., 1922, No. 1, 152.
[10] Ibid., 1922, No. 1, 151-152.

Belyj's place as usher. Sergej wrote of him as being a soul-mate also full of eschatological premonitions of the future. Almost immediately after the wedding this Count Razvadovskij apparently renounced the world, took Catholic vows and entered a monastery in Galicia. It was rumoured that he had formed a sect or brotherhood of the "New Star" bearing some resemblance to the apocalyptic aspirations of the Solov'evian circle at that time. Having read Sergej Solov'ev's enigmatic letter, Belyj felt he knew what his young friend was trying to define in such vague terms:

> ... finally I guessed: the wedding of Blok, 'who was enamoured of Eternity', to an empirical girl, prompted the question: who does this bride represent for Blok? If Beatrice—then no one is being married to Beatrice; if simply a girl, then the marriage to "simply a girl" is a betrayal of the way; true—the themes of Blok's poetry invite conjecture: by what spiritual paths was the poet himself proceeding? After all, it was natural for us to see him as a monk protecting himself from worldly seductions; but then—this wedding. On the other hand (we knew) the worldly deeps were to be transformed in the "light of the New Goddess", but how, in what forms? We filled in the transformation; and we spoke of it; and in us there arose the question of whether this was a wedding or a mystery? By the description of S. M. Solov'ev I understood that it was a "mystery" (something indescribable); thus it seemed; the bride Mendeleeva according to Solov'ev emerged in truth as an extraordinary creature; she understood the ambivalence, the paradox of her situation: being Blok's bride, being the new woman who dared to embark on radiant ways.[11]

Belyj further surmises that Blok and the others also perceived the significance of this event. Apparently it was what persuaded Count Razvadovskij to become a monk. Although in this account, written later, Belyj appears quite sober and analytical, nonetheless at the time he himself was deeply moved and in fact sought to extend the power of the event in a strange and ambivalent relationship between himself, Sergej Solov'ev, Blok and Ljubov' Dmitrievna.

The first long-awaited meeting between Belyj, Blok and Ljubov' Dmitrievna took place in January of 1904. This fateful meeting was anything but "mysterious". Both Blok's letters to his mother and Belyj's reminiscences share an unusual agreement on this point. Blok's natural reticence and introversion, Belyj's natural nervous ebullience and extroversion, and the momentous nature of the occasion appeared to daunt both. Both were taken aback first of all to find that their physical impression of the other was completely false. In fact, one could hardly imagine two people more dissimilar in nature and manner, despite their spiritual kinship in Vladimir Solov'ev. While temperamental disparity between two closely allied writers might not warrant great comment, it was quite significant in this case.

[11] Ibid., 1922, No. 1, 175-176.

Ironically enough all the most apparent differences between the two men seemed to symbolize the ever-present contradictions of the spirit of the literary movement they represented. Type and antitype, harmony and discord, avowal and denial formed the stuff of Russian symbolism and helped create the temper of their personal relationship. Moreover, both were fully aware of their contradictory natures. Throughout his reminiscences Belyj delights in highlighting these. He often calls Blok a "melancholic" and a "maximalist", while he himself is a "sanguinist" and a "minimalist". Over and over Belyj upset their precarious relationship by over-reacting and exaggerating; Blok, on the other hand, was often a victim of his own reticence, seldom speaking his mind when he should have. If Belyj's cardinal sin was clouding and obscuring the issue with words, then Blok's was his apparent inability to verbalize clearly.

The first collective meeting of Blok, Belyj and Sergej Solov'ev in Moscow, after the initial discomfiture, occurred in a whirlwind of meetings, discussions and receptions. It took place on January 16, 1904, the first anniversary of the death of Sergej's parents; a journey was arranged to Novodevichij Monastery and the graves there. It was the boisterous nature of Sergej Solov'ev, with his jokes, parodies and flamboyance, that helped to dispel the awkwardness. Ironically, it was also this youngest member of the triad who brought out those latent characteristics in his friends which clashed so markedly in their ambiguous relationship. This first meeting, however, put the seal to their symbolic friendship as Belyj describes it quite aptly in the occult symbol of the triangle: ". . . the three of us formed—a triangle, complementing one another in a natural fashion; and the 'orb' or the 'eye in the triangle'—the theme of Solov'ev's poetry ('The Beautiful Lady')—was present among us; S. M. was the cement that united: after all, he had summoned forth my relations to Blok".[12] Ljubov' Dmitrievna was obviously this "eye" which was the occult symbol for Sophia that Vladimir Solov'ev had often invoked in his poetry: "On that evening I sensed L[jubov'] D[mitrievna] to be the oneness which we had created: the background of our discussions; perhaps at times the 'eye' in the centre of the triangle; each of us had a role in our oneness, L. D.—was the symbol of the oneness".[13] Apparently on that first evening when the four of them were able to sit in private together and discuss their common ideas and interests, Ljubov' Dmitrievna remained silent, merely listening, as she was to do on all succeeding occasions. At the time it reinforced no doubt the sphinx-like mystery surrounding her symbolic nature as can be seen in Belyj's remembrance of it: "And to each she said 'be joyful' in silence. Her image is

[12] *Ibid.*, 1922, No. 1, 199.
[13] *Ibid.*, 1922, No. 1, 205.

vivid in some kind of crimson dressing-gown—at the window-curtains; beyond the window the snow turns a rosy hue; the rays of the sunset illuminate her face, young, in blossom; a rosy sunbeam settles on her head; she—smiles at us".[14]

Not only did Ljubov' Dmitrievna fill the atmosphere with mystery for Belyj and Sergej Solov'ev, but Blok himself appeared to radiate those revelatory hues that had so entranced the young symbolists in Solov'ev's poetry: "... the visage of the youthful Blok, rosy-golden from the embers of an effulgent sunset...".[15]

Sergej Solov'ev, according to Belyj's memoirs, although five years younger than the others, was the most doctrinaire, demanding constant allegiance to Solov'ev's ideas and fanning the already raging flames of their naive romanticism. In the triad he played the role of dogmatist, or theologian:

> At that time S. M. was particularly dogmatically minded in regard to the understanding of Solov'ev's ideas; we sought to develop in the life around us all that was indicated in the intersecting lines of Solov'ev's philosophy, poetry and mysticism; in regard to the concrete scheme sought after, the three of us occupied different positions: Blok was poet-clairvoyant; above all I was the philosopher; S. M. Solov'ev was the theologian who was prepared at anytime or place to proclaim in practice the "first ecumenical council" of our Church; in it Blok was the Johanine principle (so we all supposed); whereas S. M. was the Petrine principle; and I the Pauline. The threesome—Peter, Paul and John—at our sittings formed triunely the naturally emergent 'ecumenical council'; at the councils the theologian ruled; the mystic, the philosopher were always absent....[16]

Much of the time Belyj blames "S. M." for many of their excesses. Apparently he fostered his own somewhat distorted and sectarian conceptions of the new Theocracy to be built, envisaging himself at its head with Belyj and Blok, as the incarnations of the high priest, king and prophet in imitation of Solov'ev's projections.

The triad expected to discover the ideal prototype of Sophia in an earthly woman. The inflated "jargon" of symbolism was typified by Sergej Solov'ev's characteristically semi-serious word-plays and orations which, even in Belyj's transcription, offer a fair idea of the mood he wished to create:

> S. M. judged that the papal representative of Christ possessed the power of entry through the gates of the Kingdom of Christ; the coming embodiment of Sophia, her earthly form, was supposed to be (don't laugh!)—the "Mama" completely corresponding to the "Papa". In S. M.'s opinion, we formed the natural foundation of the theocracy; it remained for us but to choose the prototype; and—"Mama's" throne

[14] Ibid., 1922, No. 1, 205.
[15] Ibid., 1922, No. 1, 213.
[16] Ibid., 1922, No. 1, 200.

would be substituted; and—the seed of the coming Russia would be ready; in the seed the coming revolution of the Spirit would ripen; autocracy would be overthrown; revolution is the bridge to the Theocracy: Orthodoxy, Autocracy and Nationality would be substituted for by: Theocracy, Sophia and the People...[17]

In fact many pseudo-serious parodies were staged on the inspiration of such highly imaginative pot-pourris. Sergej Solov'ev seems to have inherited his uncle's grotesque sense of humour, the same self-satire that appears to have infected Belyj especially and, to a lesser degree, Blok. This sacriligous or serious buffoonery seems to have inspired the young Solov'evians to unrestrained parodies on themselves in a small symbolist "theatre of the absurd" that will be dealt with more extensively later. Many of their gatherings were given over to these improvisations, but the most popular one, concerning "Professor Lapan", is described by Belyj in some detail:

> S. M. began the bouffonade: and we appeared in parodies before our very selves as a sect of "Blokovians"; the outline of the sect was inquired into by an industrious professor of culture from the XVIIIth century; S. M. thought up his name: this was the academician, the philosopher Lapan, who had posed a most difficult question: whether a "sect" similar to ours had existed—on the basis of the poems of A[leksandr] A[leksandrovich Blok], the works of Vladimir Solov'ev and the 'Testament' of A. N. Schmidt. Lapan came to the conclusion: S[ophia] P[etrovna] Kh[itrovo], the friend of Vladimir Solov'ev, of course—had never existed: S. P. Kh. was a symbolic sign, a cryptogram similar to an early Christian one; S. P. Kh.—is Sophia Premudrost' Khristova [Sophia the Divine Wisdom of Christ]. 'Sophia Petrovna' is an allegorical sign: Sophia or the Third Testament, arising on the rock 'Peter': thus, the significance of 'Sophia Petrovna' from Solov'ev's biography is that it is a legend compiled by the pupils of the philosopher.[18]

This particularly meaningful parody, however, does not cease with the exegesis of Solov'ev's Sophia. It was carried on by its own inner logic to a parody on Blok and Ljubov' Dmitrievna:

> Then falling hopelessly into the joke, S. M. announced: but Lapan's pupil, the very, very learned Pampan, continuing the Lapan method, came to the conclusion that A. A. had never married: the spouse by the name of 'Ljubov' Dmitrievna' did not exist; and this was the legend of the "Blokovians": through Blok, Sophia, the Divine Wisdom, had become the new "Ljubov" [i.e. "Love"]—from the Eleusinian mystery in honour of Demeter, 'Dmitrievna'—Demetrovna.[19]

---

[17] *Ibid.*, 1922, No. 1, 201. This pun is difficult to translate. In essence it plays upon the similarity in sound of Russian *papa* ("the Pope") and *papa* ("papa" or "father"). Consequently, Sophia appears as "mama".

[18] *Ibid.*, 1922, No. 1, 215-216.

[19] *Ibid.*, 1922, No. 1, 216.

This ambivalent mixture of farce and serious discussion appears to have dominated all the subsequent meetings of the triad and their mistress. When Belyj and Blok were together without Sergej Solov'ev, the buffoonery was totally absent, but once the youngest appeared he took over the situation and invariably initiated these bizarre performances.

In describing the atmosphere of the Solov'evian Circle, Belyj noted in particular the vocabulary and symbolism of knight-errantry which often predominated. Once the oath of allegiance to the Divine Sophia had been taken by the three youthful knights, disobedience and disaffection were not to be tolerated. Sergej responded to Blok's unwillingness to perpetuate their chivalrous code by calling him "... a renegade, a fallen knight."[20] Their "crusade" was likened to the deliverance of Brunhilde from the evil dragon whom they must destroy. Belyj reported the following dialogue between himself and Blok's wife which he felt was typical, no doubt embellishing it with his own imagination:

> ... the "ideas" whereon we lived, seemed to be Brunhilde who had been seduced by an evil Dragon; we wanted to slay the Dragon.
> I recollect well that it was precisely at that time that L[jubov'] D[mitrievna] pointed to a picture hanging on the wall and depicting Brunhilde tied up; at her feet coiled the Dragon.
> She said:
> —"Free Brunhilde!"
> I understood that she was summoning us to the final and decisive struggle.
> —"What is the Dragon?"
> —It is the demon of despair, of inertia, of indolence arising from disillusionment; it is the spirit of the bourgeois mentality, of life without any great exploit..."[21]

Obviously it was not difficult for Belyj and the others to adopt this exaggerated attitude. After all, Vladimir Solov'ev himself had provided the philosophical and poetic patterns of modern-day chivalry which they were able to explore and expand in their own quest. Moreover, as can be seen from Belyj's own comments on this conversation, the knight-errantry of the Circle was in his mind, at least, connected with vaguely social ends. Here again Solov'ev had already provided the seminal pattern by linking the emblem of the Divine Sophia with the future transformation of society.

This was an atmosphere that could not long be maintained; in June of 1905 when Belyj and Sergej Solov'ev came to visit Blok and Ljubov' Dmitrievna at Blok's ancestral home in Shakhmatovo, the first major—and as it turned out, unbreachable—crack appeared in

[20] Ibid., 1922, No. 2, 249.
[21] Ibid., 1922, No. 2, 249.

the Solov'evian triangle. Before exploring the inner causes in the following chapter's analysis of the correspondence between Blok and Belyj, let us examine at this point the events.

Apparently by the time of this meeting Blok's doubts about himself and his scepticism about the beliefs and aims of this Solov'evian triad had come to a head. To be sure, they were always present, though somewhat obscured by what people took to be the dominant feeling of exultation in his poetic descriptions of his "Beautiful Lady" and by his own hesitation in broaching them with his more forthright and effusive colleagues. It seems, however, that at this gathering he expressed openly for the first time all his doubts about what they were doing and perhaps even declared himself unwilling to participate any further. No doubt Sergej Solov'ev attempted to persuade him to close ranks and probably carried on his customary leadership of their farces and parodies. His incredible behaviour during the visit in fact helped to precipitate catastrophe. One evening when Belyj was to read his new poem "Ditja-Solntse" ("Sun-Child") to Blok and his wife, Sergej Solov'ev went out for a walk because he had already heard it. When it was noticed several hours later that he had not returned, the Bloks became anxious because there were dangerous swamps in the area where accidents had already taken place. Hour after hour they waited for his return and then began a frenzied search throughout the neighbourhood that lasted all night—Serezha was not to be found. Then the next evening he suddenly turned up in a borrowed troika, his usual ebullient self, to the consternation of everyone else. This is, according to Belyj, what had happened:

> S. M. subsequently explained that he had walked aimlessly from the terrace down into the garden and gradually wandered into the forest; and suddenly saw—the sunset; and a star above the sunset; suddenly he understood that for the salvation of those sunsets that had enlightened the years for us, he had to perform some symbolic gesture, that on this gesture depended all our future;... S. M. suddenly felt that if at that very moment he did not proceed straight ahead through the forest, through the swamps (ever forward and forward)—towards the sunset, in pursuit of the star, then something immense would collapse in the future; and he marched forward, did not even return for his hat: he kept going, going and going until night overtook him in the forest; then he came out of the forest, crossed a field; and plunged into—the woods; there was no way he could turn back; then he realized that he had reached Boblovo. In Boblovo he had sought shelter; and, assured that he had saved our future, did not think about us.[22]

This was the last straw for Aleksandra Andreevna (Blok's grandmother) and for Ljubov' Dmitrievna, who were apparently fed up with Serezha's antics and grandiloquent buffoonery. No doubt Blok him-

---

[22] Belyj, "Vospominanija o A. A. Bloke," in *Epopeja*, 1923, No. 2, 259.

self took a dim view of the whole absurd affair as well. On the other hand, Belyj sided with Serezha: "I was sincerely perturbed: Aleksandra Andreevna, A. A.—how was it they were unable to comprehend the heroic lyricism of S. M. Solov'ev?".[23] Under strained circumstances, Belyj and Serezha left separately in the next few days. This first major rift in their relations could never be totally repaired. True, it was often patched over, but somehow or other always managed to come apart again.

From this point the active withdrawl of Blok from the triad can be traced. Although perhaps an unwilling member all along, it cannot be denied that he *seemed* to be tacitly in agreement with Belyj and Serezha. As the correspondence between Blok and Belyj will show in the following chapter, there was frequently considerable reluctance on his part to champion Solov'evian ideas. Yet for the other symbolists, Blok's poetry appeared to be an unmistakable espousal of the Divine Feminine. In any event, he was held directly responsible for destroying that all-important Solov'evian *collective* whose avowed task it was to transform the world. In a literary movement like Russian symbolism that continuously sought to organize collectives, communes, or unions of writers and thinkers who banded together to produce a veritable landslide of manifestoes, declarations and avowals of principles and beliefs, Blok's desertion of the Solov'evian circle was regarded as tantamount to treason, to betrayal.

In retrospect, Belyj is able to present many reasons for the breakup. As might be expected, he himself emerges from the ashes of the past with his best foot forward, but there is some degree of truth in his assessment. Where formerly Belyj, Blok and Sergej Solov'ev appeared to form an indivisible oneness, a "three-in-one", opposing pairs emerged after the business in Shakhmatovo, invariably with Belyj caught in the middle between Blok and Sergej Solov'ev:

> ... having seen A. A.'s gestures of protest against the style of S. M., I defended S. M. .... Our jargon disappeared ("Bloko-Belovian-Solov'evian"); and there appeared the jargons: first—"Belovo-Solov'evian"; then—"Bloko-Belovian"; it was anguishing and it was false to sit between two chairs... our triune relationship collapsed; "pairs" were formed. A. A. would take me aside and we would begin a conversation between the two of us and then S. M. would take me aside and begin a conversation between the two of us.[24]

Even after the split at Shakhmatovo Serezha appeared to disregard the true state of affairs and blithely continued with his plans for their Theocracy. By this time Belyj claims that he and Blok had put aside all

[23] Ibid., 1922, No. 2, 259.
[24] Ibid., 1922, No. 2, 243.

problems connected with the "resolution of 'Solov'evian' questions",[25] but Serezha kept pestering Blok with the same demands:

> ... he especially emphasized the history of the "theocracy", demanding from A. A. a strict faith in the "religious covenants"; when the impulses of this religious creativity became insipid then "duty" was brought up; thus, S. M., by emphasizing the "duty" or "obligation" to support "Solov'evianism"—was himself experiencing the waning of Solov'evian zeal.[26]

Ljubov' Dmitrievna, this earthly inspiration of their poetic dreams of the divine Sophia, also played a major role in the dissolution of their group, according to Belyj. He felt that she studied all three of them in silence, noting their differences and then deliberately manipulating them so that these would emerge more sharply. Ljubov' Dmitrievna on several occasions became quite angry when "Lapan" was mentioned or Serezha tried to carry the farce further. When she forebade Serezha to even mention "Lapan", he in turn was insulted, seeing this as a direct blow at all that held them together.

The demonic aspect of Ljubov' Dmitrievna waxes ever stronger in Belyj's memoirs. At this time, in 1905, he felt that she and Blok were drifting apart if not actually breaking up. Her evil influence was attested to by the fact that Blok's poetic talent seemed to be drying up at this time. Belyj also seems to hold her at least partly responsible for the vulgar betrayal of the closeness of their collective in an even more sinister fashion by hinting that she may have suggested that Blok write the play "Balaganchik" ("The Puppet Show", 1906), blaspheming all they had formerly held dear. More than any other work, this play aroused the paranoid fury of Belyj and almost led to a duel between him and Blok. He saw himself parodied in many of Blok's verses at this time and felt strongly that Blok was befouling the ideals of their collective.

Although Belyj tried to patch up his relations with the Bloks at the end of 1905, it was only a matter of a few months before they reached rock bottom again. It would appear that all their dreams of a realized Sophiology were dead, that their naive and romantic aspirations now entered a new period of depression expressed in the sceptical, urban verses of Blok and the frenzied theorizings of Belyj after 1905. However, the seeds of this failure were doubtless present from the very beginning, as we shall see in the following chapters, and were destined to grow at the expense of their ecstatic hopes for the realization of their painless and radiant world transformation. Sergej Solov'ev declined in influence sharply after 1906. His only hope of

---

[25] Ibid., 1922, No. 2, 242.
[26] Ibid., 1922, No. 2, 244.

real literary and intellectual survival was bound up in their collective, now permanently dissolved, as new alliances and groupings came to the fore on the literary scene in Russia.

Chapter 3

A DIALOGUE ON THE DIVINE SOPHIA

The correspondence between Blok and Belyj, particularly in the years from 1903 to 1906, offers intriguing insights into their relationship in respect to their conception of Sophiology. It likely represents both a more honest and a less censored account of their thoughts, postures and actions than one finds in Belyj's memoirs. Remarkable throughout is the symbolist "jargon" concerning ecstatic colours, premonitions, innuendoes and apocalypse. At times their language becomes incredibly vague and mystical, but once again this accords with the spirit of the times and acts as a measure of the medium of communication among the younger symbolists.

The coincidence of their first letters to each other crossing in the mails has already been mentioned. Blok's was posted on January 3, 1903; Belyj's on the following day.[1] Curiously, Blok, in fact, was primarily responsible for the early theoretical and mystical tone of their correspondence despite his later reticence on theoretical matters. In his letter of January 3, 1903 (old style), he praises Belyj's recent article "Formy iskusstva" ("The Forms of Art", 1902)[2] as the "song of the system" which he himself has long sought, but not yet discovered. He also mentions Belyj's famous "apocalyptic letter" sent to Zinaida Nikolaevna Gippius and her husband Dmitrij Merezhkovskij with the signature "a student of the natural sciences."[3] Blok was immediately captivated by the eschatological content of the letter which he describes as "all white, the entire codex of apocalyptic whiteness" (p.4). Curiously enough, Blok is quite explicit about the fact that he sees in Belyj the centre for a new development in art and thought that is free of the distasteful compromise between two opposites which typifies Merezhkovskij's theories on the union of flesh and spirit, Christ and Antichrist. The criticism he has for Belyj is positive, for he wants him

---

[1] *Aleksandr Blok i Andrej Belyj. Perepiska*, pod red. V. N. Orlova, Letopisi, kniga sed'maja (Moscow, 1940). Unless otherwise indicated, all page references are to this source.

[2] This article appeared in *Mir iskusstva*, 1902, Nos. 7-12, 343-58.

[3] Belyj apparently wrote this letter in response to Dmitrij Merezhkovskij's work on Tolstoj and Dostoevskij. The letter was printed in *Novyj put'*, 1903, No. 1, 155-159.

to say more, to be more explicit, he wants him to draw a more distinct boundary between art and that which is more than art. In other words, Belyj must justify the hopes he has given rise to in Blok with his work *Simfonija 2-ja, Geroicheskaja* (*Second Symphony, The Heroic*, Moscow, 1902) by showing what path they must travel in order to realize all their apocalyptic premonitions. And then, in those terms already defined by Vladimir Solov'ev in his differentiation between the heavenly and earthly Aphrodites, Blok introduces the entire Sophiological context of the Divine Feminine by requesting Belyj to show that "... Isida has nothing in common with the "Maiden of the Radiant Gates", for "... It is time to divine the name of the 'Radiant Mistress'..." (p.5).

This early posture of theoretical questioning is quite uncharacteristic of Blok's letters, as has been pointed out, but it cast the die for all the future relations of Blok with Belyj. His "jargon" is the same as Belyj's; his desire to participate in the search, "to divine the name of the 'Radiant Mistress' " puts him explicitly within Belyj's and Sergej Solov'ev's "collective" at this time. The abundance of quotes from Vladimir Solov'ev's poetry that punctuate this letter (and those that follow) appear to brand him unmistakably as a disciple of Solov'ev with all the attendant views and aspirations. The fact that he seems to shun any "compromise" certainly gives Belyj cause to consider him a "maximalist" in their common cause. One key sentence, however, should be highlighted in this letter because it gives a significant clue to the entire mood or attitude of Blok. While later, after the breakup at Shakhmatovo, Belyj will write Blok that he has always looked to him to lead their collective and show the others where and how to proceed, in this letter Blok puts the responsibility for leadership on Belyj's shoulders. In spite of the theoretical tone of this and the next few letters, Blok claims that he is capable only of *experiencing* and not of *creating* the euphoria promised in their Sophiology: "My questions are like a bottomless pit because I am fated to experience the Babylonian harlot and only to 'live in white' but not to create white" (p.4). In other words, Blok is forecasting his own bitter career as the impotent clairvoyant, who like Solov'ev, receives visions of Sophia, but cannot realize these visions in reality.

Belyj's reply of January 6, 1903, to this first letter takes up the questions and charges of the other poet. Writing in his highly sophisticated, theoretical and yet mystically-inspired language, he defends his symbolist view of music which he had outlined in "The Forms of Art". In fact, "music" turns out to be only one artistic symbol, one of the forms which reveal the same content as Sophia, and he takes up the requisite Sophiological terminology:

> On the one hand, music is still art insofar as it is beyond good and evil just as the feminine principle in itself is the "principle of ambiva-

lence". "The World Soul is a dualistic being" (Vl. Solov'ev). Embodying Christ, She is Sophia, the Radiant Virgin; not embodying Christ she is the Moon Virgin, Astarte, the Fiery Harlot, Babylon. The encounter with the Lord is necessarily by way of seeking for the Radiant Mistress, who in the moment of meeting will manifest the Lord. In this sense She is the "Maiden of the Radiant Gates". The meeting with the Beast takes place in Astartism. (p. 9)

With his typical syncretism, substitution and reclassification, Belyj in this letter has associated the mystical role of music with Sophia. In a diagram which he appends to his arguments it is plain to see that music is placed in that intermediate realm between heaven and earth usually occupied by Sophia the Intercessor.

As a result, Belyj's theoretical juggling appears to continue to support the "compromise" of opposite principles in the face of Blok's attack on any compromise. Moreover, he explicitly denies the role of leader or the positing of symbolist hopes in him, saying that they must group together, listen to each other and proceed patiently. However, the spirit of the final mystical paragraph appears to contradict all the careful theorizing before it:

Christ is risen! Nature is slowly purifying itself in joyous melancholy! Redemption is not in vain! It is our ecstasy and abides with us, with us! The rosy smile of the Eternal Friend, Her Easter, the greeting in the waves of Eternity's radiant blueness—this I know! ... Let us not despair! The new testament is with us! (pp. 11-12)

Within the context of the times perhaps it was not such a "contradiction" to fuse theory and mystery, but it may well have proven misleading to all concerned to have to divine the meanings of others in the effulgent and grandiloquent style of mystical rhetoric. In a later letter (February 19, 1903) to Blok, Belyj writes that although he understands Blok's letters, he sincerely doubts whether any one else would and perhaps it is not worth releasing any to be printed in one of the contemporary literary journals.

Continuing their theoretical discussion in his next letter of January 9, 1903, Blok attempts to set up a parallel theory to that outlined by Belyj in his previous letter. Belyj had indicated three stages in the development of art: 1) the formal (the spirit of music); 2) the ideological (the search for the Radiant Mistress); 3) the mystical (the ultimate music of the End). To this scheme Blok opposes one that he considers more concrete: 1) Form (for instance, the epos); 2) Content, ideology, the search for the Radiant Mistress (for instance, the lyric); 3) Synthesis, the mystical zone (for instance—the drama-mysterium). In working through these three "forms" one may enter, by means of poetry, into the realm of music. This is the theoretical scheme that begins lower than music and represents the first stage in the evolution of art. But Blok then breaks off, expressing his dissatisfaction with his inability to express his thoughts in theoretical terms. It is rather significant that he concludes his letter on a lyrical note, as though seeking recourse to the language he knows best: "Here is something that at times overfills the cup of life's enigma which wafts immutably around us, whispers day and night, blows in our faces tirelessly and sweetly, as though a state of dream and wakefulness at the same time—the unique beauty, the unique voice from Her Radiance" (p. 14). As though validating the legitimacy of his statement and the authenticity of his source, he closes his letter with a quote from Solov'ev—just as Belyj had done in the preceding letter.

After the death of Sergej Solov'ev's parents in January of 1903, Blok received a most curious letter from Belyj penetrated through and through with a mystical sense of their oneness, of an almost cathartic sense of the tragedy that has befallen them and that has drawn their collective closer together. It is one of those personal documents of Russian symbolism that is well worth quoting in its entirety in order to understand better the ritualized chant of their "jargon" that displayed all their beloved motifs in eschatological ecstasy:

> My dearest Aleksandr Aleksandrovich. All is for the best. All is illuminated and penetrated with light and is sublime.
> On the streets the whirlwind of joys is the blizzard of snows. Snows. In ecstasy they sweep away the border of life and death. The times are being fulfilled, and the appointed hours have drawn nigh. We are all together and forever.
> All is for the best. I am not anxious for Serezha. I know Serezha. He has been prepared! He told me—that he felt how a wave of sweet dreams had arisen, had come surging forward—of messianic expectations. The coming.
> All is for the best.
> And all about, ever summoning and ever swirling is the whirlwind of joys and the blizzard of snows. All is illuminated and penetrated with light and is sublime. We are all together.
> All is for the best.
> I kiss you joyfully. Boris Bugaev. (January 19, 1903, p.15).

These exuberantly mystical utterances of Belyj's must temper his avowals that he was less of a "maximalist" than either Blok or Sergej Solov'ev. Belyj's correspondence with Blok is riven with such lyrical mysticism that it surely gave Blok every reason to see in Belyj an ally for his own apocalyptic lyricism.

The letters of that year continued similar discussions and included the frequent exchanging of their poems. Belyj repeatedly requested Blok to send a photo of himself which the latter promised to do, but never did. On his photo which he enclosed in his letter of May 9, 1903, Belyj wrote the following inscription: "Sunset all through the night ... The unknown is illumined ... Wait with illumined face. Wait ... If there is no sun, if the sunset begins to fade—you will espy on the horizon the unreflecting pearly smile of parting. Boris Bugaev. The year 1903, May 9, Moscow." (p. 32, n.1)

However, the first real discussion of Sophia or the feminine principle is broached in its entirety in a letter from Belyj on June 10, 1903. He realizes that although their letters have been filled with references to the Radiant Mistress and Sophia, they have never fully analysed and compared their conception of this image so central to both their works: "Here we are writing to each other about Her, about the Radiant Mistress and between us exists a tone as though we already know *what* she is all about, know who She is, why we speak of Her and all the time it is nothing of the sort: we never look each other straight in the eye on this question" (p. 32). Belyj goes on to say that he realizes the most direct and immediate path to profundity is through imagistic speech without complicated theorizing; however, it is important for him that Blok verbalize in concrete detail what She means to him so that they may share a "collective consciousness" of Her. The direction of Belyj's own interests becomes apparent in the long list of questions which he begs Blok to answer:

> Do you sense her as an atmosphere, undefined in misty phantasies? Does she appear for you as the World Soul or as a specific personnage? (I know one 48-year-old woman who considers herself to be Her incarnation [i.e., A. N. Schmidt]). Do you sense her approach to all or only to separate individuals? Do you expect her manifestation to be to the entire world, to a group of individuals or to a separate individual? How do you connect the atmosphere surrounding her with the religio-dogmatic teaching of the Orthodox Church? How do you interpret the myths about Her among the pagans? What relationship does she occupy in your opinion with the Mother of God, with Christ, with the question of the End of the World? Does her manifestation take place symbolically or incarnately in the soul of the people, society or a separate individual? Is what you observe in life and on the faces of people drawing nigh to her or do we have here only life-like images? Are these images merely images (and distinct ones) or proto-images? Can a proto-image become that of which it is a proto-image? How does the image of Astarte become intertwined with Her? Could there be a difference between the spiritual Astarte and Artemis? (pp. 32-33)

Quite obviously a theoretical evaluation of the Radiant Mistress was most essential to Belyj who was always obsessed with the concept of a collective of like-minded people able to produce a joint theory of thought and action. Although Blok in his first few letters had not shied away from the general theoretical discussion of art, he had never voluntarily sought to elucidate his thoughts specifically on the feminine principle. The letter which Belyj received in response to his "questionnaire" significantly reveals either Blok's inability or his disinclination to *theorize* the feminine principle. This letter, sent from Bad Nauheim in Germany, June 18, 1903 (o. s.) discloses an increasing desire to remain silent on the topic because of his unwillingness to accept compromise: "I often think about such a 'logical elucidation' but the more I thought the more I felt the 'impossibility of a synthesis and any bridges', and therefore I wanted to be silent." (p. 34) What is more, Blok claims that already she does not occupy his thoughts as much as before: "Earlier I thought about Her more than now." (p. 34). As we shall see, this prevailing sense of scepticism continued to grow in his subsequent letters, in practical terms preventing him from being a member of the Solov'evian triad before he even met Belyj. The position which he occupied in replying to Belyj's questions is significant, for it discloses Blok's own basic mentality in regard to art and thought. In the letter he goes on to say that at first he thought of Belyj's questions as "dogmatic and dialectical" but then felt that in fact they resembled more a "psychological questionnaire". Thus, he attempts to answer them not by making up theoretical formulations, but rather by trying to provide answers directly as they occur to him, i.e., in a more personal and unpremeditated fashion. Characteristically, then, his responses will be prompted "mystically" and tempered by his "scepticism": "There are two dominating moods (perhaps it is the same for you as for me?)—mystical and sceptical (indifferent)—the first 'begs' not to be trammelled by thought (begs as only 'emerald-like eternity' can beg its servant, rather it orders),—whereas the second either obliges thought to be silent or despatches it so that it 'knows its place'. Therefore, to think in this direction (about Her) appears to me to be the least successful method of penetration." (p. 34).

Apparently, to the cerebral mysticism of Belyj, it never occured that one could not think or speculate on the nature and function of the Radiant Mistress, while the more taciturn Blok appears fatally crippled by his awareness of this basic impasse: "Scepticism (a characteristic of intellect) lies like a stone on the road and it is impossible to circumvent it... If this were not so then probably speculation on Her would be more accessible" (p. 34). Seeing the paradox between the mysticism surrounding Her and the desire to rationalize her function in a time when "mystical rationality" has barely been conceived of, Blok can only come to the conclusion that "She is still only potentially incarnated in the people and society" (p. 34) and therefore he also considers that She is more apt to appear incarnated in a single individual. For generally the same reasons She is more likely to draw nigh to one individual and for the time being only potentially approaches all people. In other words, Blok and Belyj find themselves essentially in the age of the precursor, before the truth has been accepted by all and has only just been announced.

Blok goes on to describe his own relationship with Her, his personal experience:

> I sense Her most frequently as a mood. I think that it is possible to catch a glimpse of Her, but not incarnated in a person and the person himself cannot know whether She is present in him or not. Only fleetingly (in a moment of ecstasy) is it possible to catch, as it were, a glimpse of Her Shadow in another person (even an uninspired person). This does not exclude phantasies of Her as of the World Soul because the world for the mystic (or the person finding himself in a mystical state) is closer than the people. The whole is more comprehensible than the part, the macrocosm (the world), like the microcosm (the individual) is closer than all the links acting as intermediaries between them (society—people—the earthly sphere!). For this reason, society, insofar as the concept of Her is concerned, does not appear to be mystically involved (to my mind) and is of no consequence. (p. 35)

More than anything else Blok's denial of a relationship between society and his own vision of the Radiant Mistress would seem to preclude any communication between himself and that society. Quite obviously he is not the person to embark on any crusade for its mystical transformation. His vision of the Beautiful Lady appears therefore to be entirely private, possessing nothing in common with Belyj's developing theories of a mystical socialism or commune. Blok was emphatically not the person to theorize his Beautiful Lady into a mystical manifesto as Belyj and other symbolists were only too willing to do.

Blok's reply to Belyj's question about the relationship of the "Radiant Mistress" to Christ is especially important. Blok's denial of Christ has always been a favourite battleground for critics. In this letter to Belyj, and in many of his letters to E. P. Ivanov (who appeared to question him frequently on the subject, perhaps in the hope of converting him), Soviet critics have seized upon his denial of Christ as a sign of his democratic and socialist leanings, whereas emigré critics have usually produced a case for Blok's inner belief in Christ by claiming he protests too much. At any rate, he views this feminine principle as his genuine "saviour", while he recognizes the "goodness" of Christ and his connexion with society:

> Here, namely, [i.e. on the question of Her and Society] arises the subsequent question of Her relation to Christ, for Christ is indivisible from society (the people). Let all those come unto me who labour—is a sign of the goodness of Christ (not a single ethical moment). Christ is always good, this is not essential with Her, for the "Unfailing Light of the New Goddess" is neither good nor evil, but more than either. I would say that I love Christ less than Her, and in "adulation, thanksgiving and entreaty" I always turn to Her. (p. 35)

Therefore it would seem that Blok is socially uncommitted, apolitical; he is more attracted to Her because She is above society and the people, and beyond good and evil. She represents a greater macrocosm, whereas Christ he associates with "goodness" and consequently with the smaller question of society and the human condition. Blok (Belyj's description of him as the "maximalist" would seem to be borne out once again) is not interested in the battle of good and evil; he is totally committed to a single mystical vision that he associates with the feminine archetype and without "syntheses" or "bridges". When (as we shall see in a later chapter) Belyj identifies Sophia with society, Blok is no longer with him, and on this point, in fact, never was. When Christ (and not the Beautiful Lady) appears at the head of the twelve brigand-revolutionaries in the mystical conclusion of the poem "The Twelve", it is quite simply because that poem is dealing with a revolutionary period of social upheaval and with the people. For Blok, Christ belongs in this context, whereas Sophia is above it.

However, the most profound conception which Blok considers worthy of being attached to Her is eschatological: "The greatest concept which we can invest [in Her] appears as the End of the World and therefore this concept is unmistakably connected with Her. In the holy scripture the references to Her are also unmistakably connected with the End .... Speculation on Her always bears in itself the seed of speculation on the End" (p. 35). Whether this End is positive or negative is impossible to say from this letter, although in the light of Blok's total work, it is certainly difficult to ignore the growing catastrophic mood. At this point, however, he does not amplify this particular aspect.

The reply which Blok offers to the question of the relationship between Astarte and their "Radiant Mistress" is predictable. In fact, it follows almost entirely the spirit of Vladimir Solov'ev's own differentiation as outlined in the preface to the third edition of his poetry. Astarte is both the physically and spiritually seductive imitation of Her in the earthly sphere, and although the two are often confused, it should be made clear that the Radiant Mistress is eternal and unconditional whereas Astarte is temporal and conditional. As Blok states more directly, Astarte is "movable", whereas She is "immovable" (p. 36). Once again, faced with the dilemma of theorizing the differences between the two, Blok takes refuge in an intuitive awareness of their opposition: "The main 'consolation', however, appears, I believe, not in the dialectical development of the difference between Her and Astarte, but in the intuitive knowledge of how different are their emanations" (p. 36). Blok appears caught between "mysticism" and "scepticism". A wholehearted espousal of the former would deny the nature of Astarte; the latter alone would logically support only Astarte; and any "mystical scepticism" (that compromising and ambivalent synthesis so distasteful to Blok) would make Her and Astarte one. This is, of course, what Blok wants to deny, but his only means of rationalizing his intuitive mysticism invariably demands a certain amount of logical scepticism. This is the dilemma from which he wishes to escape by simply not speculating on Her nature and function at all:

> And so I find myself speculating on Her more and more infrequently. But those thoughts which I have "assimilated" about Her are: She is unique in her manifestations, possessing nothing in common with anything else, the sensation of Her is strange and in the most elevated moments entirely distinct from Astarte. Here Her immovability emerges. However, if only according to the acknowledged mystical pattern, it follows that no definitions of Her essential nature are to be affixed to Her, speculation on Her simply being entwined with the roses of praise. (p. 36)

Ultimately therefore, Blok wishes to remain the mystic in all matters relating to his personal vision of the Divine Feminine. She exists for Herself and in Herself without reference to any other being, criterion or situation. Because She is "Ultimate", there can be no question of Her simply being "Good". This Blok considers one of his major points. He is not concerned with a "catharsis of conscience" in regard to Her because any such concept would only be a "standard of Good" below Her essential Nature. Although Vladimir Solov'ev never went as far as actually removing Sophia from the question of good and evil within the earthly realm, it is still quite apparent that for him Sophia was also "immovable" and "absolute" and therefore unsullied by the context of this world. The question of good and evil was limited to her lieutenant, the World Soul. As a symbol of perfection in total-unity, Sophia was not, by inference, a participant in the drama of flesh and spirit. Solov'ev intended that man be attracted to Sophia by the beauty of the idea she reflected of God's design *in order to* proceed to Godmanhood. Belyj understood this and attempted to proceed to Godmanhood *via* this path. Blok, on the other hand, was incapable of proceeding beyond Her, so captivated was he by his enamourment of the Divine Feminine.

The theme of scepticism introduced in this letter became the subject of their correspondence over the next few months. Replying to Blok's letter from Germany, Belyj goes into a typically involved discussion of it as a philosophical system, with extended references to Kant, Plato, Schopenhauer, Nietzsche, Hartmann, etc., He tries to persuade Blok that the scepticism which haunts him should not be a real obstacle to believing in Her. Blok is totally unconvinced, however, and his next letter to Belyj (August 1, 1903) is devoted exclusively to the problem of scepticism. In even greater detail he outlines the reasons underlying his doubt and why he is particularly susceptible to it:

> 1) I still do not have (not now or ever before) any awareness of Christ. I am aware of Her, Christ I sometimes only comprehend.
> 2) I suffer (?) from an extreme *individualism* (does it follow from the first point?: I love to play the fool and I do not desire any "Calvary". I am not aware of the participation of society and the people in Her Blessedness. In life I sometimes am isolated by my contempt. For the most part I write poetry.
> 3) There follows from the second point that I suffer from laziness (both in the narrow as well as the broad sense, possessing but a small reserve of areas of the natural sciences), I do not feel a deep need for them and pull metaphysical caps over my eyes at times gladly, at others painfully.
> 4) *I still fear* (perhaps I shall cease to fear) losing those Solov'evian crutches which supported me so firmly (during the life of Mikhail Sergeevich [Solov'ev]). Not ceasing to be "attracted to the azure gloom", I risk meeting the devil knows whom. The warning symptoms: I never surmise the phenomenality of the flesh, *although this is an unalterable conclusion (from the point of view of oneness)* a conclusion from Solov'ev's words which you cited (about the transference of physical relationships... the greatest abomination). (p. 44)

Blok's "confession" betrays the deepest pessimism on his part. Obviously he considers the positive philosophy of Solov'ev his "crutches", but those crutches are rapidly failing him, for his "extreme individualism" allows no room for belief in the socially and morally edifying effect of the Divine Feminine's image. What is more, he suggests that he is often a victim of the flesh, of possible seduction by the demonic aspect of the feminine principle. He further reiterates his lack of interest in the disciplines of knowledge and, therefore, by inference is prepared to follow the wilful path of his socially and morally uncommitted feelings wherever they may lead him. At the real basis of his suffering, however, is the fact that he too has had a glimpse of the noumenal realm which it is impossible to forget. This is, in fact, their collective burden. As early as 1903, Blok seems already to have given in to a feeling of pessimism from which he will never be free. Moreover, he is quite prepared to submit entirely because he believes it is hopeless to engage in the frustrating and frenzied search that is to plague Belyj for the rest of his life—to speculate, theorize, reformulate and reorganize:

> I admit the possibility of not wishing to penetrate. The possibility of desiring to circumvent, to retreat, to forget, [not] to create the banner of a crusade, to whisper the words of spells, the words of compassion. Impossible! "They" [i.e. thinkers and philosophers] steal up on one along the way, they steal up in ecstasy. "She"—Alone brings majesty, "they"—slander. Here is my "vision", it is different than yours. There are no colours.[4] It arises from within and casts a pall all about. I did not

---

[4] This is doubtless a reference to Belyj's article "Svjashchennye tsveta" ("Sacred Colours") which was written in 1903. Here Belyj outlines the apocalyptic spectrum of symbolic colours which illuminates his personal vision of spiritual transformation.

> desire "scepticism", now—I do, because I know the inescapability of the other [i.e. mysticism]. I remember—I do not forget, retreating, I cannot retreat. I want to be silent "like a human being" in a primitive fashion, more and more often I prefer this to a "hysterical frenzy". (p. 44)

Almost two years before the breakup at Shakhmatovo, Blok is voicing his "vision" of scepticism to an uncomprehending Belyj in the most direct terms. Whether insensitive to Blok's plea to be set free of any constricting Sophiological dogma fated to end negatively from the start, or too intent on building his "collective", Belyj says in his reply of August 19, 1903, that he does not understand what Blok is getting at. He claims that philosophy and theory are essential if only for "form's sake", that is, to set up the boundaries and milestones of their progress in resolving Solov'ev's Sophiology. He wants to replace Blok's desire for free flight with a measured journey:

> In regard to theory I am a conservative: it is too early to do without philosophy as Brjusov, Bal'mont and others are attempting to . . . . It is necessary to know how to overcome. It is necessary in withdrawing that one leave markers. It is too early to soar boundlessly with light baggage. (p. 47)

At the end of the letter Belyj makes the first confession of his awareness of the sombre and threatening tone in Blok's verses. He discloses his premonitions of Blok's attraction to chaos and darkness: "There is no one other than you who might in such strikingly realistic terms have pointed to the terror stealing its way in. You know, I am afraid: where will verses like these lead? What will they conceal, what will they bring with them?" (p. 48). So, Belyj was not as imperceptive as he may have seemed. In fact, he was probably the first to note a darkness in some of Blok's early poetry that later escaped a number of critics.

As the year continued another note gradually crept into Blok's letters—the sister of his scepticism, namely, fatigue or *ennui*. It is a similar atmosphere which he seems to appreciate in the verses of Gippius and Fyodor Sologub. But after the interchange on the nature of the "Radiant Mistress" and scepticism, discussion and theory largely disappeared from their letters. Although these became more personal, Belyj's did not lose any of their hyperbolic rhetoric and outbursts of mystical lyricism. Throughout 1904 they continued to exchange personal and literary news, copies of their latest poems and sundry other writings. Belyj often expressed his unbounded love for both Blok and Ljubov' Dmitrievna, especially after their meeting in Moscow in January of 1904, and speaks of them as a constant source of inspiration and consolation. If anything, Belyj appears by 1904 to have accepted Blok in the role of prophet and unreasoning clairvoyant, a position which Blok himself seems to claim in this letter of April 7, 1904:

> I have finally lost ultimate faith in the possibility of exactness in final things. I know nothing, but often I clearly see the rosy foam and the tender azure crest of the wave which bears me. Then it will sweep past and what will happen afterwards—again I do not know. But how wonderful to be on the wave, in the melodious foam. (p. 80)

Blok, however, was not done with his "Beautiful Lady". He, like Vladimir Solov'ev, appears to have fallen into an interim period of fleeting glimpses, muffled echoes and vague hints of her presence. At the end of December, 1904 (letter of December 23), he informed Belyj that he was writing a long poem on her: "I have finally come to the spot where She is supposed to appear. I know how it should be ... but here there runs a single golden strand for whose breaking there is perhaps neither any need or strength—and perhaps the same is true of continuing with it" (p. 120). Significantly, the poem was never finished. By December of 1904 seven fragments were written and subsequently grouped as a cycle under the title, "Eë pribytie" ("Her Coming", 1904).

The Sophiological rhetoric, however, had certainly not dried up for Belyj. In a letter sent to Blok on February 6, 1905, he transforms their "Radiant Mistress" into a sun-goddess and suffuses her image with the spectrum of eschatological colours already associated with her:

> Yesterday she plunged from her soaring course into the azure sea of the vernal ether—her hair—tousled by the wind, streamed upward. Thousands of radiant golden strands stretched across the horizon. Each strand more incandescent than fire, a melodious and glittering hair that melted the freezing icicles. And everything was asparkle with a celestial gold. Then all grew still. The stars faded. A silence arose in undisturbed serenity. A silver star arose. And gleamed. (p. 122)

It should be noted that this letter was written almost immediately after the revolutionary events of January, and the assassination of Grand Duke Prince Sergej Aleksandrovich Romanov. Yet there was no realistic "social awareness" in any of Belyj's writings at this time, something which he in later years attempted to obscure by insisting on his early revolutionary ardour and involvement. If indeed the events of January provoked this response, in it Belyj returns to the mood and motifs of his first important poetry collection *Gold in Azure*. The letter which he wrote Blok immediately before the one cited above (probably between the 6th and 8th of February) displayed the same mystical mood. What is more, Belyj apparently experienced a retreat from the world of everyday events into the gold-azure realm of Eternity: "Dearest, dearest—the world is apt to despise us because we are bound to be not of this world, but of 'gold, roses, azure, snow and crimson-purple'. The azure-golden, snowy-crimson roses of Eternity! Christ be with Thee. Dearest friend, be joyous, forget not —remember, remember." (p. 123). Here Belyj seems to be exhorting the "pessimistic" Blok to remember their visions of the Radiant Mistress, to keep his faith in Her and the mystical doctrine She represents, especially in these days of social upheaval. At least Blok cannot be held responsible for Belyj's position at this time; predictably, he himself does not reveal any particularly revolutionary zeal or social awareness, but remains aloof from these events. In a letter written to Belyj at the end of March, 1905, Blok makes several oblique and vague references to the intrusion of politics into his life as something he considers a burden, although he does try to come to grips with it from time to time (p. 127).

The correspondence between Blok and Belyj after the meeting in Shakhmatovo in the summer of 1905 became more rarified in mood and frequency, but for the time being it appeared as though nothing significant had taken place. Relations between Blok and Belyj do not seem to have suffered at all, though in a letter written to Belyj on July 19, 1905, Blok expresses his uneasiness over the effects which the disagreement may have had on Serezha. In succeeding letters it becomes clear that Blok and Serezha are completely estranged and do not even correspond any more. However, this surprising amity between Belyj and Blok was merely the lull before the storm which burst in October 1905. Blok offered the major provocation in his letter of October 2 which brought all the disharmony and disillusionment out into the open. He returns to the events of the summer and speaks of the positive effect which the change has had on him: "You know that in the summer something frightfully important happened to me. I underwent a transformation but I am happy because of this" (p. 141). As the letter progresses, the reason for Blok's untimely joy (apparently at the expense of Belyj and Serezha) becomes apparent. He says that he has ceased to be afraid of other people inwardly and feels that now he is much more understanding of others. What Blok is saying is that he is becoming increasingly self-confident and independent. Now he is able to free himself from the influence of the insistent leaders of various literary and intellectual movements (including the Merezhkovskijs and, by inference, Belyj and Serezha) and follow his own tendencies. This "manifesto" of maturity and independence was bound to rankle with Belyj who for so long had considered Blok part of their collective.

In his reply to this letter, written on October 3, Belyj does not explode immediately. He begins with an acknowledgement and assessment of the some twenty-one poems Blok had enclosed with his previous letter.[5] In view of Blok's declaration of attained freedom, Belyj immediately responds to his "new thematics":

> Still that same inscrutable fascination, ever in a more and more refined manner the familiar fascination with your muse is interwoven into the new themes you have taken up: the personification of the elemental forces of Russian nature awaits its orator: it seems to me that you are this orator. How to reconcile your summons to the "Beautiful Lady" with these themes which are new for you, how is the "duty" of the knight to be reconciled with "simply" the existence even of daimonic forces, how is the duty of the creativity of life (theurgism) to be reconciled with the paralysis of the duty of life (shamanism)—I do not know. (p. 155)

The gentle rebuke, which is hinted at in the word "duty", soon gives way to the spleen that has been building up since the disappointment of the summer. He wants Blok to consider whether he is not playing with mysticism and other terms, whether in fact there is no sense of "duty" at all in the individual and non-sacrificial path he has chosen. Belyj fastens on a line in Blok's previous letter in which the latter states that he is preparing his soul for the "future". This is what Blok wrote on October 2, 1905:

> I no longer love the city or country and I have slammed fast the bolt of my soul. I hope that in this tightly closed confinement it will prepare itself properly for the future. Frequently there emerge from it ever the same harmonious sensations. I shall never forget anything in the past. Someone is saying to me that very easily I can become the [Burning] Bush. There is no reason to believe otherwise. Persecuted by Apollo, I shall be transformed into the autumn bush, golden and clothed in a netting of rain in the forest glade. The wind will blow and my barb-like foliate hands will begin to dance freely. (p. 142)

These words are a source of great consternation for Belyj, for he is obviously piqued that Blok wishes to enclose himself, shut himself away from all that is around him. It is ironic that Belyj, with all his own megalomaniac tendencies, should take Blok to task for the latter's grandiloquent reference to himself as the "Unconsumed Bush" and the persecuted of Apollo. For the distraught Belyj this is nothing more than self-aggrandizement and immediately provokes a warning on his part about Blok's poetry being caught between Christ and Antichrist:

> And now I shall speak my mind on your verses. Above them there hovers a mist of the unknown, but they are full of "parentheses" and ambiguous silences which at times have pretensions to secrets.

---

[5] Several of these poems, in particular "Potekha. Rokochet truba...", Belyj considered to reflect most directly the unfortunate events which took place at Shakhmatovo. See Belyj, "Vospominanija o A. A. Bloke" in *Epopeja*, 1922, No. 2, 260-261.

> Dear Sasha, forgive me for my words which are addressed to you because of my love, but I say to you as one who bears the responsibility for the purity of one Secret which you are betraying or preparing to betray. I am forewarning you—where are you going? Come to your senses! Or you must give up, forget—the Secret. It is impossible to be with god and the devil at the same time. (p. 157)

In other words, Belyj has indeed considered Blok the "prophet", the bearer of the great Secret which he was to share with his two fellow symbolists. The "parentheses" and "ambiguous silences" he has always interpreted as the mystical yet inexpressible knowledge of the divine at first disclosed to Blok alone and then to be passed on to others. Of course, as the recipient of this knowledge, it was Blok's express duty, his *responsibility* to preserve it unsullied. That this is the operative concept in their relationship in Belyj's mind is made quite clear: "But after all I always supposed, from reading your very first poem, that you were labouring in the name of duty before the 'Beautiful Lady' " (p. 156).

Replying on the 14th or 15th of October, Blok apologizes for the "verbal abomination" of his previous letter. He pleads guilty to all the charges Belyj has levelled at him with the exception of vehemently denying that he ever amused himself at Belyj's and Serezha's expense. In discussing the rest of the charges he tries to clarify his vision of himself as the "Unconsumed Bush" by saying that he thought of it not as a symbol of the Mother of God, but rather as the symbol of a thorny bush growing by itself in the midst of forest and field and constantly ablaze. He refuses the title of "mystic" and admits that he has written a good deal of mystical nonsense in his previous letters. All of this was part of the "beautiful and aimless" life he had been leading earlier and had now ceased to lead. Nor can he be considered a "seer" for he knows nothing and, if he does know anything, it is only "what" and not "how". In particular he replies to Belyj's description of his relationship to the "Beautiful Lady": "How could you think I was 'working in the name of duty before the Beautiful Lady'? I who never did, or even now know how, to organize anything inside of me, who had in the very heat of the verses of the Beautiful Lady a desperate proclivity for 'psychological mysticism' (only now I do not love her)?!" (p. 158). He goes on to say that he did not oppose any of Belyj's or Serezha's earlier plans because he did not know how to oppose them or what to offer in place of them. As an "illiterate" he cannot lead or teach others until he learns himself. Blok apologizes for the fact that Belyj and others read their own interpretations into the vague innuendoes of his poetry, innuendoes Belyj now calls ambiguous "parentheses" and which he apparently felt contained Blok's secret knowledge of the "paths" leading to the realization of their Sophiological aspirations.

It appears then that Belyj and Serezha, among others, had read their own aspirations into the meaningful lacunae of Blok's mystical verses. Blok himself, in retrospect, considered that it was his timidity, his dependence on others, his inability to classify or define closely his innermost experiences, that led to this misunderstanding. Finally, however, he has found the courage to speak out forthrightly, to free himself from the role others had fashioned for him on the basis of his verses to the Beautiful Lady, the role of logical successor to Vladimir Solov'ev, the man to carry his vision to conclusion. Belyj appears to have ignored this search for self-affirmation despite the fact that Blok had long been hinting at it in his letters, especially when speaking of his scepticism and pessimism. The title which Blok gave to his collection of poems succeeding *Verses on the Beautiful Lady* was *Nechajannaja radost'* (*Unexpected Joy*). Its sombre mood and landscape begged for the title "Despairing Joy" as far as Belyj was concerned. What he did not understand was that, although Blok may not have attained any positive faith, although pessimism seemed to have conquered, at least now the poet had won his freedom to speak in his own voice, to express his genuine vision even though, as Blok himself admitted, that vision was suspended between heaven and hell. He no longer felt he had to submit to Merezhkovskij's vapid synthesis of spirit and flesh or the Sophiology of Belyj and Serezha.

This airing of their differences acted as a temporary balm to the wounds incurred by "betrayal", the flaunting of "duty" and so on. A meeting between Belyj and the Bloks was arranged in December, 1905, in St. Petersburg, at which friendship and forgiveness won the day for all concerned. A flood of letters ensued, all of which are expressive of new esteem and affection. However, if Blok believed that he had finally convinced Belyj and the others that he was not their "great symbolist hope", he was mistaken.

Shortly after this reunion, Blok received a characteristically Belyjesque letter of mystical inspiration. The "dream-vision" which Belyj recounts appears to have been prompted by a similar "dream-vision" that Blok had described to him in a letter dated July 19, 1905. This is Blok's dream:

> I dreamt that you and I—in a dewy and shadowy forest—had gone off a long way together and become separated from the other hikers. Then I began to show you that I knew how to fly in all different ways, both sitting and standing on air; the sensation was pleasant and effortless and you were amazed and envious. And so it continued for a long while and I did not want to bring it to an end. (p. 136)

For the sake of comparison and also for further insight into the fertile imagination of Belyj, here is the entire text of his vision:

A Dialogue on the Divine Sophia

> I see an unbounded light: a cloud is drifting, a white cloud—when it is neither night nor day, and everything is so frighteningly beautiful: the lilac and rosy-hued patches of evening have covered the cloud with a trembling net.
>
> I see the image of Eternity which has taken shape in the cloud. And you are like an image enveloped in the sunsets, dear brother,—you are kneeling at the feet of Eternity.
>
> And the cloud drifts.
>
> And I, until now motionless in the azure ether, with eyes upraised to the heavens, I catch a glimpse of the cloud drifting by, I recognize Eternity, recognize you as well irradiated by Eternity, I lower my gaze from the fathomless blue, silently I reach out for the cloud when the cloud is off in the distance. From those times if you sweep the horizon with your gaze, you will see that I am flying along the horizon, gleaming in ecstasy before Eternity, before him who is bowing down—and my ecstasy gives birth to swift, white horses. I gather the lonely fliers and on white steeds we sweep along the horizon, we describe circles around the silently drifting cloud. I am the guard on watch, I stand at the horizon, pressing the golden trumpet to my lips I announce to the world: "The true and faithful cloud flies for all eternity". I wave my sword, I see the enemies, I send against them my bright divisions. But when I am exhausted by the battle I fly to and alight upon the edge of the drifting cloud, embracing you like a brother, I pray and kneel at the feet of Eternity...
>
> Only once again to rush off to the horizon and from the horizon's boundary to trumpet and glisten in the flashes of lightning.
>
> I am the white horseman who has been sent by Someone in order to fulfil the behest, but who has met the cloud along the way and has followed after it. For the sake of the cloud I have, perhaps, betrayed Him Who has sent me, but I shall not be the betrayer a second time.
>
> I shall soar on high.
>
> And so it will be until the end of time—in life, and after life and over and over again...
>
> Dearest, are you my brother, the brother who has been sent to me (I never had a brother—be, be, be him!)
>
> Yes or no? (p. 162)

The mind boggles! Belyj has already formulated a new symbolism on the basis of their altered relationship. He is now the *active* emissary sent to do battle with the "enemy" and fulfil "Someone's" behest, while Blok has become the *static* or *passive* symbol of worship at the feet of Eternity, and is no longer the leader. Belyj had put his faith in Blok, who then betrayed the responsibility of the ideal with which he had been invested (against his will), but Belyj is not to be betrayed a second time by an aimless and self-indulgent worship which ignores this world (i.e. the image of the drifting cloud with Blok kneeling before his vision of Eternity). Instead he sets out in ritual combat to create the new Theocracy.

Belyj, however was to be "betrayed" over and over again. In Nina Berberova's apt, if vitriolic, phrase, Belyj was always seeking a "father-figure".⁶ Indeed, most of his relations seem built upon the near-worship of "significant personnages" who will reveal the true way to the realization of all his aspirations. Although Blok was his equal in age and less active than himself, nonetheless Belyj constantly reiterates the fact that he looked upon him as his elder, as someone to follow and emulate.—Perhaps an older brother? Always seeking the role of disciple or acolyte Belyj found himself attracted to men like Brjusov, Merezhkovskij, Vjacheslav Ivanov, and Rudolf Steiner, who would "show him the way". Invariably, of course, he became bitterly disillusioned and resented the betrayal of all his cherished ideals by those men.

Despite Belyj's reunion with the Bloks at the end of 1905, their relationship deteriorated rapidly within a few months. The Solov'evians had parted ways. The theme of the Divine Feminine had reached an impasse, insofar as there appeared to exist no possibility for the realization of those Sophiological aspirations which Vladimir Solov'ev had inspired. What ensued was the manifestation of her demonic aspect, the appearance of the "anti-Sophia" in her hypostasis as the Harlot, the irresistible yet destructive mask of physical beauty of which Vladimir Solov'ev had warned. It is as though the inability of the symbolists to sustain the pure image of Sophia naturally begat Her demonic opposite.

⁶ See Nina Berberova, *The Italics are Mine* (London, 1969), 158.

Chapter 4

THE BEAUTIFUL LADY

Aleksandr Blok made his poetic debut on the pages of the Petersburg literary-philosophical journal *Novyj put'* (*The New Way*) in March of 1903. However, he was already well known to a number of major symbolist-decadent writers by this time. A more or less regular visitor to the Merezhkovskijs' (Dmitrij Sergeevich and Zinaida Nikolaevna Gippius) cultural salon in Petersburg, he carried on a correspondence particularly with Zinaida Gippius who was fond of encouraging young aspiring writers and gathering youthful converts to her husband's Idea of the synthesis of spirit and flesh. In Moscow he was being promoted, privately at least, by the Solov'evs until their death in January of 1903.

Although Zinaida Gippius apparently did not believe that he had a great deal of talent, it was nonetheless decided (probably through the kindly offices of the editor of *The New Way*, P. P. Pertsov) to print some of Blok's rather vague and mystical poems in the journal. On reading some of the poems from Blok's future collection *Stikhi o Prekrasnoj Dame* (*Verses on the Beautiful Lady*), Pertsov's immediate reaction was to think of Vladimir Solov'ev:

> It was precisely as though the poetry of Vladimir Solov'ev had been resurrected—its final shafts of illuminating light. It seemed to me to be undeniably some kind of miracle: only two years beforehand the muse of the thinker-clairvoyant had fallen silent, and all of a sudden its sounds are transposed to a new lyre—someone had arrived as the direct and legitimate heir of the echoed singer; he is already omniscient and wise and will continue the interrupted song as the previously familiar song about one and the same thing.[1]

Blok's first major appearance in print was very carefully staged in order to heighten the role which Pertsov and others took for granted in him as Solov'ev's legitimate successor. *The New Way* devoted the poetry feature of each monthly issue to a single poet. Although other arrangements had been made for the March 1903 issue, it was decided to print ten of Blok's poems instead.[2] Both the nature of Blok's poetry

---

[1] P. P. Pertsov, *Rannij Blok* (Moscow, 1922), 10-11.
[2] The ten poems included "Predchuvstvuju Tebja. Goda prokhodjat mimo...",

and the role he seemed to have assumed proved the major dictates behind this move as Pertsov recalls: "... March seemed to be the most natural, even absolutely necessary month for his debut: March—the month of the Annunciation".[3] Blok's image as the knight dedicated to the feminine principle in poetry was further underscored by the editors' attempts to "illustrate" his verses: "For March we decided to collect a sort of artistic entourage for Blok's verses and placed on the pages of his verses four 'Annunciations'—the Leonardo from the Uffizi, a detail—the head of Mary from the same picture, a fresco from Beato Angelico in the Florentine monastary of St. Mark and an icon from a chapel of the Kiev Cathedral by our own Nestorov. Blok was pleased with these illustrations and he thanked me warmly for them."[4]

In spite of all these elaborate preparations, Blok's debut did not cause any great furor in the larger reading public. In retrospect it is interesting to note, as Pertsov himself writes, that these first poems, as well as the entire cycle of *Verses on the Beautiful Lady*, never did achieve any significant popularity. Nor was Pertsov alone in his assessment. Despite the narrow circle of admirers around Blok, however, the appearance of this selection of poems in *The New Way* and the subsequent first volume of his poems which appeared towards the end of 1904, established, albeit somewhat belatedly, the public image of Aleksandr Blok as the heir to Vladimir Solov'ev's title of knight of the Beautiful Lady. This role, which Blok may have been willing to accept privately or personally, was to cause him a great deal of anguish as we have already seen in the preceding chapters. Not only was it a cause of friction between him, Belyj and Sergej Solov'ev, but Zinaida Gippius, who exerted such an early influence on him and whom he certainly found intimidating, also subjected him to some painful moments. Apparently when he told her that he was planning to marry Ljubov' Dmitrievna Mendeleeva, she viewed his decision as some manner of "desertion" or "treason" before the "mystical bride" of his verses addressed to the Beautiful Lady. Given the atmosphere of the times this remark could be serious or ironic in tone.

There can be little doubt that Blok's early poetry seemed to bear all the outward characteristics of the person he himself called "the master of my thoughts".[5] The obeisance paid to a vague but divine

"Verju v Solntse zaveta...", "Gadaj i zhdi. Sredi polnochi...", "Strannykh i novykh ishchu na stranitsakh...", "Ja, otrok, zazhigaju svechi...", "Ekklesiast", "Starik", "Tsaritsa smotrela zastavki...", "Ja k ljudjam ne vyjdu navstrechu...", "Kogda svjatogo zabvenija...".

[3] Pertsov, *Rannij Blok*, 15.

[4] *Ibid.*, 23.

[5] See Blok's letter to A. V. Gippius on 13 August (o.s.), in A. Blok, *Sobranie sochinenij* (Moscow, 1960-1965), VIII, 21-23.

feminine principle, the mood of expectancy, the premonitions of manifestation, the sombre landscapes—all this seemed to corroborate the discovery of a new Solov'evian disciple especially since, as pointed out in the previous chapters, Blok did not object as energetically as he might have.

The poems which seemed to crystallize Blok's posture before the feminine principle in the eyes of his public were those like "I have a premonition of You. The years pass by..." (1902), "I, a youth, light the candles..." (1902), and "I enter sombre temples..." (1902). Even in the very first of these, however, the mood of ecstatic expectancy and revelation is tempered by that scepticism of which Blok wrote Belyj in later years but which was ignored by many critics in his early poems:

> I have a premonition of You. The years pass by—
> Ever in the same image I have a premonition of You.
>
> All the horizon is ablaze—and unbearably bright,
> And silently I wait,—*in grief and in love*.
>
> All the horizon is ablaze, and the manifestation is nigh,
> But I am afraid: You will change your appearance,
>
> And will arouse an insolent suspicion,
> Having in the end replaced Your usual features.
>
> Oh, how I fall—both sorrowfully and wretchedly,
> Not having overcome my mortal dreams!
>
> How bright the horizon! And the radiance is nigh.
> But I am afraid: You will change Your appearance
> ("Predchuvstvuju Tebja. Goda prokhodjat mimo...", 1902)

The fact that Blok not only takes as an epigraph to his poem these lines from Solov'ev: "And the oppressive dream of earthly consciousness/ You shall shake off, in grief and in love.", but actually includes the phrase "in grief and in love" in his own poem, no doubt helped to support the connection between him and the philosopher-poet.

The meetings between the poet and his vision of the Divine Feminine are often set in a church at vespers, that moment of maximum expectation and increasing mystery as day turns to night, rude reality to ecstatic potentiality:

> I enter sombre temples,
> I perform the austere ritual,
> There I wait for the Beautiful Lady
> In the flickering of the red lamps.
>
> In the shadows by the tall column
> I tremble at the creaking of the doors.

> And there peers into my face, all illuminated,
> Only the image, only the dream of Her.
>
> Oh, I have become accustomed to these robes
> Of the magnificent Eternal Woman!
> High above along the cornices there flit
> Smiles, phantasies and dreams.
>
> O Holy One, how tender the candles,
> How comforting Your features.
> I cannot hear the sighings and the words,
> But I believe: Dearest—it is You.
> ("Vkhozhu ja v temnye khramy...", 1902)

These trysts in church appear to have been inspired by Solov'ev's own description of his vision of Sophia during evening service as described in "Three Meetings". The great number of verses steeped in religious gloom provided a firm foundation for those who envisioned Blok as the youthful high priest of a new Madonna cult in Russian poetry, as the prayerful and chaste monk bowing at the foot of the Holy Virgin's icons. This impression was strengthened by yet another of Blok's best known poems of this early period:

> I, a youth, light the candles,
> The flame of incense I tend.
> Without thought and without speech
> She laughs on the other shore.
>
> I love the evening worship
> At the white church above the river,
> The village before the sunset
> And the hazy pale blue dusk.
>
> Obedient to the tender gaze,
> I admire the mysterious beauty,
> And beyond the church enclosure
> I cast white flowers.
>
> A misty curtain is lowered.
> The Groom will descend from the altar
> And from the crenelated tips of the forest
> The wedding sunset will burst into light.
> ("Ja, otrok, zazhigaju svechi...", 1902)

The vision of, and striving for, divine syzygy, for a vague yet ecstatic union, proved yet another link between him and Solov'ev that was not to be lost upon the reader already invested into the mysteries of Solov'ev's poetry and philosophy. The barest mention of "blue" or "azure" surrounding the imminent union of Bride and Groom, the approach of the "wedding sunset", the "tender gaze" of the vision, the "white flowers" (Solov'ev's white cow-bells?) certainly provided enough material to illuminate similarities and obscure differences.

Blok's poetic landscape is identical to Solov'ev's. The reader finds himself invariably in a nocturnal atmosphere of rustlings, spectres and vague summonings:

> I went out into the night—to discern, to comprehend
> The distant rustling, the nearby rumbling,
> To greet the non-existent spectres,
> To believe in the imaginary trot of horses.
> ("Ja vyshel v noch'—uznat', ponjat'...", 1902)

As Solov'ev justly commented,[6] a meeting with the Beautiful Lady in day-time would be unthinkable. For both Solov'ev and Blok the period of greatest tension and speculation was set between sunset, as the symbolic promise of the morrow, and sunrise, the actual consummation of their desires, in the pure potential of night. But, of course, while the night could give birth to the most ecstatic visions, it could also mask them with deception and obscure truths with untruths to lead the "nocturnal soul" astray:

> You passed along azure paths,
> The mist welled up behind you.
> Above us the darkening evening
> Turned into desired deception.
> Above your azure path
> Stretched the ominous gloom.
> But with deep faith in God
> The dark church is bright for me as well.
> ("Ty proshla golubymi putjami...", c. 1901)

This feminine principle which is so evocative of the new radiant day to come, can become quite another spirit at night: "The golden haired angel of day/ Is transformed into the fairy of night." ("Zolotokudryj angel dnja...", 1902). Unlike the "daytime Solov'ev" who was able to cast the light of his rational philosophy into the mysterious but potential chaos of night, however, Blok is entirely a "nocturnal soul" seized with a premonition of ecstatic apocalypse that invariably evades consummation:

> I await the summons, I seek the response,
> The heaven grows mute, the earth is silent,
> Beyond the yellow field—far off somewhere—
> For an instant my summons has come to life.
>
> From the echoes of distant speech,
> From the nocturnal sky, from slumbering fields,
> The mysteries still loom of approaching encounter.
> Of meetings bright but fleeting.
>
> I wait—and a fresh trembling besets me.
> The sky is ever brighter, the silence. deeper ...

[6] See Solov'ev, "Mifologicheskij protsess...," in *Sobr. soch. V. S. Solov'eva*, I, 13.

> A word destroys the nocturnal mystery,
> Have mercy, lord, on nocturnal souls!
>
> For a moment beyond the field, somewhere, there awoke
> My summons in a distant echo.
> I still await the summons, I seek the response,
> But the earthly silence is strangely long...
> ("Ja zhdu prizyva, ishchu otveta..." 1901)

The Beautiful Lady is entirely a spectre of night, a nocturnal companion whom Blok knows at night but who disappears with the coming of day. In one of several poems that might be considered somewhat reminiscent of Solov'ev's own supposedly "automatic" writings, the Beautiful Lady defines her presence to the poet:

> I have descended and shall be with you till morn,
> At the break of dawn I shall depart your dream,
> Without a trace I shall disappear, I shall forget all,—
> You will awaken, once again set free...
> ("Utomlennyj, ja terjal nadezhdy...", 1902)

If anything, the contours of Blok's Beautiful Lady are even more obscure than Solov'ev's. The capitalized form of address in "Thou" and "Thine" which suggested such intimate veneration in Blok's verses, proved a source of some small embarrassment with the appearance of Blok's verses in *The New Way*. Pertsov and his colleagues feared that this form of address in poems that had erotic overtones and appeared to make vague reference to the Holy Virgin, might be construed as sacriligious by the censors. Consequently, when they submitted the draft copy they substituted uncapitalized "thou" and "thine", and upon receiving permission to publish, changed them back to the original. However, as we shall see later, this capitalized form of address was not solely reserved for a separate being who in her other aliases appeared as the "Beautiful Lady", "queen", "mistress", but also designated the demonic feminine.

The inspirational colours of Blok's Beautiful Lady are identical with those of Solov'ev's. Amid forbidding landscapes dominated by gloomy shadows and mists, suggestive of greys, blacks and white, infrequent strokes of azure, blue and gold announce the imminence or passing of the Beautiful Lady:

> And you yourself—beyond the river gloom
> Direct your mountain course,
> You who in a golden azure
> Shine radiant forever.
> ("Priznak istinnogo chuda...", 1901)
>
> Someone whispers and laughs
> Through the azure mist.
> ("Kto-to shepchet i smeetsja...", 1901)

> Transparent, unfamilar shadows
> Swim towards You, and You swim with them,
> Into the embraces of azure dream-visions.
> ("Prozrachnye, nevedomye teni...", 1901)

But as though wilfully suspending his vision of the Beautiful Lady in her nocturnal atmosphere, whether for fear that his vision is a spectre without substance only to be dispersed with the coming of day, or whether irresistably attracted to and enchanted by the dream-like qualities of his private inspiration, Blok chooses increasingly to cast this feminine principle in the predominant tones of white and paleness, perhaps heightening the insubstantial nature of his inspiration:

> But is it possible that I could not recognize
> The white flower of the river
> And these pale dresses,
> And the strange, white allusion?
> ("Tebja skryvali tumany...", 1902)

Gradually a new note is sounded. The harsh power of white becomes stronger and stronger in Blok's poetry, culminating in the blinding and cathartic whiteness of the snowstorms and blizzards of later poems, including "The Twelve". But the multivalency of this "non-colour", both stern and benign, at times invades even his early poetry as suggested by the following verses:

> I search for the strange and the new on pages
> Of ancient oft-read books,
> I phantasize on white birds that have disappeared,
> I feel the moment of estrangement.
>
> Discordantly excited by a riotous life,
> Troubled by rustlings and cries,
> Rigidly chained by a white dream
> To the shore of belated times.
>
> White are You, undisturbed in Your deeps,
> In life—severe and wrathful.
> Mysteriously anxious, mysteriously loved,
> Maiden, Sunset, [Burning] Bush.
>
> The cheeks of golden-haired maidens grow pale,
> The sunsets are not eternal like dreams.
> The thorns crown the meek and the wise
> With the white fire of the [Burning] Bush.
> ("Strannykh i novykh ishchu na stranitsakh...", 1902)

Whereas Solov'ev's poetry proved to be the mystical counterpart to his philosophical Sophiology, Blok's poetry appears to be completely without metaphysical basis. Yet, even without any overtly rational structure to drape with the lyrical adornment, the "lyrical problem" Blok poses is essentially the same as Solov'ev's, namely, the problem of syzygy with its attendant polarization of opposites in divine and demonic manifestations of the feminine principle with the poet as "spiritual medium". Solov'ev was fortunate enough to formulate a rational theory of syzygy or love within his Sophiology. Blok, however, was immediately seized with an intuited perception of the same concerns without being able or willing to support the irrational with the rational. Solov'ev's vision of Sophia inspired his subsequent views of Godmanhood and the Universal Church. She inspired him not only with a premonition of the goal but with the means of achievement as well. On the other hand, Blok had only vague premonitions of the path to be followed, of the direction his inspiration should take:

> The poet stands in banishment and doubt
> At the crossing of two roads.
> The nocturnal impressions fade away,
> The sunrise is pale and distant.
>
> In the past there is still no indication,
> What to desire, where to go?
> And he in doubt and banishment
> Has stopped in the midst of the road.
>
> But already in his eyes burn hopes
> Barely accessible to the mind,
> That the day will awaken, will open his eyes
> And the horizon he will espy.
> ("Poet v izgnan'i i v somnen'i...", 1900)

Blok's Verses on the Beautiful Lady were considered his revelation of the feminine principle, while the verse cycle preceding it, Ante Lucem (1898-1900), was supposed to be only her vague stirrings. It is convenient to view a poem such as the following as indicative of a poet's searching for an ideal undiscovered in Ante Lucem and found in the succeeding Verses on the Beautiful Lady:

> Won't you bring new life to my soul?
> Won't you reveal the mysteries?
> Will you not give wings to the songs,
> That are so frenzied, so inconstant.
>
> O, believe! I shall give you my life
> When to the hapless poet
> You open the doors into the new temple,
> And show the path from gloom to light!
>
> Will you not to that distant land,
> To that land as yet unknown today
> Lead me—into the distance I shall peer
> And cry out: "Lord! an end to the desert!
> ("Nevedomomu bogu", 1899)

However, it is quite apparent from the very earliest of Blok's poems, before he even knew of Solov'ev's poetry, that the "content" or "metaphysic" of his poetry is to be *Love*:

> Alone to you, to you alone,
> Queen of love and happiness,
> To you, beautiful and young
> All the best pages of life!
>
> Neither the true friend, nor brother nor mother
> Know the friend, brother, son,
> Only you alone can comprehend
> The vague anguish of the soul.
>
> You, you alone, o my passion,
> My love, my queen!
> In the gloom of night your soul
> Gleams like the distant summer lightning.
> ("Odnoj tebe, tebe odnoj...", 1898)

This is one of Blok's earliest poems addressed to the Divine Feminine and forms part of his *Otrocheskie Stikhi* (Juvenile Verses, 1897-98). The love of which he speaks is quite explicit; it is not the love between friends or between relatives, but that of lover and mistress. Blok's "philosophy" becomes quite simply the emotion of love, the private emotion of a mysterious love which he alone experiences. If any poem is to serve as the undisputed manifesto of his poetic inspiration, then surely it is this one from *Verses on the Beautiful Lady* expounding the credo of love's exultation:

> The joyless seeds are sprouting.
> The cold wind beats in the bare thickets.
> In my soul are revealed inscriptions.
> I keep them concealed—in the villages, at crossroads...
> And I hide myself, like a shadow, at moonlit walls.
> The walls change, darken and grow lifeless.
> All changes are a source of joy to me,
> Every day gives birth to changes for me.
> Oh how alive I am, how the blood pulsates like springs!
> Here I am at one with those underground springs!
> Moments of mystery! You, oh eternal love!
> I have understood you! I am with you! I am for you!
> The great wall grows and grows.
> The cold wind beats in the bare thickets...
> I have discovered you, sacred inscriptions.
> I preserve you smilingly at the crossroads.
> ("Bezradostnye vskhodjat semena...", 1902)

However, a philosophy is not to be extracted from Blok's visions and experiences of love, at least as far as he was concerned. His vision was totally private, disclosed to him alone and jealously guarded:

> I dream that not a single soul
> Has seen Your incorruptible soul
> And I alone, mortal, know how fine
> It alone is, in all, in all the world
> ("Ty, mozhet byt', ne khochesh' ugadat'...", 1898)

Early on in his poetry Blok declares himself unsympathetic to the theorizing of the ultimate experience because he feels a basic antipathy between mysticism and rationalism. What is divine can only be accessible to sympathetic spirits and not to the mind:

> The celestial is unfathomable to the mind,
> The azure to minds is unrevealed.
> Only rarely do the seraphims bear
> A sacred dream to the chosen of worlds.
> ("Nebesnoe umom ne izmerimo...", 1901)

Blok was obviously unwilling to formulate a public vision of his Beautiful Lady.

Once having experienced the vision of the feminine principle and been stricken with this otherworldly love, the poet is immediately subject to an awareness of a dual existence, of two worlds and two contending spirits. Recognition of this divine love is not sufficient for salvation, for the poet's deliverance is irretrievably posited in the hope of intercession from the other realm:

> I seek salvation.
> My fires blaze on mountain heights—
> They have illuminated all the region of night.
> But brighter than all is the spiritual gaze within me
> And You in the distance... But is it You?
>   I seek salvation.
>
> Solemnly the celestial choir resounds in heaven.
> The people of earth curse me.
> I have lit a fire for You in the mountains,
>   But You are a spectre.
>   I seek salvation.
>
> The celestial choir has tired of resounding and falls silent.
> The night departs. Doubt is afoot.
> There you descend from distant bright mountains.
> I have waited for You. To you I have reached out my spirit.
>   Salvation is in You!
> ("Ishchu spasenija", 1900)

If, in the case of Solov'ev, love and the striving for syzygy were translated into a plan for transforming mankind and the world and returning them to oneness with God, in Blok's case the emotion exists for itself without purpose. Here we have the purest possible expression of what in Jungian terms may be considered the attraction between the masculine and feminine principles, the striving for unity exerted by some deeply imbedded impulse (between animus and anima). In Solov'ev this polar attraction is translated into a metaphysic. In Blok it jealously guards its mysterious contours in the vague and non-transferable language of his poetry. This is probably the one and only principle that Blok's poetry extolls, more mystical than metaphysical, an undefined emotional yearning that seeks a content, an object, and discovers it in the feminine principle. In yet another one of those poems that are reminiscent of Solov'ev's reputed "automatic writing", the Beautiful Lady Herself seems to tell the poet that she is the content of his formless dreams:

> Without Me your dreams would have flown off
> Into the impassive misty heights,
> Remember the evening horizons,
> Knock at my silent tower, my child.
>
> I live above the crenelated earth,
> I grow into evening in my tower.
> Come to Me, I shall console you,
> Dearest, dearest, I shall embrace you.
>
> I have gone off into the snows without return,
> But stirring the cold blizzards
> On the border of the fiery sunset
> I have inscribed my Name, my child.
> (Bez Menja b tvoi sny uletali...", c. 1902)

Having revealed to him the content of his aspirations, she has at the same time made him a slave to herself:

> But here below, in the dust, in wretchedness,
> Having momentarily caught a glimpse of immortal features,
> The nameless slave, filled with inspiration,
> Sings of You. You do not know him,
>
> You will not distinguish him in the crowd of people,
> Will not reward him with a smile,
> When he gazes up at You, a captive,
> Having tasted for a moment of Your immortality.
> ("Prozrachnye, nevedomye teni...", 1901)

Like Solov'ev before him who was transformed by his visions of Sophia and devoted his entire life to exploring the many ramifications of the single all-in-one principle which she represented, Blok too considers that he is doomed to celebrate the unique principle of Love which has been revealed to him even though there can never be any hope of consummation:

> My voice is mute, my hair is grey,
> My features terrifyingly immobile.

> With me for all my life is one Sacrament:
> The Sacrament of worship to the Unattainable Woman.

Of course, these very verses could just as well have been written by Solov'ev with respect to his life-long worship of Sophia and the principles which she represented. But Blok's despair was not always in the ascendent. Like Solov'ev at times he too seemed to espy the eternal meaning of his relationship with the Divine Feminine which would ultimately triumph over the pessimism of his earthly condition:

> She herself will descend to you.
> Then you will no longer in mortal slavery
> Entice the laughing sunrise
> In your wretched and humble aspect.
>
> She and you form one law,
> One behest of a Higher Will.
> You are not eternally condemned
> To a despairing and mortal anguish.
> ("Ne bojsja umeret' v puti...", 1902)

These verses are rather unique in that they seem to express the same metaphysic which Solov'ev spoke of in "The Meaning of Love", that is, the transfigurative process of syzygy as the salvation of this world.

Elsewhere Solov'ev's direct influence can be felt as well. In particular Solov'ev's somewhat paradoxical statements, both poetic and philosophic, on the dualistic nature of the World Soul, on the possibility of both divine and demonic development, must have found a very sympathetic response in Blok. The following poem displays Blok's grasp of Solov'ev's teaching on this aspect of the World Soul:

> I am a trembling creature. Illuminated
> With rays my dreams become frozen.
> Before Your depths
> My depths are insignificant.
> You do not know what purposes
> Lie hidden in the depths of Your Roses,
> What angels have alighted,
> Who stands silently at the threshold...
> Within You in expectation lie unrevealed
> A great light and an evil gloom—
> The unravelling of all knowledge
> And the raving of a great mind.
> ("Ja—tvar' drozhashchaja...", 1902)

What was to become one of the most obsessive preoccupations of Blok's verses is foretold in Solov'ev's own conception of the two passions, of divine and demonic love. The first is spiritual and leads to salvation, the second is erotic and leads to self-destruction. In the very earliest of his poem cycles, *Juvenile Verses*, Blok comprehends that Love, unspecified and simply emotive, is not only the most potent force within him, but is capable of assuming alternatively erotic and divine hues:

> At times my love burns like a fire,
> At times gleams like a nocturnal star,
> But forever the eternal and living flame
> Trembles in my soul, not fading for an instant.
> ("Ty, mozhet byt', ne khochesh' ugadat'...", 1898)

Aware of this counterpoint within, Blok at first attempts to declare himself in favour of a pure and divine passion: "But I am not about to pray to the passions!/ Before another I am prepared to fall on my knees!" ("Mrak. Odin ja...", 1898). This awareness of "two loves" continues to grow in strength in Blok's early verses until it informs most of his poetry as a whole. It is rather strange that his symbolist colleagues like Belyj and Sergej Solov'ev, to mention but a few, did not recognize it. Early on he is capable of considering some synthesis between the opposing passions to which he awards equal status:

> Of love both radiant and sombre
> Both paths are likewise known.
> They are both desirable to the soul,
> Yet how might harmony be found in them?
>
> Contending and disagreeing
> They are equal in good and evil,
> But the first is passively bright,
> The second—in confusion and gloom.
> ("Dve ljubvi", 1900-1916)

The dilemma in which Blok found himself with respect to the polar aspects of love may well explain his initial attraction to the Merezhkovskijs and the "white synthesis of spirit and flesh" that they were promulgating at that time. A fairly clear picture of this relationship emerges in one particularly long letter which Blok wrote to Zinaida Gippius on June 14, 1902 on the subject of synthesis and love. In his letter Blok returns to a conversation he and Gippius had earlier at the Merezhkovskijs'. Apparently Gippius had said that their "white synthesis" was to "combine" and "purify" aesthetics and ethics, *eros* and *amor*, paganism and ancient Christianity. Taking up the argument again, Blok reiterates his conviction that such a synthesis is only "pure possibility"; he does not share her belief that man already possesses the logical or rational knowledge to achieve it without destroying all connection with life as they know it. He goes on to say that he believes there already exists an "apocalyptic synthesis" which has been disclosed through inner revelation to people like Vladimir Solov'ev. Moreover, this synthesis (which he illustrates with several quotations from *Revelation*) will take place in spite of any of man's efforts or any exertion of his will. Thus, he concludes that all human effort towards any synthesis is futile and that the only philosophy is passivity: "And in the second place (and most important) any *real* synthesis *whatever it may be*, is merely a 'human' point of view. We see only the image of what is coming just as we see only the image of God and not God himself; and therefore—are we not then confined by our very nature within the framework of expectation alone and *relative* (in relation to the latter point) passivity?"[7] This statement is immensely important, for it holds the key to his conflict with Belyj and Sergej Solov'ev and his retreat from a concept of symbolism as socially transfigurative. Blok then turns the discussion of synthesis to the question of love, the intersection of those opposite passions which, judging from his poetry, had long occupied his mind:

> It would also be terribly important for me to know your resolution of a certain case in particular, namely: if in the conception of Eros there is a complete absence of "amor" (vljublennost') as you said (i.e.—"longing", the dream of the impossible, Don Quixote, the "poor knight"), then how is one to understand Orpheus and Eurydice, "Platonic" love and Sappho? (If they can serve as an exception, then is it merely conditional?) Your formula disclosed for me such enormous horizons that I have experienced a great need to test it in individual cases which very well could prove to be exceptions for obvious reasons and which I would very much prefer them to be.[8]

Blok, it seems, would dearly love to accept the "purifying" and "combining" synthesis of flesh and spirit which both Gippius and Merezhkovskij espouse. Yet, at the same time, one is aware of an unmistakably sceptical attitude towards man's ability to effect it. To avoid the misconception that Blok was wholeheartedly for the point of view expressed by the Merezhkovskijs, it is quite sufficient to read his subsequent letters to Zinaida Gippius in which he expresses his scepticism about their visit to the supposed site of the mythological city of Kitezh, indeed, about any earthly "Kitezh" ever existing within our time and space.

Thus, Blok sensed very early that it was impossible for him to be delivered by his vision of the Beautiful Lady. As deeply committed as he may have been to her, he felt only some external apocalypse, beyond his control, could effect any syzygy between him and this ideal love. As early as 1901 he sensed the inevitability of her long slumber, although he never ceased to be troubled by visions and echoes of her:

[7] See Blok's letter to Zinaida Gippius on 14 June, 1902, in Blok, Sobr. Soch., VIII, 30.
[8] *Ibid.*, 30-31.

> Silently the evening shadows
> Settle in the blue snow.
> Crowds of shapeless spectres
> Set your ashes atremble.
> You sleep beyond the distant plain,
> You sleep in the snowy shroud...
> The sounds of your swan-song
> I seem to catch.
> A voice calling anxiously,
> The echo in the cold snows...
> Is resurrection really possible?
> Is it true that what has been is not ashes?
> No, from the heavenly house
> The spirit filled with immortality
> Has emerged to excite my ears
> With a familiar and intimate song.
> Crowds of sepulchral visions,
> The sounds of living voices...
> Silently the evening shadows
> Have touched the blue snows.
> ("Tikho vechernie teni...", 1901)

A victim of his awareness of the two passions and the impossibility of their positive synthesis, Blok increasingly gave way to his mounting scepticism and turned his face from the sunsets. Poems like "Dve dushi" ("Two Souls", 1899), "Dvojniku" ("To My Double", 1901) reflect his growing obsession with the split between light and dark. Blinded by his vision of Love, he is nonetheless irresistably attracted to darkness: "Why, why into the gloom of nonexistence/ Do the blows of fate drive me on?" ("Zachem, zachem vo mrak nebytija...", 1902). He sees himself as a victim of some inexorable fate:

> I am old of soul. Some black destiny
>   Is my long road.
> An oppressive dream, cursed and insistent
>   Crushes my breast.
> ....
> Deliver me from vague spectres
>   Unknown friend.
> ("Ja star dushoj. Kakoj-to zhrebij chernyj...", 1899)

Once turned to the radiant vision of his Beautiful Lady, Blok is now hopelessly engulfed by erotic passion:

> I know not whether beyond the distant boundary
> Azure happiness does exist...
> Now I hearken to a foreign
> And ever growing passion.
> ("Ja bremja pokhitil, kak tat", 1901)

I do not believe that it is possible to find a clearly defined and satisfactory development in Blok's verses from 1898 to 1904. They certainly do not display any indisputable ascendancy of the Divine Feminine or any complete optimism about the realization of transformation. They seem, instead, preoccupied from the very beginning with the lyrical metaphysic of Love in all of its divine and demonic manifestations. From the very beginning the poet is "split", is simultaneously drawn to the radiant ideal and the dark anti-spirit. It is as though Blok has experienced the principle of syzygy in all of its possible manifestations, from divine to demonic. His passivity could not resist the alluring charms of his erotic love, once it foresaw a path "darkened with passions" (as in the poem "Moj put' strastjami zatemnen...", 1901). Unlike Solov'ev who resisted scepticism all his life in constant reformulations of his Sophiology only to submit in the end to the overwhelming sense of unavoidable apocalypse, Blok was early convinced of the futility of effort and submitted to his own overwhelming sense of catastrophe or the End:

> Let my age be lonely but joyful,
> So enamoured of destruction.
> Yes I, as no other great man
> Am the witness to the universal catastrophe.
> ("Uvizhu ja, kak budet pogubat'...", 1900)

Almost as though desiring to speed the approaching holocaust, to submit to the evil forces of darkness in order that the world might be transformed, Blok wilfully pursues his own personal degeneration. It is not enough that he has to counter Belyj's vision of a "bright" or "radiant" Blok by insisting on darkness,[9] but he seems to take an almost demonic pleasure in confirming and extolling his fallen nature, his "two-facedness":

> I love to visit
> Soul-soothing lofty cathedrals,
> To enter the sombre choir lofts,
> To disappear amid the singers.
> I fear my two-faced soul
> And carefully I submerge
> My devilish and wild appearance
> In this holy armour.
> In my superstitious prayer
> I seek protection in Christ,
> But from beneath the hypocritical mask
> The deceitful lips smile.
> And silently with altered face
> In the deathlike flickering of candles
> I arouse the memory of the Two-Faced One
> In the hearts of praying people.
> And lo—they shudder, the choir lofts are hushed,
> In confusion they rush to escape...

[9] See A. Belyj, "Vospominanija o A. A. Bloke," Epopeja, No. 2, 1922, 247.

> I love to visit
> Soul-soothing cathedrals.
> ("Ljublju vysokie sobory... ", 1902)

Most of Blok's verses bear a heavy awareness of ambivalence. His *alter ego* has long since declared himself to the poet: "I know you, my two-faced confidant,/ My dearest friend, hostile to the very end" ("Ja pomnju chas glukhoj, bessonnoj nochi...", 1901). The same is true of his vision of the Beautiful Lady and the following verses offer one of the most ambiguous statements Blok ever made not only on the nature of the Radiant Mistress, but especially on his relationship with her:

> You are Holy, but I do not believe You.
> And I have long since foreseen all:
> The day will come and the doors will swing open,
> A white file will pass through.
>
> There will be terrifying, there will be
> Indescribable unearthly masks of faces...
> I shall call out to You: "Hosanna!"
> Seized with madness, prostrate on the ground.
>
> And then having arisen above corruption,
> You will reveal your Radiant Visage.
> And, free of earthly captivity,
> I shall pour all my life into a final cry.
> ("Ty svjata, no ja Tebe ne verju...", 1902)

Although he seems to acknowledge her holiness and envisions her at the climax of revelation in his own deliverance, he also claims that he does not believe her. What does he foresee?—presumably his "path darkened with passions" and his irresistible attraction to the erotic. Although the epithets of the Divine Feminine in this poem recall both Solov'ev's Sophia and his World Soul, how is one to understand the poet's ambiguous stance of simultaneous belief and disbelief?

Blok always protested when people spoke of the exalted vision of the Divine Feminine being in a fallen state, especially after 1905 when the archetype of the demonic female seemed to predominate in the works of both Blok and Belyj. He felt it was not the Ideal that had fallen or suffered, but rather the poet who was incapable of either sustaining the divine image or consummating his relationship with it. Perhaps Solov'ev, Blok and Belyj would all have agreed that the celestial vision existed independently of them, was "immovable" (in Blok's terms) or "unconditional" (in Solov'ev's). The only conditional or movable subject was the poet himself. Affirming his passivity and believing in his powerlessness to attract the Beautiful Lady permanently into the earthly realm or to effect any transformative syzygy with her (as indicated in his letter to Zinaida Gippius), Blok predicted an age of negative apocalypse before the final and ecstatic revelation beyond his control could take place. Thus, the image of the

Divine Feminine had to be temporarily interred until the Final Judgement. Thus, Blok's disbelief is a commentary on himself alone. The other fact which must be borne in mind when dealing with such ambiguous poems as "You are Holy, but I do not believe You" is Blok's self-avowed duplicity, his simultaneous attraction to two principles despite himself. It is the sceptic and the degenerate in Blok who refuses to believe in Her, whereas the chaste mystic cannot refrain from it. This polarity within a single individual is explored by Blok in his later dramas such as "The Puppet Show," "The Stranger" and "The King in the Square". Nor was this theme exclusively Blok's. It also informs the Ableukhovs' destructive polarities in Belyj's famous novel *Petersburg* and provided Russian symbolists with a most fertile source for their literary creations.

The poetic collection "Rasput'e" ("Parting of Ways", 1902-1904) which appeared to close the period initiated by *Verses on the Beautiful Lady* in mid-1904 concluded with a final requiem in Her honour:

> Here it is—a row of graveyard steps.
> And between us there is no one. We are alone.
> Sleep, tender companion of days
> Flooded with hitherto unknown radiance.
>
> You lie at rest in the white coffin.
> With your smile you say: wake me not.
> Golden curls on your forehead.
> A golden icon on your breast.
>
> I paid my respects at the radiant death,
> Pressing the waxen hand,
> All the rest—the boundless firmament
> Has buried in the azure mist.
>
> Slumber—none will disturb your rest,
> We are the outer limits of unknown roads
> All through the inclement night
> The irradiated chamber burns here.
> ("Vot on—rjad grobovykh stupenej... ", 1904)

Surely Blok here celebrates the funeral rites of the Divine Feminine. One may well ask whether the Beautiful Lady was not fated to this end from the very outset of Blok's work; in retrospect this seems an inescapable conclusion.

When Solov'ev sought to make the terms of reference the same for Sophia, the World Soul and his earthly loves, seeing in the latter two the Sophiological possibilities of the first, it was nonetheless fairly easy to discern the identity of the object of his adulation in each case. With Blok's verses it is less so because he made so little attempt at upholding metaphysical distinctions. Quite often those love letters and poems which are apparently written in honour of a woman of

Blok's acquaintance could be construed as tribute to the Beautiful Lady. The correspondence between Blok and one of his early infatuations, K. M. Sadovskaja, in particular contains all the epithets, the familiar terms of address, and the nocturnal landscape which typify the *Verses on the Beautiful Lady*. Although of course it is merely an epistolary convention to capitalize forms of address, if the reader momentarily ignores the convention as such, he is more apt to see the remarkable connection between the letter and the poems. Blok is writing to Sadovskaja who is vacationing in France whereas he is in Petersburg:

> There You have mountains, the sea and the southern sky of France, but here—dull, grey Petersburg and the blue haze of the islands where every tree, every evening shadow, every turn of the road says to me with unbearable pain, melancholy and acuteness that "then" was the first and final—the real, youthful happiness; do You remember the park flooded with moonlight, the dark lake in which those reflections of the islands barely visible to the eye were reflected, and large white swans swim; and here on the shore You, You and You—and other than You there is nothing about of such beauty, so inaccessible to the artist's brush. And with You the night seems yet darker and more filled with a passion suffused in the air that caresses You, and Your eyes are ever more inscrutable, deeper and more brilliant...—Perhaps the swans were not swimming at night and the islands were not reflected in the dark lake, but all of this I imagine to myself to be so,—and I would have it no other way. Besides the nights and evenings there were also the mornings and days, but it is impossible to write down everything and it is unbearably boring for You to read all this empty rhetoric... If you knew how my nerves are frayed and what melancholy there is here, and how everything is vulgar and sad, and I want to embrace Your knees and "burst into tears at Your feet"... Laugh, but it is not at all laughable.[10]

All the standard leitmotifs of Blok's poetry are in this letter. He even creates the sense of two worlds, of the "here" and the "there", which is to be found in *Verses on the Beautiful Lady*. The "there" of France is idealized and romanticised, whereas the sombre and forbidding aspect of Blok's Petersburg is played up. The fact that Blok himself destroys the atmosphere of nocturnal ponds and swans by saying that perhaps it was not at all like that but at least he wishes to remember it as such, betrays the irresistible strength of an imagination that Belyj would have called "maximalist". In yet another letter to Sadovskaja the final line reads like the soulful entreaty of the poet summoning his Radiant Mistress to appear: "I now await Your letters like some unearthly joy... I await You, come."[11] This merging of realms reminds one of the reputed "automatic" letters "received" by Solov'ev

---

[10] See Blok's letter to K. M. Sadovskaja on 31 March, 1900, in Blok, *Sobr. soch.*, VIII, 12-13.

[11] See letter to Sadovskaja (date unknown, c. 1898) in Blok, *Sobr. soch.*, VIII, 9.

and those poems of Blok's which bore the same characteristics of "automatic" writing.

This same confusion of the divine and earthly was particularly remarkable in those situations and poems seemingly inspired by Ljubov' Dmitrievna Mendeleeva. One might well wonder whether the deep interest in drama that Blok and Ljubov' Dmitrievna shared before and after their marriage also helped to sublimate the roles which they assumed in the same way as Blok's "divine-earthly confusion" with Sadovskaja did. In a letter to A. V. Gippius (28 July, 1901) Blok informs his friend that he and Ljubov' Dmitrievna are rehearsing the principal roles of both *Hamlet* and *Romeo and Juliet*. The first of these plays was unmistakably Blok's most beloved and no doubt there was more than a little self-identification with the character of Hamlet whom he so enjoyed playing at private gatherings. This is a subject worth exploring in order to delve more deeply into Blok's own character and his conception of himself. The role which he preferred for his female counterpart was no doubt that of Ophelia who figures so prominently in many of his early verses. His image of Ophelia probably coloured his comprehension of the Beautiful Lady and also throws some light on his difficult courtship of Ljubov' Dmitrievna —in his mind she epitomizes the aloofness, distance and indifference that invariably characterize the early appearance of the divine feminine in Blok's poetry and, of course, most important, allow Blok to adopt the tragic attitude of a Hamlet:

> But you, Ophelia, gazed upon Hamlet
> Without joy, without love, goddess of beauty,
> And roses were sprinkled on the poor poet.
> ("Mne snilas' snova, v tsvetakh... ", 1898)

or: There, there, deep beneath the roots
Lie my sufferings,
Feeding with eternal tears,
Ophelia, your flowers!
("Est' v dikoj roshche, v ovrage... ", 1898)

Many of Blok's poems from *Verses on the Beautiful Lady* represent meetings, or at least expectations of meetings, with Ljubov' Dmitrievna and are directly inspired by her. Here again it seems as though Ljubov' Dmitrievna is the content with which Blok seeks to fill the empty form of his longing for the Beautiful Lady. Apparently a number of meetings were arranged between Blok and his future wife in church, or he would go to evening services, unknown to her, to catch a glimpse of her. "Khranila ja sredi mladykh sozvuchij... " (1901) and "Medlenno v dveri tserkovnye... " (1901) record a tryst between the two in Kazan Cathedral. These two poems are of particular interest because they are related from Ljubov' Dmitrievna's point of view rather than Blok's. Other poems, like "Na temnom poroge tajkom..." (1902), pay witness to Blok's surreptitious observations of Mendeleeva in church:

> On the dark threshold secretly
> I whisper the holy names.
> I know: we are in the temple together
> You think: you are here alone...
>
> I listen to your sighs
> In some sort of never-to-be dream...
> Words about some certain love...
> And, lord! dreams about me...

It is possible that Blok's spying on Mendeleeva in church could have inspired a similar situation in "The Puppet Show" where one set of lovers fears that they are being watched by some sinister figure during a meeting in a church. Often, Blok's bride-to-be is enveloped in a forbidding air; she is the "evil enchantress", the "evil maiden" who has bewitched him and yet who remains inaccessible. But at the same time this demonic aspect is always ambivalent, never losing connotations of divinity:

> In a white blizzard, in a snowy moan
> Again you have emerged, the enchantress,
> And in the eternal light, in the eternal knell
> Were interspersed the domes of churches.
> ("Ja dolgo zhdal—ty vyshla pozdno...", 1901)

When on the night of November 7, 1902 (o. s.), Ljubov' Dmitrievna finally consented to marry Blok after a long and stormy courtship that almost witnessed his suicide, the tones of ecstatic adulation surpass by far all that he had hitherto written in honour of the Beautiful Lady. The identification of Ljubov' Dmitrievna and his Radiant Mistress becomes complete; the coincidence of the earthly and the divine image of love is consummated as Blok extolls the climax of this long-sought syzygy. The first poem is entitled "7-8 of November of the Year 1902" and is an unmistakably apocalyptic announcement:

> Hosanna! Thou art entering my tower!
> Thou art the Voice, Thou art the Glory of the Queen!
> Let us sing, cry out and believe,
> But we are oppressed by the regal robes!
> We are blind from tears of blood,
> Deafened by the cries of corruption
> ....
> But Thou in unheard of glories
> Hast delivered to us sighs of incense!
> ("Osanna! Ty vkhodish' v terem...")

This poem was no doubt written immediately after the momentous occasion. The following day (November 8, 1902) witnessed yet another:

> I tended them in the Johanine Chapel,
> A motionless guard,—tended the fire of the lamps.
>
> And lo, She appeared, and to Her my Hosanna—
> The laurel wreath of labours is greater than all rewards.
>
> I hid my face and the years passed by,
> I spent many years in Worship.
>
> And lo, the vaults are set afire by evening rays,
> She has given me the Regal Response.
>
> I alone tended and warmed the candles here.
> Alone—the prophet—trembled in the haze of incense.
>
> And on This Day—the one participant in the Meeting—
> I have not shared these Meetings with anyone.
> ("Ja ikh khranil v pridele Ioanna...")

Notably this last poem was originally included in *Verses on the Beautiful Lady* in 1904, but subsequently placed as the first poem in the following collection *Parting of Ways*, perhaps reinforcing a significance hitherto obscured. Mochulskij believes that Blok's courtship of the Beautiful Lady was concluded with the announcement of Ljubov' Dmitrievna's willingness to marry him, thereby ushering in the subsequent period of disillusionment and despair. Whether this is true or not can be debated. What is certain, however, is that if Blok expected to find salvation from his darker side, to be delivered by this mystical betrothal from the abyss towards which he was being attracted, he was to be disappointed. Even after his marriage in the summer of 1903, the same nagging pessimism and scepticism persist. Erotic passion still darkens his path and he still seeks a way to deal with it:

> Empowered, I calculate as in former times,
> I weave spells and conjecture anew,
> How I, a wise king, shall with passionate life
> Combine You, o Love?
> ("Stoju u vlasti, dushoj odinok...", 1902)

Nor has his "double" disappeared with the acquiesence of his earthly Radiant Mistress. He is ever there, haunting their steps, a constant reminder of Blok's two selves:

> At the doors of the Incomparable Lady
> I wept in a blue raincoat.
> And swaying, with a pale face,

That same stranger imitated me.
("Potemneli, poblekli zaly... ", 1903)

Moreover, he is still plagued by unceasing rustlings and glimpses of Someone:

> And Often it seems—in the distance,
> By the dark walls, at the bend,
> Where we sang and walked,
> There still walks and sings Someone.
> ....
> I know all. But we are together.
> Now there can be no talk
> That we are not walking here alone,
> That Someone is huffing at the candles.
> ("My vsjudu. My nigde. Idem." 1902)

Apparently Blok's evil genius, Love, was not sated with the entente between him and Mendeleeva. Perhaps he had wrongly mistaken her for the manifestation of his divine Radiant Mistress, who would save him from his erotic passions, only to discover that the dark side of his nature was strong enough to drag both himself and his bride into the abyss. What he came to understand, however, was that Ljubov' Dmitrievna was not his deliverance and that she was not an earthly incarnation of Sophia in spite of Belyj's and Serezha's contentions to the contrary.

Both Solov'ev and Blok attempted to lure the Divine Feminine to this earthly realm, to work a syzygal alchemy that would bring salvation. Where for Solov'ev it was the deliverance of mankind and the world, for Blok it was his own personal salvation. Both sought the divine manifestation of the feminine principle, but found the temporary ascendancy of the demonic inevitable. This left no other course open but that forecast by Vladimir Solov'ev's "A Short Tale of the Antichrist", and indeed, by many of Blok's own early verses.

Andrej Belyj (pseud. of Boris Bugaev, 1880-1934)

Chapter 5

THE WOMAN CLOTHED IN THE SUN

Andrej Belyj was undoubtedly one of Vladimir Solov'ev's most fervent disciples. But although he adopted many of the principles of Solov'evian Sophiology and esteemed Solov'ev more highly than any other influence throughout his literary and intellectual career, the philosopher's ideas were by no means always faithfully reproduced by this ardent follower. Belyj found himself influenced from many quarters during his career. Among his own symbolist generation Dmitrij Merezhkovskij, Valerij Brjusov, Vjacheslav Ivanov and Aleksandr Blok were but a few of those who created wildly unpredictable moods of sympathy or antipathy in him. He was attracted in turn by Nietzsche, Kant, Hartmann and the Neo-Kantians, Theosophy and in particular Rudolf Steiner's Anthroposophy. At home in both mysticism and scientificism, he read the Bible side by side with Spencer. His inscrutable articles on the nature of symbolism, art and culture read like a bad distillation of all of world philosophy, bearing proof of his overexuberantly syncretic method of searching for the New Jerusalem. Art was no simple question of "art for art's sake", no adulation of artistic method and innovation, as it was for decadents like Brjusov and Bal'mont. The function of art proposed by Belyj is by no means autonomous. It serves a higher master just as Solov'ev had earlier indicated in his own aesthetic theories.

In the first years of his activity as a symbolist writer and apologist, Belyj inclined to mystical homily on behalf of Symbolism's universal task. Following Solov'ev's proclamation of Sophia and Godmanhood, Belyj too was drawn to the archetype of syzygal union as the end of world history. Accepting the essential Platonism of Solov'ev's perception of two divided yet potentially united realms, the young symbolist echoes the elder philosopher's vision in his own terms: "The union of the universal abyss, which exists where there is neither time nor condition, with the ethereally white space, as though with the symbol of an ideal humanity—this union is revealed to us in the unifying Colour of the heavens—in this symbol of Godmanhood, of two-in-oneness."[1] The colour of which Belyj is speaking is, of course, that favorite Sophiological colour, azure.

[1] Andrej Belyj, "Svjashchennye tsveta," *Arabeski* (Moscow, 1911), 128.

In those early years of Symbolism's carefree youth before the abortive Revolution of 1905, Belyj put no restraints on his ecstatic maximalism. Recalling Merezhkovskij's words from "On the Reasons for the Decline and the New Tendencies in Contemporary Literature"[2] which demanded a new idealism in art and the author's willingness to undergo martyrdom for the new literary and cultural faith, Belyj pronounces his own readiness to assume this sacrificial role: "To penetrate through all the forms 'of this world', to journey there where all are fools-in-Christ—this is our path."[3]

Belyj's article "Svjashchennye tsveta" ("Sacred Colours", 1903) is rather significant in respect to his professed discipleship of Vladimir Solov'ev. Here he deals quite specifically with Solov'ev's theories on love, yet goes far beyond the sober rational view expressed in "The Meaning of Love" with his own mystical panegyric. Solov'ev would never have allowed himself such mystic exuberance in prose; divine revelation he always reserved for his private vision in poetry.

Although in this article Belyj is ostensibly talking about the symbolism of various colours, infusing red, white, pink, azure, grey, black, etc., with both philosophical and theological content, he also turns his attention to the nature of art. Art and religion quickly combine to produce the vehicle for creating new being, namely "theurgy": "In prayer the heights of art are united with mysticism. The union of mysticism with art is theurgy."[4] Striving to develop the idea of theurgy, Belyj introduces the role of love: "In theurgy is the incarnation of Eternity. Therefore the immediate emotion of love must include in itself something of a religious nature. Love is ideal."[5] The following excerpt is particularly significant insofar as it displays the degree to which Solov'ev's theory of an idealized love, of a prototypic syzygy which could lead to Godmanhood, has become exalted in Belyj's own vision. Indeed, the archetype of the "marriage" of Bridegroom and Bride to create the New Jerusalem becomes the most important symbol for transforming mankind:

> The ideas of the world and mankind coincide conditionally for us. The idea of the world may be called the world soul. The world soul, Sophia according to Solov'ev, is perfect humanity, eternally enclosed in the divine nature of Christ. Here the mystical nature of the church coincides with the image of the eternal feminine, the bride of the Lamb. Here are the Alpha and Omega of true love. Christ's relation to the church—that of the bridegroom to the bride—is an unfathomable universal symbol. This symbol illuminates every ultimate love. Every love is a symbol of this symbol. Every symbol in its ultimate breadth manifests the image of the Bridegroom and Bride.[6]

[2] St. Petersburg, 1893.
[3] "Svjashchennye tsveta," *Arabeski*, 127.
[4] *Ibid.*, 122.
[5] *Ibid.*, 123-124.
[6] *Ibid.*, 126.

In other words, Belyj is propounding the same function for love which Solov'ev detailed in his treatise "The Meaning of Love", albeit in more grandiloquent terms.

In the final pages of this article Belyj tries to compose the unique image which will symbolize the coming salvation of the world. In view of the fact that Belyj has spoken at length of Christ without specifically mentioning his favourite feminine archetype, the Woman Clothed in the Sun, one is tempted to accept it as Christ, although Belyj does not specifically call it so:

> Proceeding from colour symbols we are in a position to formulate the image of the one who will conquer the world. Even though this image be hazy we believe that the haze will be dissipated. Its visage must be white like the snow. Its eyes are like two flights into the heavens, wondrously unfathomable, pale and blue. Like liquid honey, the joy of ancients in the heavens, are its thick golden strands of hair. But the grief of the pious for the world, this is the waxen film on its face. The bloody crimson are its lips, like that crimson which closes the line of flowers into a circle, like that crimson which destroys worlds in fire; its lips are the crimson fire.[7]

On closer examination, the reader will find that here Belyj has not capitalized the pronouns and possessive adjectives as he has in the rest of the article when mentioning Christ. (Thus I have taken the liberty of interpreting the Russian *ego* as "its" and *on* as "it", in reference to the antecedent "obraz".) Moreover, the reader will immediately recognize the characteristics of Sophia and the Beautiful Lady: the "azure-blue eyes", "golden strands" and the "white visage". In other words, there are two interesting possibilities here. Perhaps the ultimate symbol of which Belyj speaks, the ultimate sign of love, is indeed the Eternal Feminine. On the other hand, perhaps Belyj is purposely creating an ambiguous image of the Bridegroom and Bride united, the marriage of Christ and the Church, the consummation of Godmanhood. This androgynous view seems quite likely in view of the basic idea of "two-in-oneness", of divine syzygal union which Belyj has been developing in the article. It is not necessary to insist upon this interpretation; I offer it simply as a curious, but possible, view of Belyj's infatuation with Solov'evian syzygy.

Despite Belyj's obsession with Solov'evian ideas in the early 1900's, despite the complex dialogue with Blok concerning the Divine Feminine, there is little or no specific mention of the feminine archetype in Belyj's poetry of that period. "Rational" (if one may use that term of Belyj) discussion of the Divine Feminine is quite apparent in his critical articles, while all "lyrical discussion" is incorporated into the author's *Symphonies*.[8] Particularly *Northern Symphony* and

[7] *Ibid.*, 128-129.

[8] Simfonija [*2-ja, dramaticheskaja*], (Moscow, 1902); *Severnaja simfonija* [1-ja,

the fourth symphony, *Goblet of Storms*, deserve attention in examining Belyj's advocacy of the Divine Sophia.

For both of these symphonies Belyj could well have appended as an epigraph the formula he pronounced in "Sacred Colours": "Marriage and romantic love can assume the requisite inflection only when they appear as the symbols of other, as yet unattainable, suprahuman relations."[9] How indicative of the conception of these two symphonies this statement is, may be deduced from even a brief description of the *fabula* of each.

In *Northern Symphony* a young king ascends the throne of his dying father, who commands him to lead his people to the heights and not forsake them. Fearing the darkness of his kingdom, however, he flees to the north and builds a lonely tower there. A daughter is born to him and, like her father, she learns to sing songs to the sunset. With the death of her hapless father, who perishes trying to reach his former kingdom again, her mother delivers her into the protection of Eternity before disappearing in pursuit of her husband. Subsequently, a young knight falls in love with her, but is too much influenced by his father's pagan nature and an evil courtier-magician who performs black masses. He attempts to seduce the princess and carry her off, but loses her love as a result of his crudely physical action. Returning to her father's lost kingdom and preaching new truths, the princess transforms the land into a realm of light and goodness. Their love unconsummated in this world of time and space, she and her knight are united only in the realm of Eternity after death.

The symbolism of this elaborate fairy tale is fairly transparent in the light of Solov'ev's Sophiology. The young king has shirked the duty of leading his kingdom to the New Jerusalem and seeks refuge from the spectral evils which intimidated him. His daughter, a divine symbol of truth and beauty, performs the function of the Divine Feminine by restoring light and harmony. The knight, torn between the two poles of his physical and spiritual impulses, is not worthy of joining with the princess in the creation of the ideal union or syzygy, for such a union could not be the "symbol of other, as yet unattainable supra-human relations". Thus, it is only after the purging of his physical nature in death that Belyj allows him to unite with the chaste princess.

Of course, it is hardly a coincidence by now that one of Belyj's earliest literary attempts is formulated with a cast of princesses, knights, dragons and other appropriate motifs of chivalry as befitted

geroicheskaja], (Moscow, 1903); *Vozvrat* [Tret'ja simfonija], (Moscow, 1905); *Kubok metelej* [4-ja, simfonija], (Moscow, 1908).

[9] "Svjashchennye tsveta," *Arabeski*, 125.

the youthful symbolist-knight of the Divine Sophia. Indeed, Belyj found it difficult to escape this format even in his later works.

The fourth symphony, *Goblet of Storms*, presents a variation on the same theme. Both Adam Petrovich and the engineer's wife, Svetlova, are possessed of a vision, he with that of the Divine Feminine and she with that of the Christ-Groom. This creates a common mystical attraction, but an antagonist appears in the figure of the demonic and powerful Colonel Svetozarov. Svetlova, despite herself, feels both attracted and repelled by this frightening character. Adam Petrovich is killed in a duel with Svetlova's husband, but is resurrected in eternity where he meets Svetlova, now a nun, after escaping the clutches of Svetozarov. In the conclusion, Belyj openly identifies Svetozarov with the Lucifer-Serpent whom Svetlova destroys in her apotheosis as the Woman Clothed in the Sun. The mysterious attraction which Adam Petrovich and Svetlova experience symbolizes the inescapable desire for syzygy which animates both Solov'ev's and Belyj's schemes. The exemplary nature of this union is indicated in the names of the protagonists, Svetlova signifying the light and Adam Petrovich's unusual Christian name suggesting the first man reborn in the line of Peter. Interpretation is unnecessary here since the elaborate fable is explained in its conclusion when Svetlova in fact receives the designation of the Woman Clothed in the Sun and Adam Petrovich becomes the symbolic Bridegroom of this chaste Bride.

By 1905 Belyj had evolved an increasingly "politico-cultural" conception of the Divine Feminine. No doubt prompted by the events of the 1905 Revolution as well as Blok's apparent desertion of the Beautiful Lady, Belyj attempted to create a more social image of this archetype, which he now identified even more fervently with the spiritual and cultural revolution he was heralding for Russia. In this regard he came very close to Solov'ev's own "public" intentions of recreating mankind under the symbol of Sophia, while moving of course further from Blok's purely personal and intimate apprehension of the Beautiful Lady.

In "Apokalipsis v russkoj poezii" ("The Apocalypse in Russian Poetry")[10] Belyj indicates the degree to which the Divine Feminine has subsumed all of his views on the coming spiritual transformation. He still believes, in this article at least, that Russia and Russian poetry are at the crossroads, with the potential of turning to either cosmos or chaos. As yet, chaos is still a "spectre", if a very real one, hanging over the horizon like some rapacious bird of prey, waiting to swoop down and devour the culture of Russia. He believes that it is still possible to

---

[10] This article first appeared in *Vesy*, No. 4, 1905, 11-28. It was subsequently included in Belyj's *Lug zelenyj* (Moscow, 1910), 222-247. The latter source is quoted here.

avoid Antichrist's reign if only the "sleeping beauty" can be awakened: "If the veil be torn from the world, then these factories, peoples, growths, will disappear; the world, like a sleeping beauty, will awaken to wholeness...".[11] Recollecting both *Three Conversations* and "A Brief Tale of the Antichrist", Belyj awards Solov'ev the credit of first discerning the "rosy smile" of the World Soul and the banner of the Woman Clothed in the Sun. Solov'ev is also responsible for tearing the mask from the face of the enemy and warning people of the imminent dangers. In veiled allusion to the horrific Russo-Japanese War of 1904 and the Revolution of 1905, Belyj claims that Solov'ev's prophecies have been fulfilled. They are signs of the chaos about to engulf Russia.

In the face of threatening cataclysm, it is to art and poetry that Belyj turns. The goal of poetry, he feels, is "to find the visage of the muse, expressing in this visage the universal oneness of cosmic truth."[12] The goal of religion is to realize this truth in humanity, for the image of the muse can be transformed into the perfect visage of humanity, the visage of the Woman Clothed in the Sun. Arriving at the conclusion that Art is the shortest road to Religion, Belyj is able to claim that the image of the muse should crown the development of national poetry because humanity is the genuine total-unity, and "nationality" (*natsial 'nost'*) represents the first qualification on the road to humanity.

In other words, Belyj has just given Solov'ev's dialectical process, which leads to Godmanhood under the aegis of Sophia, an entirely nationalistic twist, with art playing the prominent role. Examining the history of Russian poetry Belyj claims there are two definite streams which begin from Pushkin and Lermontov, and all other poets may be categorized according to one or the other. Pushkin represents a "superficial oneness" and universality in outlook, while Lermontov signifies a "tragic split" and individualism. This rather vague description of the two is not particularly enlightening, but the main point is Belyj's conviction that they must be reconciled. Vladimir Solov'ev has begun this work by marrying philosophy and poetry. He is responsible, according to Belyj, for tearing the mask from the Lermontovian muse and revealing the Woman Clothed in the Sun as the genuine muse of Russian poetry, whose inspiration will bring the rebirth of man:

> The manifested image of the Woman Clothed in the Sun must become the focus of the mysterium, manifesting in itself the all-one principle of humanity. The Woman of whom Solov'ev has received knowledge,

[11] *Ibid.*, 222.
[12] *Ibid.*, 230.

> must descend from heaven and envelop us with the Sun of Life—with the mysterium.[13]

The Woman Clothed in the Sun must become the national soul, says Belyj, as the first stage towards the unifying of heaven and earth.

Belyj claims that Vjacheslav Ivanov has helped in her descent by indicating the Dionysian basis of the commune of the future, thereby elevating sociality to a "religious principle", or the first step in what Belyj calls the "organization of love", i.e. combining the individual with society. However, it is to Blok and Brjusov that Belyj turns his especial attention, seeing in them the duality which must be synthesized. At present, Brjusov threatens to apotheosize the Harlot astride the Beast as his muse and Belyj serves notice: "The chaos manifested in Brjusov's poetry must become the body of the Woman shining in the heavens".[14] Even though Blok has formally withdrawn from the "Solov'evian Circle" by the writing of this article, Belyj refuses to release him from his "obligations":

> In Blok's poetry we encounter everywhere the attempt to incarnate a supra-natural vision in the aspects of time and space. She is already in our midst, together with us, incarnate, living, near—this muse of Russian Poetry, recognized at last, appearing in the Sun in which the rays of a newly manifested religion have intersected, and the struggle for whom should be the task of our entire life.[15]

While implicating the unwilling Blok in this panegyric to the Woman Clothed in the Sun as the muse of Russian poetry and the symbol of man's re-creation, Belyj nonetheless warns that even in Blok's poetry chaos lurks in the form of the "chernyj chelovek" and the "krasnyj karlik" who have lately appeared. These manifestations of approaching chaos Belyj terms the "many-faced dragon attacking Her".[16]

The Pushkinian and Lermontovian streams, which appear in Blok and Brjusov respectively, must be united, but Belyj does not provide the specifics of the process. Claiming that he does not yet have a symbolist programme, he outlines the first step in only the vaguest apocalyptic terminology—battle must be done with the Beast and the Woman Clothed in the Sun must become the muse of Russian poetry.

Although Blok had vague apocalyptic premonitions which he disclosed to Belyj in their correspondence, he never attempted to create a manifesto or programme of action out of them. On the other hand, Belyj was constantly striving to formulate a platform for Symbolism. Blok or Solov'ev would never have made the burdensome

[13] Ibid., 241-242.
[14] Ibid., 242.
[15] Ibid., 243.
[16] Ibid., 244.

claim that through poetry the rebirth of mankind would be effected. In essence, however, Belyj does do this. Thus, he places Russian poetry squarely, not only on the national stage, but on the universal as well:

> Russian poetry in both of its developments is deeply immersed in universal life. The question which it raises can be resolved only through the transformation of the Heaven and Earth into the city of the New Jerusalem. The Apocalypse of Russian poetry is summoned forth with the approach of the End of World History. Only in this do we find the resolution of the Pushkinian and Lermontovian mysteries.[17]

Thus, in Russian poetry Belyj provides us with the entire spectrum of Sophia or the Woman Clothed in the Sun. She represents the principle of the unification of heaven and earth. She is both the symbol of universal oneness and the national soul of Russia. These principles are incorporated in the one ideal of Love which expresses her true nature. Finally, she is the ultimate manifestation of the Russian muse which must infuse art with all of these principles.

Despite the heavily apocalyptic imagery of Belyj's article the Christ of the Second Coming is noticeably absent. He is completely displaced by the Divine Feminine in the person of the Woman Clothed in the Sun. Just how completely the apocalyptic functions of Christ have been absorbed in Belyj's vision, becomes clear in the article's concluding invocation:

> We believe that Thou shallt reveal Thyself
> to us, that before us lie not the mists of October
> and the yellow thaws of February. Let them think
> that Thou still reclinest in Thine icy tomb
> > Thou shallt rest in the white tomb.
> > Smiling Thou callest: summon me not.
> > Golden strands upon Thy forehead,
> > Golden icon upon Thy breast.
> > > Blok
>
> No, Thou hast arisen.
> Thou Thyself promised to manifest Thyself in
> the rosy light, and the soul bends prayerfully
> before Thee, and in the light of dawn—of crimson
> icon-lamps—hearkens to your prayerful sigh.
> Manifest Thyself!
> The time has come: the world is ripe like
> a golden fruit succulent in its sweetness, the
> world languishes without Thee.
> Manifest Thyself.[18]

The ascendancy of the Divine Feminine in Belyj's works was maintained until approximately 1908, the year his fourth and final

---
[17] Ibid., 246.
[18] Ibid., 246-247.

symphony *Goblet of Storms* appeared, although he claimed in later years that this work was the belated product of earlier emotions and commitments. Blok and the Beautiful Lady had parted ways by 1904 and Belyj took his drama "Balaganchik" ("The Puppet Show") as insulting proof of Blok's betrayal of all Sophiological principles. Belyj sought desperately to maintain these, but despite his deep commitment, the image of the Divine Feminine gradually degenerated in his own works, commencing with the novel *Serebrjanyj golub'* (*The Silver Dove*) in 1910 and carrying through the following novel, *Peterburg* (*Petersburg*) in 1916. In his third major prose work, *Kotik Letaev* (1922), Belyj's earlier Sophiological ideals are ornately gilded with the Anthroposophy of Rudolf Steiner and the feminine archetype has ceded its earlier pre-eminence to the Christological archetype which Belyj himself assumes. The complete ascendency of this new obsession is then established in the succeeding work, *Zapiski chudaka* (*The Notes of an Eccentric*, 1922).

PART III
The Apostasy

Chapter 1

THE DEMONIZED IDEAL

The years between 1906 and 1910 not only witnessed the low point in the ever mercurial personal relations of Blok and Belyj, but produced the most vitriolic literary polemics on the public scene as well. In 1906 Belyj became deeply involved with Blok's wife, Ljubov' Dmitrievna, and she appeared at first to encourage his feelings. In his memoirs on Blok, Belyj hints at Blok's increasingly profligate nature at this time, when he would disappear for long periods at a time and return home drunk and dishevelled. Belyj claims that at first he was trying to "protect" Ljubov' Dmitrievna after Blok appeared to have abandoned her. Certainly he spent almost all his time with her in Blok's absence. The real details of this triangle will probably never be known since Belyj's memoirs are no doubt one-sided[1] and Blok for his part did not record them. At any rate, it appears that after an initial rebuke to Belyj, he stepped aside and did not meddle directly in the affair. Ljubov' Dmitrievna herself was rather capricious, first drawing Belyj on and then rejecting him in favour of Blok. The business was most frustrating for all three and particularly so, no doubt, for the overly-sensitive Belyj. Finally, Ljubov' Dmitrievna (and Blok) advised Belyj to leave Petersburg for at least a year. In the most shattered nervous condition, he "fled" Russia a few weeks later to spend the better part of a year abroad, principally in Munich where there was a small Russian intellectual community, and then in Paris with the Merezhkovskijs who had moved there in early 1906. In fact, Belyj seems to have been the "culprit" in this love affair, judging by the contrite and self-abasing letters with which he flooded the taciturn Blok from abroad and to which he received no reply for the longest time. Characteristically, Blok did not feel that a "baring of souls" or any amount of "frank discussion"—i.e. *words*—could mend things and he told Belyj so. Equally characteristically, Belyj sought understanding and forgiveness with customarily exaggerated verbiage.

These personal relationships were further exacerbated by the literary antagonisms that dominated the symbolist scene from 1906

[1] See p. 89.

onwards. The tension arose principally between the two "geographical" camps, Moscow and Petersburg. Valerij Brjusov had launched the journal *Vesy* (*The Scales*) in 1904 and had gathered about him many of the younger symbolists like Belyj, Sergej Solov'ev and Ellis-Kobylinskij. About the same time, another group of "mystical anarchists" were forming an alliance in Petersburg under the direction of Vjacheslav Ivanov and Georgij Chulkov. They came to particular prominence in 1906 and helped to fill the vacuum caused by the departure of Dmitrij Merezhkovskij and Zinaida Gippius to Paris. Their journal was called *Fakely* (*Torches*) and they attracted to the "tower", Vjacheslav Ivanov's regular Wednesday evening gatherings, Aleksandr Blok, Sergej Gorodetskij and others. The dissolution of the Argonauts and the Astrov Circle in Moscow, not to mention the smaller Solov'evian Circle of Belyj, Blok and Sergej Solov'ev, had temporarily caused a hiatus especially for Belyj who was still obsessed with the formation of the theurgic "collective", the symbolist phallanx that would lead the way to the New Jerusalem. At first Belyj was attracted to Ivanov and his circle in Petersburg, but especially after the affair with Ljubov' Dmitrievna and the disagreement with Blok, he threw all his energy behind Brjusov's journal *The Scales*. In a series of bitter and vitriolic articles he took every opportunity (together with Sergej Solov'ev and Ellis-Kobylinskij) to attack the views of Ivanov, Chulkov and Blok in Petersburg. So partisan were the literary politics of that period that both sides engaged in a type of "espionage" that included all the unsavory tactics of sabotage, backstabbing and using double-agents. A continuous attempt was made to lure members of one literary party over to the other: offers were made to publish more of their works, to pay higher wages, to allocate them certain columns or literary sections in the opposing journals, etc. The Moscow symbolists were horrified, for instance, when the Petersburg symbolists appeared to gain a foothold on the Moscow front by having their works published in the Moscow journal *Zolotoe runo* (*Golden Fleece*). Blok and Belyj were at the centre of this double-dealing. Brjusov at one point hoped to deal a mortal blow to the Petersburg camp by inviting Blok—through Belyj!— to publish in *Scorpion* in Moscow. Early in 1906 Ivanov attempted to lure Belyj to Petersburg—through the Bloks!—to participate in his journal *Torches* as well as the Symbolist Theatre he was organizing.

However, any possibility of a new *entente* between Belyj and Blok in the early part of 1906 had already been smashed by the destructive love affair between Belyj and Ljubov' Dmitrievna. When Belyj returned from abroad in the summer of 1907, the contention reverted to the literary scene once again. The split between the two can easily be traced to Blok's second volume of verses, *Unexpected*

Joy, and the play "The Puppet-Show". When Belyj reviews the former he once again introduces the thorny question of Blok's original commitment to and subsequent rejection of the Beautiful Lady.[2] After praising Blok and pointing out the major influences on the poet, Belyj comes to the essential point of his article. Referring to Blok's first collection, he states that *Verses on the Beautiful Lady* displays a specific and significant content. The poet intones the approach of "the eternal feminine principle, of life . . . His theme is profound. His purpose is meaningful."[3] But then Belyj claims that, although Blok's verses have become technically improved in *Unexpected Joy*, he has "cast off all ideological ballast,"[4] and revealed his true nature. However, although Blok appeared to accept Belyj's assessment of *Unexpected Joy*[5] he was very upset by the comments which were made in the same article about his play "The Puppet-Show". Here are Belyj's provocative words: "In the drama *The Puppet-Show* are [Blok's] embittered scoffings at his past."[6] Blok quickly comes to his own defense over this statement by Belyj: ". . . I only beg of you, while you are flagellating my sacrilege, not to take *The Puppet-Show*, and everything similar to it, for 'embittered scoffings at his past.' Scoffing has always been foreign to me and I know this just as firmly as the fact that I am consciously following that path of mine which has been preordained, and that I must proceed without waivering."[7] Perhaps the reader will recall that this was not the first time that Belyj had accused Blok of making sport of sacred matters (witness his letter of 13 October, 1905 after the disagreement at Shakhmatovo).[8] The response at that time also was Blok's immediate and sincere denial.[9]

In the summer of 1907, a bitter exchange of letters began between Belyj and Blok. Blok expressed his annoyance at the fact that Belyj had been criticizing him unjustly and ambiguously in his articles, while Belyj responded with an abrupt letter in which he informed Blok that they were no longer friends and that he wanted nothing to do with him. Vilifications crossed back and forth, Blok calling Belyj a "spy and a lackey" for making slanderous comments about his personal life and works and Belyj responding with the old countercharges of "disloyalty and betrayal". In August of 1907 Blok finally challenged Belyj to a duel (their second!). However, the challenge

[2] See *Pereval*, 1907, No. 4, 59-61.
[3] *Ibid.*, 59 (right column).
[4] *Ibid.*, 60 (left column).
[5] See Blok's letter to Belyj on 24 March (O.S.) 1907, in *Aleksandr Blok i Andrej Belyj. Perepiska*, pod red. V. N. Orlova (Moscow, 1940), 187-189.
[6] See *Pereval*, 1907, No. 4, 59 (right column).
[7] Blok's letter to Belyj on 24 March (O.S.) 1907, in *Perepiska* . . ., 187.
[8] See Belyj's letter to Blok of 13 October (O.S.) 1905, in *Perepiska* . . ., 155-157.
[9] See Blok's letter to Belyj on 14/15 October (O.S.) 1905, in *Perepiska* . . ., 157-160.

was subsequently withdrawn and within a few weeks, their relations returned to "normal". Now it was Blok's turn to make a clean breast of all his faults and confess his transgressions and weaknesses.

The following spring, Belyj sent Blok a copy of his *Fourth Symphony* (*Goblet of Storms*, 1908) and asked Blok's opinion of it. Blok demurred at first, but in a letter to his mother he wrote that he did not like it at all, in fact, disliked the entire spirit of the work. Moreover, he disclosed his suspicions that it contained some unsavory allusions to himself and Ljubov' Dmitrievna. When finally he summoned enough courage to tell Belyj, he turned the tables by claiming the work was "sacrilege" and furthermore lacked respect for their personal relations. He went on to express his displeasure at Belyj's latest articles in *The Scales* which attacked Gippius and Sologub among others, and then concluded with this picture of their frustrated relationship:

> But I have never had, nor have now, more confused inner relations with anyone. All my life I have had and still have a single "steadfast truth" of a mystical order, and from the point of view of this truth I find myself forced to acknowledge your symphony [*Goblet of Storms*] as being hostile to me in its very essence.[10]

Belyj's reaction was predictable. In response he wrote Blok that all contact between them was at an end. In fact, there followed an effective rupture in their relations that was to last at least for several years.

Between 1906 and 1911, Belyj produced hundreds of pages on the nature of symbolism and the task of art. The gulf between him and Blok widened as he became increasingly theoretic and fanatic, a self-appointed inquisitor dedicated to a ponderously rationalized view of symbolism. While it is frequently impossible to untangle the incredible syncretism of his more theoretic articles of this period, one can gain a sense of the bias of Belyj's mentality during this period by examining some of his more forthright articles which appeared monthly in *The Scales* under the heading of "Na perevale" ("On the Divide"). Belyj's posture in these articles certainly provokes thought once again as to who of these two symbolists, Blok or Belyj, was the greater "maximalist".

In "Detskaja svistul'ka" ("A Child's Tin Whistle", 1907)[11] Belyj attacks the Petersburg symbolists like Georgij Chulkov and Vjacheslav Ivanov because they have apparently lost all faith in sunsets and sunrises, claiming that symbolism as such has completed its cycle and a new period of "neo-realism" is beginning. Mockingly, Belyj chides those who are attacking symbolism from the "left", that is, from within its ranks, rather than from the "right" as had always been

---

[10] See Blok's letter to Belyj on 24 April (O.S.) 1908, in *Perepiska*..., 232.

[11] First appeared under Belyj's monthly by-line of "Na perevale" in *Vesy*, 1907, No. 8, 54-58. Later included in A. Belyj, *Arabeski* (Moscow, 1911), 263-268.

the case. Revealing his deep commitment to seeking out a rational and theoretic basis for symbolism, Belyj points out that these people are obviously not involved in the disciplines that should underly any concept of symbolism: "All these attacks of the new style against symbolism display the complete ignorance of the 'whistlers' in questions of psychology, psycho-physiology and the theory of cognition."[12] In fact, Belyj means to extend the limits of symbolism by freeing it from the confines of any single literary school: "Symbolism in the broadest sense is not a school in art. Symbolism—this is art itself. The romantic, classical, realist and even the symbolist schools are only a means of symbolization in images of the experienced content of consciousness."[13] The cultural task he forsees for symbolism is that it should participate in all areas of knowledge and be interpreted in the widest possible sense. In effect, Belyj calls for all symbolists, (whether "mystical anarchists", "neo-realists", "neo-symbolists" or whatever) to close ranks around Symbolism. All deviation from it is tantamount to sacrilege: "Symbolism, this is a banner around which all those forces who are struggling for the lofty purpose of art should group themselves... Symbolism is the culmination point in the growth of art; deviations to the right or left at the present time are leading to the profanation of creativity."[14]

Belyj continued to project himself as the arbiter of symbolism and its task on the pages of The Scales with an increasingly strident voice. In 1907 and 1908 his articles "Vol'nootpushchenniki" ("Emancipated Slaves")[15] and "Shtempelevannaja kalosha" ("The Stamped Galosh")[16] drive deeper the wedge between himself and the Petersburg symbolists, including Blok. The second article, "The Stamped Galosh", is particularly remarkable, not only for its forthright attack on Vjacheslav Ivanov's circle, but also for the rhetoric it employs with respect to the Divine Feminine. Belyj specifically charges the Petersburg symbolists with frivolity and self-indulgence, while he portrays Muscovite symbolism in the agonizing throes of self-sacrifice, seeking the answers to the problems of symbolism:

> In Petersburg the modernists have grown accustomed to walking over an abyss. The abyss is an essential condition of comfort for the Petersburgian literati. There they walk about admiring themselves over the abyss, they gather for visits over the abyss, arrange their careers on the abyss and set up the samovar over the abyss.[17]

[12] Belyj, Arabeski, 263.
[13] Ibid., 263.
[14] Ibid., 268.
[15] First appeared under Belyj's monthly by-line "Na perevale" in Vesy, 1908, No. 1, 73-81. Later included in A. Belyj, Arabeski (Moscow, 1911), 331-335.
[16] First appeared under Belyj's monthly by-line "Na perevale" in Vesy, 1907, No. 5, 49-52. Later included in A. Belyj, Arabeski, 342-346.
[17] Belyj, Arabeski, 342.

At first Belyj attacks all these "mystics" for defiling the sacred aims of symbolism which he associates with the Woman Clothed in the Sun: "The mystics of our God-protected capital have turned the Woman Clothed in the Sun (the symbol of the struggle with the terror) into an overshoe..."[18] Then he makes a veiled but vindictive attack on Blok:

> The brave jester has not fallen into a deep reverie; tinkling his bell, he has concluded importantly: "The final sacrilege is an advertisement: Christianity is a special type of flirt; mysticism is the teaching of three hundred and thirty-three embraces; the Woman Clothed in the Sun is an overshoe!" Everyone remained pleased and carried the overshoe into the temple. It is not surprising that soon "every little demon will be begging permission" to approach the defiled altar.[19]

Clearly, Belyj believes he is striving to maintain the positive idealistic values of symbolism undefiled before what he sees as the wanton and unprincipled attitudes of Blok, Ivanov and Chulkov. The fact that Blok has apparently allied himself with Chulkov and Ivanov seemed a direct insult. What rankled even more was that Blok's fame grew, not from his *Verses on the Beautiful Lady* which Belyj considered to be in the service of all the ideals of symbolism, but rather from such poems as "Neznakomka" ("The Stranger") and the play "Balaganchik" ("The Puppet-Show") which for Belyj represented a gross and mocking sacrilege of their aspirations.[20] Belyj could only think of this betrayal as "counter-revolutionary".[21]

Blok was capable of responding to the barbs of the Moscow symbolists with his own critical evaluations of their works. In his article "O lirike" ("On Lyrical Verse", 1907) he took Belyj and Sergej Solov'ev to task by pointing out the deficiencies of the former as a literary critic, and of the latter as a poet. Much of this controversy seems to have arisen because of Blok's praise for poets like Georgij Chulkov and Sergej Gorodetskij whom Belyj and Sergej Solov'ev, from their bastion in Moscow, loathed for their affiliation with the Petersburg symbolists. Of Belyj, Blok writes: "The poet can be a good critic (like Valerij Brjusov) or a bad one (like Andrej Belyj, who reviles Sergej Gorodetskij and praises Sergej Solov'ev to the heavens)".[22] After defending his associates, Blok then turns to the subject of Sergej Solov'ev's recently published book of poems *Tsvety i ladan* (*Flowers and Incense*, Moscow, 1907) upon which he pronounces the critic's death sentence—he does not consider it poetry at all. Indeed, it would

---

[18] Ibid., 345.
[19] Ibid., 346.
[20] See Belyj, "Vospominanija o A. A. Bloke" in *Epopeja*, 1922, No. 3, 251.
[21] Ibid., 275.
[22] A. Blok, "O lirike" in *Sobranie sochinenij* (Moscow, 1960-65), V, 134-135. This article first appeared in *Zolotoe runo*, 1907, No. 6.

serve better as a poet's manual with categories arranged to illustrate successful and unsuccessful images, good and bad rhymes. The only poem which he singles out as possessing some modicum of merit is significantly entitled "The Holy Maiden and Bernard".[23]

Naturally, both Belyj and Sergej Solov'ev were angry. While Belyj expressed his discontent in a letter to Blok, Sergej Solov'ev responded the following year with an altogether acrimonious article in his *Crurifragium* (Moscow, 1908) which was entitled: "Mister Blok on Farmers, Longbearded Arians, Beer Fumes, Me and Much Else". Like Belyj, he too has obviously never forgiven Blok for his betrayal of the Divine Feminine and their original Solov'evian Sophiology:

> The bankruptcy of Blok in the role of mystical prophet, knight of the Madonna, has recently been made apparent. No more successfully does he play the role of elemental genius. However negative the stance we may have assumed concerning the pathos of elementalism, we cannot bow before such titans of elementalism as Michaelangelo, Emile Zola, Lev Tolstoj. But what does Mr. Blok have in common with elemental titanism while he is transplanting to Russian soil the sickly, consumptive flowers of western decadence, the creator of incorporeal and bloodless spectres in the style of Maurice Denis and Maeterlinck?[24]

Writing to his mother on April 2, 1908, Blok expresses his disgust not only with Belyj's *Goblet of Storms*, but with Sergej Solov'ev's article as well: "The Moscow snideness annoys me; they are bothersome and tasteless, like 'Indian roosters'. I walk around and spit as though a bedbug had dropped into my mouth."[25]

Blok's "sacrilege" and "betrayal" did not stem from any wilful malevolence on his part. As the events surrounding the Shakhmatovo disagreement reveal, his cardinal sin was his taciturn character, his weakness of will and readiness to be coerced by others who sought to use him for their own ends. His association with the "mystical anarchists" seems to have arisen in much the same fashion as his membership in the Solov'evian Circle. It was "assumed" by the others that he was one of them on the basis of what they read into his vague and nebulous verses. Blok wrote Belyj early in 1906 about the circumstances surrounding the origin of his play "The Puppet Show". Apparently from the very beginning of his association with Chulkov and Ivanov, he felt uneasy as he indicates here after a meeting with the members of *Torches* at which he agreed, at their request, to write a play based on his poem "Balaganchik" ("The Puppet Show", 1905):

> Already I feel that they want to cut something out of me with a scalpel. All of this you know much better than I because I am writing to you in

---

[23] *Ibid.*, 156.
[24] S. M. Solov'ev, *Crurifragium* (Moscow, 1908), 162.
[25] A. Blok, *Sobranie sochinenij*, VIII, 237.

order to unload my soul. The most terrible thing for me (the reason I am suffering) is that I do not know how to be independent. Already I have given all my acquaintances an innumerable number of points in advance and they have the right to think that I belong with all my soul to mystical anarchism, I do not know how to rectify this and do not know how to express myself, especially in public.[26]

But while this lack of independence may be a personal fault, there is an even worse disease that Blok believes he shares with his contemporaries. This malady is "irony". In what is certainly one of the most significant and yet generally ignored documents of Russian symbolism, Blok treats the malaise of his generation, particularly evident after 1905. This short article, "Ironija" ("Irony", 1908), is the key to understanding not only the undercurrents of Blok's work, but Belyj's as well. The father of this transcendental irony is none other than Vladimir Solov'ev himself. One has but to recall the ambiguous admixture of farce and solemnity in the philosopher's "Three Meetings" and "A Short Tale of the Antichrist", or recollect, as Blok does, the two lines from Solov'ev's "Posvjashchenie k neizdannoj komedii" ("Dedication to an Unpublished Comedy", 1880): "Out of ringing laughter and choked weeping/ The harmony of the universe is created." The symptoms of the disease are as follows:

> The most lively, the most sensitive children of our century are infected with a disease that is unknown to physicians of the body or spirit. This disease is akin to maladies of the soul and can be called "irony". Its manifestations are fits of enervating laughter which begin with a devilishly taunting, provocative smile and end up in vehemence and sacrilege.[27]

This disease provokes the will to self-destruction, outbursts of profligacy and depravity, the desire to plunge the mind into an inebriated lethargy where all boundaries between good and evil are erased and all value judgements suspended:

> In the face of accursed irony, everything remains undifferentiated for them: good and evil, the clear sky and a stinking pit, Dante's Beatrice and Sologub's "Nedotykomka". Everything is confused as though in a tavern and in the gloom. The truth of wine, "in vino veritas", is revealed to the world, all is one, the one is the world; I am drunk, ergo, I so desire, I "accept" the world in its entirety, I shall fall on my knees before the "Nedotykomka", I shall seduce Beatrice; sprawling in a ditch I shall imagine that I am sailing through the heavens; if I so wish, I shall "not accept" the world: I shall prove that Beatrice and the "Nedotykomka" are one and the same. Whatever I feel like, for I am drunk. And what can one expect of a drunken man? Drunk with irony, with laughter, as though with vodka ... [28]

[26] See Blok's letter to Belyj on 3 January (O.S.) 1906, in *Perepiska...*, 167.
[27] A. Blok, "Ironija" in *Sobranie sochinenij*, V, 345.
[28] Ibid., 346.

The origin of the malaise of his generation he traces, as did Vladimir Solov'ev and Dmitrij Merezhkovskij before him, to the "terrifying nineteenth century, the Russian nineteenth century, in particular."[29] The mechanism, positivism and economic materialism of the preceding century have prepared the catastrophe for the twentieth. Its spirit-crushing materialism "has buried the voice of man in the rumbling of machines: a metallic century when the 'iron box'—the railway train—has overtaken the 'uncatchable troyka' in which Gogol' personified all of Russia..."[30]

Blok is somewhat vague about the cure for this disease, also termed the "disease of individualism" which he elsewhere considers to be one of the trademarks of decadence par excellence.[31] The general treatment for recovery he posits in the formula of "self-denial", the genuine discovery of the true self through a denial of a person's individual ego. It will be recalled that Vladimir Solov'ev, in his article "The Meaning of Love", also considered self-denial, the suppression of the individual ego, as the starting-point on the road to universal syzygy in human love. Moreover, the question of the human ego, the formation and development of the individual "I" together with all the ancillary considerations of "immediate experience", the sources of cognition *a priori* and *post priori* in the light of the then-burgeoning sciences of psychology, physiology, etc., were shaping many theories of symbolism, particularly as propounded by Andrej Belyj. Though in the case of Belyj these theories were made hopelessly incoherent by his heterogeneous jumbling of terminology—the typical Belyjian exaggerated overstatement—they were equally obscure in the typical understatement of Blok.

Although Blok never became involved in the ponderous theorizings of his symbolist colleagues, he did formulate those general principles which appeared to guide his own conception of art and artist. In his article "On Lyrical Verse", he proclaims his elementary aesthetic credo. Essentially, he states a claim for the freedom of poetry and the poet from all preconceived ideas. Art and the artist must be free of all "schools" and all "influences". Making an indirect reference to Belyj's earlier article "Lug zelenyj" ("The Green Meadow") in which he demanded the involvement of Russian literature in a sociocultural context, and his own verses in the collection entitled "The City" with its unsavory background of taverns and brothels, Blok seeks to liberate art from all constraint: "The poet is completely free in his creativity and no one has the right to demand of him that green

---

[29] *Ibid.*, 347.
[30] *Ibid.*, 347.
[31] The correspondence between Belyj and Blok after 1905 is particularly riven with this motif of the "disease of individualism".

meadows should be more pleasing to him than public houses."[32] Only too aware of how his personal life and his poetry had often been confused in the minds of his critics, Blok states his first law as the division between poetry and the poet; the poet's life should not be confused with his poetry: "*Lyrical verse is lyrical verse and the poet is poet*".[33] Mindful of the wrangling among the various schools of Russian symbolism and the bitterness arising out of the misconceptions concerning his associations with various of them, he expresses his second law which denies the necessity for a homogeneous and single movement in art, something Belyj, among others, had been demanding: "... poets are interesting in how they differ from one another and not in how they are similar."[34] The poet must be in a position to exercise complete freedom and this is probably the most important slogan for Blok's pragmatic view of art:

> *I so desire it.* If the poet loses this slogan and replaces it with any other,—he will cease to be a poet. This slogan—his malediction—is chaste and radiant. All his freedom and all his enslavement is in this slogan: it is his freedom of will, but at the same time in it is his imprisonment within the walls of the world, the "pale-blue prison". Lyric poetry is the "ego", the macrocosm, the entire world of the lyrical poet lies in his powers of reception. This is the enchanted, the magical, circle. The lyricist is buried alive in a luxurious grave where all the essentials, food, drink and protection, are with him. Against the walls of this grave, against the green earth and the pale-blue vault of the heavens he beats as though against an element that is foreign to him. The macrocosm is alien to him. But abundant and splendid is his reception of the macrocosm. In imprisonment is enslavement. In splendour is freedom.[35]

This thirst for the totality of experience and the absolute freedom of the poet became an obsession with Blok. As though in reaction to the unbearably exalted and idealistic partisanship of the earlier Sophiology, Blok turns to its opposite in a wanton degeneracy, hearkening not to the voice of the Beautiful Lady, but to the elemental chaos he senses as Russia's darker aspect:

> No, I embark upon my path, summoned by no one
> And may the earth be light unto me!
> I shall listen to the voice of drunken Russia,
> And rest beneath the roof of the tavern.
> ("Osenjaja volja", 1905)

Blok's second book of verse, *Nechajannaja radost'* (*Unexpected Joy*, 1904-1908), signalled for many the parting of ways between poet and Beautiful Lady. Foremost among those who believed they were

---

[32] A. Blok, "O lirike" in *Sobranie sochinenij*, V, 135.
[33] *Ibid.*, 134.
[34] *Ibid.*, 135.
[35] *Ibid.*, 133-134.

witnessing her demonization, the triumph of the demonic feminine, was Belyj: "From the first volume to the second is described the drama of Sophia's descent, Her transformation into Achmaoth, Her reincarnation in the decay of affliction..."[36] In the introductory poem to the second volume, Blok himself pays homage to her memory as she disappears, apparently irrevocably, into the depths of Russia:

> Thou has departed into the fields without return.
> Hallowed be Thy Name!
> Once again the red spears of the sunset
> Have reached out their points to me.
>
> Alone to Thy golden reed
> On a gloomy day I shall press my lips.
> When all the prayers have died away,
> Oppressed I shall fall asleep in the field.
>
> Thou shallt pass by in the golden porphyry—
> I can no longer open my eyes.
> Let me rest in this dreamlike world,
> And kiss the path illuminated with light.
>
> Oh, wrench out this rusty soul!
> Give me rest with Thy Saints,
> Thou Who Hold the land and the sea
> Motionlessly in Thy tender Hand!
> ("Ty v polja otoshla bez vozvrata...", 1905)

From the landscape of churches and dreamlike rustic atmospheres, Blok leads us into the primeval world of swamps and marshes in the first cycle of the second volume entitled "Puzyri zemli" ("Earth Bubbles"). Against this eerily pulsating background, demons, imps, witches and magicians appear and disappear in a mood of expectation and suppressed movement. Belyj was greatly disturbed by the sudden appearance of this swamp motif with its "chertenjatki" ("imps") and "bolotnye popiki" ("swamp priestlings"). He was particularly offended by the following verses, which he interpreted as a direct parody of the Solov'evian Circle:

> And here we sit, fools—
> The sprites and sickness of the swamp.
> Our dunce caps turn green
> Sitting front to back.
> ("Bolotnye chertenjatki", 1905)

However, premonitions of the Beautiful Lady have not completely disappeared and even in the midst of the bogs and swamps the poet still sings her praises:

---

[36] A. Belyj, "Vospominanija o A. A. Bloke" in *Epopeja*, 1922, No. 3, 234.

> Oh, Mistress of the days! with Your crimson band
> You have encircled the pale azure vault!
> I know, I recognize the caress of my Friend—
> The antiquity of the illuminated swamps.
> ("Belyj kon' chut' stupaet...", 1905)

In a lengthy poem, "Nochnaja Fialka" ("The Night Violet", 1906) which belongs with "Earth Bubbles" in a kinship of atmosphere and landscape, Blok records a dream sequence he actually experienced. Standing at the crossroads of his two worlds of inspiration, the divine and the demonic, he discovers himself, in fact, beyond the pale of time "... in the hour of oblivion of evil and good", in a landscape "... where the sky, ceasing to conceal/ The actions and thoughts of my fellows,/ Has fallen into the swamp ..." In this "waking-dream" Blok describes the events which befell him during his nocturnal journey in this forbidding yet fascinating landscape wherein "One can see the mauve-green/ Passive and chaste flower/ That is called the Night Violet." He discovers a hut and inside sits an "ugly girl with an unprepossessing face." He cannot recall the colour of her hair, her age or features, only that she is spinning passively. However he does recall the heady odour of the swamp and the fragrance of the blossoming Night Violet. In the dream he is a miserable wanderer, a habitué of all-night restaurants, who has turned up unexpectedly at this evening celebration without "wedding dress". Kings are gathered here and he has a vague feeling of having once moved in their circle and drunk from their cups, but now they seem not to recognize him, just as all his other acquaintances gathered there do not. In the very darkest corner, all alone, sits an ageless and unchanging man. He has been sitting over the same mug of beer, thinking the same thought for many ages. He pays no attention to Blok, but contemplating him further the poet suddenly comprehends his significance:

> Only then I understood, silently peering
> Into the depth of his dim eyes,
> That I too, like him, am fated
> To sit here—at the undrained mug
> In the darkest corner of all.
> I too am fated to contemplate the same thought,
> I too am to cross my arms,
> Likewise to direct my dim eyes
> Into the distant corner of the hut,
> Where sits beneath the flickering light
> Behind the slumbering royal pair,
> Behind the sleeping body guard,
> Behind the endless spinning—
> The princess of a forgotten land,
> Who is called the Night Violet.

Blok, his double, the kings and attendants, all sit in frozen timelessness, bewitched by the princess at her silent spinning:

> With sweet sleep she has befogged us,
> Inebriated us with the swamp's philtre,
> Encircled us with a nocturnal fairy tale,
> While she herself blooms over and over,
> And the Violet breathes of swamps
> And the soundless spinning wheel revolves
> And she spins and spins and spins.

With no sense of time, whether of moments or ages, Blok slumbers and grieves, concealing his one thought as he gazes at the illuminated horizon. But then faint sounds reach his ears, bearing premonitions of something unexpected:

> I hear, I hear through a dream
> Pealings beyond the walls,
> The distant sound of splashing
> As though of a distant surf,
> As though of a voice from a new homeland,
> As though of the cry of sea-gulls,
> Or the moanings of muted sirens
> Or the playful wind speeding
> Ships from a cheerful land.
> And unexpectedly Joy approaches,
> And the distant foam tosses,
> Far off the fires burst into bud.

With this the company seems shaken, then crumbles and disappears, whereupon Blok finds himself transported back into the swamp where the Night Violet blossoms over the marshes. The dream over, he synthesizes its phantastic details:

> But ages have passed
> And I have contemplated the thought of the ages.
> I am at the very rim of the earth,
> Solitary and wise, like children.
> The fading heaven is likewise silent,
> The same oppressive world greeted me,
> But the Night Violet is flowering
> And its lilac flower grew bright.
> And in the green caressing gloom
> I hear the rolling movement of waves,
> And the approach of enormous ships
> Like tidings of a new world.
> And the solemn distaff spins
> The life-like and momentary dream
> That unexpectedly Joy shall arrive
> And it will abide in perfection.

The dream-vision of the "ugly princess" is quite interesting and suggestive of many things. While certain aspects of this intensely symbolic poem will not yield easily to exegesis, it seems nonetheless that the major Sophiological moments are fairly clear. My feeling is that Blok has here transmuted his literary predicament into a dream-world. Belyj's symbolist "cadre", the company of kings and courtiers that Blok once belonged with, have staged a wedding banquet, but their Beautiful Lady is an "ugly princess" and their bridegroom reluctant—he has come without "wedding dress" so that the ceremony cannot take place. Perhaps this is a reference to his past obeisance before the Beautiful Lady and subsequent "desertion" of Her. His double or reflection is, of course, the man motionless over his beer, doubtless pondering the same unique thought of the Divine Feminine, the search for the Beautiful, which for Blok is synonymous with Love. What frees him, however, from the compulsion this "princess" exercises over the group are the sounds which herald the unexpected coming of Joy, the ultimate descent of the Divine Feminine, promised in the scent of the night violet. It seems as though Blok is here saying it is impossible for him as a poet to expedite the ultimate consummation of Beauty or Love that he feels is promised. Deliverance and transformation are not within his power, for the poet is simply the mirror and echo of all the influences radiating from Her. It would be wrong to think of Blok as having lost faith in the vision of the Divine Feminine. What he has lost faith in is the attempt of those like Belyj who sought to effect transformation. Perhaps this poem is his way of saying that all they have really succeeded in doing is to distort her beauty into ugliness.

While Belyj is involved in an active manipulation of apocalypse, Blok has submitted himself passively to an apocalypse beyond his control. Elsewhere, in his second book of verse, Blok reaffirms his faith in this "Unexpected Joy" which is allied again with the motif of ships arriving in the night, as in the seven poems of the verse-cycle "Eë pribytie" ("Her Arrival", 1904).

Whatever significance one may want to attach to this particular symbol, one must take into account the malevolent atmosphere of the swamp landscape and the fascinating, yet undeniably forbidding, aura of the mauve-green shade of the Night Violet, where "heaven... has fallen into the swamp". Belyj was extremely upset by this somewhat macabre symbolism and sensed an underlying demonism in the swamps, the Night Violet and the ugly maiden.[37] As we shall see, he retaliated in his novel *The Silver Dove*.

Although Blok continued to receive premonitions of the Divine Feminine after 1905, that archetype underwent an increasingly wilful metamorphosis into its demonic counterpart. It would be wrong to say that he befouled her memory or that he had given her up. Rather it is the awareness of his own fallen nature which seems driven by some fate beyond his control that takes him from church to tavern, from temple to brothel, following his own passion to move beyond good and evil:

[37] *Ibid.*, No. 2, 279ff.

> Conceived in the night, I was born in the night,
>   And I screamed when I saw
> How anguished my mother's groan,
>   How black the night's maw.
> ("Zachatyj v noch', ja v noch' rozhden", 1907)

His Ideal, however, remains the same as before. Blok's elementary metaphysic abides in "Enamourment":

> And to the summons she flew off into the aerial retreat
> Forever... O, Enamourment! Thou art more severe than Fate!
> More imperious than the ancient laws of our forbears!
> More sweet than the blast of the war-trumpet!
> ("Vljublennost' ", 1905)

In "City", the second verse-cycle of *Unexpected Joy*, Blok leads us out of the swamp of gestation to nocturnal city streets, back-alleys and taverns where the sacred icon-lamps of *Verses on the Beautiful Lady* have been replaced with the sinister electricity of a forbidding urban culture:

> In taverns, back-alleys and winding streets,
> In a waking electric dream,
> I sought without end those who were beautiful
> And deathlessly enamoured of rumour.
> ("V kabakakh, v pereulkakh, v izvivakh", 1904)

The sirens of factories pierce the air ominously as a new sub-culture appears in Blok's verse:

> A red house-porter splashes buckets
> Of drunken-crimson water,
> The fiery hips dance
> Of a prostitute in the square.
> ("Gorod v krasnye predely", 1904)

Nor does Blok hesitate to lead his reader into the Petersburg brothels with him as poems such as "Lazur'ju blednoj mesjats plyl..." ("The Moon Swam in a Pale Azure...") testify. These record nocturnal perambulations through the disembodied urban sights, sounds and smells with which he has consciously replaced the equivalent impressions of his former, more sublime, world:

> You peer into the eyes of bright sunsets
> While the city raises glimmering lights
> And in the back streets it smells of the sea,
> The factory whistles are singing.
>
> And in the unavoidable bustle
> The soul is bequeathed to mists...
> Here is a red cape, flying past,
> Here a woman's voice like a string.
>
> And your designs lack courage
> Like the folds of contemporary robes

> And women lower so often
> Their arrow-like eyelashes.
>
> Whom have you noticed in the slippery gloom?
> Whose windows glow through the murk?
> Here the restaurant, like a church, is bright,
> And the church is open, like the restaurant...
>
> To everlasting illusions
> The soul has rushed off in vain;
> And the looks of girls and restaurants
> Will fall dark—at the appointed hour.
> ("Ty smotrish' v ochi jasnym zorjam...", 1906)

Inebriated in *Verses on the Beautiful Lady* with incense and icon, with the communion wine of divine experience, in "City" he surrenders to the more conventional intoxication in which he drowns his disillusionment:

> I shall work at your side,
> Perhaps you will not remind me
> That I have seen the glass' bottom,
> Drowning my despair in wine.
> ("Kholodnyj den' ", 1906)

Rather than in cathedral services, Blok now awaits the appearance of his Beautiful Lady in the guise of the Stranger, amid the drunks and degenerates of his nocturnal haunts. The atmosphere is desperate and sinister, but it cannot dispel the mystery and magic of the Stranger who appears at the same hour every evening in the tavern where Blok sits. Although "Neznakomka" ("The Stranger") is Blok's best known poem, I quote it here in a plain prose translation in order to recall its atmosphere with all the attendant motifs of Blok's second meeting with this divine-demonic feminine:

> In the evenings above the restaurants
> The scorching air is frenzied and choked,
> And the corrupting spirit of spring
> Holds sway over drunken cries.
>
> In the distance, above the backstreet dust,
> Above the boredom of suburban houses,
> Faintly glistens gold a bakeshop's pretzel sign
> And a child's sobbing echoes aloud.
>
> And every evening, beyond the road barriers,
> Cocking their bowler hats,
> Among the canals there stroll with women
> The established wits.
>
> Above the lake the scrape of oar-locks,
> And a woman's shriek rings out,

And in the sky, accustomed to anything,
The disc grimaces senselessly.

And every evening a single friend
Is reflected in my glass
By the acrid and mysterious moisture,
Like me, hushed and deafened.

And at the neighbouring tables
Sleepy waiters loom up,
And drunks with eyes like rabbits
Shout "In vino veritas".

And every evening, at the designated hour
(Or do I only dream this?)
A girl's figure, enveloped in silks,
Moves by the steamy window.

And slowly, passing among the drunks,
Always without escorts and alone,
Breathing of fragrances and mists,
She sits by the window.

And her resilient silks
Waft of ancient beliefs,
And her hat with funereal feathers
And her slender hand in rings.

And chained by the strange proximity
I gaze behind the dark veil,
And I see an enchanted shore
And an enchanted horizon.

Mute secrets are trusted to me,
Someone's sun is in my care,
And all the recesses of my soul
Are suffused with the acrid wine.

And the drooping ostrich feathers
Sway within my brain,
And the bottomless blue eyes
Flower on a distant shore.

In my soul lies a treasure-vault,
And to me alone the key is trusted!
You are right, drunken monster!
I know: truth is in wine.
(1906)

For some the stranger is only a typically flamboyant prostitute; for others she is the symbol of the Divine Feminine degraded to a frequenter of taverns. Some find her an amalgam of all the intertwining aspects of the feminine archetype, both divine and demonic, that twist through Blok's fevered imagination. Above all, she is Blok's own inspiration; he alone appears to see her in the tavern; he alone, even in his fallen condition, holds the key to her mystery. This he announces at the end of the poem just as he formerly announced that he alone tended the icon-lamps of the Beautiful Lady.[38] The image of Ophelia, so significant for Blok's Beautiful Lady, is no less evident here in the aloof and sorrowful homeless Stranger.

Though she seems suspended between divine and demonic, Blok's feminine archetype, like Solov'ev's World Soul, can also swing completely into the abyss and assume the aspect of the Harlot:

> Revelry in a night tavern.
> Over the city a blue haze.
> Beneath the red sunset in the distance
> The Invisible Woman walks in the fields.
>
> She dances over the marshy swamps
> Surrounding the houses like a ring,
> Protractedly she calls and sings
> In a voice, in a familiar voice.
>
> Is it sweet for you to sigh of love
> Blind, mercenary creatures?
> Who has stained the sky in blood?
> Who has hung out the red lantern?
>
> And she howls like an abandoned dog,
> Miaouhs like a lascivious cat,
> Clusters of evening roses
> She flings to the whores through the window...
>
> And into the black haunt bursts
> A pack of revellers and drunks,
> And all are drawn in the gloom
> By a mob of crimson-cheeked prostitutes.
>
> In the shadow of a graveside lantern
> The rumbling grows still over the city...
> Against the red sunset band
> A soundless laughter sways...
>
> The evening sign is drunken
> Above the door opened into the shop...
> There has intruded upon the mad throng
> With a splashed cup of wine
> On a crimson beast—the Woman.
> ("Nevidimka", 1905)

Once loosed, the erotic passions can immerse the chaste in a swirling snowstorm in which the Stranger becomes "The northern daughter of tempests" and the "Snowy maiden."[39] In the third and

[38] See Blok's poem "Ja ikh khranil v pridele Ioanna..." (1900).
[39] See Blok's poem "Proch'" (8 January, 1907).

fourth cycles of the second book of verse, "Snezhnaja maska" ("Snowy Mask", 1907) and "Faina" (1906-8), Blok creates a tempestuous and phantasmagoric landscape of driving swirling snow that obliterates all the urban geography of "City". These two cycles were written primarily under the influence of his love affair with N. N. Volkhova, an actress he met during his close association with the Kommissarzhevskij Theatre. No doubt she assumed the earthly role of the Stranger just as Ljubov' Dimitrievna had formerly assumed that of the Beautiful Lady. The thirst for catharsis and catastrophe, together with the loosening of all erotic passions, is the major concern of these two cycles.

But in the first cycle Blok responds as well to the earlier demands of Andrej Belyj's and Sergej Solov'ev's knightly collective. He purposely uses motifs of the knight-errantry to describe his departure from among the followers of the Divine Sophia. Under the spell of passion's alluring daughter, Blok has lost his knightly accoutrements: "My sword of iron/ Has drowned in the silvery blizzard .../ Where is my sword? where is my sword!" ("Golosa", 1907). He becomes the "dark knight" in a fairy-tale world where vices and virtues are disguised behind masks, confounding the hapless poet who cannot separate dream from reality. In his romantic but ridiculous garb he is taunted by passion:

> And lo, the king passed by
> In his pointed, bobbing crown.
>
> The jester passed by in a winged cape
> With a round bell.
>
> Ladies with veils, with pages,
> Lurked in the rosy shadows.
>
> A knight with dark chains
> On his steel arms.
>
> Ah, knight, how well a long sword
> Would suit your walk.
>
> Beneath your vizor, oh knight,
> Is the tender gaze of wishful encounters!
>
> Alas, the cockscomb, oh knight,
> Has adorned your helm!
>
> Alas, speak, dear knight
> Why have you come hither?
>
> To our fairy-tales, dear knight,
> Bend your ear ...

> These roses, dear knight
>> A friend has given me.
>
> These roses, to me, oh knight,
>> A dear friend has borne...
>
> Alas, you are a fairy-tale yourself, oh knight!
>> You need no roses...
> ("Teni na stene", 1907)

Blok is obviously all too aware of the haplessness of chivalrous devotions to the Divine Feminine and parodies his own earlier worshipful attitudes.

Blok's female companion in "Snowy Mask" is undeniably sinister as the poet joins physical drunkenness with spiritual release in the passion of "Snezhnoe vino" ("Snowy Wine", 1906):

> Glistening again from a wine cup,
> You engendered fear in my heart
> With your innocent smile
> Amid serpent-heavy hair.
>
> Plunged in dark streams am I,
> And once again I inhale without loving,
> The forgotten dream of kisses,
> Of the snowy storms encircling you.
>
> And you laugh your wondrous laugh,
> You become a serpent in a golden cup,
> And over your sable fur
> Passes the pale-blue wind.
>
> And how, gazing into the life-like streams,
> Can I not see myself laurel-crowned?
> Not recall your kisses
> On a face thrown back?

Indeed, the theme of erotic passion completely displaces the earlier ideal passion throughout the second book, plunging into the depths of a frenzied sadism in poems like "Devushke" ("To a Girl", 1907) or a masochistic oblivion beyond the pale of good or evil:

> What means it to be passionless? What to be winged?
> Whip me and reproach me a hundred times
> That I might be for at least an instant accursed
> Together with you—in the fire of a nocturnal sunset!
> ("Zakljatie ognem i mrakom", 1907)

The wine of released passion has bespattered all of Blok's world in "Snowy mask". It is the potion that has released him from objective judgement and allows him to submit to his demonic double and aspire to self-destruction:

> And in what other monastery
> Am I fated to drag myself,
>> If the heart desires destruction,
>> Secretly begs to drink the dregs?
> ("Obrechennyj", 1907)

Other images carry this same desire for catastrophe and destruction: "The heart is given to the tempest... I myself approach your fire!/ Consume me in flames!... Pierce me/ Wingéd eyes/ With an icicle of snowy fire!". Once again Blok reiterates that he does not know the path to universal salvation. Those who sought leadership from the youth who lit the candles before the Beautiful Lady in the Johannite temple are rebuffed by a poet extinguishing those same lights:

> You shall say nothing, people,
> You shall not understand that my temple is dark.
> The breast's throbbing and sighs
> Are bared to red-rimmed eyes.
> ("Zakljatie ognem i mrakom", 1907)

Once again Blok's encounter with his feminine apparition takes place in the gaping néant of night, once again in the Solov'evian "pure possibility of night" that can spawn either demonic or divine. The poet longs for this supernatural time of release:

> Yes! the night is with us! And with a new power
> The daily night will embrace us
> So that in an anguishing passion
> The impotent day is extinguished—
> And for long hours above us
> Night rings and beats its wings...
> And once again it is evening...
> ("I ja provel bezumnyj god", 1907)

The poet's female companion in his soaring flight through the nocturnal tempest, his companion in drunkenness, is also the daughter of night driving him on to madness:

> I shall go mad, mad I shall be,
> In a wild frenzy I love the fact
> That you are all night and you are all darkness,
> And you are all—besotted.
> ("Zakljatie ognem i mrakom")

Apparently inspired by the exotic image of Cleopatra and a masked ball held once for the colleagues of the Kommissarzhevskij Theatre, as well as presumably his affair with N. N. Volkhova, Blok's demonized imagination creates a sinister but fascinating nocturnal bride whose ambivalent nature is defined by her "serpent-like" and "wingéd eyes". The serpent-motif in "Faina" is heavily exploited for its erotic and hypnotic qualities:

> ... I recognize
> In the flickering light of the backstreet
> My beautiful serpent.
> ....
> And the reddish murk of your eyes
> Conceals a serpent-like flicker
> And a night of stormy surrenders.
> ....
> And I meet you at the threshold
> With the frenzied wind in your serpent-like curls.

These eyes are the only regularly recurring physical characteristic one finds in "Snowy Mask" and "Faina" other than the reference here to the snake-like hair. In contrast to the mysterious and serenely azure eyes of the passive Beautiful Lady, these are unmistakably sinister in their erotic allurement:

> From her winged eyes
> Shines the gloom.
> ....
> Then burn and slumber the poppies
>   Of evil eyes.
> ....
> Gazing silently into me
> Is a dark-eyed woman.
> ....
> The wind languishes for you
> My dark-eyed one.
> ("Pesn' Fainy")

Exhausted from his tempestuous and erotic courtship of this seductive serpent-bride of the night, plunged into an impotent melancholy, the vision of the Divine Feminine, the "Snow Maiden", somehow still wavers before his eyes, still hovers in the background in the poet's remote landscape of salvation:

> And with a secret sorrow, with a tender sorrow,
> Like snow falling from a petal,
> The life-like name of the Snow Maiden
> Still slips from my tongue...
> ("Zakljatie ognem i mrakom")

Although inescapably in the grip of his own erotic passions and given completely to the allurement of evil, Blok nonetheless believes in some "second baptism" whereby even the fallen can be resurrected:

> And entering into the new world, I know
> That there too people and activity exist,
> That probably the path is open to paradise
> For all who travel the ways of evil.
> ("Vtoroe kreshchenie", 1907)

The ironic twist is, of course, that "salvation" had once been sought through submission to what were presumably the chaste ideals of the

Divine Feminine, whereas now deliverance consists of an almost Dostoevskijan "salvation through sinfulness", in complete surrender to the demonic feminine. Blok allowed for this very confusion of demonic and divine in his article "Irony", but to understand it completely an examination of his major dramatic works appears a prerequisite.

Chapter 2

FARCES AND FOOLS

Before turning to Blok's "lyrical dramas", attention should be drawn again to the atmosphere in which they were created. One should recall the symbolist farces (with their hero, Professor Lapan) that Belyj, Blok and Sergej Solov'ev indulged in, seemingly profaning their most fervent ideals.[1] These private jokes were by no means created in a vacuum. Indeed, they may well have been inspired by Vladimir Solov'ev's fondness for self-parody. However, one of Vladimir Solov'ev's specific "vices" was self-indulgence in farcical and heretical one-act dramas which he frequently composed for the amusement of his intimate friends. In these he seldom spared either himself or his ideals from an ironic and derisive mockery. Although only a few of the more incisive of these farces were published, and then not until after his death, they were doubtless familiar to Blok, Belyj and Sergej Solov'ev who had access to all his unpublished manuscripts in the keeping of Mikhail Sergeevich Solov'ev. It is worth summarizing one of the more sacriligious of these dramas that appeared in print only in 1922.[2]

The play is entitled "Al' sim" which is the name of its poet-hero. It is remarkable for its desecration of the feminine ideal, its vulgarization of the love relationship into a parody of syzygy as hermaphroditism, and certainly serves to confirm the startingly eccentric nature of Solov'ev. In this play the devil concludes an agreement with a professor who finds himself in financial straits. The professor has just sold his house, which is worth 57,500 roubles, for a fictitious price of 25,000 roubles in order to escape taxes. His buyer, who knows of the fraud, at first agrees to pay the under-the-table sum of 57,500, but after the papers are signed, refuses to pay anything above the 25,000 roubles officially entered in the contract. Due to this financial turn-about, the professor now finds himself in an exaggeratedly presented metaphysical despair, with his former comfortably bourgeois mode of life completely upset. Hereupon, the devil displays his usual

[1] See pp. 114-15.
[2] *Shutochnye p'esy Vladimira Solov'eva*, ed. S. M. Solov'ev (Moscow, 1922).

excellent sense of timing and proposes a deal. Although the devil claims that he cannot simply give the professor any money, the professor could, with his aid, employ his "passionate emotions" to gain the vast wealth of the rich mistress of the house in which they now find themselves, namely the *bearded* Eleonora. The devil allays the professor's misgivings by convincing him that the beard is simply a style accepted locally there in Trapezundia and that Eleonora will shave once they return to Moscow. On reconsideration, the professor finds this impending affair rather piquant; it appeals to his bizarre, if not perverted tastes:

> Actually, you know, from the very tenderest age I have loved only masculine women—feminine women were always rather distasteful to me. The senseless difference between woman and man dismays me to the depths of my soul. I believe that all the disorders in the world are a result of this. My favourite heroine in world history became the virgin-maiden of Orléans after the most recent historico-medical investigations showed that she was a . . . .[3]

At this point he is conveniently interrupted by the devil before he finishes his scandalous remark.

The fact that the professor is already married seems to present no obstacle to his courtship of the bearded Eleonora. He has conceived a brilliant plan for doing away with his wife impunitively. By reducing her diet by one-quarter every day, she will soon perish of her own accord, simply the victim of "economics", which is, of course, not punishable by law. (No doubt Solov'ev is enjoying his dig at all the mechanistic and materialistic economic theories which were the result of French positivism and ignored the spiritual values he proposed for man!)

The second scene takes us to Moscow and the study of Al'sim, a young poet and the husband of Eleonora. He is rejoicing at his good fortune—all his dreams of marriage have come true, all that his soul desired has been realized. The world seems new and vibrant, full of fresh promise. At this point, a peasant intrudes to disturb his reverie and warns him to beware of women like his wife, who smoke a pipe and swill vodka. After Al'sim gets rid of this simpleton, he continues his poetic reminiscences of their journey from Trapezundia to Taganrog on a steamer. The poet recalls the captain's cryptic reply to his remark that the long autumn night had seemingly swept by like half an hour:

> "Don't you know about this, young man? Incidentally, this manifestation is rooted in the very nature of things. After all, we are on the sea, and it is quite natural that the flow of sea-waves, when linked to the flow of time, creates this acceleration; and of course this is only at

[3] *Ibid.*, 18.

night because in the daytime the sun's rays, expanding from the heat, paralyze the application of this law."[4]

The conflict of appearance and reality, of wakefulness and dream, obviously underlies this aside, but Al 'sim does not understand; he simply rejoices at the sight of his Eleonora with the thought: "She is in me, I in her—and this is no dream". Thirsty from his joy, he cries out for water and Satan in disguise appears to give it to him. When he drinks, however, he instantly changes; the devil has prepared a philtre to poison his mind as part of his agreement with the professor. Now Eleonora's beard upsets Al 'sim and he begins to condemn her vicious nature—revealed in her inclination to beat him once they are in Moscow. Eleonora is rapidly disenchanted with Al 'sim. She curses him and her own bad fortune and cannot even think what she once saw in him. When an argument arises between them, she beats him soundly. Having sown this discord with the aid of the devil, the professor now appears on the scene and wins Eleonora with compliments. As they kiss and hold hands, the professor adds the final insult by mocking the young poet for his lack of academic knowledge. Eleonora completely rejects Al'sim. In a quandary as to whether he should surrender to complete despair or revolt like a Titan, he decides to bide his time for revenge. The play ends with these lines:

> And thus she is a vision of perfection,
> My radiant paradise, my wondrous ideal.
> Al 'sim, Al 'sim, you thirsted only for bliss,
> But malevolent fate gave you suffering.[5]

Such farcical disillusionment, with an equally farcical transcendental ideal, could well have been the prototype for Blok's own dramas, particularly "The Puppet Show" and "The Stranger", not to mention "The Rose and the Cross" as well. Even if one rejects any direct connection, the parallel experience of the two poets is remarkable in itself.

Beginning in 1906 Blok's involvement with the theatre as a symbolist art form became quite intense and proved to be a further bone of contention between him and Belyj. Apparently Blok was initially attracted to Vjacheslav Ivanov's idea of drama as the ultimate expression of symbolism, a ritualistic enactment of the ultimate "mysterium" which would lead to theurgy.

In several articles, from 1907 and 1908, Blok outlined his basic conception of the theatre, or rather of aesthetics in relation to the theatre. "Tri voprosa" ("Three Questions", 1908) views the development of modern Russian art as the resolution of three questions. The

[4] Ibid., 26.
[5] Ibid., 28.

first was "how?" or the "question of forms" which might have been the principal slogan of the first modernists. The second was "what?" to write, or the "content" of the new art. But the final question was "why?" which could be expressed as the "duty" or "task" of art in relation to form and content. This is art's most difficult phase. What most people had once considered irrevocable enemies, namely "art" and "usefulness", were now confronting each other. Although Blok is willing to admit that art's ultimate destiny must be navigated on a course that lies between the useful and the beautiful, nonetheless the artist is as yet living in a transitional era when the beautiful is still useless and the useful still unbeautiful. The resolution of this basic antipathy lies in the future and the present can only be considered a preparation for it. The art form which he believes might possibly resolve the conflict is theatre, but the "abyss of contradictions" must still be plumbed, the agony of the present division must of necessity be experienced first, before the heights of art can be reached, before beauty is gained:

> The voice of duty draws us on to tragic catharsis. Perhaps on the heights of future tragedy the new soul will come to know the oneness of what is beautiful and proper, of beauty and benefit . . . Perhaps we are excited by the "theatre of the future" because through the noise from the collapse and destruction of the old and the contemporary theatre we hear somewhere in the nocturnal fields the incessant horn of an errant hero.[6]

In "O teatre" ("On the Theatre", 1908) Blok reiterates much the same hopes for the future based on a transitional apocalyptic role for the contemporary theatre. Here too he realizes that the ultimate goal is the reconciliation of art and duty, but the solution is not the destruction of the beautiful because "life is beauty":

> And in this struggle we are plagued with a new, perhaps the most profound, contradiction: the *anguish over beauty*. After all, life is beauty. As though "destroying" aesthetics, annihilating duality, were not to kill beauty as well—life, wholeness, strength, power. The whirlwind of emotions, thoughts, transports of inspiration, passion, impotence, despair: where is good and where is evil? At what can we level a straightforward "yes"? To whom can we shout our honest "no"?[7]

In other words, Blok is still unwilling to compromise himself by declaring for or against all values. Instead he wants to explore the entire contradictory spectrum of human emotions and actions.

In his preface to the collection *Liricheskie dramy* ("Lyrical Dramas", 1907), containing "The Puppet Show", "The Stranger" and

---

[6] A. Blok, "Tri voprosa" in *Sobranie sochinenij*, V, 240.
[7] A. Blok, "O teatre" in *Sobranie sochinenij*, V, 261.

"The King in the Square", Blok reiterates and expands these same ideas. Referring to the title of this collection, he emphasizes the word "lyrical" which, as he had already proclaimed in his article "On Lyrical Verse", belongs to that area of artistic creativity which does not teach about life. Rather it signifies the "immediate experiences of the soul". Moreover, these experiences tend to be "complicated and chaotic" and to best comprehend them one must be "somewhat in this manner". Especially in dealing with the contemporary soul, one is, according to Blok, on very loose footing since, as he implies, his generation is particularly given to complexity and chaos. Blok admits that there are bound to be those who find the lyric mode intolerable, especially Russian readers who usually seek in literature "directions on the road of life". They are apt to curse his dramas, but at the same time there are bound to be others like himself who are spellbound by the lyric experience.

The greatest task of lyricism is "to enrich the soul and complicate immediate experiences". However, Blok warns, it does not always sharpen these experiences, but is just as capable of dulling them by overloading the soul with formlessness:

> The ideal lyrical poet is a complicated instrument which simultaneously produces the most contradictory experiences. And all the complication of the contemporary soul, rich with the impressions of history and reality, undermined by doubts and contradictions, suffering protractedly and painfully when it suffers, dancing, juggling and sacrilegious when it rejoices—a soul which has forgotten the voluntary agonies of death and the voluntary joys of life—is it really possible to describe all of this confusion?[8]

Consequently, Blok envisages the three dramas, "The Puppet Show", "The Stranger" and "The King in the Square", as being "lyrical" within these terms:

> ... the three small dramas, which are offered for the reader's perusal, are *lyrical* dramas, that is, dramas in which the immediate experiences of the individual soul, the doubts, passions, failures, falls, are merely represented in a dramatic form. Here I draw no ideological, moral, or any other conclusions.[9]

Clearly Blok wishes to remove from himself the burden of reconciling the beautiful and the useful or necessary. This he does by shifting the onus to the "future theatre". Because he lives in a transitional time undergoing an apocalyptic catharsis to prepare the way for the syzygy of art and duty, he can only reflect this in his own dramas. Belyj was quick to attack Blok for his self-indulgence in the

---

[8] A. Blok, "Predislovie" [k sborniku *Liricheskie dramy*] in *Sobranie sochinenij*, IV, 433-434.
[9] *Ibid.*, IV, 434.

so-called symbolist theatre in Petersburg. He felt that the time was not yet ripe for the theurgical mysterium of a symbolist theatre, and that any attempt to employ drama as an art form towards the realization of an ultimate symbolism was premature. Apparently, Belyj was also convinced, like Blok and Ivanov, that drama represented the ultimate artistic form, the synthesis of the lyric and the epic which would herald the final consummation of their symbolist aspiration. However, as his other articles show, he believed the Petersburg group was merely being frivolous. No doubt he was contentious and pedantic in his rigid attitude towards these experiments because of his animosity towards the mystical anarchists. In fact, he considered Ljubov Dmitrievna largely responsible for leading Blok into the theatre and never forgave either of them for what he considered an ill-timed move.

In his preface to *Lyrical Dramas*, Blok offers the reader ample material for comprehending the basic mood behind the plays. He points out that the three are interconnected and that they all represent variations on a single theme: the search for a beautiful, radiant and unconstrained life which is incarnated for lyrical souls in the image of the Divine Feminine, but which they are unable to attain for one reason or another. For Pierrot in "The Puppet Show" this Eternal Feminine "... is *Columbine*, the radiant bride whom only the diseased and foolish imagination of Pierrot has been able to transform into the 'cardboard bride'".[10] In "The Stranger" the incarnation of the beautiful is "... the Stranger, a star which has fallen from the sky and has been incarnated only to disappear once again, leaving behind the Poet and Astrologer as fools".[11] Finally, in "The King in the Square" it is "... the *Architect's Daughter*, the beautiful lady lilting a biblical dream and perishing together with the Poet".[12] Blok particularly stresses the romantic "transcendental irony" of the three plays, which are clearly riven with parody.

The circumstances which generated "The Puppet Show" have already been mentioned: a gathering of the members of "Torches" in Petersburg in January 1906 asked for a play on the theme of Blok's poem of the same name. The first performance was directed by Meyerhold at the Kommissarzhevskij Theatre in December of 1906.

The play opens to find mystics of both sexes in stylish dress sitting at a table, waiting in deep concentration for the appearance of the Woman whom the chairman of the gathering calls Death. Also present on stage is Pierrot in the traditional costume of all Pierrots and he is beseeching his bride, Columbine, to appear. It is near

[10] Ibid., IV, 434.
[11] Ibid., IV, 434.
[12] Ibid., IV, 434.

midnight and hints of her approach, transmitted in vague rustlings, footsteps and sighs, excite the assembly. Suddenly she appears—"an unusually beautiful girl with a simple and gentle face of a dull whiteness. She is in white. The expression of her calm eyes is indifferent. Down her back hangs a braid [kosá]".[13] Pierrot is ecstatic with the recognition of the bride he has sought for so long. But the chairman of the mystics contradicts him, saying that she is the death they have all been awaiting. The irony of these opposing views is based on a pun on the word *kosá* which can mean either "braid" (as it does to Pierrot) or "scythe" (as it does to the mystics). The baffled Pierrot is distraught at the chairman's differing interpretation and expresses his confusion about this ambiguity:

> I am leaving. Either you are right and I am a luckless madman. Or you have gone mad and I am a lonely misunderstood romantic. Sweep me away, o tempest, through the streets! Oh, eternal terror! Eternal gloom![14]

The passive silent Columbine is about to follow Pierrot offstage when their path is blocked by the sudden appearance of a handsome youth in the dress of Harlequin who addresses her:

> I await you at the crossroads, beloved,
> In the grey shadows of winter's day!
> My tempest sings above you,
> Tinkling the bells for you![15]

With a single touch he renders Pierrot powerless and leads the unresisting and smiling Columbine away.

At this point the play is interrupted by the unexpected appearance of the author to protest the action which has just taken place:

> Gracious ladies and gentlemen! I beg your profound pardon, but I disclaim all responsibility! I am being made sport of! I wrote an entirely realistic play, the nature of which I consider it my duty to expand before you in a few words. It concerns the reciprocal love of two youthful souls! Their path is obstructed by a third figure, but the obstructions finally disappear and the lovers are united forever in lawful wedlock! I never arrayed my heroes in fools' costume! Without my knowledge they are enacting some kind of ancient legend! I do not recognize any legends whatsoever, nor myths, nor any other such vulgarities! Much less any allegorical play on words: it is indecent to call a woman's "braid" the scythe of death![16]

The author's tirade is interrupted and the play continues. Pierrot relates the events which followed Harlequin's seduction of Columbine as he sits in the midst of a costume ball with the dancing figures

[13] Ibid., IV, 12.
[14] Ibid., IV, 13.
[15] Ibid., IV, 14.
[16] Ibid., IV, 14.

of clowns, knights, ladies and other masked figures swirling about him:

> Between a pair of street-lamps,
> I stood listening to their voices.
> As they whispered, wrapped in cloaks,
> The darkness kissed their eyes.
>
> The silver tempest wove
> Their fingers a wedding ring
> And through the night I watched
> Her smile into his face.
> ....
> He had caught her in his nets,
> And, laughing, rang a bell,
> But as he bundled her up
> She tumbled on her face.
>
> Not even once did he insult her,
> But his lady-love fell in the snow:
> For she could not hold her balance,
> And I could not hold my laughter!
>
> To the dancing of icy needles
> Round my cardboard lady-love—
> He rang his bell and leapt,
> And after him I danced around the sleigh.
>
> And we sang in the sleepy street:
> "Oh, what a misfortune has befallen!"
> And up above my cardboard love
> A star gleamed green.
>
> All the night, through snow-white streets,
> We wandered—Harlequin and Pierrot...
> And he pressed against me tenderly
> And tickled my nose with a feather.
>
> And he whispered: "My brother, we are together,
> Inseparable for many a day...
> Let us mourn for the bride,
> For your cardboard bride!"[17]

The audience is then presented with three symbolic pairs of lovers who apparently explore the various aspects of the love relationship. The first is significantly arrayed: the man all in pale-blue; the woman all in rosy-pink. They imagine that they are sitting in a church and gazing up at the vaults. Doubtless they represent love in a pure and idealistic moment, yet not unthreatened by the sinister figure lurking behind the columns who temporarily disturbs their idyll:

[17] Ibid., IV, 15-16.

> She: My dear, you whisper—"bend this way"
> And I gaze at the cupola, face upturned.
>
> He: I gaze into fathomless heights—
> Where the vault has met the evening dusk.
>
> She: How ancient is the gilding there above.
> How the icons glitter there above.
>
> He: Our dreamy tale flows softly.
> You have chastely closed your eyes
>
> (A kiss)
>
> She: ... A dark figure stands by the column
> And winks a cunning eye!
> I fear you, beloved!
> Shelter me beneath your cloak!
>
> (Silence)
>
> He: See how gently glow the candles
> How the sunset has spread through the vault.
>
> She: Yes. Our meetings are sweet,
> Though I myself surrendered to you.[18]

They are then swept up in the dance of masked figures and replaced by the erotic passions, or demonic love, portrayed in the second pair of lovers:

> He: Let me go! Do not torment! Do not pursue!
> Do not foretell my dismal fate!
> Exultant in your triumph! Will you remove
> The mask? Will you withdraw into the night?
>
> She: Come after me! Catch up to me! I am
> More passionate and melancholy than your bride!
> Embrace me with your whole arms' strength!
> Drink to the dregs my shadowy cup!
>
> He: I am sworn in passionate love to another!
> But you dazzled me with your fiery eyes,
> You lured me into a cul de sac,
> You poisoned me with a deadly bane.
>
> She: I did not entice you—my cloak blew
> Like a whirlwind after me—my fiery friend!
> You yourself desired to penetrate
> My spellbound circle.[19]

---

[18] *Ibid.*, IV, 16.
[19] *Ibid.*, IV, 17.

So great is the power of this passionate and demonic seductress that he eventually capitulates and agrees to follow her wherever she wills.

The third pair of lovers appear to recall the medieval relationship of knight and lady in chivalrous love, but ironically, he sports a cardboard helmet and a wooden sword. The knight is trying to turn his lady's attention to the significance of the play in which they are participating, but the only response he elicits is the passive echo of his own words, perhaps suggesting the nature of a love that is purely formalized ritual without real content:

> He: Do you understand the play in which we fulfil not the final role?
>
> She: (Like a soft and distinct echo) Role.
>
> He: Do you know that the masks have made our meeting today wonrous?
>
> She: Wondrous.
>
> He: So you believe me? Oh, today you are more beautiful than ever.
>
> She: Ever.
>
> He: You know everything that was and will be. You understand the significance of this outlined circle.
>
> She: Circle.
>
> He: Oh how captivating your words are! Diviner of my soul! How much your words speak to my heart!
>
> She: Heart.[20]

The mood immediately returns to farce when the knight deals a series of blows to one of the clowns who has stuck out his tongue at him. Instead of blood, the clown "bleeds" cranberry juice. The action is then swept up in a torchlight procession and Harlequin appears in response to the chorus, addressing them all:

> Harlequin: Through dreamy snowy streets
> I dragged the fool with me!
> The World was revealed to the mutinous eye,
> Over my head sang the snowy wind!
> Oh how the young breast desired
> To breathe deep and enter the world!
> To enact in the lonely void
> My cheerful springtime feast!
> Here none dare comprehend
> That spring is asail on high
> Here none know how to love!

---

[20] Ibid., IV, 18.

> Here they live in gloomy dreams.
> Hail, world! Again you are with me!
> Your soul has long been close to me!
> I shall go breathe in your spring
> At your golden window.[21]

Upon concluding this speech, he leaps through the window, and the horizon there which turns out to be simply painted on paper so that he plunges through it and flies feet upward into nothingness. Through the tear in the paper horizon, the sky can be seen growing light as night gives way to morning. Against the backdrop of the first light of dawn stands Death, the pale face of a woman, in long white folds and a scythe on her shoulder. All the dancers and lovers either flee or cower on the stage. The profile of a pale-blue masquer becomes faintly etched on the morning sky. At its feet is a frightened, kneeling, rosy-pink masquer pressing its lips to the hands of the pale blue masquer. At this point Pierrot reappears from nowhere and slowly approaches Death with outstretched hands. The "scythe" fades in the morning light as he draws nearer, and *Her* features come to life until finally standing there, with a silent smile on her calm face, is Columbine. Here the author pops up gleefully to declare triumphantly that at last all obstacles have been removed with the disappearance of Harlequin and now the audience will witness the "joyful union of two lovers after a long separation." But at the very moment when he is about to join the hands of Pierrot and Columbine, the stage set flies upward and the masked figures scatter. When the author comes to his senses, he finds Columbine gone and Pierrot lying motionless at his feet. Distraught, he takes to his heels. Pierrot sits up and delivers the final monologue:

> Where have you brought me? How to guess?
> You have delivered me to an inconstant fate.
> Wretched Pierrot, enough of submission,
> Go and seek out a bride of your own.
>
> Oh, how bright is she who has disappeared.
> (My ringing companion has led her away).
> She fell (she was made out of cardboard).
> And I came to mock her.
>
> She lay face down and white.
> Oh, joyful was our dance!
> But she could stand no more.
> She was a cardboard bride.
>
> And now I stand with my face pale,
> But you sin to laugh at me.

[21] Ibid., IV, 19-20.

> What's to be done? She fell upon her face...
> I'm very sad. But are you entertained?[22]

The action concludes as Pierrot "thoughtfully takes a pipe from his pocket and begins to play a song about his pale face, his burdensome life and about his bride."[23]

Irony functions on a number of levels in "The Puppet Show". Its roots lie in misunderstanding and misinterpretation. Blok appears to have fragmented himself (that is, the contradictory aspects of his "contemporary lyrical soul") into Pierrot, Harlequin and the Author. As Pierrot he is the pathetic romantic entirely devoted to his idealized vision of the Divine Feminine, typical of the chaste reverential *Verses on the Beautiful Lady*. His "double" is incarnate in Harlequin, the dark seducer of the Beautiful Lady, reflecting the sinister passions of *Unexpected Joy*. As the author he protests that he is completely misunderstood, that it was simply his intention to portray the "reciprocal love of two young people" the path to whose union was at first blocked by a third figure who is subsequently removed in order that the union might be consummated. He disavows the play on the grounds that its entire conception has been perverted with allegory, symbolism, costume-dress and puns, no doubt reflecting Blok's own dismay at the manner in which his verses honouring the Beautiful Lady were manipulated and interpreted by Belyj and Sergej Solov'ev, as well as the mystical anarchists. This intrusion on the privacy of Blok's own vision is further parodied in the debate over the meaning of *kosa*. For the sentimental but pathetic Pierrot, this incarnation of the Divine Feminine in Columbine is an answer to his own personal anima-complex, his private search for syzygy beyond the pale of any metaphysic; whereas for the mystics, she is the visible sign of the End, the manifestation which they have, as a group, come to expect from their interpretations of mystical sources. As already mentioned, the dialogues of the three pairs of lovers are doubtless intended as an ironic survey of the nature of love in its entire spectrum from divine to demonic, or, perhaps more aptly, the contradictory experiences of Blok himself. Furthermore, the three episodes seem to reflect once again the poet's varying experience. The first love duet recalls the atmosphere of Blok's poems in *Verses on the Beautiful Lady* and in particular the church setting of the more prominent of these verses. The second duet, demonic and sinister, presages in particular the verses to follow in the collections of "Snowy Mask" and "Faina". Finally, the third duet, chivalrous and courtly, prompts comparison with the "knight-motif" of Vladimir Solov'ev's poetry which had been taken up by the Symbolists in their assessment of the

[22] *Ibid.*, IV, 21.
[23] *Ibid.*, IV, 21.

poet-philosopher.²⁴ This theme was especially developed by Blok and in fact served as the basis of one of his later plays "Roza i Krest" ("The Rose and the Cross", 1912). So pervasive is the irony of "The Puppet Show" that no one escapes censure, Blok least of all, inasmuch as he parodies the naive romanticism of Pierrot which turns Columbine into a "cardboard bride"; the modest ambitions of the Author whose well-intentioned creation grows and multiplies beyond his control; the absurd salon-style mystics in their foppish dress. Not even Columbine/Death herself escapes, although, in fact, she is degraded by the preconception and abuse of Pierrot, Harlequin and the mystics, rather than by her innate nature. As Blok points out in the preface to the plays, it is Pierrot's diseased imagination that alters Columbine.

"The Puppet Show", in spite of its kinship with Belyj's "Second Symphony", nonetheless completely disillusioned him more than any other work of Blok's. Again he charged "sacrilege" and "betrayal". So devastating did he find the irony, so unsubtle the satire on the theme of the Radiant Mistress, which had inspired his earlier relationship with Blok, that he never forgave either of the Bloks for this play. He felt that both of them were consciously denigrating all that he had once held sacred and were deliberately destroying his aspirations towards a new "collective":

> Then—the reading of "The Puppet Show" or the blow of a mighty hammer in my heart; it came early, when I was still in an inspired mood; after all, Ljubov' Dmitrievna had written: "*The Puppet Show* is good"; "good" was connected with the thought that the drama was a "mysterium" for staging in the Intimate Theatre which the Bloks, Ivanov and I had once desired; here I had envisaged important work together; this was the affirmation of the love of the collective whose life according to Vladimir Solov'ev consisted of syzygy.²⁵

Irony is in no less degree the inspiration of Blok's third play, "Neznakomka" ("The Stranger", 1907). Interestingly enough, it was originally entitled "Three Visions" and invites, for that reason alone, comparison with Solov'ev's poem "Three Meetings". Finished at the end of 1906, published in *The Scales* in 1907 (Nos. 5-7), the play was not performed until 1913 because of censorship. One of the original comments of the censor shows how obvious the confusion of divine and demonic in the feminine archetype had become in Blok's work: "This play represents such decadent murkiness that I am not about to analyse its content. The fact, however, judging by several hints, that the author has depicted the Mother of God in the person of the

---

²⁴ See Blok's article "Rytsar'-monakh", in *Sobranie sochinenij*, V, 446-455. The same motif doubtless helped to inspire Belyj's *Severnaja simfonija* (1-aja, geroicheskaja), (Moscow, 1903).

²⁵ A. Belyj, "Vospominanija o A. A. Bloke" in *Epopeja*, 1922, No. 3, 131.

"Stranger", should be recognized as sufficient reason for the prohibition of this play."[26]

The play opens with the "first vision" in a street tavern where there sits an assortment of typical customers from all social levels. Many of those present are drunk and boisterous. Snatches of typical tavern conversation can be heard. A seminary student is trying to convince some derisive and sceptical co-drinkers of his exalted love for some dancer whose performance he has just witnessed.[27] A man and woman enter. He has a vulger and abrupt manner and she is shallow and talks too much. He tells her to shut up and finish her drink. The Poet enters, pulls out his notebook in preparation to write, takes a drink and eulogizes on women:

> To see many women's faces. Hundreds of eyes, large and deep, blue, dark, light. Narrow like the eyes of a lynx. Wide-open, childlike. To love them. To desire them. There cannot be a man who does not love them. And you must love them ... And in the midst of this flame of eyes, in the midst of this whirlwind of eyes, suddenly there arises, as though flowering beneath the pale-blue snow—a single face: the uniquely beautiful face of the Stranger, under a thick, dark veil ... Then you see the feathers swaying on her hat ... Here is the slender hand, accentuated by a glove, holding her rustling dress ... Now she slowly passes by, passes by ...[28]

The Poet becomes drunker and drunker; the company grows more boisterous. Suddenly a tout announces he has a miniature to sell, depicting a woman in a tunic sitting on the earth and holding a sceptre. The Poet proclaims her the Mistress of the World who holds all in her power and, half-drunk, he buys the piece. Vulgar jokes about love and marriage amuse the tavern rabble as the drunken Poet sits in stupefied ecstasy over his cameo: "The eternal return. Once again She will embrace the earthly globe. And once again we are under her spell. Here She waves her flowering staff. Then she spins me in a circle ... And I turn in a circle with Her ... Under the pale-blue ... beneath the evening snow ..."[29] The scene concludes in the midst of drunken confusion, with the seminary student's avowals of love for the dancer, with the Poet beseeching *Her* to manifest *Herself*.

The second vision shifts to the outskirts of the city near a bridge over a large river. It is the same evening and snow flurries are falling. Standing on the bridge is an astrologer whose astral observations are temporarily disturbed by the sight of the Poet being dumped into a

---

[26] See A. Blok, *Sobranie sochinenij*, IV, 576.

[27] Compare this situation with Belyj's own ecstatic account of a dancer whose performance he witnessed during the 1905 Revolution and subsequently included in his ultra-mystical article "Lug zelenyj" which appeared in *Vesy*, 1905, No. 8, 5-12.

[28] Blok, "Neznakomka" in *Sobranie sochinenij*, IV, 76-77.

[29] Ibid., IV, 79.

snowdrift by a pair of watchmen. The Astrologer is entranced by the appearance of a new star in the heavens, brighter than all the others. He watches in fascination as the star streaks through the heavens, making straight for earth. After an instant a beautiful woman, all in black, with a wide-eyed look of wonderment, appears on the bridge. This Stranger still preserves something of her pale gleam of descent as the snow envelops her figure. She stands motionless on the bridge and waits until "Pale-Blue", a handsome man covered in snow and as mysterious as the Stranger Herself appears:

Pale Blue

Lurking in the gleam of winter's night,
Turn your face to me.
You who waft so softly of snow,
Grant to me your weightless snow.
(She turns her eyes to him)

Stranger

Eyes are the dying stars,
Bending from their path.
For you, my softly fluttering one,
I mourned up above.
(His pale-blue cloak is sprinkled with snowy stars).
....

Pale Blue

The centuries have flowed past like dreams.
Long have I awaited you on earth.

Stranger

The centuries have flowed past like instants.
Soared like a star through space.
....

Stranger

Can you speak to me earthly words?
Why are you all in pale-blue?

Pale Blue

Too long I have gazed in the sky:
Hence—my pale blue eyes and cloak.

Stranger

Who are you?

                          Pale Blue

A poet.

                          Stranger

                     Of what do you sing?

                          Pale Blue

Everything about you.

                          Stranger

                     Have you waited long?

                          Pale Blue

Many centuries.
. . . .

                          Stranger

The falling maiden-star
Desires earthly speeches.

                          Pale Blue

Only of mysteries know I the words.
My speeches are only solemn.[30]

The interchange between Pale Blue and the Stranger continues in this dream-like and symbolic fashion as she questions him on the nature of his passions:

                          Stranger

Do you see my handsome figure?

                          Pale Blue

Yes, you are blinding.

                          Stranger

(In Her voice an earthly passion is sprinkled)
Do you wish to embrace me?

                          Pale Blue

I dare not touch you.

[30] *Ibid.*, IV, 84-86.

Stranger

You may touch my lips
(The cloak of Pale Blue flutters, disappearing under the snow)

Stranger

Do you know passion?

Pale Blue

(softly)
My blood is silent.

Stranger

Do you know wine?

Pale Blue

The celestial drink is sweeter than wine.

Stranger

Do you love me?

(Pale Blue is silent)

Stranger

The blood is beginning to sing in me.

(Silence)

Stranger

My heart is filled with poison.
I am more comely than all your maidens,
I am more beautiful than all your ladies
I am more passionate than all your brides.

(Pale Blue trembles, all sprinkled with snow).

Stranger

How sweet it is on your earth![31]

Pale Blue disappears as the snow swirls around and the Stranger stands there alone, until she is suddenly accosted by a vulgar dandy whom she asks to kiss and embrace her. He is only too happy to seduce her. When asked what her name is she replies after some

[31] *Ibid.*, IV, 86-88.

hesitation that among the stars she bore the name of "Maria". They depart and the Astrologer reappears to bemoan the star he discovered and saw fall from the heavens, his celestial inspiration whom he calls by the exotic name "Maria":

> "Maria"—let her name be.
> In the yellow scrolls
> Will be inscribed
> By my solitary hand:
> "Maria has fallen, the star.
> No longer will she gaze into my eyes.
> The Astrologer remained alone."[32]

As he weeps at his loss, the Poet approaches him to enquire whether he has not seen a woman all in black, a Stranger. So deep is his grief that at first the Astrologer will not answer him. Finally he says that he did see such a Stranger and a "pale-blue gentleman", but now they have disappeared and the wind has swept away their tracks. They both commiserate with each other over their respective losses, not realizing that they are speaking of the same maiden-star, the same Stranger, each believing that he suffers the greater tragedy.

The third vision opens in a private home with a gathering of friends and acquaintances. The company is rather bourgeois and pretentious. An argument is taking place about the Italian dancer Serpantini (no doubt the subject of the seminary student's adulations). One prissy youth calls her shameless, while another is in ecstasy over her. The hostess expresses her consternation at the idea of interpreting music with dance, let alone dancing in the nude. In order to make the parallel perfect between the first vision in the tavern and the third vision in a home of "good taste", the vulgar gentleman with the shallow girl in a kerchief reappear. Once again he tells her to shut up. The irony is completed, however, by changing their appellations from "girl" and "man" (in the tavern scene) to "lady" and "gentleman" (in the house gathering) obviously in deference to their surroundings. The young dandy who accosted and presumably seduced the Stranger, enters and boastfully whispers his most recent conquest to a friend. Finally the Poet appears and is requested to recite his latest verses. He complies:

> Already the snow had scattered
> From the pavement.
> Baring themselves, the roofs glistened,
> When in the Church, in a dark niche,
> Her pearls glistened.
> And from the icon, in tender roses,
> Slowly She descended...[33]

---

[32] Ibid., IV, 90.
[33] Ibid., IV, 99.

Presumably these are the verses that inspired the censor to make the connection between the Mother of God and the Stranger who appeared in such an unsavory light with both Pale Blue and the dandy. And this point, the Poet's reading is interrupted by a ring at the door. Unannounced, Maria has turned up and throws the entire company into confusion. The dandy, fearing a scandal, hurriedly makes his excuses and disappears; the Poet is stunned and cannot recite further. While the rest turn their attention to the refreshments, he studies the Stranger, trying desperately to recall something. Just as he is about to remember, prompted absurdly by the irrelevant French word "brie" uttered by a fat guest indulging himself at the table, his concentration is destroyed by the sudden appearance of the Astrologer. The latter has just arrived from a meeting of the Astronomical Society where he reported on the fall of the star Maria. He and the Poet chat and both request the other's silence concerning the compromising incidents on the bridge that night. When questioned by the Astrologer concerning the results of his search for the mysterious woman, the Poet answers in the negative and stares hopelessly into the depths of the room where Maria had been lingering in the shadows by the window. When the hostess comes to summon them to the table, the two men have disappeared out the door. Maria is not to be seen, but in the window a bright star is gleaming through the blue-tinted falling snow.

Once again, as Blok stated in his preface to the collection *Lyrical Dramas*, this play reveals "the most contradictory experiences" of the lyrical poet who is mirroring the condition of the contemporary soul. Blok projects the entire spectrum of his own experience of the Divine Feminine in the various figures of the play and, as in the "Puppet Show", irony inhabits all levels of speculation on Her nature. In the first vision, speculation is hindered by the drunken haze that prevents the inspired but impotent Poet from discovering Her whereabouts. The incongruity of an ethereal love being voiced in the unlikely surroundings of a tavern is further reflected in the attempts of the drunken seminary student to convince his rude companions of the ideal love which the dancer has inspired in him. The laughter that meets this ideal image of love is echoed in the second vision by the dandy who accosts and seduces the mysterious Maria, misunderstanding her request to be passionately loved as the desire of a loose woman. The Astrologer has directed his gaze at the heavens for so long, at this distant, unattainable new star, that he is incapable of perceiving her on earth. If the tavern rabble and the dandy are shortsighted when confronted with a "divine love", then the Astrologer and Pale Blue are longsighted when in the proximity of an "earthly love". Here Blok presents again the chaste youth of *Verses on the Beautiful Lady* whose love is entirely ideal and pure, whose adulation of the Divine Femine is so rarified that he is incapable of responding to her desire to be loved as a woman. The nature of the "maiden-star", Maria, no doubt reveals something of Blok's mind concerning the permutations of the vision of the Divine Feminine. It is as if he were experimenting with the hypothesis: "What would happen if an incarnation of the Divine Feminine were to appear suddenly on earth and seek union with man?" The results have been amply illustrated in the responses of characters who represent all the contradictions of a single soul. Having explored all the possibilities from sterile chastity to vulgar degeneracy, Maria returns to her position in the heavens, the life-transforming syzygy she sought remains uneffected. The Poet, the Astrologer and Pale-Blue, after having summoned Her, are unable to unite with Her, to consummate their dream. Consequently, the reader is led to believe that it is not Maria or the Stranger who is lifeless and sterile, who has degenerated, but rather her would-be admirers who are impotent and fallen.

Blok's second lyrical drama, "Korol' na ploshchadi" ("King in the Square") was first written in the late summer and early fall of 1906, just before "The Stranger", but first appeared in *The Golden Fleece* in 1907 (No. 4). A staging at the Kommissarzhevskij Theatre was planned but never carried out, presumably for censorship reasons. Blok's constant revision of the play probably reflected his basic doubts about it and, indeed, it is definitely the weakest of the three. Perhaps its most interesting aspect is its heretical Sophiology which appears to have been inspired beyond a doubt by Vladimir Solov'ev, for the cosmology is identical with the philosopher's. Particularly the ship-motif of Blok's poem-cycle "Her Arrival" (1904) is picked up and utilized in "The King in the Square". The play opens in a large city square. A gigantic ancient king with grey-green curls sits motionless on his throne. It is just before dawn and the town is seized with excitment at the expected arrival of ships that are supposed to bring news of a momentous event. A Poet and an Architect appear. The Poet is upset and disillusioned, but nonetheless he has put all his faith in the ships' arrival. The Architect chides him for stirring up the populace with his personal delusions. Calling the Poet a madman, he insists that he should bow down before the people: "But they are all better than you. You are broken, you can breathe neither of the sea nor of the dust. At least they breathe the yellow, stinking dust—bow down before them on your knees!"[34] He further accuses the Poet of dreaming constantly about the end of the world, while other people are working, starving and suffering all around him. He then makes the significant remark that he can believe only in those capable of differentiating between good and evil, something the poet, presumably, is incapable of.

[34] Blok, "Korol' na ploshchadi", in *Sobranie sochinenij*, IV, 38.

A sinister jester appears who attempts to influence the action towards destruction. First he calls himself "Common Sense", then appears in priest's garb and finally claims the role of "Truth in red and gold nakedness". He tells the Poet he must choose one of two ways that are open to him. These courses of action are symbolized in two costumed figures that plead their cases before the Poet. The first is a birdlike man dressed in black who tells the Poet to join the party and overthrow the King. All the Poet has to do is to sing his verses of freedom and the crowd will follow. The second figure, also birdlike, but dressed in gold, seeks to convince the Poet to guard the "shrine" and support the King with his verses. The Poet follows the latter course.

The ships do not arrive that first night and rumour has it that the King has sent them away. Everyone believes that the ships bring salvation; it seems that if they do not arrive the following night, it will be too late and chaos will engulf the city. The crowd, however, is full of hope and rushes off to await the arrival. The Poet, apparently, once sought wisdom from the Architect, but now finds him too old and proud. When the Poet claims that he can no longer love him because the feeling is obviously not returned, the Architect responds that it was only his love that allowed the Poet to come to know him at all. The meaning of this statement becomes apparent at the end of the play. Finally the Architect advises the Poet not to follow the crowd:

> Remain here. Follow not the mob. Do not sing rebellious songs for it. I command you to remain with the night. And may that solitary one be saved who utters words of love on a night like this.[35]

The Architect's daughter appears to the Poet to tell him that she has come to him for the last time. In their dreamlike and symbolic language they speak of their former love, the Poet still affirming his, but the daughter saying that they must now part. As the darkness thickens and a storm rises over the sea, she advises him to forget the past when she saw him as a hero and he envisioned her a princess. Now she calls herself the beggar daughter of the crowd. At these words a wild mob surges into the square with the bird-like black figure urging them to throw the motionless King from his throne. When the Architect's daughter appears before them, however, they fall still. She approaches the silent and motionless King, offering her chaste body to revive his powers. Bowing at his feet, she exhorts the crowd to let him slumber because she has recognized the seal of the Father on him. The crowd stands in awe as the jester departs, bitter that the people will not listen to Common Sense and warning that

[35] Ibid., IV, 53.

they will miss him. The black bird-man tries to enflame the crowd by saying that they have been deceived, Common Sense has departed and they are without food and shelter, but the golden bird-man suddenly appears to announce the ships' arrival and the people's long-awaited salvation. The ecstatic poet begins to ascend the steps towards the Architect's daughter and the King, while she beckons him on by saying that once he reaches her, he will be able to pass on to the Father. The crowd, however, has listened to the inflammatory accusations and disregarded the golden man's announcement; they rush the steps of the throne. The entire platform, with the King on his throne, the Architect's daughter and the Poet, is swept away. All that remains of the King are fragments of a stone body and broken limbs and the people cry out in terror, "Where is the King?". As the Architect appears, a hush falls over the crowd. He then reveals the symbolism underlying the action and characters:

> I sent you my beloved son and you have killed him. I sent you another consoler—my daughter. And you did not spare her. I created power for you. I hewed the solid marble—and every day you admired the beauty of those ancient locks which emerged from beneath my chisel. You have shattered my creation and lo, your house stands empty! But tomorrow the world will be green as before and the sea will be just as calm!
>
> Various Despairing Voices
>
> But who will give us to eat? Who will return to us our husbands and children? Who will console our grief?
>
> The Architect
>
> You will be given to eat by Him Who causes the heavenly bodies to move, by Him Who waters the black earth with the rains, by Him Who gathers the clouds over the sea. You will be given to eat by the Father.[36]

The Sophiological context is transparent in "The King in the Square". The Architect is the mind behind the great universal design symbolized in the carved image of the King. His "daughter" is Sophia, the Wisdom of God, created as a source of inspiration to all mankind. Particular notice should be taken of the "architectural" imagery of *Proverbs* 8:22 ff. describing the relationship between God and Sophia, which inspired Solov'ev and here apparently inspires Blok's choice of symbols. The Poet is the "son", the natural complement to Sophia, in the basic formula for universal syzygy and the future harmony of the world. The Architect loves him as his son, imperfect though he is, but admonishes him for arousing the people with his visions of apocalypse. The position of the Poet is quite

---

[36] *Ibid.*, IV, 60.

ambivalent; as the Architect points out, he is lower than the people and should bow down before them, but at the same time his place is not with them, but with the night. This problem is further illustrated in his choice between serving the people with his verses or the "shrine" and the King. Reflected here, no doubt, are Blok's own misgivings in the aftermath of the 1905 Revolution. His sense of guilt over his non-civic and "undemocratic" verses clashes with his desire to remain aloof, to follow his private muse. The Architect's statement that he does not believe in people who cannot differentiate between good and evil appears to put the Poet below the people, while at the same time, the role of potential bridegroom to the Architect's daughter seems to elevate him above them, beyond the pale of civic duty. The détente between the Poet and his love which takes place in the play bears overtones of the disengagement between the Poet of *Verses on the Beautiful Lady* and his early visions. Afterwards, however, the near-consummation of this transformative syzygy as the ships arrive in the harbour and the Poet mounts towards the daughter and through her to the Father, seems to confirm all his premonitions and desires. The ambivalence of the whole play is summed up in its final action—the thwarting of union and the destruction of the great design by a people roused to rebellion.

Thus, in all three plays there is no positive hero who actually participates in the action. To be sure, there is an ideal, the Divine Feminine, but her role is invariably limited or distorted by the nature of her beholder. She is not responsible for transforming the world; he who receives the vision of her must act accordingly. As the symbol of the Beautiful, she serves to inspire and influence, but in the end is powerless to act. Unfortunately, as Blok himself pointed out, the foolish imagination of Pierrot transforms his bride into "cardboard", and the Poet loses the Stranger because of his drunkenness. However, this pattern is not as obvious in "The King in the Square". Blok was never really satisfied with this drama, so that even more than the preceding plays, it is the victim of numerous contradictions. For instance, the Architect's daughter turns from the Poet to the same people who are intent on destroying the King, claiming to have become their servant. She then supposedly infuses new life into this King with her own chaste self-sacrifice. Finally, it is the Poet, lower than the people, whom she beckons to herself, only for them both to be swept to their destruction by the raging mob. The only conclusion would seem to be that either the mob has destroyed all hope for attaining the Beautiful, or that the Daughter and the Poet are victims of their own illusions, as Blok claims in the preface to the plays. Despite this, the final speech of the Architect seems to vindicate them and accuse the crowd of destroying the great design, albeit this condemnation is tempered by the promise of succour and restoration by the Father.

In retrospect, it would appear that Blok here suspends himself between the courses outlined by the two bird-like men. While he cannot dedicate himself to the liberation of the people, he nonetheless sympathizes with their predicament and indirectly censures the "mysterium" created by the Poet and the Architect's daughter. At the same time, despite his scepticism, he cannot disassociate himself from the aspirations and sentiments of the Poet and the image of the Divine Feminine in the Architect's daughter. Once again, as in the other dramas, he is a victim of his own duality. The Architect's final grandiloquent speech has a hollow ring, as though Blok is paying lip service to something he finds difficult to believe in. However, possibly he here admits of a greater design including the possibility of specific values, but finds that he personally cannot deal with the question of duty and art, that he is the victim of the apocalyptic interregnum which precedes that "future theatre" where responsibility and beauty can be synthesized. This is his recognition of the historical path open to him, one which is essentially self-destructive.

Whether simply by coincidence of Blok's long desire to write an historically based operatic drama of XIII Century France, or by force of some on-going inner logic, "The Rose and the Cross" ("Roza i krest") begs inclusion in any discussion of symbolist knight-errantry. After torturous years of intense discussion of Solov'ev's Sophiology, with the frequent invocation of fairy-tales, knights, princesses, chivalrous duty and the like, it seems difficult not to catch the echoes of the "poor knight", Vladimir Solov'ev, in this play as well.

After having worked intensely on "The Rose and the Cross" throughout 1912, Blok completed the drama early in 1913. He originally conceived of his work as an opera rather than a drama, which caused a certain amount of confusion in his own mind, particularly in the depiction of the principal character, Bertran: "... at one time it seemed to me that a drama rather than an opera would come of this, but all the same an opera is emerging: I had been led astray by one of the *dramatis personae* who by his very character is more dramatic than musical; this is the hapless soul, Bertran."[37] In an attempt to be as historically accurate as possible, Blok did a great deal of research into the life and culture of XIII Century France, even supplying scholarly notes for his sources. He hoped that the opera-drama would be produced at the Moscow Art Theatre by Stanislavsky, but the latter was very equivocal about the work and apparently unwilling to stage it. A few years later, in 1915, Nemirovich-Danchenko invited Blok to submit it again to the Moscow Art Theatre. Due to the Revolution, and

[37] *Sobranie sochinenij*, VII, 394-5.

various other reasons, the work never did achieve public performance during Blok's lifetime, even though it was rehearsed for the stage on several occasions.

The play is set in early XIII Century France where the action alternates between sunny Languedoc in the south and misty, snowy Brittany in the north. The conflict between the Albigensians and the papal supporters provides the external framework to the sequence of events in the play. The principal character is the lowly knight Bertran who also bears the nickname of the Hapless Knight (Rytsar'-Neschast'e). While Bertran's nature and position can be extracted from the play, Blok wished to afford his readers a more complete background for this curious representative of knighthood. In an afterword entitled "Notes Written by Bertran Several Hours Before Death", Blok stressed the humble origins, the undistinguished career and the ultimate humiliation of Bertran:

> I, Bertran, am the son of a simple Toulouse weaver . . . My initiation into knighthood passed without notice and no lady awarded me either her scarf or belt, but I, myself, unbeknownst to others, chose for the lady of my heart the beautiful wife of my master—the Countess Izora.[38]

Bertran's duties included that of castle warden and he spent many sleepless nights on guard, particularly beneath the window of his beloved lady. During a tournament, Bertran suffered the worst humiliation for a knight—defeat in manly combat:

> . . . an unknown knight—a giant with a dolphin on his coat of arms —struck me from the saddle with a foul blow and placed his foot upon my breast. Burning with shame and wrath, I begged him to pierce my heart; but my mistress waved her handkerchief and I was spared. From that time no one stood aside for me, everyone began to laugh right to my face. Probably she too was laughing at me behind my back, but my love for her did not perish, only a feeling of bitterness was added to it, because I felt myself indebted to her for my life, miserable though it was . . .[39]

Bertran's master is the cruel, jealous and insensitive Count Archambaut who fears an uprising of the oppressed peasants and the attack of the Albigensian forces. Closer to home he suspects his young and neglected wife, Izora, a passionate Spaniard, of amorous designs and imprisons her in the Tower of the Inconsolable Widow. Apparently under the spell of some minstrel's mysterious song, she is oppressed by dreams and visions of an otherworldly and perfect love. She can only recall snatches of the song which has plunged her into melancholy and whose leitmotif is: "Joy-and-suffering . . ./ Is the heart's immutable law." In her restless dreams, Izora has a vision of an

[38] "Zapiski Bertrana, napisannye im za neskol'ko chasov do smerti," *ibid.*, IV, 521.
[39] *Ibid.*, IV, 521.

unknown knight who will not respond to her entreaties as to his identity. On his chest he carries the sign of a black rose and she calls him the "Wanderer". The same inscrutable yet haunting lines oppress Bertran who cannot fathom their meaning.

Concerned at the approach of his enemies, Count Archambaut despatches the lowly Bertran to gain intelligence of the whereabouts of the Count's allies, thus offering Bertran a chance to redeem something of his lost honour. Though Bertran does not approve of his master's cruel treatment of his subjects, he still feels it is his knightly duty to serve him faithfully. However, before he can set out on his mission, Izora, who has been locked in the tower, takes advantage of Bertran's dedication to her and charges him with discovering the whereabouts of the mysterious "Wanderer" of the black rose she has seen in her dreams. This Bertran agrees to as well, even though it seems futile.

In search of Izora's fabulous knight who is also the author of the song, Bertran travels to the misty, snow-covered shores of Brittany. There he chances upon the knight, Gaétan, whom he bests in combat only to discover that Gaétan is a feeble, but endearing, knight with no possessions to speak of and who boasts a most bizarre origin. They become fast friends and Gaétan relates to Bertran the story of his life:

> A fairy bore me off, infant I was,
> To her palace beneath a lake.
> And in misty captivity she raised me...
> ....
> A knight I did desire to be...
> But long the fairy held me in her arms,
> And covering me with her hair she wept...
> I know not what she divined
> As over her distaff she hunched...
> And then she said: "Go forth now
> Into a world of rain,
> Into a world of mist...
> For thence leads the threads of the Fates..."
> ....
> And further she said:
> "With the boundless ecstasy of the world
> Shall I fill thy heart full!
> Hearken to the songs of the ocean,
> Peer into the crimson sunsets.
> To people thou shallt be an aimless summons!
> Perhaps thou shallt move
> The heart of an earthly maiden,
> But thy own heart
> Will be moved by none...
> It remains within my power...
> A Wanderer in this world shallt thou be!

> Therein is thy design,
> Thy Joy-and-Suffering."⁴⁰

This dual role of inspiration and duty, is emblazoned on Gaétan in the symbol of the cross he must bear on his chest, a symbol of the "immutable law" of Joy-and-Suffering:

> Bertran
>
> Joy-and-Suffering!
> What does that mean?
>
> Gaétan
>
> "The heart's immutable law,"—
> So she said.
> And amid tears she repeated:
> "Thy future path is that of wandering!
> What lies before thee?
> Don thy powerful armour
> With the sign of the cross on thine breast!"
> My breast I did adorn with the cross
> And entered this misty world.⁴¹

Bertran now realizes that Gaétan is none other than the author of the mysterious song and the Wanderer of Izora's dreams. He persuades Gaétan to return to Languedoc with him to perform before the Countess.

The Hapless Knight, that is, Bertran, thus fulfills both his missions, for he brings good news to Archambaut of the proximity of his allies, and he has discovered the "Wanderer". As a special favour he requests Archambaut to release the pining Izora from the tower in time for the May celebrations. At the festivities Bertran brings Gaétan forth to sing his haunting melody before the assembled company and for the first time we hear the mysterious lines in their entirety:

> The hurricane's roar
> The ocean's song
> The snowy swirl.
>
> An eternity flashes past in an instant,
> We dream the dream of a blessed shore!
> In the dark clefts of night
> The spinning wheel hums and sings.
> The invisible spinner gazes into your eyes
> And spins our destinies one and all.
>
> At the frontier of fire the sunset
> Peers into eyes of the knights,

---

⁴⁰ "Roza i krest," *Sobranie sochinenij*, IV, 202-3.
⁴¹ Ibid., IV, 203-4.

And over fateful destiny
Burn the lights of starry nights.

The boundless ecstasy of the world
Is given to the trilling heart.
Upon a fateful yet aimless path
The roaring ocean does summon.

Surrender to the impossible dream,
What is decreed will come to pass.
The heart's immutable law—
Joy and Suffering are but one!

Thy path to come is one of Wandering.
The roaring ocean sings.
Joy, oh, Joy-and-Suffering—
The pain of unknown wounds!

Misfortune and loss are all about,
What lies before thee yet?
But set thy crude sail,
Don thy powerful armour,
With the cross thy chest adorned!

The hurricane's roar
The ocean's song,
The snowy swirl.

An eternity flashes past in an instant,
We dream the dream of a blessed shore![42]

Disillusioned that the singer of this tormenting melody is an old man and not the radiant knight of her passionate dreams, yet greatly moved by the song, Izora faints. On regaining her senses she seems purged of her former, otherworldly love and now turns her passionate attention to the handsome page, Aliscan, who has long been courting her.

At the conclusion of Gaétan's performance, Archambaut's castle is attacked by his enemies. However, Bertran removes entirely the stain of former dishonour by defeating the strongest knight and thus winning the day for Archambaut who continues, however, to belittle Bertran's efforts. Grievously wounded, yet ever faithful to his mistress, Izora, Bertran agrees to stand guard that night under the window while she and Aliscan make love in her chambers. In his death-agony, Bertran falls to the ground in the courtyard, the noise of his sword crashing to the stones warns the young lovers of the approach of the suspicious Count Archambaut and thus allows Aliscan to make good his escape. Just before his death Bertran plumbs the meaning of

---

[42] Ibid., IV, 232-3.

Gaétan's mysterious song that "Joy-and-Suffering—/ Is the heart's immutable law."

As in Blok's poetry and earlier dramas, the same contentious forces of reason and intuition, of earthly and unearthly love, rule the characters and animate the plot. Despite the serious attempt at historical accuracy in detail and atmosphere, Blok himself stressed on several occasions that the play's time and setting should assume a secondary importance to the inner truths of the work which obtain for all times and all places.

"The Rose and the Cross", like the earlier dramas "The Puppet-Show" and "The Stranger", appears to be once again a "riddle-play". In the two earlier dramas, the major characters were at odds in solving the question as to the symbolic identity and function of both Columbine and the Stranger. In "The Rose and the Cross", the riddle is not embodied in a person, but in the meaning of Gaétan's song, particularly the refrain: "The heart's immutable law—/ Joy and Suffering are one!" The two principal characters who must solve the riddle are Izora and Bertran. The haunting leitmotif drives the young and passionate Izora almost to distraction and for her it becomes synonymous with the handsome and mysterious knight of her reveries, the "Wanderer" who bears a black rose on his chest. In short, it is her desire for love's romantic consummation. She comes to this realization unconsciously when Gaétan does not coincide in appearance with the handsome knight of her dreams, yet with his song he does unite her in earthly love with the page Aliscan. Or as Blok expressed it very succinctly: "The seventeen-year-old Izora, daughter of a simple Spanish woman, having read too many novels, comprehended the song of Joy-and-Suffering in her own fashion: 'It is joy to love, and suffering not to know love.'"[43]

Nor can Bertran fathom the riddle of the song at first. According to Blok, he is too consumed with his own grief and humiliation to understand how joy can come of suffering.[44] His error derives, perhaps, from the fact that he attempts to understand the meaning of Joy-and-Suffering with his head, rather than his heart. Indeed, herein lies an important sense of the play as Blok indicates:

> "The Rose and the Cross" above all represents the drama of the person of Bertran. He is not the hero of the drama, but its Reason and Heart. The poor Reason wished to reconcile the Rose of beauty and immortality with the Cross of suffering. Reason sought reconciliation with the Heart, but the Heart alone discovered it. Bertran's consolation comes in Death.[45]

---

[43] [K postanovke v Khudozhestvennom teatre,] *Sobranie sochinenij*, IV, 528.
[44] *Ibid.*, IV, 528.
[45] [Interv'ju s A. Blokom o drame "Roza i krest"], *Sobranie sochinenij*, IV, 530.

In the light of Blok's own description, Bertran's mortal wound, while obviously grievous, is symbolic as well. Inside his tunic, next to his heart, was a black rose plucked by Izora. With this rose over his heart, yet unloved by Izora, Bertran had gallantly restored his honour by defeating the strongest of the opposing knights, but not before his opponent had pierced the rose and Bertran's heart as well. Thus, the meaning of love and duty, the rose and the cross, are united in the leitmotif of Joy-and-Suffering at Bertran's death. However, it was only with this mortal blow to his heart, that Bertran understood the riddle. It is difficult to mistake Blok's own sympathies here. How often he had struggled to comprehend with his mind, had been forced by the other Solov'evians to rationalize his intuitions into metaphysical statements and aesthetic positions! The disclosure of the riddle, of the mystery, had come to him, as it had to Bertran, only after a long and painful conflict between reason and intuition.

While Bertran accepts the idea of the Cross, with its inherent demands for suffering and duty, Izora rejects it outrightly, seeking only the joy and the fulfilment of love's desires which she intuits in the Rose. Thus, when she has a vision of her mysterious knight with a cross adorning his breast, this passionate lady attempts to efface the foreboding Cross with the symbol of the Rose:

> Izora
>
> You! You!—Are you some dream or not!
> Oh, Wanderer!—Where is thy rose?—
> On thine breast a cross does burn!..
> Oh, frighten me not with that stern cross!
> ....
> Take this rose!
> As black as my blood is she!—
> Do not leave! I shall go mad!—
> Closer, come closer to me!—
> Let me cover thy terrifying cross
> With this black rose![46]

The haunting and beautiful song which afflicts both Bertran and Izora, deserves, together with its author, Gaétan, special attention not only within the context of the play, but within the larger scheme of Blok's involvement in Sophiology. Blok, once again, offers insight:

> Here, in short, is the content and basic idea of the drama "The Rose and the Cross".
>
> There are songs wherein echoes a vague call to that which is desired and unknown. It is possible to forget entirely the words of these songs, one may recollect merely disconnected snatches of the words: but the

---

[46] "Roza i krest," IV, 221-2.

> melody itself will go on echoing in one's memory, summoning and oppressing with its summons.[47]

That oppressive and unrelenting summons to something "desired and unknown" is one which Blok himself knew all too well and responded to constantly throughout his poetry, sharing the same poignancy of experience with Vladimir Solov'ev. Of course, Vladimir Solov'ev, Andrej Belyj and Sergej Solov'ev chose not only to flesh out the vague contours of these mysterious summonses with the image of Sophia, but to clothe her in their own complicated metaphysics. For his part, Blok had also intuited a feminine presence in the inscrutable echoes, but resisted the rationalization of his muse into a coherent system. The "melody... echoing in one's memory", and not the words, was all that he required and felt at ease with.

The image of Gaétan, whom Blok called "... not a human being, but an apparition and a kind of pure summons, a singer, without knowing himself of what he sings..."[48] can likewise claim a special significance for Blok. He is a curious creation of Blok's because the motif of summonses and pure song, so long associated with Sophia, loses its "femininity" and now becomes attached to this spectral being. The nature of the summons is no less elusive, mysterious, or certainly open to interpretation than before. However, while the questions of love, otherworldly and earthly, of duty and wilfulness, of fate's inescapability, are as omnipresent in this play as in the previous ones, that overwhelming and familiar imminence of the divine or demonic feminine certainly is not. Moreover, one can hardly fail to catch something of Blok's reflection in Gaétan as well. Like Gaétan, Blok fancied that he too was "... a singer, without knowing himself of what he sings", but as he always protested to Belyj and Sergej Solov'ev, he could only catch the otherworldly melodies and not discern their meaning other than intuitively in his verse. Moreover, fate's impress, which Gaétan's fairy stepmother had emblazoned on his breast in the symbol of the cross, also rang true for Blok's own sentiments:

> ... Now go forth
> Into a world of rain,
> Into a world of mists...
> Thence leads the thread of the Fates.[49]

How often did Blok himself refer to his own desperate fate, feeling that his path to destruction, to wilful suffering, was somehow preordained!

---

[47] [K postanovke v Khudozhestvennom teatre], IV, 527.
[48] Ibid., IV, 527.
[49] "Roza i krest," IV, 202.

The poetic imagery of Britanny's "northern" landscape, with its snows, mists, echoes of distant shores, together with an atmosphere fraught with vague and otherworldly summonses, recreates those all-too-familiar leitmotifs shared by Vladimir Solov'ev, Alexandr Blok and the other early Solov'evians. To this typically Solov'evian syndrome Blok adds yet another familiar *topos*, namely, that of the fairy-tale or *skazka* whose literary "decent" can be traced back through Blok's own poetry to Belyj's *Northern Symphony* and Solov'ev's frequent references to his "fairy-mistress" and the "fairy-tale" of his fabulous visions of Sophia. The fairy-tale, with its mysterious and otherworldly atmosphere, with its unconditional or ideal time and space wherein beautiful maidens were rescued from dragons of both the legendary and apocalyptic variety, provided the young poets with a convenient allegorical framework for creating their own literary magic. The danger lay, however, in a rigid faith and stern interpretation of what, after all, was really only a "fairy-tale" of medieval knight-errantry and damsel-rescue and did not necessarily coincide with contemporary reality as Belyj often coerced it into doing. Not that a kind of truth did not reside in fairy-tales, as Blok reminds us through Bertran's words when the latter is despatched by Izora to find the "Wanderer" with the black rose: "This mission seemed to me to be a children's fairy-tale, but knowing that in children's fairy-tales there is greater truth than people think, I gave her my word to perish or to fulfil her mission..."[50]

However, irony, that ever-present and self-annihilating dilemma of Blok's work, not to mention Vladimir Solov'ev's and Belyj's, forces its way once again into this play. In her feverish imagination, Izora has envisioned her longed-for knight in the usual, legendary fashion. But Gaétan is anything but her knight in shining armour. Hence the disparity between the ideal and the real, so destructive, yet so typical of Russian symbolism. This confusion of legend and reality is best exemplified in a dialogue between Gaétan and Bertran, when Gaétan is requested to sing before Count Archambaut and Izora:

> Gaétan
> So then tomorrow
> I shall sing before the king?
>
> Bertran
> Before the Count
> You mean to say?

---

[50] "Zapiski Bertrana...," IV, 523.

Gaétan

> Then she is not the daughter
Of Grallon of old?

Bertran

> Those are all tales!
Not of a king is she the daughter
But of a simple seamstress of the Tolosana Martyrs.

Gaétan

> Of a simple seamstress!
Yet she did not destroy the old man?

Bertran

On the contrary, he wished her ill.
He locked her up in a lofty tower.

Gaétan

> I understand!
I must free the golden-haired maiden
From her captivity!

Bertran

> She is swarthy. And her locks
Are blacker than the night.

Gaétan

> But still
Her name is Morgana? Or is it not so?

Bertran

It makes no difference to you whom you shall
Free with your song. Believe me.[51]

In this interchange, Gaétan has confused a legendary tale, born of nocturnal Brittany's northern mists, with the sunny reality of southern Languedoc, and to pick up on the ironic ring of his unsuspecting words, *it was not so* that the legendary and the ideal must be made to accord with the real world. The song will be sung in any event and it will exert its magic on each person in its own fashion. Thus, Izora will turn her affections to her earthly lover, Aliscan, and Bertran will understand that his joy can only be achieved in fulfilling his preordained fate of selfless duty to his master and mistress.

While often troubled by certain aspects of the play, Blok never once doubted what he was frequently to refer to as the "truth" of the

---

[51] "Roza i krest," IV, 218-19.

play, namely, the meaning of Joy-and-Suffering which he ultimately came to understand with his heart rather than with his reason and which he signified in the emblematic conflict of the rose and the cross, of love and duty. The life-long and self-sacrificing service to a dubious or unattainable ideal—apotheosized in Vladimir Solov'ev, the "poor knight"—could not have been far from Blok's mind in this play. The image of Sophia or the Beautiful Lady may have faded or been obscured, yet the atmosphere and the motifs of knight-errantry seemed ever-appropriate for robing the basic concerns of "The Rose and the Cross." It was, after all, a language of Solov'evian conventions that Blok knew all too well and had practiced for so long.

Chapter 3

THE TRIUMPH OF THE DEMONIC FEMININE

The displacement of the Divine Feminine by the Demonic, the degeneration of the poet and his headlong flight to self-destruction, were concerns by no means exclusive to Blok between the Revolutions. Undoubtedly prompted by Blok's example, Belyj too set out to explore the sinister aspect of the feminine archetype and the poet's will to chaos.

In *The Silver Dove*,[1] the first part of his projected trilogy *East or West?*, Belyj provides his own history of the search for the Divine Feminine, reflecting the events and transitions within Russian symbolism. Ostensibly, as the title suggests, the trilogy was to deal with the old Slavophile question of East versus West within contemporary society and the course of Russia's history plotted between the two. *The Silver Dove* examines the "eastern course". Pjotr Dar'jal'skij, a young decadent poet, jaded by the effete intellectual society of Moscow, forsakes Westernized city life for Russia's pastoral depths. At first he seeks salvation from his past in the courtship of the chaste Katerina who is of good family and lives in the country, far from the coquettish circles of Moscow society. However, at a church service, Dar'jal'skij sees Matrjona for the first time and she immediately exerts a hypnotic power over him and arouses his desires:

> ... and suddenly in the far corner of the church there swirled a shawl, red like snow apples, over a red cotton basque. Some peasant woman was staring at him. He was about to say to himself, Oho! What a woman!, and then grunt and assume a dignified air so that having forgotten all else begin to bow to the Holy Virgin. But he neither grunted nor assumed a dignified air and did not even bow. A sweet but eerie flood of warmth spread through his chest and he was not even aware that he was growing pale, and pale as death he was barely able to remain on his feet. Her browless face which was covered with large pock marks stared at him in a terrible and greedy excitement.[2]

---

[1] *Serebrjanyj golub'* was serialized in *Vesy*, Nos. 3-12, 1909. The first separate edition appeared Moscow, 1910.

[2] Belyj, *Serebrjanyj golub'*, reprinted in the series *Slavische Propylaen*, vol. 38 (Munich, 1967), I, 19.

The source for Belyj's Matrjona can probably be found in Blok's poem "The Night Violet" which disturbed Belyj very much. The homely yet compelling aspect of the peasant girl at the spinning wheel seems to have provided the inspiration for the creation of the demonic Matrjona. Should there be any doubt on this point, the background of Dar'jal'skij's search is an exact parallel to the geography of swamp and mist in Blok's verse-cycle "Earth Bubbles" as well as in "Night Violet", both of which Belyj considered proof of his desertion of the path of brightness (*Verses on the Beautiful Lady*) for that of darkness (*Unexpected Joy*):

> Like a wanderer surrounded by a multitude of tree-trunks, bushes, forests and swamps which bewitch him with the icy breath of the mist... he seeks that forest path from which he has long since wandered. Like this wanderer, Dar'jal'skij had given to Katja the life, light and nobility of his soul, for she became the path of his life and now this path was no longer a path. In one day, in an hour, in a brief moment which kisses the soul, his life's path had become the path of mists... a day, a glance, a moment of the pock-marked peasant woman—and, lo, the light, path and nobility of his soul had turned into the forest, into the night and marsh, into the mire of the swamp.[3]

Dar'jal'skij tries to erase the demonic, erotic image of Matrjona from his mind in the church with invocations to his chaste Katerina, but her divine talisman is impotent before the all pervasive power of Matrjona:

> ...her red, smirking lips trembled slightly, as though drinking up his soul in long draughts; and he could not remember pressing his lips to the pure cross and the priest summoning him to the bread or what he replied to the priest; he only recalled that the pock-marked wench had claimed his soul. In vain he resisted, summoning in his soul the image of Katja: "My wonderful bride, my good bride!"—the beloved image, so it seemed, proved to be inscribed in chalk on a school blackboard: the evil teacher had erased it and now only emptiness turned up there.[4]

In a passage unmistakably inspired by Blok's *Unexpected Joy*, Dar'jal'skij loses his way in the swamps at night while returning from the church service on Katja's estate. His fevered mind is haunted by the feminine image in the form of the divine Katja, the demonic Matrjona, and his own succouring mother, who contend with each other for his consciousness.[5]

A silly misunderstanding between himself and Katerina's matriarchal aunt leads to his abandoning the estate and Katerina after a bout of drunkenness. Forsaking "civilized Russia", he plunges head-

[3] *Ibid.*, I, 129-130.
[4] *Ibid.*, I, 21.
[5] *Ibid.*, I, 130ff.

long into the mysteriously chthonic Russia of the East. He adopts peasant dress, dons a red shirt and places a wreath of oak-leaves on his head to symbolize his transformation. The architects of this conversion make up a religious sect called the Silver Doves, led by a sinister carpenter, Kudejarov, living with the buxom young pock-marked Matrjona. He has no child by her. The irony of the Christian symbolism becomes grotesque parody with the appearance of Dar'jal'skij. In order that the Silver Doves might become a full-fledged sect, they believe that Matrjona must give birth to a Messiah-child. For various obscure reasons, Kudejarov is not the man for the job. Dar'jal'skij has been chosen, unknown to him, to father this Messiah on Matrjona, because the sectarians discern that particular blend of religion and eroticism in him which they are searching for:

> There were, to be sure, other people here who better understood what my hero needed (perhaps love and something else), where the languishing stare of his velvet eyes was striving as he stared passionately directly in front of himself when there was not even a single girl before him or even anywhere within sight and there was only the evening sunset aglow in flames all about. They understood a great deal more in Dar'jal'skij and, so to speak, surrounded him with an invisible net of surveillance for reasons unknown to anyone else. These people were simple, not educated in the least—but about them later. Let us merely say that there were such people and let us say also that if they had understood the subtleties of poetic beauties, if they had read what was hidden under the bookcover inscribed with the fig-leaf written by Dar'jal'skij, well then, they would have smiled, oh, with what a smile! They would have said: "He is one of us...".[6]

It is no passing curiosity or infatuation which this peasant woman arouses in Dar'jal'skij. Belyj's conception is akin to that of *Goblet of Storms* where the archetype is deeply buried in the pysche and emerges in response to external stimulus. What Dar'jal'skij is experiencing is the externalization of the mysterious anima-complex because of which the sectarians have intuitively chosen him to father the Messiah:

> Again you have peered into my soul, you evil mystery! Again you are looking at me out of the dark past.... From childhood right from my cradle you have pursued me in rustlings.... —Right from the first moments of life I was filled with dread and my eyes were directed into the darkness from the first days of my childhood. From those very first days of childhood a sweet but mocking song called me in the sunrise and in the gloom... —And I continued to wait and lo, out of the shadows people took form. But I continued to wait for the arrival of that terrible but languorous and summoning one who would come to me from afar out of the darkness... —I waited, I called, but no one came. I grew and became a man, but no one came. I called and then listened—to the rustling of the trees and I understood, but when I

[6] Ibid., I, 28-29.

spoke of that rustling no one understood me. And just as I was calling someone, the rustling of the trees summoned me and like some unknown and sweet lament above me someone was weeping out their life—but what, what was the lament about?"[7]

Once he joins the Silver Doves and goes to live in the forest hut of Kudejarov and Matrjona, Dar'jal'skij surrenders himself completely to a primitive communal life close to the soil and to an irrational intoxication of body and spirit in the frenzied rites of the sectarians. He repulses all Katerina's attempts to win him back to herself and the civilized west and sinks ever deeper into the morass of his released passions. His relations with Matrjona assume an ambivalent nature as she becomes for him not only the satisfaction of his all-powerful and irrational erotic desires, but a mysterious chthonic mother-figure. Not only does Belyj perceive the multivalency of the feminine archetype that obsesses Blok, but he acknowledges as well the commonly accepted homologous nature of the Virgin Bride and Virgin Mother in his description of Matrjona becoming both mistress and mother to Dar'jal'skij. Significantly, on those two occasions when "religious matings" between the two are arranged, the love act is preceeded by an overt mother-child relationship so that her *compassion* transforms the demonic Matrjona into a sympathetic mother-figure:

> And he burst into tears before this bitch like a big abandoned child and his head fell on her knees; and in her there was a transformation. She was no longer a bitch; those large, intimate eyes: full of tears those eyes sailed into his soul; and her face was not distorted with aroused passion, but bowed before him sweet-scented. —Oh, my sick one! Oh little brother: here is my cross for you ... [8]

And at the second tryst:

> Pjotr gazed at Matrjona and wept: she had such fragrant eyes, like corn-flowers; whether with a paradisal ecstasy or a hellish abyss she had betwitched him: her dove ... She seized him; she rocked him like a child; she pressed his head to her breast.[9]

Dar'jal'skij, however, is incapable of begetting the desired Messiahchild. This physical impotence no doubt mirrors the bankruptcy of his attempt to eschew the learning of the West and return to the soil and paganism in the East. The consequences of his "betrayal" of Katja and wilful pursuit of his unbridled passions prove more lethal than this mere impotency. Once disenchanted with his primitive mode of existence, he longs to return to the West and Katja and sets about effecting this. Kudejarov, however, decides that he must be silenced.

[7] Ibid., I, 128. Compare also with I, 21, the passage beginning "Rjabaja baba, jastreb, s ochami bezbrovymi...".
[8] Ibid., I, 283-284.
[9] Ibid., II, 119-120.

He is lured to a house where, in a chilling ritualistic act, he is "executed" by being smothered to death and dressed in the ceremonial garb of the Silver Doves for his interment.

Belyj claimed that Dar'jal'skij was inspired by the example of Sergej Solov'ev, who in 1907 was obsessed with the idea of going out to the people or returning to the soil.[10] To this end Solov'ev exchanged his city garb for peasant dress, moved in peasant circles, became interested in sectarianism and even prepared to marry a simple peasant girl. It will be recalled that he had exhibited this type of maximalism on more than one occasion in the past. (Of course, he did not come to the same end as Dar'jal'skij.)

Other factors as well may have been among the multiple influences that formed Dar'jal'skij and *The Silver Dove*. The example of the erstwhile decadent poet, Aleksandr Mikhajlovich Dobroljubov (1875-?), who like Dar'jal'skij forsook his past and went out to the people and formed his own religious sect of "dobroljubovtsy", must have contributed something to Belyj's creation as well.[11]

Belyj himself figures prominently in all of his novels and there are many connections between his personal experiences and those of Dar'jal'skij. Nevertheless, it is no doubt Blok who proves telling in Belyj's novel. The parallels between Katerina and Matrjona and Blok's "Beautiful Lady" and "serpent-eyed mistress" are too arresting to be ignored. The longing for spiritual and physical intoxication, the plunge into the storm, the irresistible dark passions of Blok's *Unexpected Joy* are shared by Dar'jal'skij: "He gazed somewhere off into the empty space, into the tempest, he gazed into the howling wind, into the blizzard ...."[12] Not even his vision of the "Radiant Mistress" could swerve Blok from his ecstatic but catastrophic plunge into the abyss, lured on by the demonic feminine of his second book of verse. Thus, Belyj prophesied his destruction if he continued on this path away from light into darkness. The words which Dar'jal'skij's friend Schmidt speaks to the distraught Katerina concerning the poet's nature and fate can be considered in essence as Belyj's assessment of and warning to Blok:

> —Pjotr thinks that he has left you forever; but there is no infidelity here, no flight, only a terrible hypnosis that is oppressing him; he has stepped out of the circle of salvation—and for the time being his enemies are triumphing over him just as the enemy is triumphing over and jeering at our homeland.... Reconcile yourself Katerina Vasil'evna, do not despair! all that is dark is befalling Pjotr; but Pjotr can still conquer; he must conquer himself within himself, he must

[10] See Belyj, "Vospominanija o A. A. Blok", in *Epopeja*, 1922, No. 3, 183.

[11] See S. D. Cioran, "A. Dobroliubov: A Prophet of Silence", *Canadian Slavic Studies*, V.2 (Summer 1971), 178-195.

[12] Belyj, *Serebrjanyj golub'*, I, 143.

refrain from a personal creation of life; he must reevaluate his relationship to the world; and the spectres which for him have assumed the flesh and blood of persons will disappear; believe me, only great and powerful souls are subjected to such an ordeal; only giants collapse like Pjotr; he did not accept the hand of help extended to him; he himself wanted to experience everything for himself.[13]

One could hardly ask for a more penetrating analysis of Blok in the post-1905 period. It is as though Belyj is consoling the Beautiful Lady for what he considers Blok's abandonment of her. Schmidt's remedy is that very remedy which Belyj urged on Blok, namely, the reassessment of his relationship to the world, a return within the pale of good and evil once again and a rejection of his own individual forms for the sake of rejoining Belyj's collective so that they might rediscover their original sophiological aspirations. Dar'jal'skij's "enemies" Belyj no doubt envisaged as Blok's so-called "friends" in Petersburg, the mystical anarchists and others, who like the sectarians believed they had discovered a soul-mate and encouraged what Belyj felt to be dangerous tendencies in the Lyrical Dramas and Unexpected Joy.

Belyj was not the only symbolist to reflect the conflict of a divine and demonic feminine archetype in a major work. Valerij Brjusov responded to the theme of sophiology in his novel The Fiery Angel in 1907.[14] Brjusov was no party to the visions of the Divine Feminine that occupied Blok, Belyj, Sergej Solov'ev, Ellis-Kobylinskij and others. Nor did he apparently owe anything to Vladimir Solov'ev, for his aesthetic credo did not really extend beyond the concept of "art for art's sake". Although in his theoretic articles, paramount among which are "Istiny" ("Truths", 1901) and "Kljuchi tajn" ("Keys to the Mysteries", 1904), he intimated some mysterious transformative function of art, in fact, he was more deeply involved in the sophisticated refinement and development of new forms and the introduction of French models into Russian literature. One has but to recall Vladimir Solov'ev's parodies of the first booklets of "Russian Symbolists"[15] to realize the difference in ultimate purpose between those Russian "symbolists" who viewed art as the *metaphysical* or *religious* Word for the transformation of the world and the Russian "decadents" (like Brjusov) who championed the *aesthetic* Word for its own sake. While Blok and Belyj, in particular, always considered Brjusov the first poet in contemporary Russian literature and their natural leader in symbolist art, his poetry and prose had little or

[13] Ibid., I, 298-299.

[14] Brjusov's Ognennyj angel was serialized in Vesy, 1907-1908, and the first separate edition appeared Moscow, 1908-1909.

[15] V. Solov'ev, "Russkie simvolisty", first appeared in Vestnik Evropy, 1895, No. 1, 421-424 and No. 10, 847-851. The two articles can be found in Sobranie sochinenij V. S. Solov'eva, VII, 159-170.

nothing in common with Belyj's "Woman Clothed in the Sun" or Blok's "Beautiful Lady". In the poem "They see Her!", Brjusov admits his isolation from the sophiological visions of his younger colleagues, who are apparently initiated into mysteries undisclosed to him. However, his novel The Fiery Angel provides a much more interesting response to their concerns.

In a striking parallel to Belyj's The Silver Dove, which relates the personal lives of Belyj and Blok with the metaphysical theme of the Demonic Feminine, Brjusov's novel too concerns his private relations with Belyj and Nina Petrovskaja as well as the paramount theme of the Demonic Feminine. Apparently Belyj was involved with the symbolist authoress, Nina Ivanovna Petrovskaja, during the latter half of 1904.[16] The exact nature of the relation is not known, although at least on the basis of Brjusov's novel and Belyj's general character, it was probably a platonic although deeply emotional tie for Belyj. Rumours were that he was attempting to deepen her mind and develop her character. Unfortunately, Brjusov was actually carrying on a physical relationship with her at the same time Belyj was involved in this spiritual tutoring. No doubt it proved a source of sardonic amusement to Brjusov, who had gained a notorious reputation for his decadent mentality and life-style. According to Belyj, Brjusov tried to provoke him to a duel by salacious remarks and to affront him with his wilful conduct and vulgar attempts at experimental psychology. Brjusov appears to have earned his title of "black magician" by deliberately provoking situations that would disillusion the idealistic Belyj:

> My struggle with Brjusov did not come easy for me: before me at times Brujsov the "magician" was revealed. Not scintillating with hypnotism but rummaging through dubious occult books like a lynx through the forest in search of devices for some entirely suspicious psychological experiment; his inner "face" was revealed to me, dark and reminiscent of the faces of the Stranglers he had depicted in the drama "Earth".[17]

In Nachalo Veka[18] Belyj claimed that Petrovskaja herself was not entirely without fault in the affair and even incited Brjusov to a duel with him. Whether this was fact or based on Belyj's reading of Brjusov's novel, it is difficult to say.

In the preface to the Fiery Angel Brjusov disclaims authorship of the novel, stating that it is an anonymous 16th century manuscript. It

---

[16] See Belyj's oblique references to the affair in Nachalo veka (Moscow-Leningrad, 1933), 351-352; "Vospominanija ob Aleksandre Aleksandroviche Bloke" in Zapiski mechtatelej, 1922, No. 6, 95-96; "Vospominanija o A. A. Bloke" in Epopeja, 1922, No. 2, 158-159. See generally Belyj's correspondence with the Bloks during the second half of 1904 in A. Blok i A. Belyj. Perepiska (Moscow, 1940).

[17] Belyj, "Vospominanija o A. A. Bloke", in Epopeja, 1922, No. 2, 158.

[18] Belyj, Nachalo veka, 351.

concerns the incredible experiences of the young German Rupprecht, a former student of Cologne University who is forced to give up his studies. He runs away and becomes a free *Landesknecht* in the army of a German knight that participates in the Italian campaign and the sacking of Rome by Lutheran forces. His subsequent travels take him to the New World where he makes his fortune before returning home after some eight years in the service of the Spanish Crown.

On his journey to his parents' home, he is overtaken by darkness and stops at a disreputable forest inn. During the night he is roused by the sounds of a struggle in the neighboring room. Investigating, he finds a young woman apparently possessed by devils, writhing and moaning in agony. When the devils finally leave her and she regains consciousness, she addresses Rupprecht by his name, although they have never met. His curiosity aroused, Rupprecht remains and the woman, Renata, subsequently recounts her life history to him.

As an eight-year-old she received a visitation from an angel who called himself Madiel. This angel henceforth appeared to her at frequent intervals and in various incarnations, leading her to believe that she would become a saint if she followed his counsel. Enamoured of the angel and taking his intimations to heart, she submitted herself to the most severe religious regime of fasting, praying and scourging of the flesh. The angel often passed nights with her without sexual intercourse, but Renata, who desired physical union with him, managed to trick and seduce him. Madiel was greatly offended at this and disappeared for several days. When he finally returned, he told Renata that she would next recognize him in a certain Count Heinrich who would come for her. When the Count appears, they elope to his castle and enjoy a blissful, if shortlived, relationship. Moreover, in spite of Renata's insistence, Count Heinrich denies that he is the angel Madiel. For mysterious reasons Heinrich soon grows despondent and suddenly abandons Renata. From then on she is possessed of evil spirits that wrack and distort her body in epileptic-like, yet almost erotic, fits.

Intrigued by the woman's strange story, Rupprecht agrees to escort her as far as Cologne where she is headed in search of Count Heinrich. Soon his curiosity gives way to a growing love, but although they spend their nights together, she will not let Rupprecht seduce her, for she must keep herself chaste for her Count Heinrich. Despite the fact that Rupprecht and Renata are in communication with tiny demons that promise Count Heinrich's return to Cologne, their search is unsuccessful. Finally, Renata concludes that they must resort to black magic in order to discover the whereabouts of her lover. Rupprecht agrees to risk eternal damnation by anointing himself with a magic ointment in order to participate in a Witches' Sabbath and then question Satan himself. Although he is successful in gaining an audience and participating in all manner of erotic rituals, he does not receive a conclusive answer to his questions.

Rupprecht then sets about a serious study of the occult sciences, believing that their attempt to find Heinrich through the medium of the black arts will be facilitated by mastering those illegitimate sciences. Once again, however, he fails in his experiments and decides to consult a famous scholar who has written on the occult sciences. This is none other than Agrippa von Nettesheim. In an interesting aside, Rupprecht meets a certain Dr. Faustus in the company of a rather sinister character during his journey to Bonn and Agrippa. Without receiving any help from the German scholar, Rupprecht returns to Cologne only to discover that, according to Renata, the Count is in the city and has rejected and insulted her. She forces Rupprecht to challenge the Count to a duel with the object of killing him, but at the last moment remorse forces her to make Rupprecht promise not to harm Heinrich. As a result, Rupprecht allows himself to be wounded by his opponent. When he recovers, Renata declares that she has always loved him and was only testing him with the duelling affair. Having seen that Rupprecht was prepared not only to sacrifice his soul, but his body as well, for her, she finally surrenders to him and they indulge their passions to the full. The insatiable Renata drives Rupprecht to near-exhaustion, but soon she reverts to her earlier religious mania and with Rupprecht's help begins reading all the Church writings. Invariably, however, their periods of religious abstinence give way to ever wilder sexual passions which prove to be a source of great remorse for Renata. Finally she flees from Rupprecht and he embarks on a frustrated and melancholy search for her just as she had for Count Heinrich. As Rupprecht is about to leave Cologne he is engaged by Dr. Faustus and his friend, Mephistopheles, to show them the city. Their travels eventually take them to the castle of a Count von Wellen where Rupprecht soon finds himself employed as secretary. Shortly he and his employer are invited by the Archbishop of Triers to witness an exorcism he is to perform in a local convent. A certain Sister Maria who has recently joined the order, appears possessed of the devil. The sister turns out to be Renata. Rupprecht tries to save her when the matter is turned over to the Inquisition, but Renata herself seems to desire the scourging of her flesh for her sins with an almost masochistic delight. She is tortured horribly and admits to all manner of crimes for which she is to be burned at the stake. In a Faustian ending, Rupprecht attempts to rescue her from her cell, but she refuses to leave and dies.

Having squandered all his fortune and in deepest melancholy over the loss of Renata, Rupprecht decides to gather enough money to return to the New World. While he is engaged in business dealings to earn his passage, he meets Count Heinrich once again and they smooth over the past. Just before departing for Spain and the New World, Rupprecht also witnesses the end of Agrippa von Nettesheim who on his death bed sees an evil demon in his pet-dog and curses it. The dog then drowns itself in the river. This final touch is once again inspired by the Faust legend and is no doubt meant to signify that such things as evil spirits do exist even though Agrippa denied it earlier.

If, indeed, Belyj was the inspiration behind Madiel-Count Heinrich, with Nina Petrovskaja as Renata and Brjusov as Rupprecht, their relationship must have been bizarre to say the least. Allowing for distortion and exaggeration, one can nonetheless accept the rather naive and chaste Belyj as desiring to be her spiritual tutor while Brjusov stands ready to experiment with the occult and the sensuous as her physical tutor. The curious mixture of fanatic religiosity and eroticism in the feminine archetype was very much to Brjusov's decadent taste and Renata's sensuous masochism was doubtless his response to the poets of the Divine Feminine. As Belyj himself recalled, Brjusov frequently championed the demonic and black arts in reaction to the younger symbolists' preoccupation with the divine and ideal. If Christ and the Woman Clothed in the Sun were the emblems of the early Blok and Belyj, then his banners were adorned with the tragic egoism of Beezelbub and the sensuousness of the Great Harlot.

Nor was Brjusov alone in his reaction to the vision of the Divine Feminine. With his characteristically melancholic perversity, V. V. Rozanov rebelled against the cold and lifeless chastity which he perceived in the adulation of the Divine Feminine. If others sought only to elevate the spiritual aspect of the Divine Feminine and scourge the flesh, he would champion the flesh, sanctify it in preference to the spirit. Consequently, his views rest on the blessed fruitfulness of nature, the joy of physical union with the conception and birth of the flesh. It was as though he perceived the impossibility of subjugating the physical to the spiritual and therefore made a cult of the spiritual subjugated to the physical, a pagan rejoicing in the flesh. In his sombre treatise *Ljudi lunnogo sveta* (*People of the Sub-Lunary Realm*, Petersburg, 1911) he attacks Vladimir Solov'ev for spiritual views on love that ignore the joys and sanctity of the flesh, calling the philosopher a "eunuch".[19] To counter the purely divine aspect that is

---

[19] V. V. Rozanov, *Ljudi lunnogo sveta* (Petersburg, 1911), 43. Elsewhere in this work Rozanov attacks Solov'ev for the foreword to his book of poems (see pp. 61-62). He is irked by Solov'ev's avowal that his verses do not serve that "prostonarodnaja Aphrodite". Rozanov points out that according to Plato this is the Aphrodite who bears children. Consequently, Rozanov takes this to mean that Solov'ev's verses serve the

usually ascendent in the image of the Eternal Feminine he outlines briefly the sacred history of prostitution and the "Holy Prostitute" as positive concepts equal in value to chastity and the Holy Virgin.

But while Rozanov's vision of the physical tended to an extreme version of Merezhkovskij's conception of the synthesis of flesh and spirit, N. M. Minskij (pseud. of Vilenkin), another associate of the author of Khrist i Antikhrist (Christ and Antichrist, 1895-1905), responded with a more orthodox view of dvuedinstvo ("Two-in-oneness"). His attempt to bridge the traditional separation between divine spirit and demonic flesh, was perhaps best outlined in his article "Ideja Salome" ("The Idea of Salome", 1908) which appeared during the "ambiguous period" of Russian symbolism between the two Revolutions.[20] Wilde's play "Salome" provided Minskij with a context for the discussion of the two-in-oneness of flesh and spirit. His argument, although contrived, is significant for revealing the basic awareness of the problem of opposites which so obsessed the symbolist mentality. Minskij claims that both the physical sensuality of Salome and the spiritual asceticism of Iokaanen represent equal values: "Salome and Iokaanen are both proceeding towards one and the same harmony, but are approaching it from different directions."[21] Their individual failings, however, arise out of the mutual exclusiveness of their natures. Salome is doomed because she cannot conquer Iokaanen's spiritual nature with her beauty:

> Salome proceeds from a pagan sentiment; along her path she overcomes obstacle after obstacle, but comes to a halt before the final obstacle, powerless. Her tragedy arises from the fact that she, although spiritually enlightened, still perceives the world through her eyes alone. She wants only to see and therefore has overlooked her own soul.[22]

Iokaanen's sin is his ascetic disavowal of physical beauty: "Iokaanen's tragedy arises from the fact that, although being beautiful, he still does not see beauty. He does not wish to see it and therefore he has overlooked Salome's soul."[23] According to Minskij, Salome is the more perfect of the two apparent opposites and closer to the ultimate syzygy of flesh and spirit, body and mind:

---

other Aphrodite, the Aphrodite-Urania who is barren. Therefore Solov'ev's verses pay homage to an abstract, lifeless Aphrodita Sodomica who perpetuates mere "images, phantasies, philosophies, prayers". For Rozanov, then, Solov'ev does not worship that same earthly fertility and life-affirming vision of the motherly-wifely Aphrodite who crowns Rozanov's philosophical system.

[20] N. Minskij, "Ideja Salome", in Zolotoe runo, 1908, No. 6, 55-58.
[21] Ibid., 57.
[22] Ibid., 57.
[23] Ibid., 57.

> If they are to be compared with each other, then one must consider Salome more perfect, closer to the goal than Iokaanen. She loved the prophet, she has seen into his soul, even though, as it were, through the prism of physical forms, while Iokaanen has not even noticed a related soul standing before him, he has cruelly looked right through her and rudely shunned her.[24]

Apparently Minskij feels that Salome's attraction to beauty in fact equals her attraction to divinity, since the two are so closely related. Iokaanen, not seeing the connection between beauty and divinity, turns away from the beautiful because he believes it sinful. Thus, he is responsible for his own end. Both are excused their failings because they are only the precursors to the final syzygy—she with her love of *beauty*, and he with his love of the *divine*. Although Minskij acknowledges that contemporary culture is still in the midst of a tragic contention between opposites, he feels that ultimate salvation will be forthcoming in this vision of their union: "On the eve of proclaimed harmony, divinity and beauty have met in disharmony and enmity. But are they not fated, with the incarnation of the mystery of two-in-oneness, to meet in love and understanding?"[25]

While the three-in-one syzygy of Vladimir Solov'ev or the two-in-one of Merezhkovskij and Minskij proposed to bring about a positive spiritual transformation, they were irrevocably displaced by the supremacy of the demonic feminine in the interim. The Woman Clothed in the Sun was a future possibility, but the Harlot was a present reality for symbolists like Blok and Belyj. Within the apocalyptic scheme of things outlined by Vladimir Solov'ev and reluctantly embraced by Blok and Belyj, the temporary reign of the Antichrist and the Harlot had to be recognized.

[24] Ibid., 57.
[25] Ibid., 58.

PART IV
The Faithful

Father Sergej Bulgakov (1871-1944)

Chapter 1

THE CHURCH CONTROVERSY

What began as a "public debate" on Sophiology, conducted by Vladimir Solov'ev in the final quarter of the nineteenth century, was assimilated by the Russian symbolists in the first two decades of the twentieth. Sophiology, and in particular the Divine Sophia, did not die with Symbolism on the eve of the Revolution. Instead they returned to the public arena in the 20's and 30's through one of the most important controversies within the Russian Orthodox Church in this century. Indeed, even in certain Church circles it is not difficult to sense that very same spirit of an inspirational crusade for change that Solov'ev had earlier invoked in his own search for spiritual transformation. While the terminology of knight-errantry is obscured by theological language, nonetheless the unwavering faith in an ideal that struck many as being feminine seems unmistakable even here.

Although Sergej Bulgakov may be considered the chief exponent of theological Sophiology after Solov'ev, he was by no means the only devotee of the Divine Sophia. His first treatise, *The Unfading Light* (*Svet nevechernyj*, 1917), was preceded by a major work by Pavel Florenskij, *The Pillar and the Affirmation of Truth* (*Stolp i utverzhdenie istiny*, 1914). While Bulgakov's works on Sophiology were to attempt a *rational* and *theoretical* exegesis, Florenskij's work revealed itself inspired by a pure intuition of religious experience. In combination, Bulgakov's rationalism and Florenskij's intuition provide the same subtle contrapuntal play that was earlier combined in a single man—Vladimir Solov'ev.

In his introduction to *The Pillar and the Foundation of Truth* Florenskij does not hesitate to reveal the inspired basis of the work at hand: "*Living religious experience as the unique and legitimate means for the knowledge of dogmas*—this is how I would like to express the general striving of the book, or more precisely, of my sketches recorded at various times and in various moods. Only in the recourse to immediate experience is it possible to survey and evaluate the spiritual treasures of the Church."[1] In prose that slips irresistibly

---

[1] P. Florenskij, *Stolp i utverzhdenie istiny*, (Moscow, 1914), 3.

over the divide into poetry, Florenskij duplicates the ecstatic vision of religious experience which is found in Solov'ev's verses. While Bulgakov will dot his theoretic landscape with patristic writings and traditional Church dogma—albeit viewed from a new perspective—Florenskij's geography is the otherworldly realm of mysterious nuance and divine revelation that exists unashamedly by virtue of its own inner beauty and the power of love:

> The most secret expectations, the most treasured bursts [of joy] towards godliness, those azure moments, ensuing after storms, of angelic purity, of the ecstasy of divine communion and the sacred torments of piercing repentance, the sweet fragrance of prayer and the silent longing for heaven, the eternal search and the eternal discovery, the infinitely profound insights into eternity and the childlike repose of the soul, reverence and love—love that knows no end... The ages have washed by and all this existed at one time and was stored up.[2]

Florenskij relies upon his inner voice to disclose the meaning of all things; immediate experience reveals all in a mute revelation. What he seeks to communicate from his intuitive and mysterious vision is the meaning of *tserkovnost'* ("ecclesiasticism") which at times seems to parallel Bulgakov's concept of *sobornost'* ("communality"). Florenskij defines this "ecclesiasticism" as a new life, a "life in the Spirit", whose criteria are invested in the concept of Beauty. The beauty of which he speaks, however, is an inner or "spiritual" beauty which defies all rational formulae and at the same time is the one way to the genuine apprehension of Orthodoxy: "The flavour of Orthodoxy, the countenance of Orthodoxy, can be sensed, but it cannot be subjected to any arithmetical calculation; Orthodoxy manifests itself but does not prove itself. This is why for everyone wishing to comprehend Orthodoxy, there is only *one* means—the direct Orthodox experience."[3]

Our attention is drawn here to one particular chapter of Florenskij's work, "Tenth letter: Sophia" ("Pis'mo desjatoe: Sophia"),[4] which contains the writer's mystical or intuitive apprehension of Sophia. There is no development of a logical or rational theory here, but rather an atheoretic panegyric. Sophia emerges in all her mystery, endowed with all her traditional epithets and yet performing precisely the same functions as Solov'ev's or Bulgakov's Sophia. Unlike Bulgakov, who will strive purposely to avoid charges of gnosticism and heresy by de-personalizing his feminine principle, Florenskij restores her divinely personalized motifs, the aura of the Divine Feminine: "Sophia is the Great Root of the whole creation. Sophia is the first-created being of the creaturely world, the creative

[2] Ibid., 4.
[3] Ibid., 7.
[4] Ibid., 319-392.

Love of God.... In relation to the creaturely world Sophia is the Guardian Angel of the world, the Ideal nature of the world...".[5] In Florenskij's vision, Sophia is omnipresent and omnicreative. She is the "image of God in man", the intermediary between the two realms. Closely following Solov'ev's concept of Sophia as the ideal expression of oneness, Florenskij also makes Wisdom synonymous with ideal total-unity: "... for all the enumerated ways of comprehending the word 'Wisdom', in fact, are all one and the same Sophia as the God-created oneness of ideal definitions of the creaturely world,—one and the same Sophia but perceived under various aspects—the complete nature of the creaturely world".[6]

Florenskij also describes his revelation of Sophia in relation to the Holy Trinity. For the mystic-sophiologist not entangled in careful theological structures, her function in the Trinity becomes immediately manifest in the triadic formula "foundation-mind-holiness". Quite simply, in relation to the Father, Sophia is the "ideal substance, the basis of the creaturely world, the power or force of its existence".[7] In regard to the Word she is the "mind of the creaturely world, the meaning, truth or verity of it".[8] Finally, for the Spirit, Sophia contains "the spirituality of the creaturely world, the holiness, purity and chasteness of it, i.e. of beauty".[9]

Bearing in mind that Florenskij is not well-known in the West and in order to show how Sophia usurps the whole system, I shall quote one passage at length:

> If Sophia is the entire Creation, then the soul and conscience of Creation—Humanity—is above all Sophia. If Sophia is all of Humanity, then the soul and conscience of Humanity—the Church—is above all Sophia. If Sophia is the Church, then the soul and conscience of the Church—the Church of Saints—is above all Sophia. If Sophia is the Church of Saints, then the soul and conscience of the Church of Saints—the Intercessor and Mediatrix on behalf of the creation before the Word of God, who judges and divides creation in two, the Mother of God,—is once again above all Sophia. But the true sign of the Blessed Mary is manifested in Her Virginity, the Beauty of Her Soul. This too is Sophia. Sophia is "the hidden man of the heart, in that which is not corruptible, even the ornament of a meek and quiet spirit" (1 Peter, 3;4)—the true adornment of the human being which penetrates through his whole body, radiant in his gaze, pouring forth in his smile, rejoicing in his heart with an inutterable ecstasy, reflected in his every gesture, enveloping man in the moment of exultation with a sweet-scented haze and radiant nimbus, creating him "above worldly union" so that remaining in the world he becomes

[5] Ibid., 326.
[6] Ibid., 344.
[7] Ibid., 349.
[8] Ibid., 349.
[9] Ibid., 349.

> "not of this world", he becomes supra-worldly. "And the light shineth in the darkness and the darkness comprehended it not" (John 1:5), such is the not-of-this-worldness of the spirit-bearing and beautiful individual. Sophia is Beauty. "Let the adorning of yourselves", the Apostle Peter addresses the women, "be not that outward adorning of plaiting the hair, and of wearing of gold, or of putting on of apparel; But let it be the hidden man of the heart, in that which is not corruptible, even the ornament of a meek and quiet spirit, which is in the sight of God of great price" (1 Peter 3:3-4). Only Sophia, only she alone is substantial Beauty in all of creation; and all the rest is but tinsel and putting on of apparel and a person shall be divested of this spectral radiance in the trial by fire.[10]

Florenskij also attempts to trace the development of Sophia in the Russian as opposed to the Byzantine tradition, an aspect of her nature which was of great importance to Vladimir Solov'ev in *La Russie et l'Eglise Universelle* and will interest Bulgakov as well. Florenskij believes that the Byzantine Greeks conceived of Sophia "from the aspect of her speculative-dogmatic content. Sophia, in the understanding of the Greeks was above all an object of contemplation".[11] On the other hand, the early Russians, who received their dogmatic formulae ready-made from their spiritual leaders in Byzantium, were attracted not only to the chastity and holiness of Sophia, but to her wisdom and beauty as well. The third aspect which Sophia has revealed to the Russians is their contemporary belief in oneness:

> Finally, our contemporaries, dreaming of the oneness of all the creaturely world in God, directed all their thought to the idea of the mystical Church. And Sophia turned to them in her third aspect—the aspect of the Church. Fedor Bukharev, F. M. Dostoevskij, V. S. Solov'ev, the "neo-Christians", the Catholic Modernists and so on —these are the currents which once again are discovering for themselves a symbolic expression in the icons of Sophia.[12]

Clearly Florenskij finds in Sophia the most significant and multivalent symbol of the religious renaissance of his age. With regard to the interwoven strands of both philosophical and literary Sophiology, it is worth attention that Florenskij footnotes the names of Dostoevskij, Solov'ev and the others mentioned above, with that of Anna Schmidt.

Thus the all-consuming idea of Florenskij's work is also "oneness" under the sign of Sophia. He envisions the amalgamation of all religious concepts and dogmas into a single whole which he calls "ecclesiasticism". Love, or in Florenskij's terminology, "Friendship" ["Druzhba"], is the spirit of Sophia which infuses the scheme. Echoing Solov'ev's "Meaning of Love" and anticipating Merezhkovskij's "Mystery of the Three", Florenskij identifies the submergence of the

---

[10] Ibid., 350-351.
[11] Ibid., 389.
[12] Ibid., 389.

single "I" into the dual "Thou" as the means whereby the Sophianic oneness of the creaturely world with the divine will be realized:

> Sophia—this true Creaturely World or the creaturely world in Truth—manifests herself beforehand as a premonition of the transfigured, inspired world, as that manifestation of the sublime in the earthly which is invisible to others. This revelation is achieved in the personal and sincere love of two people,—in a friendship when beforehand the one who loves is able, at no great cost, to overcome his self-identification, is able to dismiss the boundaries of his "Ego", is able to issue forth out of himself and achieve his own Ego in the Ego of another person—his Friend.[13]

In other words, the sophiological process begins in man, in his relationship with a second person. It is based upon the premise of a dyad which when constituted creates the transfigurative synthesis or triad whose joint and divine nature Sophia reflects in herself.

Thus, Florenskij is entirely within the sophiological tradition of striving for wholeness, for the meaningful and transfigurative synthesis. While he does not call his scheme "Godmanhood" as Bulgakov and Solov'ev do theirs, nonetheless the contours of the three are quite identical.

The chief architect of the sophiological controversy in the Church was Sergej Bulgakov. Perhaps this was to be expected in view of the fact that he had followed so closely, and even participated in, the symbolist controversy over Vladimir Solov'ev in 1905[14]. In fact, Solov'ev was one of the major influences on his intellectual journey from Marxism to Idealism. It was largely through Bulgakov's efforts that the works of Anna Nikolaevna Schmidt were published; together with the symbolists, he had been fascinated by the mystical and religious implications of the relationship between the philosopher-poet and the Nizhegorodian mystic.[15] In retrospect, the epithet which Blok had earlier applied to Vladimir Solov'ev, namely, that of the "knight-monk", seems even more appropriate in the case of Sergej Bulgakov. The chivalrous devotions to the ideals represented in the Divine Sophia found both their secular and sacred representatives in a single personnage who entered the church in order to realize Solov'ev's inspired teachings.

As part of a generation nurtured on the writings of Solov'ev, Bulgakov's spiritual search carried him to theology and, eventually, to the priesthood. Ordained in 1917, he spent several years in the Crimea teaching theology and political economy. In January of 1923, however, he was finally forced to emigrate to the West. Settling in Paris, he became a member of the faculty of the Russian Theological

---

[13] Ibid., 391-392.
[14] See pp. 71-74.
[15] See pp. 102-104.

Institute under the patronage of Metropolitan Eulogij, remaining there off and on until his death in 1944. During the second half of the 20's and throughout the 30's, Bulgakov gained prominence as one of the foci of the dissension that plagued the Russian Orthodox Church between the two wars. His teachings on Sophia became the major point of theological contention among the warring factions of Russian Orthodoxy outside of Russia.

Bulgakov's development of his sophiological theology is overwhelmingly massive. The first of his two voluminous trilogies contains The Burning Bush (Kupina neopalimaja, 1924), The Friend of the Groom (Drug zhenikha, 1927), and Jacob's Ladder (Lestnitsa Iakovlja, 1929). The second triology is made up of The Lamb of God (Agnets Bozhij, 1931), The Comforter (Uteshitel', 1936) and The Bride of the Lamb (Nevesta Agntsa, 1945). This, however, by no means exhausts Bulgakov's teachings on the Divine Wisdom of God.[16] Mention should be made of at least two very significant preliminary works, The Unfading Light (Svet nevechernij, 1917) and Hypostasis and Hypostatic Nature (Ipostas' i Ipostasnost', 1924), as well as his defense against charges of heresy contained in On Sophia, the Divine Wisdom of God (O Sofii, Premudrosti Bozhiej, 1935). Fortunately for English readers, Bulgakov wrote a book on Sophiology for English translation entitled The Wisdom of God (London, 1937). This text is fortunate in many respects, for it not only represents Bulgakov's most mature ideas, but also provides the essence of all his thought on Sophiology. It is a curious coincidence that Solov'ev's quintessential work on Sophia, La Russie et l'Eglise Universelle, was also published in a language other than Russian, although no doubt censorship and Church opposition would otherwise have prevented its publication.

For Solov'ev and Bulgakov, Sophiology became tantamount to announcing a religions manifesto of belief and action for the transformation and salvation of the world. The urgency which sounded in Solov'ev's proclamatory letter to E. K. Romanova[17] is echoed in Bulgakov's words on Sophiology as a theology of crisis and salvation in his time:

> The future of a living Christianity rests with the sophianic interpretation of the world and of its destiny. All the dogmatic and practical problems of modern Christian dogmatics and ascetics seem to form a kind of knot whose unravelling inevitably leads to Sophiology. For

---

[16] An excellent bibliography and thorough summary of Bulgakov's works are to be found in L. A. Zander, Bog i Mir (Mirosozertsanie otsa Sergija Bulgakova). In two volumes (Paris: YMCA Press, 1948). A briefer biographical sketch and summary of Bulgakov's theological activity is contained in an obituary written by L. A. Zander, "In Memory of Father Sergius Bulgakov," Sobornost', No. 32, December, 1945 (new series), 5-12.

[17] See pp. 11-13.

this reason, in the true sense of the word, Sophiology is a theology of crisis, not of disintegration, but of salvation.[18]

Like Solov'ev, Bulgakov also devoted his entire life to the formulation of his sophiological teaching. Like Solov'ev, he too attempted to give a rational expression to what had traditionally been the hegemony of gnostics and mystics and had remained obscure to modern Christianity. If Bulgakov was often attacked for this very "rational" and "intellectual" approach, for what was deemed in the Church undesirable "modernism", on the other hand, he was charged as well with mystical "gnosticism".

In spite of the fact that Bulgakov did not practice *belles-lettres* as did other followers of the Divine Sophia and even though his sophiological teachings were supposedly rationalistic and textually exegetical, there is no denying the irrational experience underlying Bulgakov's own apprehension of the Divine Wisdom of God. Within the vivid tradition created by Vladimir Solov'ev, Belyj and Blok, he too claims to have experienced "encounters" or visions of Sophia. In his youth a fateful viewing of Raphael's sistine Madonna in the Dresden Gallery helped to start him on his journey from Marxism to Idealism.[19] Furthermore, in various of his autobiographical writings it is possible to uncover accounts of the mystical experiences and intuitions which led him to both Orthodoxy and Sophiology.[20]

Both Solov'ev and Bulgakov attempted to inspire modern Christianity, to infuse new life into the flagging spirit of the Church, to reveal what they believed was God's divine plan for Godmanhood. They did not seek to work against the traditional Church and its ancient dogmas, but merely to renew and re-interpret them in a more meaningful fashion. Solov'ev was perhaps the more explicit of the two; he clearly subjugates everything to total-unity and a striving for synthesis. Bulgakov, on the other hand, steers a more careful theological course than his precursor. It should be remembered that he not only worked from within the Church, but was an ordained priest and recognized theologian. The student will discover that Solov'ev, the poet-philosopher, glossed over many intricate questions such as the conception of Christ by the Virgin, the nature of the Mother of Christ and so on, because he was not primarily interested in theology, but rather in the broader philosophical and cosmic principles upon which he constructed his Sophiology. The task of the theological

[18] S. Bulgakov, *The Wisdom of God*, (London, 1937), 39.

[19] S. Bulgakov, "Dve vstrechi," in *Avtobiograficheskie zametki*, ed. by L. A. Zander (Paris, 1946), 103-113.

[20] See. S. Bulgakov, *Svet nevechernij* (Moscow, 1917), particularly the introduction. The chapters "Zovy i vstrechi" (61-66) and "V Aja-Sofii" (94-102) in Bulgakov's *Avtobiograficheski zametki* (Paris, 1946) merit comparison with the mystical experiences of Vladimir Solov'ev.

vindication of his teachings on Sophia was left to Bulgakov, who spent the greater part of his creative life in expanding and correcting the original system.

However, the obvious presence of Vladimir Solov'ev's Sophia in Bulgakov's scheme does not mean that the Orthodox theologian accepted his predecessor's work in its entirety. Bulgakov esteemed Solov'ev as his own spiritual father-confessor and as the first expounder of modern Sophiology, but at the same time he discerned certain dangers in his system and tried to avoid them himself. He decried Solov'ev's "syncretism", his indiscriminate mixing of ancient Orthodox thought with gnosticism and with Western Sophiology taken from the writings of Boehme, Pordage and others, and tried to restrict himself to reinterpretation of traditional Orthodox sources. Moreover, Bulgakov felt that "in his poetry Solov'ev is indeed very far from the Orthodox conception of Sophia",[21] because of the highly personal relationship established there between poet and Sophia/muse that resulted in a Sophia too much incarnate. He himself sought to avoid this problem by depersonalizing his presentation of Sophia as completely as possible. Ironically enough, however, despite all his efforts, precisely those criticisms which he levelled against Solov'ev were turned against him by the more conservative theologians in the Russian Orthodox Church.

In *The Wisdom of God* Bulgakov pleads an earnest case for a new approach to Christianity. He forthrightly denies any "heresy", but expresses his deep conviction that in our time "nothing less than a change and renewal of men's hearts"[22] is required: "Our modern age stands in need of a new apprehension of the dogmatic formulae preserved by the Church in its living tradition".[23] He offers Sophiology as a new *Weltanschauung* within Christianity, a point of view that in no way seeks to undermine the traditional Church dogmas, all of which he unequivocally accepts, but strives instead to offer new life and spirit through a fresh interpretation.

The central concept of Bulgakov's Sophiology parallels that of Solov'ev's, for he too is concerned with total-unity, the synthesis of heaven and earth. Occupying the focus of his system is the idea of Godmanhood, the relationship between God and man, the theandric union between God and the entire creaturely world:

> The central point from which sophiology proceeds is that of the relation between *God* and the *world*, or, what is practically the same thing, between *God* and *man*. In other words we are faced with the question of the meaning and significance of God-manhood—not only

[21] Bulgakov, *Wisdom of God*, 23-24.
[22] Ibid., 28.
[23] Ibid., 35.

in so far as it concerns the God-man Himself, the incarnate Logos, but precisely in so far as it applies to the theandric union between God and the whole of the creaturely world, through man and in man. Within Christianity itself there is a never-ending struggle between the two extreme positions of dualism and monism, in a constant search for truth, which can only be found in the synthesis of God-manhood.[24]

Although Bulgakov is disturbed by the rise of materialism and secularism, he is nonetheless determined not to reject this world in favour of the divine. Like Solov'ev, he is bent upon a course of union, not selection. However, he faces the fact that Christianity appears ineffectual in his time and a great abyss separates the everyday world from it. His means of bridging this abyss echoes Solov'ev; he turns to the resurrection of an ancient message lost in modern times. This message is contained in the teaching of sophiological Christianity that "the creaturely world is united with the divine world in the Divine Sophia".[25] Man must realize that he is not rejected, cast off, living in a self-contained void independent of God: "Heaven stoops towards earth; the world is not simply a world in itself, it is also the world in God, and God abides not only in heaven, but also on earth with man".[26] Bulgakov reiterates Solov'ev's concern with ecumenism, considering it the fundamental ecclesiastical problem of his time, another phase of the sophiological question of spiritual union.

In *The Wisdom of God* Bulgakov treats the major dogmas of Orthodox thought in the light of Sophiology. More specifically, he expounds Sophia in relation to the Holy Trinity, the individual hypostases of the Holy Trinity, the relationship between the divine and the creaturely Sophia, the incarnation, Pentecost and Godmanhood, the veneration of the Mother of God, and finally the Church.

In examining Sophia's relation to the Holy Trinity, the theologian points out that the doctrine of consubstantiality has not been sufficiently developed. Moreover, Sophia's function has been generally ignored so that her role is more apparent in iconographic art and liturgy than in actual theology. On the basis of two postulates —that the Holy Trinity unites three distinct persons to form one God and that the Holy Trinity possesses but one substance—Bulgakov approaches the question of Sophia. From the very outset, he wishes to establish that Sophia is not a person and therefore does not make a quaternity of the Trinity. Furthermore, while he admits that there is often some confusion between the second hypostasis and Sophia, he stresses that Sophia does not occupy this position and should not be

[24] *Ibid.*, 30.
[25] *Ibid.*, 34.
[26] *Ibid.*, 34.

identified with any single aspect of the Trinity, but only with the three in their totality.[27] Thus, he contends that Sophia expresses the unity or consubstantiality of the Holy Trinity, its all-in-one nature or *Ousia*. At the same time, it must be remembered that Ousia-Sophia is distinct from the hypostases and yet eternally hypostatized in them; she cannot exist apart from them. To clarify this moot point Bulgakov earlier introduced the concept of *ipostasnost'* ["hypostasis-like in nature"] as opposed to *ipostas'* ["hypostasis"].[28] The other important quality which Sophia possesses within the trinity as a whole is Love. God is love and Ousia-Sophia also belongs to the realm of God's love, but "love in a special and unhypostatic embodiment."[29]

It may be worthwhile to offer Bulgakov's own summation of the role of Sophia in the Holy Trinity in order to show the complexity of the thought underlying her non-hypostatical function:

> To sum up, the nature of God (which is in fact Sophia) is a living and, therefore, loving substance, ground and "principle". But it might be said, does this not lead to the conception of a "fourth hypostasis"? The reply is "certainly not"; for this principle in itself is non-hypostatic, though capable of being hypostatized, in a given Hypostasis, and thereby constituting its life. But, it might still be urged, would this not result in "another God", a sort of totally "other" Divine principle within God? Again we reply, no; for no one has ever attempted to maintain such an idea in connection with the Divine ousia in its relation to the hypostases while the very conception of ousia itself is but that of Sophia, less fully developed. The whole strength of the dogma of the Holy Trinity lies in this insistence on the one life and one substance of the Divine tri-unity, as well as on their mutual identity: God possesses the Godhead, or he *is* the Godhead, is Ousia, Sophia. This does not imply that the three Persons own in common, and separately make use of, a certain common substance—on the basis, so to speak, of collective ownership. This would lead to tritheism, not trinitarianism. The living tri-unity of the Holy Trinity is founded on a single principle of self-revelation with one life in common, though in three distinct Persons. The Holy Trinity has one ousia, not three, or three distinct Persons. It likewise possesses one Wisdom, not three. Thus of its own accord falls to the ground the first misconception which arises on the very threshold of sophiology.[30]

Thus Sophia is possessed in common by the three aspects of the Trinity; they have but one nature or substance which is Sophia.

Despite the fact that Sophia is possessed simultaneously by Father, Son and Holy Spirit, it is in a different manner that each does

---

[27] Bulgakov's assertion here is primarily that of Solov'ev's concept of the total-unity of the Holy Trinity. However, the issue becomes somewhat more complex and confused in Bulgakov's position because alongside Sophia he introduces the concept of "Glory" as also being an essential quality—but not an aspect—of the Holy Trinity.

[28] See Bulgakov's article "Ipostas' i Ipostasnost' ".

[29] Bulgakov, *Wisdom of God*, 58.

[30] *Ibid.*, 59-60.

so. Consequently, Sophia achieves a certain degree of three-in-oneness herself: "We should learn to think of the divine Sophia as at the same time three-fold and one".[31] As before, Bulgakov reiterates that she "is not a Hypostasis, but only a quality belonging to a Hypostasis, or an attribute of hypostatic being".[32] The Father possesses Sophia as his *source* of revelation. She represents the mystery of His Hypostasis, His nature which is to be made manifest in the Hypostases of the Son and Holy Spirit, since the Father remains unmanifested in Himself and reveals Himself only in the Dyad of the second and third Hypostases. The Father's Ousia remains within Himself in the capacity of Sophia. Thus, Bulgakov offers this formula for Sophia and the Father: "Sophia, so far as the Father is concerned, connotes predominantly Ousia—prior to its own revelation as Sophia".[33]

Bulgakov firmly denies the identification of the second Hypostasis or Logos with Sophia. This appears contrary to the traditional Russian Orthodox view of Sophia as the Logos or Son.[34] The Logos is a hypostatic revelation of the Father, the hypostatic Word of the Father, the first manifestation of the Father's divine nature. But the divine nature or Ousia of the Father has already received the designation of Wisdom or Sophia. Consequently, the Logos is hypostatized Wisdom: "This Word spoken constitutes part of the hypostatic life of the Logos in his Ousia. It is precisely this content of divine thought which is disclosed in the Hypostasis of the Word in the form of Sophia or the Divine Wisdom."[35]

The role of the Holy Spirit in the Holy Trinity is to display the love which proceeds from the Father to the Son, that hypostatic love which unites the first and second Hypostases. Thus, the Holy Spirit together with the Son "discloses the Father in the divine Sophia. The Son *and* the Holy Spirit, together, inseparable and unconfused, realize the self-revelation of the Father in his nature".[36] The quality of Sophia in the Holy Spirit displays the "principle of reality": ". . .[the Holy Spirit] transforms the world of ideas into a living and real essence, into a self-sufficient creation of God, the *ens realissimum*, into a world existing with the life of God".[37]

In summary then, the divine Sophia is the Godhead revealing itself, and belongs to all three Hypostases of the Holy Trinity "both in

[31] Ibid., 63.
[32] Ibid., 83.
[33] Ibid., 68.
[34] See p. 272 of this chapter (footnote 82), where Serafim attacks Bulgakov on this very point of Orthodox dogma.
[35] Bulgakov, Wisdom of God, 69.
[36] Ibid., 74.
[37] Ibid., 78-79.

their tri-unity and in their separate being and to each one in a way peculiar to himself".[38] In other words, the entire Holy Trinity in its tri-unity is Sophia, just as all three separate Hypostases are: "The Holy Trinity possesses her as its triune subject, as it exists in three different Hypostases; and in its tri-unity has her as its one Ousia which in its revelation is the divine Sophia."[39]

Although Bulgakov introduces the idea of Ousia-Sophia where Solov'ev simply designated Sophia's role in the Holy Trinity as all-in-oneness, the two schemes differ in very little except detail. Bulgakov's alteration of some terminology does not disguise the fact that the general concept is substantially the same for both. Their similarity becomes clearer the further one proceeds, particularly in the chapter devoted to "The Divine and Creaturely Sophia" which provided Bulgakov's opponents with grounds for a charge of theological Platonism,[40] a charge not entirely unjustified as we shall see. Solov'ev's concept of the World Soul is easily recognizable even though it is presented in new vestments as the "creaturely Sophia". Like Solov'ev, Bulgakov states that God created the world out of "Nothing". "Nothing" here should be understood as the character of a lower created being with its attendant relativity and incompleteness in a state of becoming: "... its emergence represents the filling of a void by some positive but still incomplete being".[41] The creaturely world cannot exist independently of God, but derives its existence from Him. This concept is essential because it forms the basis of the denial both Solov'ev and Bulgakov make of the independent existence of any principle of evil or any Manichaean duality of good and evil. Both prefer to view evil as the absence of good. Moreover, the creaturely world is a reflection, albeit imperfect, of the divine: "That world only receives, according to the mode proper to it, the divine principle of life. Its being is only a reflection and a mirror of the world of God ... the world bears within it the image and, as it were, the reflection of the divine Prototype".[42] Since Sophia is the divine expression of the triune nature of the Holy Trinity, she becomes the divine prototype of creation: "the doctrine of Sophia as the prototype of creation finds ample support in the tradition of the Church ... the Wisdom of God is represented precisely as a prototype of creation existing with God prior to the creation of the world".[43] Thus, Bulgakov's position appears to be exactly that of Solov'ev, namely that "God in his three persons created the world on the *foundation* of the

[38] Ibid., 82.
[39] Ibid., 84.
[40] See pp. 267 and 271 of this chapter.
[41] Bulgakov, Wisdom of God, 97.
[42] Ibid., 99.
[43] Ibid., 101.

Wisdom common to the whole Trinity".[44] He argues this role of Sophia with increasing emphasis, insisting that Sophia be considered not simply as some abstract nebulous quality, "but as the ever present power of God, the divine essence, as the Godhead itself".[45] Eventually Sophia emerges as the multivalent and multipurposed centre of the divine macrocosm, for she contains the fullness of the ideal forms which are eternal in God: "In Sophia the fullness of the ideal forms contained in the Word is reflected in creation. This means that the species of created beings do not represent some new type of form devised by God, so to speak *ad hoc*, but that they are based upon eternal divine prototypes."[46] Divine Wisdom or Sophia becomes the blueprint or plan for the creation of the "creaturely world in Wisdom's image" and, consequently, the creaturely realm bears the imperfect but divinely originated seeds for its own growth towards perfection and oneness with the heavenly realm. The imperfect "World Soul" of Solov'ev, which contained the possibility for good or for evil, for initiating the movement towards union with Heaven (Godmanhood) or chaos (Mangodhood) has, therefore, simply been converted into the "creaturely Sophia" in Bulgakov's work. The created world is synonymous with the creaturely Sophia: "The created world, then, is none other than the creaturely Sophia, a principle of relative being, in the process of becoming...".[47] This concept of the two Sophias seems undeniably Platonic in inspiration, recalling as it does the two Absolutes of Platonism which also were operative in Solov'ev's scheme. The mediator between the two realms remains the same for Bulgakov as Solov'ev; both posit Sophia as the principle of mediation between the divine and creaturely:

> The principle we require is not to be sought in the Person of God at all, but in his Nature, considered first as his intimate self-revelation, and secondly as his revelation in the world. And here we have at once Sophia in both its aspects, divine and creaturely. Sophia unites God with the world as the one common principle, the divine ground of creaturely existence. Remaining one, it exists in two modes, eternal and temporal, divine and creaturely. It is of the first importance for us to grasp both the unity and the "otherness" in this unique relation of the creature to its Creator.[48]

As though to soften Sophia's seeming usurpation of all major functions, Bulgakov reminds one that man, like Sophia who cannot exist without her Hypostases, also needs his hypostases. The hypostasis which man must receive is that of the Logos who is the divine-

---

[44] *Ibid.*, 104.
[45] *Ibid.*, 102.
[46] *Ibid.*, 107.
[47] *Ibid.*, 110.
[48] *Ibid.*, 112-113.

human example of Godmanhood which man must seek to emulate. Thus the Logos is the human prototype. The third Hypostasis does not form a hypostatic centre for heavenly mankind, for Godmanhood; however, it does manifest and actualize Godmanhood as a reality in God, to the Son, and through him to the Father also.

Out of the Dyad of the Logos and the Holy Spirit in which is revealed the Father, Bulgakov generates an interesting reflection of Solov'ev's original teaching on androgyny. Solov'ev, of course, viewed the opposition of masculine and feminine as a symbolic disinheritance from original oneness; the union of the two aspects represented a synthesis that ultimately led to Godmanhood.[49] Bulgakov considers the masculine and feminine aspects in their dyadic contour as a reflection in their unity of the fullness and unity of God. Like the Son and the Holy Spirit they are but aspects of a single principle: "... the Son and the Holy Spirit together constitute Godmanhood, as the revelation of the Father in the Holy Trinity. These two hypostases can be considered, as in creaturely mankind, the relationship between masculinity and femininity".[50]

The same mystical formula of dyadic synthesis to create a transformative three-in-one may be remarked in Bulgakov's reiteration of the principle of Christ and the Church forming the dyad which reveals or manifests the fullness of God. It is extremely important to view this dyadic principle as not simply passively symbolic, but quite the contrary, as theurgic and procreative, for it represents the "theologian's stone" whereby synthesis can be achieved in order to usher in the Heavenly Jerusalem:

> This same relation [i.e. between masculine and feminine], since the Incarnation, is reflected in that between Christ and the Church. Human hypostases are reflections of the Logos, the Heavenly Man, the "new Adam". But the Holy Spirit, since he abides in the Son, is also a prototype of human hypostases. Thus man, created in the image of God, has been created male and female. Husband and wife, though they differ as two different exemplifications of human nature, manifest in their unity the fullness of humanity and of the image of God enshrined in it. Their union is sealed by the dyad of the Son and of the Holy Spirit, which reveals the Father. They bear within themselves the power of procreation, the image of the unity of the tripersonal God which is to be traced in the whole of mankind as such.[51]

Not only is Divine Wisdom cast in the role of intermediary between Heaven and Earth, she also comes to symbolize the potential course of "universal history", a term identical in both Bulgakov and Solov'ev. For both men the consummation of universal history was at

---
[49] Ibid., 120-121.
[50] Ibid., 120.
[51] Ibid., 120-121.

first the realization of Godmanhood and the union of Heaven and Earth. Although both were hesitant by the end of their lives on the possibility of achieving this within the course of the "world process" as opposed to a sudden apocalypse or eschatological upheaval outside the course of history, nonetheless, it was their fervent hope that such a "peaceful apocalypse" could be realized: "The world of becoming must travel by the long road of the history of the universe, if it is ultimately to succeed in reflecting in itself the face of the divine Sophia and be 'transfigured' in it".[52]

Christ is the prototypic Godman in whom the two natures, divine and creaturely, exist in one. This is the kenotic basis of Bulgakov's Godmanhood—man must strive to perfect the same theandric notion within himself. The basis for this structure is once again provided by Sophia in both her divine and creaturely modes. In fact, Bulgakov views the process of Godmanhood as being perfected through the offices of Sophia:

> "All power is given unto me in heaven and earth" (Matt. 28: 17). This "and" points to the link between heaven and earth, to Godmanhood, the unity of divine and created Wisdom. This unity is realized in the progressive penetration of the world by Wisdom, bringing it gradually into conformity with its prototype in Wisdom.[53]

Once again Sophia seems to underlie even the function of the Logos in the process of Godmanhood, so that Christ himself appears pale in comparison.

Another important question elucidated sophiologically is that of the Holy Virgin. In Orthodox theology the Virgin occupies an intermediary position between Heaven and Earth, higher than the creaturely but lower than the divine. She is the "heart of the Church" because of her epithets: in relation to the Father she is named Daughter; in relation to the Word, Mother and Bride, unwedded Bride of God; and in relation to the Holy Spirit, Spirit-bearer, the Glory of the World. Together with the saints, she acts as intercessor for man's petitions to God. The Virgin is neither divine nor theandric; she certainly has no separate hypostatic life. Moreover, she is not yet entirely manifested to the world. In what is no doubt a reference to the Woman Clothed in the Sun of *Revelation*, Bulgakov posits an apocalyptic role for her: "The complete manifestation of the Mother of God to the world will only be possible when the world itself enters into the kingdom of glory by virtue of the general resurrection and all creation is transfigured".[54] This apocalyptic manifestation of the Virgin is to be understood, however, only as "complete revelation" and

[52] Ibid., 114.
[53] Ibid., 143.
[54] Ibid., 182.

not as "incarnation", which would threaten to make a hypostasis of her.

The Virgin is exceedingly important in Bulgakov's exegesis, for, largely on the basis of Russian iconography, Russian Orthodox ritual and even Russian religious architecture, he is able to show that the shrines dedicated to Sophia in Byzantium were Christological in nature, but in Russia they assumed an undeniably Mariological quality, so that Sophia was often simultaneously interpreted as both Christ and the Mother of God.

In order to comprehend the sophiological function of the Virgin it must be remembered that the two natures in Christ correspond to the two forms of Sophia—creaturely and divine. The created humanity of Christ the Godman derives from the Mother of God; it is from her that the Godman assumes his human nature, which is in fact the counterpart of created Wisdom. Thus we arrive at Bulgakov's sophiological formula for the Holy Virgin: "it is in this sense, as sharing the human nature of the Godman, that his holy Mother is the created Sophia. In this way the different aspects of Sophia, the Wisdom of God, its two faces are at one in the person of the Mother of God".[55] This is, according to Bulgakov, the Russian Orthodox conception of Mary; he interprets the veneration paid her in Russia as accorded to the "created Sophia."

Like Solov'ev, Bulgakov considers the Church as divine and human, theandric in nature. It represents Godmanhood in history. Bulgakov, however, is not willing to restrict the Church by considering it merely as the "Bride" of Christ, making it Christ-centred. He seeks to broaden its entire scope according to his sophiological views:

> We may say that in the present age the Church is the body of Christ precisely as being that eucharistic body on which are bestowed the eucharistic gifts of the Holy Ghost, the giver of life in Christ. To the Church as a whole the plenitude of the manifestations of divine Wisdom is present. Accordingly it is granted not only full communion with God in Christ in the power of the Holy Spirit, but also full communion in the divine and created Wisdom of God. This latter is disclosed to the Church in the person of the Mother of God, together with the whole of the Church triumphant, angels and saintly men. The full significance of the sophianic character of the Church cannot be restricted to its relation to Christ, or defined so to speak, Christocentrically.[56]

In other words, the Church appears to reflect Sophia in her role as intermediary between Heaven and Earth, for it too represents that intersection of the divine and the creaturely which is to give birth to Godmanhood. Its function is to develop this conjunction of divine

---

[55] Ibid., 189.
[56] Ibid., 206.

and human within the bounds of history and through the historical process. The Church is responsible for fostering *sobornost'* or "communality" within man, who must recognize "his own communal existence, not as an individual, but in the union of humanity in the bond of its own common nature and of a subsistent love".⁵⁷ Thus the Church becomes the focal point of a divine-human community, of a sociality in its historical life, an inward community of mutuality "whereby mankind is unified to such a point that love for God and for neighbour are inseparable and the second commandment is 'like unto' the first (Matt. 22:39)".⁵⁸

At the conclusion of *The Wisdom of God*, Bulgakov very briefly introduces the questions of evil and of eschatology, but in very ambiguous fashion. Like Solov'ev, he preferred to see the attainment of Godmanhood within the natural course of history, but here, nonetheless, there is a foreboding of apocalypse and a supra-historical vision of the final struggle between good and evil. Until this point he has denied any separate existence to evil; furthermore, there has been no discussion of the concept of a "fallen Sophia", that is, a parallel to Solov'ev's designation of the World Soul as capable of inclining either to good or to evil in order to establish a theoretical freedom of movement that would avoid constraining man to Godmanhood like a puppet in some divine comedy. Now this ambiguous note does enter:

> The history of the humanity of Christ is the history of the Church as it is figured in the Apocalypse. The apocalyptic content of history is the drama of the world conflict between the forces of Christ and those of Anti-christ. And since Christ is a conqueror, therefore it is the history of his victory and his conquest, the triumph of the Kingdom of God. This can also be presented in the sense of a struggle between two rival principles; between the true Sophia which irradiates the world with wisdom, and the forces of evil, "Sophia fallen". The "woman clothed with the sun" and pursued by the dragon is opposed to "the great whore", "Babylon the great, the mother of harlots and abominations of the earth" (Rev. 17:5. With which compare the analogous figures of Proverbs 7:6-27 and 9:13-18).⁵⁹

Here evil seems to grow in strength, rather than languish as Bulgakov suggests. Evil exists, he would believe, only as a "parasite", resulting from a "confusion of good and evil, as shadows, and darkness itself, are only apparent by contrast with the light. The overcoming and suppression of evil, therefore, consists in separating it from good, whereupon it must inevitably languish and die".⁶⁰ And yet, the ultimate resolution of this struggle between unconditional good and

---

⁵⁷ *Ibid.*, 212.
⁵⁸ *Ibid.*, 212-213.
⁵⁹ *Ibid.*, 215.
⁶⁰ *Ibid.*, 216.

conditional evil comes only apocalyptically, outside the course of history by a supernatural and divine act which alone can effect their separation. Bulgakov's posthumously published *Apocalypse of John* (*Apokalipsis Ioanna*, 1948) arrives at the same eschatology as did Solov'ev's final work *Three Conversations*, with its appended "Brief Tale of the Antichrist". Sophiology alone can elucidate what is finally eschatological, i.e., what lies even beyond the separation of good and evil, namely the fulfilment of the ultimate synthesis of Heaven and Earth:

> Only in the light of sophiology can we grasp all the scope of the eschatological fulfilment of all things, which is not limited to the final separation of good and evil in the last judgment at the end of this age, but, in ways invisible to us, transcends even that separation, for then God shall be all in all, and divine Wisdom fulfilled in the created.[61]

Both Solov'ev and Bulgakov expound Sophiology as the divine plan which is not yet fulfilled, but is to be fulfilled in the future. Essentially it is their inspired but rational prophecy of those things yet to come, based upon the conviction that the creaturely world bears within itself the imperfect reflection of the divine. If man can be made aware of his potential for divinity, if he can read the religious symbolism of the perfect Godman in Christ as his own goal and purpose, then created Wisdom, or the striving for total-unity, lies within his grasp.

The sophiological patterns of Bulgakov and Solov'ev seem to coincide perfectly, for both posit Sophia at every important theurgic juncture. She explains all. The omnipresence of Sophia, regardless of any protests as to her hypostatic or non-hypostatic nature, is so overwhelming that all of Christian theology appears to be suspended on a single thread spun out of the imaginative theologizings of thinkers like Solov'ev, Florenskij and Bulgakov. Given this state of affairs, it is not surprising that more conservative theologians in the Russian Orthodox Church should express their concern, even their fears of heresy. The result was a lengthy and complex battle, charges and countercharges that ran through the emigre Russian journals and Church publications in the 1920's and 1930's. Like Bulgakov's own writings, the literature of this controversy is voluminous, spread over many years and great distances.[62] Some of its background can be

[61] *Ibid.*, 216.

[62] The most important threads of the Sophia controversy can be traced through the Russian emigre journal, *Put'* (Paris), particularly in the Nos. 47-50, 1935-1936. *Russie et Chrétienté* (nouvelle série), also published in Paris, carried less partisan reviews of the debate in Nos. 1-3, 1937-1938, than did the liberal *Put'* which tended to support Bulgakov. *Orientalia Christiana Periodica* (Rome) also recorded the strife within the Orthodox Church in its volumes III-IV-V 1937-1939. B. Schultze, writing in *Orientalia Christiana Periodica*, sided with more conservative Orthodox opinion against Bul-

found in Bulgakov's defense of Sophiology, *On Sophia the Divine Wisdom of God*[63] as well as the very informative and lengthy article "Evêques russes en exil" by M. De Herbigny and A. Deubner.[64] The reading of the latter in particular makes it clear that internal Church politics no doubt played a significant part in stoking the fires of theological controversy.

Briefly, this was the situation. The Holy Synod of the Emigre Russian Church situated itself at Sremski-Karlovtsy in Yugoslavia after the Revolution with the blessing of the Serbian patriarch. Considering itself the head of the Russian Church abroad, it demanded the allegiance of the other ecclesiastical provinces including America, Western and Eastern Europe, the Near East and the Far East. However, it encountered stiff resistance from Metropolitan Evlogij, who was in charge of the diocese of Western Europe from his seat in Paris. Metropolitan Antonij in Sremski-Karlovtsy wished to have a strongly centralized Church leadership to avoid the disintegration of the Church outside Russia into independent factions. Evlogij was interested in preserving a large measure of the co-operative independence he had gained by virtue of being awarded the status of exarchate by the Byzantine Patriarch. He had also become head of the newly founded Russian Theological Seminary in Paris whose professorial staff included some of the most "liberal" and "modern" emigre Russian theologians Sergej Bulgakov, Pavel Florenskij and P. Kartashev. The Seminary itself was a bone of contention because the Holy Synod at Sremski-Karlovtsy asserted that it alone could authorize and confirm the statutes and professorial body of the Seminary after a close examination not only of its regulations, but also the writings of its professors. Thus, in 1925 the Synod refused to recognize the Seminary until these conditions had been met. On the reports of Archbishop Teofanij, who had been made responsible for investigating the Seminary and its teachers, the Synod published an important pastoral letter in March of 1927 denouncing its "modernism" and accusing it of freemasonry, which was to be purged together with the

---

gakov. Needless to say, the official Church publication *Tserkovnaja zhizn'* (Sremski-Karlovtsi, Yugoslavia) carried full details of the conservative Church view during the years of dissension in the 1930's. Its views were opposed by *Tserkovnyj vestnik* (zapadno-evropejskoj eparchii), which reported on Church news from Western Europe, principally from the camp of Bulgakov's superior, Evlogij. A fairly complete background of general dissension within the factions of the Emigre Russian Orthodox Church is chronicled by S. Lialine in his two articles, "Chronique religieuse" (Orthodoxie Russe-Emigration) and "Le Debat Sophiologique" for the influential religious journal *Irenikon* (Belgium, Amay-sur-Meuse) in No. 6, XIII, 1936, 675-705.

[63] Sergej Bulgakov, "O Sofii, Premudrosti Bozhiej (Ukaz Moskovskoj Patriarkhii i Dokladnye zapiski prof. prot. Sergija Bulgakova Mitropolitu Evlogiju), Paris, 1935.

[64] In *Orientalia Christiana* (Rome), No. 67, 1931.

"Brotherhood of Sophia". More specifically, they attack Kartashev's "Reform, Reformation and the Fulfilment of the Church, a Statement of the Eurasians" ("Reforma, reformatsija i ispolnenie Tserkvi, utverzhdenie evrazijtsev") for its desire to renew the Church completely from within and without. Bulgakov is then singled out as the one who is attempting to effect this "renewal" with his new teaching on Sophia:

> Until now, in accord with the Apostle Paul and the Church Fathers, we have recognized only "Christ crucified, unto the Jews a stumbling-block, and unto the Greeks foolishness.... Christ the power of God, and the wisdom of God," (I Cor 1: 23-34) They, to the contrary, ennunciate a new doctrine of "Sophia, the feminine principle in God". At times, for them this feminine principle (zhenstvennoe nachalo) is an individual substance, a hypostasis who while not being con-substantial with the Holy Trinity is at the same time not removed from it. At times this feminine principle appears to them only as a "hypostatic" mode analogous to the hypostasis. In the first case, Wisdom is a being superior to the Mother of God and worthy of cult and adoration, in the second case she is practically identified with the Holy Virgin. They themselves do not provide an exact account of their doctrine. But whatever it may be, both interpretations of "Sophia" are absolutely foreign to the tradition of the Apostles and the Patristic teachings.[65]

Metropolitan Evlogij is condemned in the letter because he takes no step to halt this "modernism". In fact, he supports these deviations and allows them to be taught to future priests of the Church. Evlogij is called upon to change his ways or be subject to judgment.

In spite of more meetings and the intervention of Archbishop Anastasius who had come in the role of peacemaker from Jerusalem, no reconciliation could be found between the two sides. Evlogij continued to assert his independence and to support his followers. The entire controversy reached a climax in 1935-37 when Metropolitan Sergij of Moscow intervened. Again his reasons appear as much political as theological, for the Moscow Patriarchy claimed, of course, that it was the only legal representative of the Russian Orthodox Church and that even the Emigre Church had to recognize this. In 1935 Metropolitan Sergij, apparently hearing of the rumoured heresies of Bulgakov, requested Metropolitan Eleutherius of Lithuania to provide him with a report on the writings of the Russian theologians in Paris.[66]

[65] From *Tserkovnye vedomosti*, Nos. 7-8, 1927, page 3. As quoted in d'Herbigny and Deubner, "Evêques russes en exil," *Orientalia Christiana*, No. 67, 1931, 148.

[66] Metropolitan Sergij's request, together with Eleutherius' report and Bulgakov's refutation are contained in *O Sofii, Premudrosti Bozhiej*... (See footnote 63). This volume also contains an earlier report on the Sophiological controversy and refutation by Bulgakov made in 1927 which is entitled "dokladnaja zapiska predstavlennaja professorom prot. Sergiem Bulgakovym mitropolitu Evlogiju vesnoj 1927 g."

In Eleutherius' denunciation Bulgakov faces numerous charges. One of the most interesting attacks concerns his condescending intellectualism: "like a true intellectual he [i.e. Bulgakov] looks down somewhat on Church tradition from above as though on a stage which he has traversed and left behind".[67] Like an ironic echo of Bulgakov's own criticism of Vladimir Solov'ev, Eleutherius claims that the theologian's system is not simply an unorthodox syncretism garnered from semi-Christian, semi-Gnostic and semi-pagan sources, but the product of an entirely overactive imagination: "Bulgakov's system as well is created not only by philosophical thought but by a creative imagination as well. Here we have as well a poem [sic] which is attractive in its exaltation and external form".[68] Predictably, Bulgakov is accused of having created a fourth hypostasis or at least of attempting to infuse into each hypostasis a masculine and feminine principle. Thus, Bulgakov's attempt to deal with Sophia as the "Ousia" of the Holy Trinity in general, and of each individual hypostasis in particular, is rejected out of hand. Furthermore, his differentiation between hypostatical and non-hypostatical being is found entirely unacceptable to traditional Church dogma. Eleutherius believes that the formulation of the divine and creaturely natures of Sophia, particularly the latter concept, could lead to the false belief that the responsibility for man's fall lies ultimately with the Creator and not with man himself. In any event these ideas have no place in Orthodox theology. Finally he provides a three-point summary of Bulgakov's heresy. The following is my paraphrase:

> 1. Bulgakov has manifestly shown that he is unwilling to contend with the genuine traditions and teachings of the Church and has propagated false teachings specifically condemned by the Church.
>
> 2. Bulgakov has reverted to Gnosticism (also condemned by the Church) as displayed by the basic principles of his interpretation and misleadingly operates with customary and traditional ideas and concepts.
>
> 3. His ideas are seductively attractive in their apparent depth and innovation and holiness. The fact that the responsibility for man's fall could be interpreted as lying with God and therefore reduces in man his consciousness of his own sinfulness. Moreover, making it seem as though redemption comes in the form of a universal Divine process in creaturely nature and in man, the way is open to all manner of distortion in this life.[69]

On the basis of these charges the Moscow Patriarchy recommended that Bulgakov be deprived of all his students and parishion-

---

[67] Bulgakov, *O Sofii, Premudrosti Bozhiej*, 6.
[68] *Ibid.*, 7.
[69] *Ibid.*, 18.

ers in view of the unorthodoxy of his teachings. Moreover, all the laymen and ecclesiastics who had supported Bulgakov in any way were now to be called upon to repent of their mistakes and, what is more, to submit to a "healthy cleansing". Although the Moscow Patriarchy could not exercise its authority over Bulgakov at that particular moment, it was made clear that should he ever wish to enter into communion with the Soviet Orthodox Church he would be required to recant his beliefs and reaffirm his allegiance to the Church in writing.

With "heaviness of heart" Bulgakov takes up his pen, at the request of his spiritual leader, Metropolitan Evlogij, to defend himself against these charges of heresy. Upset because he feels that his system as a whole was ignored and only separate points taken out of context, he demonstrates specifically how he was misquoted. But he takes special umbrage at being labelled a "true intellectual" for he personally considers the rift between the Church and the Russian intelligentsia as one of the major cultural catastrophes of Russian history. One of his main reasons for taking orders was to try to bridge this gap. In this 1935 report to his Metropolitan, Bulgakov reiterates many of the points of defense he had already used in 1927.[70] He objects that although a great deal of the criticism of his teachings on sophiology is based on his book *The Unfading Light* (Moscow, 1917), yet when this book appeared nothing was said against it. In fact, he felt that he was allowed to join the Church because of that particular work and even points out that he was under the direct patronage of Tikhon, then Patriarch of Moscow. He adds that Pavel Florenskij was apparently promoted within the Church for *The Pillar and the Foundation of Truth*, but is now attacked for the same reason. Thus it appears that previous to the Revolution and immediately afterwards while he was serving in Southern Russia, nothing whatsoever was said concerning his sophiological teachings. It was only after he was forced to emigrate in 1923 that he became embroiled in controversy. In the fall of 1924 Metropolitan Antonij attacked Bulgakov and others for what he claimed was a new heresy involving a fourth feminine hypostasis in the Holy Trinity[71], but just as inexplicably as he had made his charges he withdrew them and expressed his full confidence in Bulgakov's sincerity and ability.[72] The damage was done however and the controversy flared up anew with Archbishop Teofanij at its head in 1926.

Bulgakov's denial of the charges contained in the report to Metropolitan Sergij of Moscow is counter-charge rather than self-

[70] I.e., in "Dokladnaja zapiska, predstavlennaja prof. prot. Sergiem Bulgakovym...". See footnote 66.

[71] See Antonij's attack in *Novoe Vremja*, Sept. 4 (No. 1005), 1924.

[72] See *Vechernee Vremja*, Nov. 13 (No. 170), 1924.

explanation. He claims that the report was not based upon any genuine knowledge of his writings, since most of his works are unavailable in Soviet Russia because of censorship. Therefore, Sergij himself could not have read the texts in question. He disposes of the charge that his world-view is both pagan and gnostic by reiterating his complete faith in all the genuine dogmas of the Orthodox Church. He is not interested in creating new dogma, but only "theological interpretation" of what already exists. Moreover, he insists on his right as a theologian—the right of interpretation. Before any conclusion concerning his teachings can be reached, all his works including the trilogy *On Godmanhood* must be thoroughly examined. In addition, he points out that his interpretation is also based upon "ecclesiastical architecture, liturgy and iconography" and these areas of religious knowledge must also be taken into consideration. Finally, he rejects Metropolitan Sergij's condemnation because it does not correspond to the spirit of Orthodox *sobornost'* and bears instead the stamp of papal authority and infallibility, all of which is alien to the historical freedom of the Orthodox Church: "Orthodoxy, according to its spirit and dogmatic foundations, permits a corresponding freedom of thought whose diminuation or destruction threatens the life of the Orthodox Church and affects the essential interests of all theologians independently of the difference in their theological views."[73]

Unlike the ambiguous insinuations made by his theological enemies,[74] Bulgakov's counter-charges are quite forthright. Nor was he alone in his defense of religious freedom of thought. Nikolaj Berdjaev was perhaps the most notable of the Russian emigre intellectuals who came to his defense. This is hardly surprising in view of their common roots—both came from the same intellectual generation, made the same philosophical journey from Marxism to Idealism and now they found themselves leaders of the Russian philosophical and religious emigration. In an article entitled "The Spirit of the Grand Inquisitor",[75] Berdjaev voices his opinion on the controversy. Signifi-

---

[73] Bulgakov, *O Sofii, Premudrosti Bozhiej*, 53.

[74] Attacking Bulgakov, his "inquisitors" even make the outrageous statement that he is of the same philosophical persuasion as V. V. Rozanov who had affronted the Church with his paganistic belief in the sacredness of flesh and fertility. All his life Bulgakov was a staunch opponent of Rozanov and proclaimed it publically in *Voprosy zhizni*, No. 2, 1905, in the column "Bez plana" (Po povodu vykhoda v svet 6-go toma sobranija sochinenij Vladimira Solov'eva), 361 ff. Such outright misrepresentations were often accompanied by others, less overt but equally suggestive, such as the following statement contained in the denunciation of Bulgakov which speaks for itself: "But this is the question: is it an ecclesiastical content which Bulgakov is investing in this new form? Is it possible for our Orthodox Church of Christ to recognize Bulgakov's teaching as its own? For the solution of this question *it is not necessary to analyse and examine Bulgakov's entire system*. In order not to be hypnotized by it, *let us approach from the side*. [my italics]" *O Sofii, Premudrosti Bozhiej*, 7.

[75] "Dukh Velikogo Inkvisitora," *Put'* (Paris), No. 49, 1935, 72-81.

cantly enough, he believes that the implications of Metropolitan Sergij's condemnation of Bulgakov go beyond the question of Sophiology. He feels that Sergij's position threatens the entire concept of the possibility of religious thought within Orthodoxy as well as the question of "freedom of conscience". Like Bulgakov, he decries the stance of infallibility taken by the Metropolitan and his lack of acquaintance with the writings in question. The "behind-the-scenes" politicking and issuing of denunciations brings Berdjaev to accuse the Church of "ecclesiastical fascism". He too is incensed at the pejorative tag "intellectual" which the Church applies so indiscriminantly, for he and his colleagues all fall squarely into this category. He is goaded into outlining the course of Russian intellectual history in which an autocratic, conservative and jealous Church was able to wield its power behind the scenes to persecute intellectuals like Khomjakov and Solov'ev who were unable to publish works on religious subjects within Russia. This, plus the Church's suppression of intellectuals who desired to work within its structure, has resulted in an internal theological dictatorship. Like Bulgakov, Berdjaev is adamant in his counter-attack, implacable in his demand for freedom within the Church: "I remain within the Church of Christ which is based upon love and freedom. For freedom and creativity in religious life, for human dignity it is necessary to conduct an heroic battle".[76] The Russian Church must reexamine itself, must turn away from its "degenerative provincialism, its unChristian nationalism"[77] and go out into the world if the rebirth which Russian Christianity seeks is to be realized.

The controversy, however, was far from over. That same year an enormous work was published by Archbishop Serafim (Sobolev) entitled *The Defence of the Sophianic Heresy by Archpriest S. Bulgakov Before the Archepiscopal Synod of the Russian Emigre Church.*[78] Two years later a more modest outline was published under the same title containing the same basic arguments. The work was apparently inspired by Bulgakov's defence of his ideas on Sophiology in response to the condemnation by Metropolitan Sergij.

The introduction is of interest insofar as it reveals Serafim's reasons for attacking Bulgakov's heresy, reasons that once again are based on extra-theological considerations. Here he attempts to show how the worship of science and reason were in large part responsible for the destruction and loss of Russia. The culmination of this

---

[76] Ibid., 81.

[77] Ibid., 76.

[78] Arkhiepiskop Serafim [Sobolev], *Zashchita Sofianskoj Eresi Protoiereem S. Bulgakovym pred litsom Arkhierejskogo Sobora Russkoj Zarubezhnoj Tserkvi*, Sofia, 1937.

materialistic catastrophe was the Revolution. Faithlessness and immorality spread through the land as materialistic philosophy gained control. Drawing on the writings of several pre-Revolutionary ecclesiastics, Serafim concludes that the Revolution came about because people were essentially anti-religious and religion was generally ignored. Thus, it is in the interests of salvation and resurrection that the Church must now condemn heresies such as Bulgakov's: "In the designated sect our Synod simply rejects from the Church the sophianic heresy of which it has full knowledge, professes the truth of Orthodox faith and summons all to its profession for the purposes of the resurrection of Holy Russia, the Russian Orthodox people and all Orthodox Christians, for the sake of salvation".[79]

Although Serafim's examination of Bulgakov's teachings is more thorough and serious than those of his predecessors, and in spite of the fact that his knowledge of the Church Fathers and other sources is unimpeachable, his criticisms of Bulgakov are generally the same as we have already encountered, only better supported. Serafim is also quick to condemn the sophiologist for Gnosticism: ". . . the theological teaching of Father Bulgakov on Sophia is in no way rooted in these sources [i.e. Divine Revelation and the works of the Church Fathers] of theology, but is borrowed by him from gnostic fantasy and from those sources which have nothing in common with the rule of genuine orthodox theologizing. . .".[80] Moreover, Bulgakov's trespass is viewed in the most serious light, as the "most serious sin", for it is committed against Orthodox faith and belief. Therefore it must lead to destruction and loss of salvation for those who would practice it. Finally, Serafim even concludes that it could destroy the entire Orthodox Church.

More specifically, Serafim deals in great detail with approximately ten major charges made against Bulgakov and the latter's refutation of these. He reargues each point and reestablishes each against the theologian. Essentially Bulgakov is once again attacked for expounding both the Cabala and Plato in his scheme, as well as drawing on gnostic sources. He puts aside Bulgakov's charge that his opponents are not familiar with his writings by claiming to have examined all of his works very carefully. As far as Bulgakov's interpretation of the Holy Trinity is concerned, even that is in grave error according to Orthodoxy. The heretical teachings of the Varlaamites and "Godnamers" are repeated and while Serafim does not make a great deal of the second heresy, it would certainly seem to parallel not only Bulgakov's confusing array of epithets applied to the concept of the Divine Wisdom of God but Solov'ev's and the symbolists' as

[79] Ibid., 8.
[80] Ibid., 8.

well. Serafim certainly seems to believe that the abyss is unbridgeable between Bulgakov and the Church and that the former is quite recalcitrant. Nonetheless he calls upon Bulgakov to recant publicly his teachings on Sophia, "this gnostic intermediary between God and the world".[81] Bulgakov "must accept the teaching of the Orthodox Church on the Second Divine Hypostasis, the Son of God, as the true Sophia, the Divine Wisdom of God... and must adhere to the genuine teachings and traditions of the Church without any addition or alteration to this teaching from the judgments of his mind".[82]

It would appear that the conservative members of the Church feared greatly what they considered the "revolutionary spirit"[83] of teachings like Bulgakov's. Perhaps made even more conservative by their tenuous position outside Russia after the Revolution, many were ill-disposed to such "modernism". Here one finds essentially the same retreat to conservatism and provincialism that characterized the attempt to arrange a meaningful dialogue between the intelligentsia and the Church in Petersburg during the first decade of the twentieth century. At that time, intellectuals like Z. Gippius, D. Merezhkovskij, V. V. Rozanov, etc. attempted to exchange ideas with the Church at the famous Religious-Philosophical Meetings held under the watchful eye of Pobedonostsev. However, the Church was not forthcoming, suspicious of intellectuals and intellectualism. Nevertheless, some of the more cosmopolitan and liberal of the Church's junior membership survived to carry on the continuing debate after the Revolution. With the onslaught of World War II and Bulgakov's death in 1944, the controversy lost much of its impetus and apparently has receded into the background behind more intrusive questions like ecumenism.

[81] Ibid., 121.
[82] Ibid., 121.
[83] Ibid., 122.

CONCLUSION

While Vladimir Solov'ev's avowed task had been to transform the future of mankind with his philosophical and poetic system of the Divine Sophia, doubtless even he would have been amazed at the results of his Sophiological investigations. When he embarked on his personal quest in search of Godmanhood and the union of heaven and earth he did not foresee the power which the figurehead of his vision, the Divine Sophia, would exert on a succeeding generation of symbolist writers and theologians. Yet, both the strengths and weaknesses, both the chastity and seductiveness inherent in his devotions before this symbol, appeared to prescribe most prophetically the subsequent fate of the Divine Feminine. Just as Sophia seemed to overpower Solov'ev's entire philosophy with her omnipresence, the aesthetic systems of Aleksandr Blok and Andrej Belyj, as well as the theological system of Sergej Bulgakov, experienced the alluring yet distorting attendance of the Divine Sophia in their individual quests.

The passionate obeisance of certain symbolists before this seemingly all-embracing feminine symbol often bordered on idolatry. Indeed, the frequent religious motifs stemming from such biblical sources as the *Apocalypse*, the prayerful attitude of the poets, the mysterious visions of the Divine Sophia, apparently shared by all the principals in this study, contributed to an atmosphere of religious experience. Yet, when this religious experience was wed to the desire to bear arms, if only in the exaggerated "symbolist jargon" of those times, to sally forth with the Divine Sophia emblazoned on their shields in order to do battle with the beast, then a modern-day knighthood of the Divine Sophia was born. However, the "swords" of these crusaders were not made of steel. They proposed to strike a blow for mankind's future with the inspired word, in the prose and poetry of divine inspiration.

The times had provided a convenient conspectus for this philosophical, literary and theological knight-errantry: the turn of the nineteenth century to the twentieth; the growth of unrest and revolution in Russian; the Russo-Japanese War; the disastrous revolution of 1905. While it would be distorting facts to overemphasize the "political-awareness" of the symbolists in particular, nonetheless that age of social injustice and unrest often made their quest seem more real. However, it can hardly be denied that symbolists like Andrej Belyj were more practiced at tilting with spectral and elusive enemies than with genuine enemies of society. Nonetheless, the loss of the original vision of the Divine Sophia, so romantic, mysterious and inspired, and the ascendancy of her opposite, the Anti-Sophia, or Harlot, seemed a natural and logical consequence of the same events which eventually brought catastrophe to the old tsarist system in Russia.

BIBLIOGRAPHY OF WORKS CITED

Belyj, Andrej. *Arabeski*. Moscow, 1911.
―――――. "Formy iskusstva," *Mir iskusstva*, 1902, Nos. 7-12, 343-58.
―――――. *Kubok metelej [4-ja simfonija]*. Moscow, 1908.
―――――. "Lug zelenyj." *Vesy*, 1905, No. 8, 5-12.
―――――. *Nachalo veka*. Moscow-Leningrad, 1933.
―――――. *Serebrjanyj golub'*. Moscow, 1910.
―――――. *Severnaja simfonija [1-ja, geroicheskaja]*. Moscow, 1903.
―――――. *Simfonija [2-ja, dramaticheskaja]*. Moscow, 1902.
―――――. "Vospominanija o A. A. Bloke." *Epopeja*, 1922, No. 1, 123-273; 1922, No. 2, 105-299; 1922, No. 3, 125-310; 1923, No. 4, 61-305.
―――――. "Vospominanija ob Aleksandre Aleksandroviche Bloke." *Zapiski mechtatelej*, 1922, No. 6, 7-122.
―――――. *Vozvrat [Tret'ja simfonija]*. Moscow, 1905.
Berberova, Nina. *The Italics are Mine*. London, 1969.
Berdjaev, Nikolaj. "Dukh Velikogo Inkvisitora." *Put'* (Paris), 1935, No. 49, 72-81.
Blok, Aleksandr. *Pis'ma k rodnym*. 2 vols. Leningrad, 1927.
―――――. *Sobranie sochinenij*. 8 vols. Moscow, 1960-63.
Brjusov, V. *Ognennyj angel*. Moscow, 1908-1909.
Bulgakov, S. N. *Avtobiograficheskie zametki*. Edited by L. A. Zander. Paris, 1946.
―――――. "Ipostas' i Ipostasnost'." *Sbornik statej posvjashchennykh P. Struve*. Prague, 1925, 353-371.
―――――. *O Sofii, Premudrosti Bozhiej (Ukaz Moskovskoj Patriarkhii i Dokladnye zapiski prof. prot. Sergija Bulgakova Mitropolitu Evlogiju)*. Paris. 1935.
―――――. *Svet nevechernij*. Moscow, 1917.
―――――. "Vl. Solov'ev i Anna Schmidt." *Tikhie dumy*. Moscow, 1918.
―――――. *The Wisdom of God*. London, 1937.
Chulkov, Georgij. *Gody stranstvij. Iz vospominanij*. Moscow, 1930.
Cioran, S. D. "A. Dobroliubov: A Prophet of Silence." *Canadian Slavic Studies*, V, No. 2, 178-195.
Florenskij, Pavel. *Stolp i utverzhdenie istiny*. Moscow, 1914.
Gippius, Zinaida. *Dmitrij Merezhkovskij*. Paris, 1951.
Herbigny, M. de and Deubner, A. "Eveques russes en exil." *Orientalia Christiana*, 1931, No. 67.
Ivanov, Vjacheslav. *Dionis i pradionisijstvo*. Baku, 1923.
Janzhul, L. I. "Vospominanija L. I. Janzhul." *Russkaja starina*, No. 3, 1910, 475-490.

Lialine, S. "Chronique religieuse (Orthodoxie Russe-Emigration)" and "Le Debat Sophiologique." *Irenikon*, 1936, No. 6, XIII, 675-705.
Minskij, N. "Ideja Salome." *Zolotoe runo*, 1908, No. 6, 55-58.
Mochulskij, K. M. *Aleksandr Blok*. Paris, 1948.
_____ . *Vladimir Solov'ev*. 2nd ed. Paris, 1951.
Orlov, V. N., ed. *Aleksandr Blok i Andrej Belyj. Perepiska*. Letopisi, Vol. VII. Moscow, 1940.
Pertsov, P. P. *Rannij Blok*. Moscow, 1922.
Rozanov, V. V. *Ljudi lunnogo sveta*. Petersburg, 1911.
Schmidt, A. N. [A. Timshevskij]. "O budushchnosti," *Novyj put'*, 1904, No. 6.
_____ . *Iz rukopisej Anny Nikolaevny Schmidt*. Moscow, 1916.
Serafim, Arkhiepiskop [Sobolev]. *Zashchita Sofianskoj Eresi Protoiereem S. Bulgakovym pred litsom Arkhierejskogo Sobora Russkoj Zarubezhnoj Tserkvi*. Sofia, 1937.
Solov'ev, S. M. *Crurifragium*. Moscow, 1908.
_____ . *Shutochnye p'esy Vladimira Solov'eva*. Moscow, 1922.
Solov'ev, Vladimir. *Pis'ma Vladimira Sergeevicha Solov'eva*. Edited by E. L. Radlova. 4 vols. Moscow, 1908-1923.
_____ . *La Russie et l'Eglise Universelle*. Paris, 1889.
_____ . *La Russie et l'Eglise Universelle*. 2nd ed. Paris, 1906.
_____ . *Sobranie sochinenij V. S. Solov'eva*. Edited by S. M. Solov'eva and E. L. Radlova. 2nd ed. 10 vols. Petersburg, [1911].
Trubetskoj, Pr. Evgenij. "Lichnost' V. S. Solov'eva." *Sbornik Pervyj. O Vladimire Solov'eve*. Moscow, 1911.
Valentinov, N. *Two Years with the Symbolists*. Stanford, California, 1969.
Zander, L. A. *Bog i Mir (Mirosozertsanie otsa Sergija Bulgakova)*. 2 vols. Paris, 1948.
_____ . "In Memory of Father Sergius Bulgakov." *Sobornost'*, 1945, No. 32 (new series), 5-12.

INDEX

Aksakovs (Ivan Sergeevich and Konstantin Sergeevich), 41
Antichrist, 6, 40, 62, 64, 65, 66, 92, 98, 134, 168, 244
Anti-Sophia, 62, 92, 110, 138, 274
Antonij, Metropolitan, 268
Aphrodite Anadyomene/Pandemos, 15, 34, 62, 97, 122, 242-43
Aphrodite Urania, 15, 34, 97, 122, 242-43
Arnold, Gottfried, 16
Astarte, 123, 125, 128, 129

Beautiful Lady, 7, 57, 69, 102, 112, 116, 127, 132, 134, 135, 136, 139-61, 165, 167, 171, 184, 185, 188, 190, 192, 193, 195, 196, 232, 238, 239
Belyj, Andrej (pseud. of Boris Bugaev), 2, 5, 6, 7, 14, 18, 42, 51, 69, 71, 76, 77, 83, 85, 86, 89, 94, 96, 98, 100, 101, 102, 105, 105-19, 121-38, 140, 151, 152, 155, 161, 163-71, 175, 176, 177, 181, 182, 183, 184, 185, 188, 193, 199, 201, 203, 204, 230, 233, 238, 239, 242, 244, 253, 273, 274
— "Apocalypse in Russian Poetry, The", 90-93, 167-70
— "Child's Tin-Whistle, A", 178-79
— "Emancipated Slaves", 179
— "Forms of Art, The", 121
— *Gold in Azure*, 132
— "Green Meadow, The", 183, 212

— *Kotik Letaev*, 91, 171
— *Notes of an Eccentric*, 171
— *Petersburg*, 86, 156, 171
— "Sacred Colours", 130, 164-65, 166
— *Silver Dove, The*, 77, 86, 171, 188, 233-38, 239
— "Stamped Galosh, The", 179-80
— *Symphonies*, 85, 86, 99, 122, 165-67, 171, 178, 181, 211, 235
— "Vladimir Solov'ev. Reminiscences", 90-91, 96
Berberova, Nina, 137
Berdjaev, Nikolaj, 1, 39, 102, 269
— "Spirit of the Grand Inquisitor", 269-70
Blavatsky, Mme., 79
Blok, Aleksandr, 2, 7, 14, 18, 50, 54, 57, 67, 69, 71, 76, 83-85, 89, 91, 92, 100, 101, 102, 103, 105-19, 121-38, 139-61, 163, 167, 169, 171, 175-97, 199, 201-32, 233, 236, 238, 242, 244, 251, 253, 273
— "Ante Lucem", 146-47
— "City, The", 183, 189-92, 193
— "Earth Bubbles", 185-86, 234
— "Faina", 193, 195-96
— "Irony", 182-83, 197
— "Juvenile Verses", 147-48, 151
— "King in the Square, The", 156, 203, 204, 218-22
— "Knight-Monk, The", 93-95, 211

278 • Vladimir Solov'ev and the Knighthood of the Divine Sophia

— *Lyrical Dramas*, 202-204, 217, 238
— "Night Violet, The", 186-88, 234
— "On Lyrical Verse", 180-81, 183-84, 203
— "On the Theatre", 202
— "Parting of Ways, The", 156, 160
— "Puppet-Show, The" [drama], 118, 156, 159, 171, 177, 180, 181, 201, 203, 204-11
— "Rose and the Cross, The", 201, 211, 222-32
— "Snowy Mask", 193-95, 196
— "Stranger, The" [drama], 156, 201, 203, 204, 211-18
— "Stranger, The" [poem], 180, 190-92
— "Three Questions", 201-202
— "Twelve, The", 67, 128, 145
— *Unexpected Joy*, 136, 176-77, 184-96, 234, 237, 238
— *Verses on the Beautiful Lady*, 84, 136, 139-61, 177, 180, 189, 190, 217, 221, 234
— "Vladimir Solov'ev and Our Times", 93, 95-96
Boehme, Jakob, 16, 17, 78, 254
Brjusov, Valerij, 2, 77, 85, 89, 131, 138, 163, 169, 176, 238
— *Fiery Angel, The*, 77, 85, 238-42
— "Keys to the Mysteries", 238
— "Truths", 238
Bulgakov, Sergej, 1, 2, 7, 18, 51, 53, 72, 74, 76, 77, 89, 247, 248, 250, 252-73, 273
— *Autobiographical Notes*, 253
— *Bride of the Lamb, The*, 252
— *Burning Bush, The*, 252
— *Comforter, The*, 252
— *Friend of the Groom, The*, 252
— *Hypostasis and Hypostatic Nature*, 252
— *Jacob's Ladder*, 252
— *On Sophia, The Divine Wisdom of God*, 252, 265
— "On the Publication of the 6th Volume of V. Solov'ev's Collected Works", 102-103
— "Several Remarks on the Occasion of G. Chulkov's article on the Poetry of V. Solov'ev", 103-104
— "Two Meetings", 253
— *Unfading Light, The*, 247, 252, 268
— *Wisdom of God, The*, 252-64

Cabbala, 41, 271
Chulkov, Georgij, 42, 77, 83, 84, 92, 102, 103, 176, 180
— On Sophiology", 98
— "Poetry of Vladimir Solov'ev, The", 96-98
Christ, 6, 7, 15, 19, 29, 31, 35, 36, 62, 65, 66, 67, 73, 74, 75, 76, 125, 127, 128, 129, 134, 164, 165, 167, 242

Demonic Feminine, 2, 233-44
Divine Feminine, 1, 2, 7, 12, 34, 49, 67, 82, 83, 103, 106, 117, 122, 129, 130, 138, 141, 150, 154, 155, 156, 158, 161, 165, 166, 167, 170, 171, 179, 188, 191, 194, 196, 197, 204, 218, 221, 233, 238, 242, 248, 273
Dobroljubov, A. M., 237

Earth-Mistress, 58, 60, 62
Eleutherius, Metropolitan, 266-67
Ellis-Kobylinskij, L. L., 7, 176, 238
Evlogij, Metropolitan, 265, 266, 268

Florenskij, Pavel, 1, 7, 53, 89, 247, 265
— *Pillar and the Foundation of Truth, The*, 247-51, 268

Gichtel, Georg, 16, 78
Gippius-Merezhkovskaja, Z. N., 121, 131, 139, 140, 151, 152, 155, 176, 178, 272
Gnostics, 15, 17, 51, 52, 75
Godmanhood, 14, 17, 29, 30, 33, 35, 36, 45, 78, 80, 129, 146, 163, 164, 165, 251, 254, 255, 260, 261, 262, 263, 273

Harlot, The, 123, 138, 169, 192, 242, 244, 274
Hecate, 56
Hippolytus, 18
Holy Virgin, 7, 15, 22, 29, 31, 35, 36, 75, 98, 142, 144, 243, 261, 262

Ivanov, Vjacheslav, 163, 169, 176, 179, 201, 204

Janzhul, L. I., 41, 48

Khitrovo, Sophia Petrovna, 67-68, 107, 110, 114

Martynova, Sophia Mikhajlova, 67-68
Mendeleeva-Blok, Ljubov' Dmitrievna, 54, 85, 109, 110, 111, 112, 113, 114, 115, 116, 118, 131, 140, 158, 159, 160, 161, 175, 176, 178, 193, 204, 211
Merezhkovskij, Dmitrij, 6, 7, 89, 121, 136, 138, 139, 151, 152, 163, 176, 183, 243, 244, 250, 272
— "On the Reasons for the Decline... in Contemporary Literature", 164
Minskij, N. M. (pseud. of N. M. Vilenkin), 243
— "The Idea of Salome', 243-44
Mochulskij, Konstantin, 53, 160
Mother Nature, 15, 58

Pan-Mongolism, 40, 64-66
Paracelsus, 16, 18
Petrovskaja, Nina, 85, 239, 242

Pertsov, P. P., 139, 140, 145
Plato (Platonism), 73, 92, 129, 163, 259, 271
Pordage, John, 16, 78, 254
Proverbs, 18, 21, 22, 36, 220, 263

Radiant Mistress, 122, 123, 125, 126, 127, 128, 129, 130, 131, 132, 155, 157, 159, 160, 161, 211, 237
Razvadovskij, Count, 110, 111
Romanova, E. K., 11, 39, 252
Rozanov, V. V., 242, 269, 272
— *People of the Sub-Lunary Realm*, 242-43

Sadovskaja, K. M., 157-58
Schmidt, Anna Nikolaevna, 7, 42, 71-86, 110, 114, 125, 250, 251
Serafim (Sobolev), Archbishop, 270-72
Sergij, Metropolitan, 266, 268, 269, 270
Sologub, Fedor, 178, 182
Solov'ev, Mikhail Sergeevich, 42, 43, 76, 77, 85, 90, 105, 107, 108, 109, 124, 130, 199
Solov'ev, Olga Mikhajlovna, 85, 90, 105, 109, 124
Solov'ev, Sergej Mikhajlovich, 76, 85, 89, 101, 103, 105-19, 124, 133, 135, 136, 140, 151, 152, 161, 176, 181, 193, 199, 237, 238
— *Crurifragium*, 181
— *Flowers and Incense*, 180-81
— "Reply to G. Chulkov, A...", 98-100
Solov'ev, Vladimir Sergeevich
— "Al'sim", 199-201
— "General Meaning of Art, The", 4
— *Lectures on Godmanhood*, 15, 21-30, 71, 83
— "Meaning of Love, The", 30-35, 45, 67, 71, 83, 97, 110, 150, 164, 165, 183, 250

— "Mythological Process in Ancient Paganism, The", 15, 16-17, 56, 143
— "On Lyric Poetry", 44-45
— "Poetry of F. I. Tjutchev, The", 43
— *Russie et l'Eglise Universelle, La*, 15, 21-30, 71, 72, 83, 252
— "Short Tale of the Antichrist, A", 43, 63-67, 75, 90, 161, 168, 182, 264
— *Three Conversations*, 63-67, 75, 90, 168, 264
— "Three Meetings", 16, 40, 47-51, 53, 55, 61, 83, 85, 94, 97, 98, 142, 211
Solov'evian Circle, The, 85, 98, 102, 105-19, 126, 181, 185
Sophia, The Divine Wisdom of God, 1, 2, 7, 12, 14, 15, 18, 19, 20, 21, 22, 23, 24, 25, 26, 27, 28, 29, 30, 31, 33, 34, 35, 36, 37, 39, 42, 43, 45, 46, 47, 48, 49, 50, 51, 52, 54, 55, 56, 57, 58, 59, 60, 61, 62, 63, 66, 67, 71, 74, 80, 81, 82, 83, 86, 89, 91, 97, 98, 100, 102, 108, 110, 113, 114, 115, 118, 122, 123, 125, 128, 129, 138, 142, 146, 149, 150, 155, 161, 163, 164, 165, 166, 167, 168, 170, 185, 193, 232, 247, 248, 249, 250, 251, 254, 255, 256, 257, 258, 259, 260, 261, 262, 266, 267, 272, 273, 274
Sophia-Mythus, 18-20

Sophiology, 1, 2, 3, 7, 14, 17, 31, 35, 45, 49, 69, 72, 73, 94, 97, 100, 104, 109, 118, 121, 122, 131, 136, 145, 146, 154, 163, 166, 184, 218, 247, 250, 252, 253, 254, 255, 264, 270
Steiner, Rudolf, 163, 171
Strakhov, N. N., 40
Swedenborg, 16, 18

Tolstoj, A. K., 107
Tolstoj, L. N., 64
Tolstaja, S. A., 16
Teofanij, Archbishop, 268
Trubetskoj, Prince Evgenij, 41

Universal Church, 14, 17, 22, 30, 35, 36, 45, 67, 78, 80, 81, 146

Valentinian Gnosticism, 18-20, 73, 74
Valentinov, Nikolaj, 42, 71
Volkova, N. N., 193, 195

Williams, Charles, 41
Wisdom of Solomon, 22
Woman Clothed in the Sun, 6, 7, 62, 69, 91, 92, 106, 163-71, 180, 239, 242, 244, 261
World Soul, 15, 22, 24, 25, 26, 27, 28, 45, 46, 47, 58, 59, 60, 61, 62, 63, 67, 71, 73, 82, 92, 94, 95, 96, 97, 103, 123, 125, 127, 129, 150, 155, 168, 192, 258, 259, 263

www.ingramcontent.com/pod-product-compliance
Lightning Source LLC
Chambersburg PA
CBHW051421290426
44109CB00016B/1386